eight women philosophers

eight women philosophers

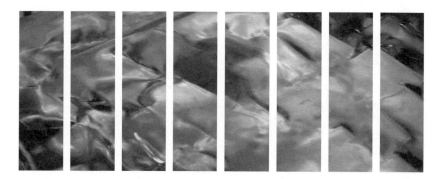

THEORY, POLITICS, AND FEMINISM

Jane Duran

University of Illinois Press • Urbana and Chicago

Library of Congress Cataloging-in-Publication Data

Duran, Jane.
Eight women philosophers :
theory, politics, and feminism / Jane Duran.
p.   cm.
Includes bibliographical references and index.
ISBN-13: 978-0-252-03022-2 (cloth : alk. paper)
ISBN-10: 0-252-03022-2 (cloth : alk. paper)
ISBN-13: 978-0-252-07265-9 (pbk. : alk. paper)
ISBN-10: 0-252-07265-0 (pbk. : alk. paper)
1. Women philosophers—Europe.
I. Title.
B105.W6D87   2006
190—dc22   2005009411

For the Golden Bears

University of California at Berkeley
Class of 1968

contents

preface

New work on women philosophers proceeds apace, and much of the work bears a double burden. On the one hand, it is necessary, and even desirable, to attempt to place women philosophers in the canon, if only because so little effort in this direction has previously been made. On the other hand, without a goal of articulating what is different about the contribution that women have made, and continue to make, there is a question-begging air about the aim of placing women philosophers in the general rubric in the first place.

A good deal of the initial effort has consisted of anthologies devoted to introducing the reader to the work of philosophers who happened to be women, or of attempts to delineate stylistic differences between women thinkers and the more traditional male philosophers. Thus far, there has been little effort to move in two or more directions simultaneously: it ought to be possible to set out some of the philosophical content of a number of women thinkers, to be precise about how it contrasts with that of some better-known thinkers of their various times, and then again to spell out what might be the gender-related content, if any, of such thought. But until now it has not been possible to find one volume that performed these tasks; instead, an astute and careful reader would have to peruse a number of anthologies and some single-author works to obtain an overview, and even then some women philosophers whose work has been rightly considered to be more standardly philosophical—for example, Anne Conway—are virtually left out.

In the present work, the goal is to bring together in a single book introductory material with respect to eight women thinkers. The women in question, almost without exception, are indisputably philosophical thinkers of their time, and yet (with few exceptions) there is very little available on them currently that has been done by writers with philosophical, as opposed to historical or literary, training. In some cases, part of the difficulty has been simply that the work of the woman in question was difficult, and that most of those with the necessary philosophical background would probably have chosen to work on other, better-known figures. This is certainly the case with Anne Conway and Edith Stein, and to some extent even with Simone Weil. In other instances, it has not been until recently that an adequate amount of material by the woman in question was readily available for study; this can be said of Harriet Taylor Mill, and also of Mary Astell, at least insofar as her more political work is concerned.

Finally, many have probably been reluctant to tackle the questions alluded to earlier: how and in what ways have these women written work that might be considered philosophical? If they have composed such work, how does it differ from that of a number of male thinkers of the relevant period? And if it does differ, is the fact that the work was written by a woman relevant to our valuation of the work, or even to its comprehension?

Because this text attempts to answer these questions in some detail, no outline will be provided here of the responses. But it is important to note that, in a sense, each chapter is itself a stand-alone work, while the introduction and conclusion of the book respond to the questions about the importance of gender categories—and of philosophical categories—in outlining thought of given periods. Each chapter is divided into eight sections, and the sections proceed in a direct manner to adumbrate the thought of the philosophers in question along parallel paths. The opening, general section is followed by sections on metaphysics and ontology, theory of value, and comparisons with other (usually female) thinkers of the time. Then a second quartet of sections follows: the first section provides an overview of the ways in which the thought of the philosopher might be deemed to mesh with feminist theory; the next shows the relationships to feminist theory of knowledge, and the third, to today's third-wave feminist concerns. Finally, the last section of each chapter provides a summary and a set of concluding remarks about the thinker in question.

Work on women philosophers asks us to retain an open-mindedness about what is constitutive of philosophical thought that is often sadly lacking in professional philosophical circles, while at the same time asking us to be prepared for some surprises insofar as theory is concerned. In the cases of Conway, Wollstonecraft, Stein, and Beauvoir, for example, a great deal of what the philosopher has set out is more standardly philosophical—and in some startling ways—than a reader might naively think. In other cases—such as Weil and Hildegard—the thought is, although in general "philosophy," decidedly different from most of the philosophy of its era.

Women philosophers were certainly neglected until recently, but one of the greatest conundra with respect to their work is the fact that, in many cases, they were better known, and more straightforwardly accepted as philosophers, in their own time than they later became. This alone must give us pause when we consider the forces that give rise to canon formation and to the compiling of lists of philosophers of given eras. But new lists and new canons can and do emerge. When such categories are constructed in the future, we can only hope that all eight of the women whose work is examined here will be among those listed.

acknowledgments

As is the case with most of the books written at the University of California at Santa Barbara, this one at least partially owes its genesis to the research discussion groups on campus. There, a series of talks or meetings, some of which focused on feminist theory, prepared the way for its chapters. Most helpful were the Political Theory Reading Group and the 1998 meetings of the Science, Technology, and Culture Studies Group; in each case, although some meetings focused on topics having little to do with feminist thought, the process of discussion and focus was helpful to the germination of this work.

My teaching at UCSB has helped me focus philosophically directed material through student discussion. Of particular assistance have been classes taught in the Department of Black Studies, the Women's Studies Program, and the Gevirtz Graduate School of Education. The courses I have frequently taught on black women writers and on black philosophy and social thought have been especially helpful in developing the capacity to identify conceptual questions in guises in which they do not often occur in standard philosophical texts. My graduate seminars on educational issues have allowed me to focus, for example, on philosophies of education and on race and ethnicity in education, both crucial to an understanding of how some women thinkers, such as Weil, have preceded us in addressing relevant issues without having received adequate credit.

It is customary to thank individuals while acknowledging that no thanks is sufficient: for help over the years, and, in some cases, for assistance that was particularly relevant to this project, I thank Kourtney Bristow, Kerry Callahan, Jenny Cook-Gumperz, Sylvia Curtis, Martha Swearingen Davis, Sara Ebenreck, Debra Jones, Greg Kelly, Oyeronke Oyewumi, Cedric Robinson, Earl Stewart, Cecile Tougas, and the members of the Society for the Study of Women Philosophers. Without the meetings of the latter group—most of which have occurred in conjunction with gatherings of the Eastern Division of the American Philosophical Association—it is difficult to know how many of us would have come to any adequate realization of the rich presence of women philosophical thinkers throughout history. *Presenting Women Philosophers* (2000), edited by Cecile Tougas and Sara Ebenreck, was of inestimable assistance in developing the ground for this project, not least because of the valuable focus on the work of Mary Astell that I was able to develop in a chapter for that work.

Although the work herein is significantly different, I also did work on some of the other women thinkers cited here for *Ratio,* the *Newsletter on Feminism and Philosophy of the American Philosophical Association,* and the anthology *Hypatia's Daughters,* edited by Linda Lopez McAlister. In addition, I wrote pieces on Kierkegaard, Quine, and Augustine for the Pennsylvania State University Press series Re-reading the Canon, and although these individuals certainly are not women thinkers, the work undertaken at that time helped to sharpen my ability to be precise about feminist and feminist-oriented lines of thought. In 2001, Armen T. Marsoobian, editor of *Metaphilosophy,* published my paper on John Dewey, which had a similar orientation.

While we as women philosophers write, we engage in projects similar to those examined in this work. It has been inspiring to read Hildegard, Anne Conway, Mary Astell, Mary Wollstonecraft, Harriet Taylor Mill, Edith Stein, Simone Weil, and Simone de Beauvoir in the spirit of instruction. We can only be glad that we can be students of their work.

eight women philosophers

introduction

The current project of retrieving the work of women philosophers is in many
ways similar to earlier projects of recovery. In a sense, the work of women philosophers has been buried, literally and metaphorically, and its finding requires both actual excavation and careful archival search. Other such projects,
including those having to do with persons of color or victims of societal transgression, remind us of the importance of salvaging work from the past.[1]

Contemporary work has helped us come to grips with the notion that
much of the writing done by women thinkers in the past may be philosophical in the large sense, without necessarily being categorizable as "philosophy" proper. Nonetheless, it is clear now that many women who wrote and
thought extensively about philosophical topics were considered to be philosophers during their own time—there are certainly more such women than
we might at first think—and their work was lost or ignored only at a later
point. In reclassifying their work, examining it, and presenting it for readers
today, we must remember why it is that the work needs such presentation. In
this effort, the aim is to give a clear account of the thought and context of
work for eight women, many of whom were labeled philosophers during
their time, but whose work, until recently, was seldom covered in courses of
philosophy taught in American colleges and universities.

The eight women in question have been selected partly because of their importance, but also in part because of the very qualities alluded to above; in most cases, these thinkers were recognized as having contributed to philosophical thought during their own era, and it was only at a later point that their names ceased to be listed among those who wrote during a given period. To be sure, among the twentieth-century women thinkers to be examined here, at least two have fairly regularly been conceptualized as philosophical thinkers even during their own lifetimes. Nevertheless, what these eight women have in common is something greater than their femaleness or their quantity of written work. For a variety of reasons, their work is only now receiving its approximate due.

If the notion of retrieval reminds us of various other sorts of reconceptualization patterns that have resulted in the production of volumes on individual thinkers and their cultures, the analogy is a valuable one. But the lot of women thinkers, although it may vary from culture to culture, has tended to be a difficult one, even when we conceive of it in global terms.[2] Global male dominance has meant that women who pursued the scholarly life were frequently regarded as unusual or even deranged. Thus the project of trying to retrieve the work of women thinkers in particular is of more than ordinary importance. The work of figures within a given culture will have some immediate appeal for members of that culture. But the androcentrism of almost all human cultures has meant that women's work has been derogated everywhere. Thus there is some urgency to the task of its resuscitation.

In attempting to weave together concepts having to do with a wide variety of women thinkers, many gaps must be bridged by our own desire to create a fit. Thus large gaps in time, such as we find between, for example, the life of Mary Astell and that of Harriet Taylor Mill, must not be allowed to become so formidable that we are unable to place these women thinkers under some of the same rubrics. At least insofar as the European countries and their offshoots are concerned, cultural factors will persevere over time; although conditions will have changed to some extent between, say, the early part of Mary Astell's life in the middle of the seventeenth century and that of Harriet Taylor Mill's time approximately a hundred fifty years later, the force of custom against women, particularly women scholars, will remain generally the same. We are also faced with some differences within the European cultures in general, and particularly with respect to twentieth-century France, the home of two of our thinkers; we might be tempted to think that these differences are so large as to militate against the belief that women working at this time and place faced obstacles similar to those faced by women in seventeenth-century England. But even a cursory examination of the periods and places will show that, sadly, there is a strong similarity in the conditions.

What women have accomplished in the "philosophical" realm has often been done under categories that might be thought to be nonphilosophical. Some of the early scholarship on the amalgamation of work by women philosophers was collected in a special issue of the journal *Hypatia* in the late 1980s; there the dearth of such previous work was made obvious.[3] In my work here, despite the multitude of writings by women that are philosophical in the large sense without being narrowly philosophical in the more professional sense, I will concentrate on the work of women who, by and large, were considered to be philosophers even by the male thinkers of their time. There are more than enough women philosophers to go around; the title of this work could contain a vastly larger number and still not do justice to this barely explored topic.

Part of the difficulty stems from the obvious fact that women writing on philosophical issues have been forced, by the very regnant nature of male thought, to respond largely to male thinkers. Thus, in many instances, their work has been believed to be an attack on the work of some noteworthy male, or perhaps a failure to understand his work completely. This, combined with female authorship, has no doubt led to the work's being "lost" or "misplaced." In other cases, especially with the French thinkers of more recent times, such writings were recognized as falling under the general rubric of philosophy, but simply as not being "standard" enough or, sadly, "good" enough. Anne Conway and Mary Astell, in particular, should have been cited more frequently than they have been.

The project of searching for the work of women philosophers, expounding on it, and tying it to other contemporary work inevitably raises a number of questions having to do with contemporary theory and its relevance. Essentialism is, of course, an area that would require investigation, since it is obvious that a project that proceeds by gender category must be making at least a minimal statement in that regard. All of the theoretical questions having to do with poststructuralism/postmodernism also come to the fore, especially since the notion of an authorial voice will be a prominent one. Given that we are dealing with women thinkers from diverse eras and times, it is hard to draw connections without forcing them. Finally, since much of the work here is historical, even the literary investigations usually labeled the "New Historicism" are more than relevant, since, although they are often mentioned in contexts more purely literary, there is sometimes not as sharp a distinction between the literary and the philosophical as we might imagine.

Examining the work of a number of women philosophers also demands that we exercise care to avoid believing that women's work will somehow es-

chew certain hallowed areas of philosophy, such as metaphysics and epistemology. Indeed, since so much of what has been done in feminist philosophy
in recent years is related to these two areas, they may prove among the most
fruitful for investigation. In any case, any given thinker may have worked in
one or more of the traditional subareas of philosophy, and yet again the de-
marcations here may not be as precise as we might wish, particularly with respect to thinkers at an earlier point in time.

Hildegard of Bingen, Anne Conway, Mary Astell, Mary Wollstonecraft,
Harriet Taylor Mill, Edith Stein, Simone Weil, and Simone de Beauvoir are all
women, and all thinkers whose work is recognizably philosophical. But they
span the late eleventh or early twelfth century to the twentieth, and encompass, nationally, France, Germany, Great Britain, and an area that later became
part of contemporary Germany. Their work has received a variety of labels,
from "mystical" to "derivative" and "literary," and they were in various ways
celebrated, scorned, and ignored in their own lives. Yet each of these women
has more recently been the subject of a fair amount of written commentary,
and four of them, at least (Weil, Beauvoir, Stein, and Conway), are now frequently cited in compendia of philosophical works.

The point of my work is to provide a ground or basis from which other students may proceed. If there was a time when it was possible to take a course in
philosophy at an American college or university without ever hearing a
woman's name, it may be hoped that future circumstances will make this
much less likely. Each of these women received at least some recognition and
philosophical correspondence in her own time. An accurate story is that, as
time went on, many became less well known than they had been in their own
lifetimes. Anne Conway, for example, had been mentioned to Leibniz and
others, and she is frequently credited with being the originator of the term
"monad."[4] But by the early twentieth century she had become more or less
forgotten, and although her name was revived somewhat by the publication
in 1930 of Marjorie Hope Nicolson's *The Conway Letters,* a work that tied her to
the circle of Cambridge Platonists, her more extensive and tightly constructed
philosophical work seems to have been ignored.[5] In sum, the project of reviv-
ing the work of women philosophers is a necessary one. But it demands attention to a number of difficult areas.

Why Women?

One of the chief problematic areas of this endeavor is the grouping together
of women thinkers in one category, a category, to be sure, of social construc-

tion. But ample evidence indicates that it is not merely our contemporary look at things that impels us to notice the differing status accorded to women scholars; rather, there is a long history of women's having noticed such problems themselves.

Part of what drove the seventeenth-century women thinkers to whose work I will be referring was an awareness of their status as women. But such awareness has been part and parcel of, at least, the Western tradition, and it has certainly affected the work of many women whose writings would not ordinarily be deemed to be philosophical. As Mary Ellen Waithe notes in her *History of Women Philosophers,* even the Pythagorean women showed an awareness of women's different social station, and that awareness manifested itself in their writings.[6] With respect to their interests and their conceptual style, she writes: "[T]he Pythagorean women were concerned with applications of the prevailing ethical theory to everyday life. . . . They are particularly concerned with how to best implement that principle in fulfilling their preordained social roles as women."[7]

By no means all women theorists or writers exhibit as much overt concern, but the fact that we can trace these sorts of concerns to the ancient era is testimony to the powerful force of social constructs and their underlying tie-ins to what, in some cases, are physical demands. Women thinkers, writers, and scholars, from the times of the Pythagorean school and the Buddhist canon to the Renaissance and modernist periods, have very frequently demonstrated a strong awareness of the combined forces of male oppression on their lives and their thought.[8] Although many women have, perhaps somewhat defensively, tried to steer clear of overt commentary on their problematic status as women writers and scholars, others have been much more forthcoming about the difficulties involved. From Sor Juana Ines de la Cruz to Ida B. Wells to Sylvia Plath, a line can be drawn that not only connects them in terms of their biological status as women, but casts them together insofar as they acknowledged the existence of this problematic area in their writings. When Plath writes, "I am jealous of men. . . . It is an envy born of the desire to be active and doing, not passive and listening," she is simply articulating, in her particular terms, a recurring theme throughout the writings of women across time and even across cultures.[9]

Because so much has been done in contemporary feminist theory on the possibility of differing conceptual styles defined largely by gender, and on the ramifications of this for the education of girls, it might be thought to be too naive to introduce this problem in a work concerned almost entirely with the productions of women who can readily be classified as philosophical thinkers. Nevertheless, there may be some reason to believe that such differing styles manifest themselves in the work of women. This contentious and difficult area is one with which we will have to struggle throughout this work, but one can initially hypothesize a number of ways in which such differences might manifest themselves. Differences of subject matter are obvious, but mode of presentation, style, and even length are all possible areas of demarcation. Much of this sort of conceptualization moves directly into questions of essentialism, with which I will deal shortly. Nevertheless, a common bond linking most women thinkers—a stated realization occurring in their texts that they are female and that this has affected their work—may translate into other sorts of differences, both acknowledged and unacknowledged.

The unifying factor between both sorts of concerns—being female in a male world, and possible employment of differing styles or modes—is best articulated in a passage by Sian Miles, anthologizer of the work of Simone Weil: "It was about this time [upon entering the lycée] that Simone was to fall into what she subsequently described as a bottomless despair at being excluded from the 'transcendent realm only great men enter and where truth resides.'"[10]

Weil's use of the term "transcendent" here is doubly evocative. It is not only that the great men reside in such a realm; it is also the case that their thought is aimed at those heights. And yet if this philosophic tradition, of which Simone Weil was already well aware, has always excluded women, then there may indeed be something to the notion that the style developed by women thinkers tends to differ from the transcendental. That "all accounts," removed-from-the-material style has been thought by many to be quintessentially androcentric. In any case, remarks such as these can be found throughout the works of the thinkers whose writings I will examine here.

Women traditionally were denied access not only to levels of education, schools, bodies of decision making, and arenas of discussion, but many women were deprived as well of the physical conditions that make intellectual work possible. Simple demarcators, such as the possession of writing equipment, places in which to work, and uninterrupted time, show up in the work of women scholars as desiderata rarely encountered. Most destructively, the passion of women to think, write, and engage in an active mental life has usually been seen as a sign of deficiency or abnormality on the part of the woman in question, and, in many cases, it has meant that the individual was not truly a woman. Miles also writes that Weil's giftedness, intellectuality, and inattention to conventions of personal appearance and social life in general made her "conspicuous" and "miserable."[11] Traits that would go comparatively unremarked upon in an intellectual male become debilitating and stigmatizing in women.

The personal lives of women philosophers thus become fodder for criticism that would not be leveled against men, no matter what sort of life the male scholar led. The four thinkers to be examined here who come last chronologically all lived in times close enough to our own that comparisons can be more easily made, and the thread of opprobrium that one might expect attaches itself significantly to their lives, particularly in the cases of Harriet Taylor Mill and Simone de Beauvoir. If Simone Weil's case is marked because, as near as can be made out, she had no significant close relationships with any adults in the years before her early death, Taylor Mill and Beauvoir received extensive and harsh criticism precisely because they did have such relationships.[12]

In general, it seems that whatever path the intellectually oriented woman takes, she will suffer from some degree of ostracism and public shaming. Until recently, there simply has been little or no accepted role for the woman scholar; to be a woman scholar was itself a contradiction in terms. As Jo Ellen Jacobs writes with respect to Harriet Taylor Mill, "[l]iving independently of her husband from her mid-twenties until her husband's death was not an easy task for a Victorian woman. If she were to prevent open scandal, Harriet must tread carefully."[13] But treading carefully has been the natural path of almost all women intellectuals and certainly of the women philosophers whose work spans the nineteenth and twentieth centuries.

If it is difficult to find a way in which to discuss easily the contentious issue of the allegedly different style of women thinkers, at least taken as a tendency, it is also difficult to discuss differences in subject matter between male and female philosophers. Again, alluding for the moment only to the four women philosophers closest to us in time, there does appear to be a tendency to focus on areas of philosophy that, in today's terms, might be thought to be constitutive of theory of value. Although some women philosophers have unquestionably dealt with the carving-up-of-reality issues that in general comprise metaphysics—and Anne Conway is a notable example—Harriet Taylor Mill, Edith Stein, Simone Weil, and Simone de Beauvoir all wrote extensively on such issues as ethics, the nature of the religious life, and education. If we may think of androcentrism as having "stylistic aggression" as one of its foci, many women thinkers have failed to exhibit this Complete Account style of thought in their work.[14] Although there are obvious variations, it is probably the case that the majority of women philosophers examined here have not been particularly concerned with grand schemes and systems. But this is nothing more than a tendency—and, again, Conway and, to some extent, Hildegard of Bingen are exceptions.

If the time period of a thinker's work is crucially important, as it obviously is in doing this particular work, we must think carefully about how we can get a clearer picture of what has transpired during a given time. Recently, the work of Stephen Greenblatt and others—work that has come to be labeled "New Historicism"—has made great inroads in our understanding of the sixteenth and seventeenth centuries, and the approach in general may be a worthy one.[15] Particularly salient to any work done during this era is the awareness throughout the Continent of the encounter with the New World and its peoples. Although one might naively think that this would not be particularly relevant to philosophizing and philosophical issues, part of what the New Historicists have succeeded in showing us is that such events inevitably cast their shadow, and this shadow must be noticed and remarked upon. Anne Conway and Mary Astell cannot have worked in a vacuum— their work must be read in light of what we now know about Europe in general during this period, and Europe's encounters with other lands.

Thinking Through the New Historicism

Writing in the *New York Review of Books* in 2001, Frank Kermode lets us know that the technique of literary criticism known as New Historicism may have had its day. He cites evidence that it is on the decline when he notes: "New Historicism has been a dominant interest among academic literary critics for something like a generation, so it is not surprising that some of them are showing signs of restlessness and hinting that it's time to move on. . . . [T]he fashion is said to be passing its zenith [but Catherine Gallagher and Stephen Greenblatt] provide compelling instances of what, in the right hands, the method or practice can still achieve."[16]

A fashion, literary or otherwise, cannot be said to be passing its zenith unless its ascendancy was a noteworthy event, and this much can truly be said of New Historicism. This way of writing about matters literary, as Kermode has it, "refuses to isolate literature from other forms of discourse, and assumes that the entire culture . . . can be regarded as text."[17]

Until recently, no style of treating literary history would have been thought to be relevant to philosophy, even historical views of philosophy, for professional philosophers have tended to regard the pronouncements of other philosophical thinkers as pristine matters emanating from the great void. Other turns in philosophy itself, however, such as the genuine rise in interest in historical matters, and new areas of investigation, such as feminist theory and multicultural matters, have altered philosophical thinking. Although it might not be accurate to say that philosophers are in general aware or even apprised of styles of theorizing that might be thought to be acute forms of literary criticism, such as New Historicism, such styles can no longer be said to be completely irrelevant to philosophy.

A good deal of the writing about such figures as Marlowe and Shakespeare, for example, now assumes that such historical watersheds for Europe as the discovery and encounter of the New World are directly related to the texts of the authors' plays, and can be spoken of and commented upon to elucidate areas within those plays. It is also considered permissible to move texts back and forth between chronological eras—in Greenblatt's *Learning to Curse,* one of the essays makes explicit comparisons between Marlowe's *The Jew of Malta* and Marx's "On the Jewish Question," despite the centuries intervening between these two pieces of writing.[18]

The work of Richard Rorty, Richard Bernstein, and Cornel West—to name but three thinkers professionally trained as philosophers—is both historically sensitive and aware of the need to see philosophy as a sort of text. West's work on Emerson in *The American Evasion of Philosophy,* for instance, has the illuminating quality that it does because it is aware of and sensitive to the historical period of Emerson's writing.[19] Taken in toto, recent trends in both literary theory and philosophy seem to indicate a renewed awareness of the impossibility, especially in cases of texts that are themselves historical, of writing about these texts as if they sprang full-blown from the theorist's conceptualization process without allusion to the surrounding culture.

To name but one woman philosopher with whom I will be concerned, Mary Astell constitutes a case in point. Much of the commentary on her work has focused on her own involvement with, and citation of, the lives of others at the time, of whom we have some historical record. Her work on marriage, women's role in marriage, and the ethical stance that might be pursued by a woman trapped in a "shipwrack'd" marriage was influenced greatly by the accounts available to her at that time of the marriage of the Duke and Duchess of Mazarine.[20] This aristocratic marriage was the topic of much discussion in London circles, and we can imagine that the set of circumstances it represents was not unique, although it certainly became exemplary. The point is that undertaking scholarship on the life and work of Mary Astell will require an investigation into much that surrounded her at the time—even if it seems, on the surface, to be irrelevant. As Kermode has written, a great deal of New Historicist work comes from the "'outlandish,' . . . well outside the range of normal historiography."[21] Marriages, births, accounts of the plague, of various royal progresses, of Roundheads and others—all of these will inevitably make their way into an historically sensitive account of the life and times of Mary Astell, who was born in 1666.

The strong a priori tradition in philosophy, and the tendency to pit one "great system" against another, even when writing of matters historical, has militated against a sensitivity to context. It is not an exaggeration to say that context in the past was, in general, ignored. Two forces currently working in academic circles (and even occasionally in strictly philosophical circles) have done much to alter this sort of approach. The first is the new attention to matters historical, some of which derives in itself from Continental traditions of thought. The second, which may pertain more peculiarly to philosophy, is simply the reemergence, as important and valued thinkers, of figures such as Dewey, who were never allied with the classical a priori tradition to begin with. Thus it is much less recondite now to attempt work that is sensitive to milieu and to the lives of others, whether scholars or not, who were contemporaries of the person in question.

To take one more example, much that has been done on Anne Conway has been sensitive to era, and we already know, through the writings of Marjorie Hope Nicolson and others, of Conway's correspondence and acquaintance with a number of the Cambridge Platonists.[22] But a fresher take, and one more in tune with work being done on literary matters, will ask us to look not only at Henry More, Leibniz, and others, but to look at the general temper and tone of their times, as well. In other words, to quote Kermode again, we may well have to incorporate some of the "outlandish" to get a feel for the period in which Conway lived.[23] Because we already have so much historical information on this particular period in Great Britain, it should not be difficult to fill in the blanks on a great deal that would inevitably have transpired in circles frequented by a viscountess; even a learned viscountess who corresponded with Continental philosophers must have gone to the royal court, for example, or known those who were present at court. It is by attending to details such as these that we can create illuminating portraits both of the thinkers in question and of their thought.

Attending to matters historical does not necessarily mean that less attention is paid to matters philosophical, or that the attention that is paid to them is somehow less rigorous than it would have been. Rather, it means that the thought is seen in context, and it simply is not possible for any human being—male or female, European or otherwise—to theorize without at least some influence from the surrounding environment. When we write of the work of the Rationalists, for example, we attempt to give an account of their ontologies, which, seemingly divorced from influence derived from the senses, appear to have sprung full-blown from some alabaster slate. But this is only in comparison to theorizing that makes its actual debt to the senses better known. Rather, it is the case that no work, whether a priori or not, can possibly be divorced from at least some of the social influence of the time, and it is only recently that philosophers have come to grips with this.

Finally, there is the matter of philosophical style. Some of the tropes employed by philosophers are clearly borrowed both from literature of the time and from the work of other philosophers, and twists of argument or strands of rebuttal are all rhetorical devices that owe their generation to the style of the period. Asserting this does not mean that one has to assent to the notion that philosophical argument is nothing more than rhetoric, although many are currently making this claim. The idea is simply that lines can be drawn that connect the styles of a given period with each other, whether those styles are found in works that are usually considered philosophical, literary, or neither.

New Historicism had the impact that it did because the outlandish quality of some of the examples cited seemed to shed light on a good deal of what was being proffered as text. Debates about the status of Native Americans (their falling under such rubrics as "human" or "animal," for example) might at one time have been considered irrelevant to a discussion of *The Tempest,* but citation of the work of Bartolomeo de las Casas and his opponents during the period after the discovery of the New World makes the character of Caliban much more intriguing.[24]

Just so, an inquiry into, for example, many of the practices and policies of the Vichy government in the years 1940–43 is not only interesting work in and of itself, but may aid us in understanding what many have perceived as Simone Weil's complete disavowal of her Jewish heritage. The work of women philosophers has probably, by all accounts, been even more influenced by context on the whole than that of male philosophers. Women have rarely had the time or leisure to attempt the complete divorce from the realm of the senses that some male philosophers appear to have attempted. Although there are individual exceptions, many women thinkers have not only been more immersed in the world of day-to-day functioning, but have also been wives and mothers, roles that clearly cannot be discarded as easily as those of husbands and fathers. To fail to take into account the importance of context is to fail to get any clear account of what it is that an individual thinker is saying. Our attempts to develop portraits of the work of women philosophers should culminate in no less than the fullest and clearest portrayals that we can make. In order to create these portrayals, it is imperative that we steep ourselves in a given period, find out as much as we can about that period, and then use the information to assist us in developing an account of the female thinker in question.

Post Post-Theory

All of our inquiries may be for naught, at least according to some, since much of the contemporary French theory that has made its way into the United States undercuts notions of a self, of authorial integrity, and invalidates attempts to grasp some concept of what it might mean to be a woman philosophizing. At this point in the American academic scene, these concerns are not new, and they have been discussed, debated, and rehashed to the point of ceasing to be of compelling interest. Nevertheless, a project such as this one will have to make an investigation of the essentialist notions that surround it, and, in so doing, at least some questions with respect to poststructuralist/postmodern theory will have to be raised.

According to much that is being written currently, one defect of an inquiry such as this one is that it assumes, from the outset, a sort of binary oppositionality that is probably more of a construct than an actuality. In addition, it might be argued, in assuming such a bifurcation, it makes it less likely that other bifurcations, real or imagined, can be dispensed with in the future. To cite just a bit of the work that moves in this direction, Alice Jardine, writing in *Gynesis,* asserts that: "'Woman,' as a new rhetorical space, is inseparable from the most radical moments of most contemporary disciplines. . . . Caught between the predominantly American feminist's 'know thyself' (your *true* self versus 'false images') and the modern discovery that there is no more self to know, she may even feel obliged to opt for one camp over the other [emphasis in original]."[25]

When Jardine writes that "there is no more self to know," she is, of course, borrowing from a number of thinkers, including Lacan, Derrida, and Deleuze, all of whom are cited in her work. Although a work written in the Anglo-American analytic tradition, such as this one, cannot be heavily influenced by such theory, since its presuppositions run in a different direction, it would be unfair and unjust to begin a categorization of the work of women philosophers without noting that, according to some, such a label is virtually meaningless.

Regardless of the notion of authorship, there is a difficulty inherent in looking for strands of commonality across thinkers separated by culture and time, and in a work in 2001 on global feminist epistemologies, I set out the problems inherent in such a task.[26] But the polarity caused by the appearance of gender disparity, especially with regard to European societies, is real, and cannot be overlooked. Thus in an area of endeavor as hypermasculinized as philosophy, it should be immediately apparent that gender is important, and that there is little difficulty in inquiring into the lot of women in the discipline, and wondering if their fate has been different. The sheer paucity of citations of women thinkers assures us that it has.

In addition to the putative problem posed by attempting to find areas of commonality among women, another problem brought to the fore by contemporary theory is that of absence rendered as a positive. In other words, there is something in itself androcentric—at least according to some—in attempting to turn the marginality of women into a statement, one that then participates in the regnant hegemony of (male) dominance. Those trained in the Anglo-American tradition may have genuine difficulty in seeing this as any kind of theoretically troublesome area, but its recurrence in the literature, and especially, for example, in Cixous, assures us that it is regarded as being a recondite matter by some.[27] Citing Michel Leiris, Jardine again provides us with a gloss when she writes: "Always writing at the very edges of traditional narrative, he [Leiris] addresses himself to a woman, but 'only because she is absent'; 'she' is not in any way 'an object,' but rather the 'melancholic substance' of that which is missing for 'him': that which forces him to desire, that is, to write. . . . And that place, the emptiness of that abyss in his self, is female."[28]

How does that which is absent become a subject? This is not, obviously, a philosophical problem in the sense of the tradition with which most American philosophers are familiar. Nevertheless, this rather strained literary problem, taken at least partially from Lacanian theory, does present a difficulty that is not incomprehensible. Women philosophers have been more or less forced by circumstances into the adoption of a male gaze, or at least a male style of thought. There will indeed be a problem in trying to unpack their work with the simultaneous awareness of their anomalous status as females in a male realm and their (already understood) adoption of a male overview that is, in a sense, hypermasculinized.

Still another area of "post-" theory presents itself, at least marginally to us, when we undertake the project of looking at the work of women almost all of whom wrote during the European period of colonial expansion. Although we may find virtually no overt mention of matters colonial in their work, colonialism cannot help but form part of the intellectual backdrop for their thinking and writing, and this is particularly true of nineteenth- and early twentieth-century thinkers. Colonial expansion allowed Europe to continue to see itself as the source of light and reason, while the inhabitants of other parts of the world were routinely grouped under the rubric "natives."[29] Postcolonial theory, such as the work of Edward Said, not only highlights for us the dependence of Europe on this relation, but the extent to which internalized oppression affected the mind-set of individuals in colonized areas.[30] Although, as indicated, we may be unable to find any one instance of advertence to colonial matters in the philosophical work of European women thinkers, these areas of concern necessarily form an important part of the underlying cultural current, and must be reflected in the works of writers of the periods in question in a number of ways, even if those ways are indirect.

One time period in which we might be able to find at least some advertence to matters best dealt with by the postcolonial is the nineteenth century. Said, in "Jane Austen and Empire," notes the extent to which the liberal and reformist thinking of the period—much of it attributable to John Stuart Mill, and thus, as we will argue, to the Mills, and even Harriet Taylor Mill—rested on a certain set of assumptions about those who were not to fall under the reforms.[31] As Said is careful to argue, assumptions about who was left out were the underpinnings of much that was accomplished, intellectually and otherwise, during the era of colonial expansion. He notes this when he says: "If there was cultural resistance to the notion of an imperial mission, there was not much support for that resistance in the main departments of cultural thought. Liberal though he was, John Stuart Mill—as a telling case in point—could still say 'The sacred duties which civilized nations owe to the independence and nationality of each other, are not binding towards those to whom nationality and independence are certain evil, or at best a questionable good.'"[32]

The reader of European ancestry and education may not be discomfited by Mill's remarks (after all, remarks like those are a staple of such educational backgrounds), but this is precisely why Said is taking the trouble to point them out. We revere both the Mills for their progressive thought, their championing of women's issues, and their work against tyranny. But all of this work took for granted the "backwardness" of certain groups of people, their lack of fitness for self-rule, and so forth.

Contemporary French theory undercuts our notions of the self, the feminine, and authorial proprietariness; postcolonial theory is similar in some ways, written in larger terms. It goes against the grain of the theorizing that permits Eurocentric thought to hold dominant sway and to define itself against Others. But both of these sorts of theorizing owe much to Marx, and at least some parts of contemporary Continental thought owe something to Freud. Marx has been appropriated and reappropriated, to be sure, by groups for whom his work could never have originally been intended: theorists of the African Diaspora, for example, have been among the leaders in articulating a new vision of Marx that has come to be known as "Black Marxism."[33] What Marx has in common with these other lines of thought is that all of them cut against the solidity of the previous regnant lines of thought. Marx taught us about false consciousness; poststructuralism, indeed, most of what is now termed "postmodern," tells us that much of what passes for ordinary intellectual categorization is a sort of false consciousness. The tie-in between Marx and postcolonial theory is probably more obvious; although the Asian, African, and Native American inhabitants addressed by much of postcolonial theory almost never constituted an actual proletariat, their degree of oppression parallels that of the European or industrialized proletariat, and it is this degree of oppression that allows a theorist such as Said to work with, for example, Palestinians as a point of departure.[34]

Such radical attempts at theorizing may initially look as if they have little to offer us in our quest for the historical, but they are of assistance in helping us decide how to read the historical now. The project of attempting to find women philosophers is of no use if we cannot make their work relevant to our lives. The "post-" theories can be of great assistance here.

Essentialism Amok

Any project that attempts to look at women over time or over a multiplicity of cultures is bound to run up against the current bogey of feminist theorizing (and of some other sorts of theorizing as well), essentialism. This term is not meant in the technical sense in which analytic philosophers have tried to deal with such issues using techniques of contemporary philosophy of language or philosophy of logic. Rather, the idea is that there are "totalizing" currents in thinking about women cross-chronologically or cross-culturally that impede us and prevent us from seeing particular cultures, specific time periods, individual women within those cultures and time periods, and so on.

Part of the flavor of "essentialism" in this use is captured to some extent by the work of Frankfurt School theoreticians, for example, who had no compunctions about discussing Reason or "the ego." Thus, in his work "The End of Reason," in which he attempts to discuss how calculative empiricism combined with the market led to some of the horrors of the twentieth century, Horkheimer writes: "Nevertheless, reason has not been cancelled altogether from the vocabulary of those who are up to date, but has only been reduced to its pragmatic significance much more radically than ever before."[35]

It might seem odd to claim that what Horkheimer means by "reason" here amounts to an essentialist use of the term, but this example is instructive, for Horkheimer is attempting to posit an old-fashioned, rationalist use of the term in which reason has an almost transcendental power and is capable of being reified. In this vein many of those who are most critical of projects involving some use of the term "woman" make a similar claim; their assertion is that it amounts to a reification of the term, as if there were some fundamental underlying womanness at which all uses of the term could get.

There are at least a couple of rejoinders to these lines of argument, and it is important to set them out so that intellectual work in this area is not vitiated from the start. The first rejoinder is perhaps the most important: it can readily be conceded that, indeed, projects about "woman" or "women" may very well be tracing areas of commonality across cultures or eras, for without such tracing it is difficult to establish the pattern of intense and overt discrimination that has undermined the works of women in almost every area of human endeavor. It may well be the case that at least some of these attributes reduce to the biological, for it is clear that women's capacity for childbearing—menstruation, lactation, pregnancy, and menopause—is the object of ritual taboo and belief in almost all cultures. Thus, at least superficially, there is nothing so nonsensical about the concept of woman.

The second rejoinder is related, but slightly to the side. It may also be the case that, in attempting to discuss woman, at least some totalizing errors are made. But the price of avoiding these errors is simply that of failing to engage in the project. If the rubric "woman philosopher" is too essentialist, we can eschew the investigation into the works of women philosophers. But, oddly enough, this is what has already happened, so to speak, since much of the work of women thinkers has either been discarded or ignored. Thus a rebuttal to those who attack essentialism is to note that without some essentialist theorizing as a base, much important work cannot be done.

One common error among those who want to accuse theorists of unnecessary essentializing is to assume that thinkers who choose to pursue areas of commonality are making the claim that something (x) holds true for every individual (y) in a given category. Thus some who have been concerned with feminist essentializing have seemed to assume that claims are being made for all women throughout time. The truth is that very few, if any, feminist theorists have attempted to make such claims, because it is obvious that cultural responses to women are enormous and vary over geography and chronological change. Thus almost all generalizations, if read carefully, are couched in qualified language. It may, for example, be the case that almost all women have been on the receiving end of at least some oppression in human cultures simply because of the biological dictates of pregnancy, lactation, and so forth. But even work going back to the time of Margaret Mead's early studies indicates enormous variation in the way in which these levels of discrimination are carried out.[36] In addition, simple advertence to chromosomal structure will not do, as we can see from the historical record that some individuals very likely manifested phenotypic differences for what would today be considered chromosomal anomalies, and these differences may well have played out in historical roles assigned to the individuals by the societies in question.[37]

Some contemporary authors, such as the sociologist Oyeronke Oyewumi, have written of the hegemonic influence of Western feminists who purportedly have tried to foist a view of "women" on females of differing societies that simply will not go.[38] But the oversimplification here, it would appear, is in the assumption that the majority of feminists, even those writing from a developed or first-world perspective, have failed to recognize the existence of at least some cultural differences. An enormous amount of work in this area has already been done, and many of the leading feminist journals in the United States have addressed these issues again and again.[39] It may be accurate to say that some oversimplification has taken place in the past, but current efforts to ameliorate this difficulty are well under way, and, as indicated, there is an historical record of work in both the social sciences and philosophy that indicates that enormous differences exist, with respect to views on women, from culture to culture.

In general, it might seem that fears of essentialism or totalization are a bit of a bogey. If the fears are given into, it is clear that they prevent valuable work from being accomplished. The phobias with respect to these issues might alert us to one genuine danger, however: the danger that the social power and force of work done in the so-called developed nations has a hegemony of its own that prevents close reading of, or even dissemination of, work done in other areas. This seems to be the most accurate kind of worry targeted at contemporary feminist work done in the United States or English-speaking nations taken as a whole.

This worry has some merit. It is very difficult for most academics, in whatever discipline, to work with material from other cultures, regardless of language barriers. A great deal of feminist theory is currently being done in India, for example, yet many American feminists would find it problematic to delve into this material.[40] The worry probably is less an accurate source of dismay, however, when chronology is more of an issue than is culture. Thus the work of European women thinkers of earlier time periods should, at least in principle, be somewhat more familiar to American feminists than some contemporary work driven by other cultural concerns.

Whatever the results of the foregoing thought experiment, one thing seems certain: without examining work by women thinkers from other cultures and eras, the hegemony of contemporary Euro-American thought will continue. (And there is a hegemony here, as we can see from the extent to which such thought drives feminist theorizing throughout, for example, Latin America.) Thus this particular argument can be turned on its head: what needs to happen is for more women investigators to look both cross-culturally and cross-chronologically at the work of women theorists.

At the core of the essentialism debate seems to be some sort of question of value. We value work by women because it presumably tends to exhibit at least some differences, on the whole, from work by men, and because it has, in general, been less excavated. (And at least part of the reason for its smaller frequency of appearance probably is, in fact, its "difference.") Thus, in order to be clear about why we want to forward the overall project of investigating the work of women writers, thinkers, and philosophers, we must get clearer about what it is that makes their work valuable.

The answer seems to be that such work often exhibits differences of style, content, and presentation, and that these differences may be significant. Although not all the work done on women thinkers by any means even begins to address these issues, one can simply scan titles to see that a significant proportion of the archaeological work done does show a concern with the notion of difference. Even if little or no difference could be shown, the project of retrieving women's work will still be a worthy one, simply because so little work is in the historical record. And that brings us full circle—we can guess that much work by women was either lost, ignored, or destroyed simply because the author was female. This may not indicate much in terms of content, but, ironically, it does tend to indicate that there is, after all, a commonality to being female. The results of a thinker's being female have tended, on the whole, to be infelicitous and less than happy for both the individual thinker and the work.

PART ONE   Early Women Philosophers

HILDEGARD OF BINGEN   one

In approaching Hildegard of Bingen (1098–1179) philosophically, one immediately runs into the oldest and most cherished conundrum with respect to female philosophers. It appears to be the case that many female thinkers whose
work might be deemed to be philosophical wrote in styles that were somewhat nonstandard, even for their respective times. Thus, arguments have frequently been made that such women are absent from the canon because of
the fact that their work was demonstrably nonphilosophical, rather than due
to their sex. Counterarguments to the effect that at least some minor male
thinkers normally found in any group of philosophical names also employed
unusual or nonphilosophical styles often fall on deaf ears, no doubt because
one is preaching to the already antifeminist converted.

There is now an enormous amount of literature available in English on
Hildegard of Bingen, and at least some of it attempts to show that Hildegard's
thought is philosophical. Comparatively little of this work, however, has actually been done by those trained academically as philosophers; the bulk of
her English-language commentators have been medievalists with literary
training. There will probably tend to be a question-begging air about contro-

versies surrounding Hildegard's status well into the future. Her work is largely visionary, and the portion of her work that is not drawn from visions (such as the *Physica* and *Causae et Curae*) repeats a great deal of the then-empirical matter taken from handbooks of medicine and close observation.[1] The difficulty with respect to placing Hildegard's work is, then, the paradox just alluded to: if we claim that we cannot properly call her a philosopher because of the vision-derived sources of much of her thinking, we are excluding her on the basis of a factor that, apparently, did not seem sufficient to exclude such thinkers as Rupert of Deutz or Hugh of St. Victor.[2] If we deny that her being a woman has anything to do with the apparent contradiction in allowing male visionaries a place in the canon, we are failing to take into account the obvious relevance, historically, of the one overwhelming difference between, for example, Hildegard and Rupert, that would valorize the placement of the one in histories of philosophy and not the other. To put it more simply: if Hildegard was not excluded primarily because she was female, what then can serve as a plausible basis for her exclusion?

In any case, the new commentary on Hildegard of Bingen, whatever its source in the academic world, seems to be pushing in the direction of her acceptance as a woman philosopher of the medieval period. The sheer volume of her work is overwhelming: in addition to the visionary *Scivias,* which has now been widely produced, even by those whose interest in it stems more from the popular culture, Hildegard composed several other lengthy works which have received at least some share of attention: the aforementioned *Causae et Curae,* the *Liber Vitae Meritorum,* the *Liber Divinorum Operum,* a great deal of music, a morality play, a voluminous correspondence, and so on.[3]

In order to try to place Hildegard within a philosophical framework, it is necessary to try to navigate simultaneously, as it were, in two different areas: the *Scivias,* for example, which is an account of her visions, provides us with a cosmology, although this cosmology is admittedly rudimentary from a philosophical point of view since it cannot be said to be buttressed by argument. On the other hand, her medical and technical works are informed by a great deal of the preceding Hellenistic and even Augustinian philosophical learning of her time, and yet they tie in to the *Scivias* in obvious ways. Thus the discerning reader must attempt to weave together a visionary cosmology with some thinking that is much more overtly philosophical to come up with a coherent whole. This is no easy task, since Hildegard's style did not encompass the type of thinking that is prevalent even, for example, in early Renaissance philosophers and since it may very well be the case that her status as a woman within the Church has something to do with her mode of composition. In any case, this intellectual undertaking is well worth the effort.

The contemporary commentary on Hildegard usually makes one of at least two sorts of comparisons, both of which may be helpful in particularizing Hildegard's place in the canon. As we have seen, despite Hildegard's failure to employ such notions as "category" and "substance," there is real merit to a comparison of her work with that of male philosophers of the medieval period, since many of them wrote at least some work that might best be described as visionary. Then again, it might be argued—and some would claim more plausibly argued—that Hildegard is best compared with other church visionaries whom we think of as women mystics of the same period. Catherine Villanueva Gardner, for example, in a work on women philosophers of the past, writes of Mechthild of Magdeburg, and in so doing makes extensive comparison with Hildegard.[4] Gardner notes with respect to Hildegard:

> When these medieval women speak of their divine inspiration to write, it seems that they are well aware of the literary tradition that emphasized their intellectual inferiority, and the theological tradition that prohibited women from teaching and preaching. For they frequently emphasize that they are merely a channel through which God speaks directly to others. Thus God says to Hildegard of Bingen, "Thou art timid, timid in speech, artless in explaining, unlearned in writing, but express and not according to art but according to natural ability, not under the guidance of human composition, but under the guidance of that which thou seest and hearest in God's heaven above."[5]

In making this comparison, Gardner is letting us know that the style employed by Hildegard was, alas, the only style she could readily employ that would not create a level of hostility that would prove to be insurmountable. Thus some points that one would like to see made in a more standard philosophical mode may have to be made in some other way—and this Hildegard does.

Berger notes, in her introduction to an English translation of *Causae et Curae,* that much of what Hildegard wrote was an interweaving of both medical traditions that themselves derived in some sense from the philosophical, and material that might be deemed to be more overtly philosophical. Thus, as she writes, "*Cause et Cure* interweaves medical and theological conceptions: health care and the cycle of human life are seen against the background of salvation, from world's beginning to world's end."[6] The traditional scope of philosophy in ancient and medieval times—seen in its often used title of "natural philosophy," meaning the thought that later gave rise to what we now call the natural sciences—helps to fill in the blanks on how an amalgam of thought from a variety of sources can, indeed, be philosophical.

I have examined Hildegard's oeuvre, then, from two vantage points. I take it as a given that, for a variety of reasons, women thinkers may have had to work in nontraditional formats, and much of the new work on women philosophers emphasizes this point.[7] In addition, it is also the case that a great deal of what was done by male philosophers, already in the canon, during the medieval period was driven at least partially by visions. The upshot of combining these two lines of argument is that the reasons for taking Hildegard's work seriously, and for at least attempting to afford her a place in the philosophical canon, far outweigh any arguments that might be made against such a place. Indeed, the fact that she received at least minor citations in the canon in previous historical periods would seem to indicate that others have made similar positive arguments. Our task now is to try to be more precise about what sorts of philosophical principles can be derived from Hildegard's work. Here, again, we will have to read with a generous spirit, and we may be required to do much filling in of blanks.

Metaphysical and Epistemological Ramifications

Putting together the two main works that are available to us in English translation, the *Scivias* and *Causae et Curae,* we can see that Hildegard had her own metaphysics, and one that enabled her to develop a relatively consistent account of what it meant to be human in the framework of God's divine plan. The most interesting part of her metaphysics is that which we would ordinarily try to gloss under some kind of label with respect to substance. Hildegard does not use this term, but it is clear from her writings that the view she espouses is, in a sense, a complex monistic vitalism, similar to that which will later be developed by Anne Conway. A crucial difference is that it might well be argued that Hildegard's account has stronger dualistic tendencies.

What Hildegard tries to do—and this is especially evident in her medical works—is to develop a hierarchy for creation that allows for humankind's having an important role in it, but that does not necessarily separate humankind from the rest of creation. She is aware of the typology of her time with regard to "humors" and their effects on human personalities, and this informs her medical writings. But putting the larger parts of her doctrine together, we are able to see how she posits human beings as those who have fallen from grace yet still retain a spark of the divine fire (the soul). As Mews writes in his fine piece on Hildegard and her place as a religious thinker:

Hildegard is more interested in the relationship of God to creation than in the doctrine of the Trinity as such. It is instructive to compare her use of the Pauline text "the invisible things of God are revealed through the created things of the world" (Romans 1.19–20) to that of her contemporaries. While Abelard explicitly uses this Pauline text in his *Theologia* to justify his exploitation of texts like Plato's *Timaeus,* Hildegard alludes to its phraseology to justify her interpretation of different parts of the natural world, which she presents as a cosmic Egg.[8]

Part of the challenge of Hildegard's work is presented in passages like the preceding. Because she mixes her visionary work, to some extent, with the drier and more precise medical work, it is sometimes difficult to know how much to take literally; even *Causae et Curae* has many symbols. Mews mentions the "egg" because it is important as a symbol and metaphor, and at some points it may appear to be more than a metaphor. But of this much we can be sure: taking Christian doctrine as a point of departure, Hildegard places human beings in the natural world, but at a step well below the divine. What human beings possess of the divine spark is, in the natural world, often *viriditas* (greening). It is here that the Hildegard best known to the contemporary ecological movement, for example, shines; all of creation possesses viriditas or the capacity for it, and in this sense all of creation falls in a direct descent from the Creator. Hence, rather than using a more technical term such as "hylomorphism," it might be instructive to think of Hildegard's ontology as a sort of vitalism, since she can draw a virtual line from the Creator to those things created.

The human being, of course, has a special ontological status not only because of his relationship to the divine, but also because, possessing a soul, the human being has a greater component of the fiery element than other creatures. For example, in *Causae et Curae* Hildegard notes, "Spirits consist of fire and air; the human being consists of water and clay," and "[t]he elements—namely fire, air, earth and water—are in the human being."[9] Thus Hildegard's outline of the human's physiology is completely consistent with the typical medicine of her time, derived partially from Galen and from other translations; but where Hildegard differs is to give an analysis of this physiology in terms of the Fall and of the metaphysical relationship between the first created human, Adam, and the rest of creation.[10] Were Hildegard the sort of dualist that many philosophers were to become in the early modern period, it would be difficult for her to construct links between human beings and other life forms. But her sense of a sort of semi-Aristotelian hylomorphism and her desire to account for all of creation simultaneously lead her, without positing substance and accident, or writing in those standard terms, to a much more monistic view.

If *Scivias* and portions of the visionary work are taken more literally—and it may well be argued that they should be—Hildegard's ontology becomes a good deal more complex, since it appears that she has room not only for standard sorts of beings, such as angels, but the Virtues (fully personified) and other types of entities. If it is difficult to know what to make of this in overtly philosophical terms, it helps to realize that these beings are also part of the graded hierarchy that, for Hildegard, constitutes life. There is obviously room in this hierarchy for a number of sorts of beings, and Hildegard has generously seen and accounted for many. Newman notes that, with regard to the figures taken from the "illuminations" and visions of *Scivias,* the Virtues are personae such that "wherever [they] appear, we will find the Platonizing cosmology that captivates 12th century thinkers: the divine ideas, eternal in the mind of God and bodied forth in creatures."[11] That cosmology is not too Platonizing, however, for as we have noted, Hildegard still has a great deal of room for the empirical and at least the rudimentary physical sciences.

It might seem easy to caricature Hildegard's epistemology as a sort of slow-motion version of the "natural light" thinking that will be more prevalent in later philosophical views. But although it is clear that Hildegard regards her visions as emanating from the divine, this sort of reception of knowledge is little related, if at all, to the inner light of reason of the rationalists precisely because Hildegard's light is, at bottom, irrational. In other words, Hildegard values her visions because she assumes that their source is divine, and for no other reason. However, as we have seen, this kind of thinking was not uncommon during the medieval period, and is employed to at least some extent by other thinkers. Nor, clearly, are visions the only source of Hildegard's knowledge. She does at least minimally valorize empirical knowledge when she writes of matters medical, despite the fact that the historical record makes clear the odd and somewhat maligned place that healing, as an activity, held in most convents. As Florence Glaze claims, "The rich mixture of new medical literature and scholarly activity provides the appropriate backdrop against which we must measure Hildegard's own activities as a medical thinker and writer."[12]

Hildegard's views, although somewhat unusual in their juxtaposition of more standard theorizing and the vision-driven, are by no means inconsistent with a great deal of the other recorded thought of the twelfth century. Indeed, it is this aspect of Hildegard's work that allows us to categorize her as a philosopher, for along with the more common sorts of conceptualization patterns to which we have advertence in histories of philosophy, a number of thinkers, already cast as philosophers, wrote on many topics. Copleston's somewhat hoary history of philosophy has the virtue that it allows us full rein, with respect to both the type and style of categorization of the period in question. I might also, somewhat parenthetically, remark that if a figure is included in Copleston's work, we would have no hesitation in thinking of the person in question as a philosopher, since Copleston's placing is canonical in that regard. It is here that we can obtain some of our most valuable insights into Hildegard's work, because it is obvious that the rich mixture of thought of the eleventh and twelfth centuries, spurred by the rise in powers of the universities and the papacy at an almost simultaneous pace, yielded some work that is difficult to categorize. With respect to the school of Chartres and one of its key figures, Hugh of St. Victor, Copleston says the following:

> This growing and expanding university life naturally found an intellectual and academic expression in the attempt to classify and systematize . . . science. . . . [Hugh of St. Victor composed a work known as the] Didascalion, [which] more or less follows the Aristotelian Classification. [In its] Practical Science [it is] subdivided into Ethics, "Economics," and Politics, while Mechanics comprises the seven "illiberal arts" or *scientae adulterinae,* since the craftsman borrows his form from nature. These illiberal arts are . . . Armoury and Carpentry [and] Medicine.[13]

There is no question, then, that Medicine was already a part of philosophy, as broadly construed during that period, and following the path of the ancients. But what makes Hildegard's medical work quite striking is that she attempts to incorporate the ontology of her visionary work as a guiding overview, and thus one is left with the sense that no mere substance/accident account can give a complete picture of how the human, full of ills though she is, came into being. Whereas Hugh of St. Victor, as Copleston informs us, might think of Medicine as part of Mechanics, medical thought cannot be separated, on Hildegard's view, from notions of the creation of humankind and the fall from divine grace. Glaze is impressed by the extent to which *Causae et Curae* wants to make the case that the human body would not be so frail and prone to ills if it were not for its metaphysical trajectory; it is unnecessary for Hildegard to complete this picture, and yet she does so. As Glaze notes with respect to one section of *Causae* in which Hildegard accounts for the occurrence of phlegm in the human body as a result of the Fall, "[w]ith this explanation Hildegard eloquently asserts that the Fall altered history, and changed the state of the body and the enjoyment of health . . . by introducing illness into the realm of human experience."[14]

Thus we find that Hildegard's metaphysics, implicit as it sometimes is, and less than fully articulated, is an original view with a noteworthy propensity for a sort of wholistic structure. As has been said, this is what makes Hildegard a popular thinker of the moment, but it does not do her justice to let matters rest there. The visions of the *Scivias* propel Hildegard to a concern for all creation, and it is this concern that manifests itself in the medical treatises. Whereas a thinker such as Hugh of St. Victor sees the more practical parts of "philosophy" as of less importance than the more sophisticated Dialectic and Logic, Hildegard is inclined to skip over sophistication, as it were, and get to the heart of the matter by proceeding from an account of creation and man's fall to an account of what man is made of, in the literal sense, after the fall. This aspect of her work points us in the direction of what many find most redeeming today.

Viriditas and Value

As I have indicated, Hildegard's thought has become increasingly noticed—not to say popular—as commentators on her work have striven to draw connections between, for example, the ecofeminist movement and the visions of *Scivias,* or between her thought on sexuality and concepts of health in general. Although the work has often been pronounced inadequate from the standpoint of scholarship, since it relies on translations from the German instead of from the original Latin editions, commentary and editions done under the leadership of Matthew Fox have probably received the most publicity. Whatever the merits or demerits of such work, it is important to make note of it, because, as has been stated time and again, few women thinkers of any era have received due attention or notice. Hildegard can scarcely be thought to have constituted an exception, and it is only recently that a full evaluation of her work has begun.

Stated simply, the emphasis on wholistic metaphysics in Hildegard's work, and her refusal to separate her discussion of physical matters from such issues, provides a great deal of the impetus for what has now come to be a discussion of Hildegard and value. It is not, of course, that her work is feminist in anything like today's sense. It is rather that a great deal of what she says supports such contemporary notions as the Gaia movement and what has come to be known as "deep ecology."[15] In his foreword to the edition of *Scivias* provided by the Santa Fe publishers Bear and Company—the edition that, according to some, is less than adequate— Fox writes: "Wisdom for Hildegard constitutes the very definition of what church ought to be—a gathering of those rejecting the folly of dualism and corruption and war-like attitudes and what we today would call patriarchy in favor of the ways of healing and celebration and cosmos and peacemaking."[16]

Although this passage may not be illuminating from the standpoint of detailed scholarship about Hildegard's thought, it does give us some insight into her current popularity. It may very well be that one could accuse Fox and other thinkers who have moved down the same path of overdramatization and a failure to contextualize, but an adequate assessment of the situation would seem to be that Hildegard's thought does indeed lend itself to this sort of commentary.

The reasons for this are easy to see. The very factors that I have cited already that might make Hildegard nonphilosophical in some eyes are at work here. Because she refuses to engage in the substance/accident theorizing so typical of medieval thought, one has to pull her ontological views out of her. But those views emphasize the interconnectedness of all things, and it is clear that her medical treatise is no mere compendium of nostrums. In contemporary language, Hildegard refuses to divorce the health of the body from that of the soul. Furthermore, her vitalism—if we may employ that term—allows for a suffusion of spirit within the body, rather than a separation of spirit from the body. However metaphorically we might be inclined to read such work today, it is important in the sense that it runs counter to much of the thinking both of her time and of ours.

Because of Hildegard's emphasis on health, and because she followed the rule of St. Benedict, moderation was the key to all human endeavors for her. Commentators are struck by the extent to which her emphasis on moderation comes in part from her metaphysical views and in part from simple views of illness, such as those found in the more practical parts of *Causae et Curae.* As one might expect, Hildegard's overarching principle is that the temple—or "tent"—of the body is destroyed by a failure to adequately maintain it, but this flat take on the body and its relationship to the cosmos is undergirded by a number of points taken from her work as a whole. Because the soul suffuses the body (and because she refuses to see the body/soul relationship in dualistic terms), Hildegard posits an unusually strong relationship between ills of the soul and ills of the body. This allows her, as has been often noted, to take sexuality into account to a much greater extent than might have been predicted for her chronological period. In addition, and perhaps more important, Hildegard sees "sin" as a result of failure of moderation, and, of course, ultimately as a result of the sort of cosmos originally envisioned by the divine. But if a human remains in touch with the force of viriditas—the well-known "greening" to which Hildegard frequently refers—a sort of healing can take place. Ultimately, Hildegard sees recognition of viriditas for all living things as crucial to the human being's functioning on earth. It is because of this that we can see contemporary echoes in her thought.

Heinrich Schipperges, working from the Latin version of *Causae et Curae* published in Leipzig in the early part of the twentieth century, provides a helpful gloss on Hildegard's views on sexuality and the relations between the sexes when he writes:

> Men and women were spiritually ordered toward each other and came together as sexual beings. This view, unambiguously expressed, was most unusual for the Middle Ages. Man and woman were so involved with each other that one of them was the work of the other (*sic ad invicem admisti sunt, ut opus alterum per alterum est*). Without woman, man could not be called man; without man, woman could not be named woman (LDO IV, 100: *quia vir sine femina vir non vocaretur, nec femina sine viro femina nominaretur*). Man and woman obviously had been created for each *other* (*propter virum creata—propter mulierum factus*). Therefore there was only one love (*una dilectio*). In any case, that was the way things were meant to be (CC, 136).[17]

Although this particular part of Hildegard's thought may not strike us as having contemporary resonance for its reliance on a sort of complementarity that many now find offensive, it is powerful in the sense that it clearly intimates the necessity for a recognition of human sexuality. Again, this recognition is itself twofold: it encompasses part of human health, but it also obviously recognizes the fashion in which humans came to be. Thus we can see that what Hildegard deems unhealthy is in part a failure to take into account the nature of humans' relationship to the rest of creation, whether it is in the form of other humans, plants, animals, or an inanimate object, such as a lake or a rock. Her style of expressing matters of health in terms of "waves" and "fire" is poignant insofar as metaphor is concerned, but it is intended by Hildegard to be more than metaphorical. *Causae et Curae* indicates that women and men differ somewhat in the expression of their sexuality because its force is somewhat different. In a well-known passage, she writes, "For man's pleasure resembles a fire that now and then is extinguished and now and then flares up." She sees women's sexuality as "more easily held in check," and clearly feels that health cannot be maintained if an adequate understanding of the various sorts of sexuality is not had.[18]

Because we are accustomed to thinking of matters of value in contemporary philosophical terms, we may have some difficulty understanding Hildegard's point of view. Later thinkers will divorce value from a number of other realms of philosophical thought. Spinoza will conceptualize the passions in terms of "inadequate" ideas, and Descartes will try to give an account of them in terms of animal spirits. Even in times closer to those in which Hildegard lived and wrote, many thinkers will assume that the force of the passions is destructive, and that it is a human duty to try to keep them in check. But because Hildegard never loses sight of the totality of creation, she sees a role for the passions if they are a part of the moderate life that the healthful human being will endeavor to live. They are indeed caused by the various interminglings of the body and are, of course, a part of nature.

Now we can see more clearly why there has been a resurgence in interest in Hildegard's work. She not only ties together a number of threads of medieval thought, but her work is also oddly resonant with that of twentieth-century thinkers whom we might not ordinarily term philosophical, but who have had a profound impact on contemporary culture—Alan Watts, for example. Informed by visions as it is, and devoid of standard philosophical terminology, each area of her thinking is driven by its relationship to the larger view and its place in the scheme of things. This prevents *Causae et Curae,* for example, from literally or figuratively being part of Mechanics; it is too important for that. The standard divisions of thought not only reflect a hierarchy of areas of knowledge as promulgated by the schools, but a hierarchy in importance for certain topics. On Hildegard's view, particulars are so intertwined with each other that it does not make sense to try to examine them in isolated terms or even, in general, to write about them in such terms (although, clearly, she does allow herself some divisions).

Nevertheless, despite the unusual scope, volume, and breadth of Hildegard's thinking, her work does bear comparison with that of other writers and scholars from the eleventh and twelfth centuries, including other women thinkers. As we have seen, reliance on visions was not at all uncommon—Hildegard's wholism is rare, but not an impossibility if one takes the sources of the visions and their interweaving seriously. In contemporary examinations of her work, she has been compared with both male and female thinkers from similar time periods. This allows us to come to some conclusions about the importance and richness of her work.

Hildegard and Her Contemporaries

There are at least two major ways in which we can address the notion of parallels between Hildegard and other thinkers of the eleventh and twelfth centuries, and each way yields its own fruits. We can proceed with a more standard analysis, attempting to find ties between Hildegard and thinkers who have already been subsumed under the rubric "philosophers," especially when—as is the case with some of those whom I have already mentioned—their work is at least touched by the visionary. On the other hand, we can proceed with an analysis of Hildegard and her thinking in comparison to women mystics of her time, a project that has been made a great deal easier by the fact that a number of trained medievalists, including Peter Dronke, have already engaged in it. Both projects, of course, are valuable. And the existence of both speaks to the very issues I have here elucidated—the projects are seen as exclusionary precisely because of the ways in which previous thinkers have used the rubric "philosopher." It may very well be the case that this term should be employed for a great many of the women mystics, for example, and yet the reluctance to employ the term in the past indicates that something else is afoot.

In any case, some work has already been done that may indeed be helpful to us. Catherine Villanueva Gardner provides us with an intriguing analysis of the work of Mechthild of Magdeburg—another visionary, whose life only approximately a century or less after Hildegard gives us glimpses into the mystical frame of mind.[19]

Hildegard's wholism, as I have termed it, makes it relatively easy to assign to her at least truncated versions of views regarding ethics and, indeed, matters metaphysical and cosmological. But although it is clear that visions as a source of knowledge do indeed provide a great epistemic problematic, other thinkers now recognized as philosophers have employed visions, and, at a much later point, we will examine the work of Edith Stein, who also devised an epistemic place for knowledge born of faith. If visions themselves are not immediately troublesome, other questions may arise. Gardner notes, for example, that although Mechthild's work parallels the thought of Hildegard in a number of ways, it contains a set of conundra of its own. Since Gardner is largely concerned with literary genre as an unexplored area of investigation in the work of women thinkers, she is easily able to focus on questions of authorship, for example, that I have yet to examine here. With respect to Mechthild's *The Flowing Light of the Godhead,* Gardner writes:

> If we accept that *God* wrote the book, as her contemporaries seem to have done, then we can have no questions about the authority of the author, or the fact that *The Flowing Light* offers its audience a divine message. However, this means that we must accept that Mechthild is simply a passive channel. Yet if we think that in fact *Mechthild* wrote the book (as I suspect most of a modern audience will do), then this then brings with it Mechthild's confusing claim that the sup-

posedly general moral knowledge (whatever this is) offered to the audience is based solely on her privileged personal experiences and emotions.[20]

Gardner goes on to say that the way out of this paradox is to abandon the "individualist concept of the self" with regard to authorship that clearly gives rise to the set of problems in the first place.[21] But Gardner's articulation of the problem points us to a parallel area of difficulty in Hildegard's work: although Hildegard does not make as strong a claim as Mechthild with respect to her own work, we can see that part of the difficulty here is simply the notion of visions themselves as a source of information. What Mechthild and Hildegard share is a concern for divine revelation—there is, then, not only an epistemological problem but a problem with the notion of women chosen as a "conduit." Mechthild resolves this problem by not even claiming the role of conduit; Hildegard thinks of herself as a poor woman to whom this gift has been given.[22] So, one might inquire, even if visions themselves are the sources of the thought of these two women, and even if we can accept the notion that the complexity of the thought and the thought and the issues with which it grapples warrant the category of philosophy, why should we accept this work as the work of the individual in question (especially since, at least to some extent, the putative author denies authorship)?

The answer, apparently, lies in an analysis of the complex relationship between the church and the authorial during the Middle Ages. Mechthild's case is simply one of the more extreme of a number of such cases, almost all of which have already been cited in other contexts. The short response is that most medieval philosophers did claim divine inspiration, and they would have had little difficulty in the notion that their philosophical work originated in impulses prompted by the divine. The long response might try to drive a wedge between those, like Hildegard, who at least admit to being the authorial repository of the visions, and those, like Mechthild, who deny authorial responsibility. But however interesting these matters are, they all point to larger philosophical concerns that Hildegard, for one, attempts to address in her *Causae et Curae.* If we as human beings are the products of divine authorship, how do we respond to the rest of creation? If one person has visions that attempt to spell out the nature of some of the interconnections, should others take these visions as having some authority? Helen John, for example, has tried to make note of possible responses to this question, in still another piece on Hildegard, by writing, "But Christian authors typically recognize God as source of *all* truth *and* recognize too that all teachings must be tested and validated in the light both of Christian faith and of human reason and experience. Male authors of Hildegard's time typically held positions of authority in the teaching Church; women who realized they had something important to say must, by that very conviction, have seen themselves as divinely powered and mandated to say it."[23]

Still another woman thinker who was more or less a contemporary of Hildegard's provides us with a fructifying basis for comparison, even if the comparison may not, at first, seem apt. That is the abbess Heloise, of Heloise and Abelard fame. It probably says something important that we can scarcely think of her without her relationship to Abelard coming to mind, but Heloise is indeed critical here simply because she represents another woman thinker from roughly the same time period, and we do have records of her work.

It is also crucial that what we do know about Heloise represents something completely different, both insofar as sources are concerned, and insofar as the structure of her written work is concerned. The largest portion of her extant work is part of her correspondence with Abelard after Abelard's mutilation as punishment for having been her lover. Nevertheless, the letters reveal enough of her own personal philosophy that Andrea Nye has used them as the basis for work on Heloise's thought.[24] Nye argues that we can discern traces—or more than traces—of rejection of male authority, and the mistake of thinking that reason alone can displace passionate thought, in Heloise's letters. More important for our purposes, however, Heloise's thought, even if it differs strongly from Abelard's, is in a sense much more conventional than Hildegard's. She does not claim to have visions, and her work is much more argumentative and hence more conventionally philosophical than Hildegard's. In response to Abelard on the notion of marriage, and their particular relationship, for example, Heloise gives a moving reply that is actually quite recognizably a form of argument: "God knows I required nothing from you but yourself, purely you, not anything of yours, no marriage contract, no dowry, nor did I study how to gratify my own desires, but rather yours, as you know. And if the title of wife seems more saintly or respectable, sweeter for me always is the name of friend, or, if you won't take offense, even concubine or whore."[25]

As Nye acknowledges, it appears that Heloise's intent here is to remind Abelard of their original relationship, and to distance it from the conventional and arranged marriages of their time. She also, unlike Abelard, chooses not to forget their physical relationship, however violative it may have been of mores of their era. In any case, the point for our purposes is that we do have written records of women thinkers from the twelfth century who did not cite the authority of vision for at least some of their thought. But what we can see is this: in the case of Mechthild, although her work might initially appear to be much more susceptible of comparison, we do not have the developed body of work such as was given to us by Hildegard, nor do we have an overarching view. Although Mechthild experiences God as love, and desires to communicate this experience to her readers, we do not have, for example, any work from her that attempts to tie her ontology into the physical world.[26] In the case of Heloise, we admittedly have work that, however truncated, is superficially more philosophical, but again it addresses only a narrow range of issues—understandably, those issues that she found relevant to her relationship with Abelard, since that was the origin of the correspondence. And, of course, a great deal of analysis has already been made of Heloise's work.

Hildegard's work, then, presents us with an interesting case, so to speak, since the body of work is much greater than it is for almost any other medieval woman thinker, and yet we must pick the philosophy from the work. But this task is far from impossible—it merely requires a sympathetic reading of the work in order to gain a sense of what the author intends. John Caputo, in his *More Radical Hermeneutics,* argues that deconstructive and poststructuralist thought allows us to create open-ended interpretations of Christian material because the loss of the sense of "authoritative text" requires us to construct our own "text."[27] Although he is primarily thinking of, for example, attempts to grapple with difficult portions of the New Testament, much of what Caputo says is relevant to an understanding of these medieval thinkers whose work was clearly infused with a powerful sense of Christianity. Because we can go to the "margins," we can come to understand that works such as those composed by Hildegard require powerful readings-in, and that to engage in this task is to do simply what is required to glean something from the text. We can move easily from the visions of *Scivias* or the other *Libers* to *Causae et Curae* if we bear in mind that Hildegard leaves it up to us to weave the threads that make her ontology hang together. In this sense, we are for once aided by the portions of contemporary French theory that many contemporary American philosophers such as Caputo use in their work, and it pushes us in useful directions.

A Feminist Hildegard

Since it has been very largely feminist theory, and ecofeminist efforts, that have succeeded in bringing Hildegard to the fore again, it might seem to be an effort in redundancy to try to make the argument that Hildegard's work lends itself to feminist theorizing. It is overly simplistic, however, to make the claim that such an effort is not needed. In the first place, it is clear that what is now meant by such thought would have been more or less incomprehensible to Hildegard in her time, and in that sense the placement of the two types of thinking together is somewhat gratuitous. More important, however, is to try to get clear on what types of feminist thought might mesh most closely with Hildegard's work. If it seems superficially easy to achieve such an interlocking, it becomes more difficult when we realize that much of what Hildegard—or thinkers of her time and affiliation—took for granted with respect to metaphysical and ontological matters is directly tied to the patriarchal structures at issue.

Nevertheless, there is a genuine sense in which those who have tried to achieve an intersection between Hildegard's thought and the deep ecology movement, for example, have been on the right track. Recent attempts by feminist thinkers to write on topics that touch on a number of issues simultaneously (racism, speciesism, animal rights) show how difficult it is to pit one set of concerns against another. It is clear that a more wholistic view is needed. Greta Gaard, for example, in a piece on indigenous whale-hunting societies and greater ecological concerns, notes: "But ecofeminism's critique of dualistic thought and 'truncated narratives' suggests that rather than seeing these different narratives as competing, a more holistic approach would be inclusive of all these layers of relationships, examining the interrelationship between the ethical context and the ethical contents."[28]

In other words, it is not simply a case of one group of interests being set off against another. Gaard is writing about a specific indigenous group of the American and Canadian Northwest, the Makah, and the importance to them of their traditional hunting of the gray whale, an endangered species. Those who have been concerned about any whale hunting have been labeled by some as "white middle-class" activists who can afford to be insensitive to issues involving indigenous persons and persons of color. Others have felt that it is the indigenous persons themselves who are lacking in sensitivity, and that in the name of tradition, many wrongs have been perpetrated.

Although it may initially provide little more than prismatic clarification, it is here that an overview similar to Hildegard's is needed. One set of concerns is no more valuable than another, since all are part of the viriditas and the vitalism that constitutes creation. Within a given context, some concerns may appear to have greater merit than others, but no one set of concerns ever is so privileged as to preclude debate or to hold off, indefinitely, another set of concerns. This sort of stance is not only close to those that have been articulated by many philosophers who take an interest in ecology, it is in fact similar—insofar as westerners can make them out—to many of the ontological views cherished by indigenous societies.

That Hildegard herself, although a human motivated by human concerns, kept certain concepts in the fore of her thinking is manifest by even a cursory appraisal of her correspondence. The superb English translation of her letters, edited by Joseph Baird and Radd Ehrman, helps us to understand how Hildegard lived through her beliefs on a daily basis. In a letter to the archbishop of Bremen, attempting to prevent a favorite nun's removal to another convent, Hildegard writes: "Therefore, may your eye see God, your intellect grasp his justice, and your heart burn brightly in the love of God, so that your spirit may not grow weak. . . . Be a bright star shining in the darkness of the night."[29]

These are no mere metaphors for Hildegard, as we know; she fully expects that heart and intellect can cooperate in God's plan, and that the soul's fire will assist. Hildegard, then, is a wholist through and through, and it shows in her everyday life as well as in her analysis, for example, of medicine.

Intriguingly enough, we have views in contemporary feminist philosophy of science that at least point us in a direction similar to the one in which Hildegard is moving. Throughout her important work of the 1980s, *Reflections on Gender and Science,* Evelyn Fox Keller writes of "static objectivity" and "dynamic objectivity."[30] She is at pains to point out that there are various styles of doing science, and the use of the work of Barbara McClintock, later a Nobelist, helps her make clear her aims. For Keller, there are different ways in which what purports to be the objectivity of the sciences can manifest itself, and one of them is in a careful noting of and interaction with a number of the different relationships among phenomena. The thinker seeks to get a better comprehension of things from the inside out, as it were. McClintock, for example, had said, with respect to her work on genetics, that she could write the "autobiography" of a corn plant. Her use of the phrase "autobiography" rather than the simpler and less marked "biography" indicates, obviously, that she felt a certain sympathy and connection with the plants the growth of which she was observing. In certain ways, Hildegard is an early exponent of this type of thinking. Because she sees all of nature as interconnected, she sees attempts to detach oneself from the phenomena as mistaken. Baird and Ehrman, in noting that Hildegard rejected a certain Catholic dualist heresy of her time, maintain that "[o]ne could scarcely conceive of a doctrine more distasteful to the seer who taught the essential goodness, the sanctity, of all creation."[31] The importance of these stands for Hildegard is constantly reaffirmed, not only by her commentators, but by the thinker herself.

If feminism is a way of seeing, then, as well as a doctrine with overt political ramifications, we can perceive a deep gynocentrism in Hildegard's view.

As indicated in an earlier part of this text, the debate over whether or not it is essentialist—in the current academically popularized meaning of the term—to try to impute such views to women thinkers misses the point. In many (certainly not all) cases, the views are there to be seen, and they frequently stand out in such a way that the woman in question has thought patterns noticeably different from those of other thinkers of her time. The point of the work on medieval women mystics, presumably, is to try to explain the preponderance of such thought during that time period. Gardner and others claim that the devalorization of women's voices has much to do with this mode of cognition for medieval women. It is also noteworthy that a scholarly investigation into Hildegard's command of Latin underscores the notion that she herself was correct when she frequently referred to herself as a person of little formal learning. Baird and Ehrman indicate, for example, that it is indeed sometimes difficult to make sense of Hildegard's Latin. It thus is most likely true that, although she had the bare-bones elements of a writing style, she did not have the training of many male clerics of her time.[32] It is easy to see why she might have been tempted, as was Mechthild, to give an authorial role to God. Writing could not have been an easy task for her, nor could it have been for the vast majority of women during her period, whether daughters of the nobility or not.

Although, as we have seen, both Hildegard's conceptual patterns and the manner in which they were derived seem to underscore the type of gynocentric concern for interrelations and connections that has been one of the hallmarks of contemporary feminist theory, her thought in general has scarcely been examined philosophically, let alone from the standpoint of philosophically developed feminist theory. *Causae et Curae* stands out among her works because of her apparent effort to tie what she has observed empirically, as one engaged—at least at the monastic level—in healing, to the ontology that she uses in her visionary works. Employing the typology of the humors, she achieves a medical compendium outstanding even for its time. Such a work seems to call out for an analysis from the standpoint of feminist epistemology, especially since it is clear that Hildegard intends her work as one that is suited for actual medical use. Current feminist epistemology has, in its more naturalized aspects, focused on women's immersion in the world of the senses, and the importance to women of knowledge derived from that world—standpoint theory, for example, is noteworthy in this regard. It is no stretch, then, to see Hildegard in the light of this contemporary work; rather, her work virtually demands that we employ this prism in order to view it properly.

Hildegardian Gynocentric Epistemics

Work in feminist epistemology is probably too easily bifurcated into naturalized and nonnaturalized approaches, but the ease with which this split can
be made signals to us something of profound importance for contemporary
feminist thought: it can, speaking broadly, either draw or fail to draw on a
number of empirical traditions that precede it. It is facile to mesh together
empirical views with all things oppressive and reactionary, but women in almost all societies have had to remain in contact with the world around them
to a much greater extent than have men, and they have seldom had the luxury of divorcing themselves from that world.

As a religious, Hildegard did indeed have the privilege of leading a contemplative, or largely contemplative, life at a time when few women or men
could do so. In that sense, she, too, was able to participate in that speculative
realm of thought that—especially in societies possessing long histories of
written languages—has tended to be the purview of men.[33] But we can see
that the range of Hildegard's thought exhibited a concern for the natural and
for interaction with the world in at least two major ways: her visions encompass a startling use of notions of creative force and growth, many of which are
clearly derived from some knowledge of the patterns of life of plants and animals. In addition, and perhaps more important, a work like *Causae* is intended to be a source book of that which actually has curative powers, and
the compilation of such a source is an empirical exercise.

Contemporary standpoint theory, although it would seem irrelevant in
some sense because of its obvious debt to nineteenth-century work, does indeed have something to tell us about Hildegard's medical projects. As developed by Hartsock and others, this theoretical construct emphasizes the extent to which women's lived lives exemplify, especially in developing
countries, immersion in a certain sort of labor. That labor is not only reproductive, as Marx and Engels had originally categorized it, but it is labor involving deliberate contact with the world—the feeding, clothing, and caring
for of small children, animals, and a variety of other living things. Because
this labor carries with it a certain set of conceptual patterns (here, above all,
there is seldom room for the devoid-of-contact speculation that is the hallmark of traditional metaphysics, for example) it also has its own rough-and-
ready epistemology. Women, traditionally, have had to be empiricists, because one cannot easily find more foodstuffs through speculation and
hypothesis alone. Thus, this sort of view is a very good index of the type of intellectual work in which Hildegard was engaged. Hildegard would not, of

course, have seen herself in this light, any more than she would have seen herself as a "woman thinker." Nevertheless, such conceptual apparatuses may be helpful to us in attempting to come to grips with her work.

Hartsock has pointed out that the significance of standpoint views is that they take account of the "importance of specific material conditions," and this specific feature is one that distances them from a number of contemporary views of Continental origin.[34] Although women religious of Hildegard's time would have been spared the family lives that led to the sort of intense immersion on which a great deal of standpoint theory is based, it is clear that a woman with medical interests attached to a convent that served as a place of medicine and healing would have had a great deal of the sort of experience of "material conditions" to which the theory refers. Consider a well-known passage from *Causae* on men with the melancholic temperament: "Then there are other men whose brains are fatty. Both the membrane encasing the brain and their blood vessels are turbid. The color of their faces is dark, even their eyes are firelike and viperlike. They have hard, strong blood vessels containing black, dense blood. . . . They are unable to practice restraint with women."[35]

The first two sentences here indicate an extensive history of medical work with individuals having the temperament in question, and although today we find the thought pattern driving categorization through humors ancient, and even quaint, it is clear that the compendium was arrived at through careful cataloging of the physical traits of a number of individuals. If, as Marx was later to say, labor is the "living, breathing fire," the labor of medical practice yields a highly empirical worldview, whatever era is involved. That worldview can never be completely divorced from the realm of the senses, for it relies on that realm for its data, and it relies on inferences made from the accumulation of that data for its epistemic strength.

In that sense, much of the contemporary debate between feminist epistemologists who find the alleged politicization of the standpoint views excessive is somewhat beside the point. Hildegard's life and the lives of other women religious were indeed lives of labor, and by thinking in terms of the labor performed we can gain insight into the epistemological stance that drove their writing and thinking.

It might be thought that the epistemics of the visionary works, such as *Scivias,* is of an entirely different stripe, and so it is if taken crudely. But the point of *Scivias* is also to work with the divine light—the light that provides for ways of knowing and seeing. As has been noted, in the later rationalist tradition this same divine light, albeit shorn of much of its imagery, will allow male (and a few female) theorists to come to major conclusions about existence and reality. But in Hildegard's time both the thought patterns and, so to speak, the use of the light were different: the visionary qualities imparted an authority to conceptual patterns that, in many cases, were mixtures of material derived from empirical observation and the Scriptures. In a sense, then, *Causae* and *Scivias,* although not all of a piece, are very closely related. *Causae* is simply a fuller articulation of some of what is contained, in seedlike form, in the metaphysical views of *Scivias.*

Years ago, in *The Science Question in Feminism,* Sandra Harding wrote: "We shall also see that a key origin of androcentric bias can be found in the selection of problems for inquiry."[36] What Harding meant in this passage was that the traditional view of androcentrism in science, by some liberal feminists, as a problem largely of exclusion of women did not do justice to the sophisticated nature of tangles that actually constituted masculinism in the sciences and science-like endeavors. But although Hildegard's forays into the sciences and natural philosophy are extremely rudimentary, she displays her lack of such bias in her selection of problems—*Causae* is filled with passages on sexuality that, although they again employ the causal analyses of the humors, display much knowledge and awareness of women's sexual pleasure. As Berger claims, "The text is replete with discussions of human sexuality and the role of pleasure in reproduction."[37] Hildegard sees both women and men as part of God's creation, but as a woman she refuses to slight other women or to deny them an equal place in the text and in the discussion of such matters. As a religious, she tends, of course, to focus on the special role of women as potential mothers, and hence she is somewhat more concerned about the possibility that a woman's sexuality might be led astray. But the combination of her empirical observations, her medical experience, and the wholistic overview on which it is based—itself partially derived from strands of philosophical thinking that go back to Empedocles—leads her to say a great deal more about women than would have been said by most thinkers of the time.[38]

Hildegard has, then, a feminist epistemological view that precedes, in odd ways, some views that are in fact contemporary. We cannot, of course, do too much forcing here; the reliance on a church-centered cosmology undercuts a great deal of the naturalism, and there is no question that the source of Hildegard's visions has been a puzzle to all and was, at least even in her own time, an inexplicable phenomenon.[39] But Hildegard through her work does accomplish at least two major categorical goals, easily articulated: she retains a place for the role of women in all her writings, and does this to a much greater extent than many of her contemporaries, and she writes medical/philosophical tracts based on her experience as a medical worker and researcher. In that sense, she is among the first to write from a "standpoint"; the standpoint that she uses is that of a woman intellectual simultaneously immersed in the world of the senses.

The Wave of the Future

Much has been written in contemporary feminist circles about "third-wave feminism," postfeminist thinking, and the like. The general category breakdown that pervades a good deal of philosophical thought influenced by Continental theory has also influenced feminism, and to no less a degree. But if current concerns center around the notion that Eurocentric thinking, for example, has dominated feminist theory, or that the "totalizing" or "one size fits all" views have to go, one might wonder how views of women thinkers from preceding eras—almost all of whom were working within the framework of what later came to be considered the European tradition—can be categorized for today's work.

It is simplistic to say that Hildegard has something for everyone, or that there is some easy way around the paradox posed by her work, which does of course center around a Christian ontology. But one way to view her work that may make it more accessible for the new feminisms is to focus on those very characteristics that I had noted in the preceding section—the rootedness of the work in life, and its potential for the lives of others. Patricia Hill Collins has argued, in *Black Feminist Thought,* that an Afrocentric feminist epistemology would have to make note of the importance of oral tradition for the African-derived cultures, and of the strength of women's learning and teaching within the tradition.[40] Work like Hildegard's is more amenable than some to employment by such a tradition, since she comes from a part of Eurocentric thought that is itself rooted in oral tradition.

This same rootedness may be helpful for coming to grips with other sorts of questions that now begin to surface with respect to feminist theory, especially the paradox or set of paradoxes that is frequently posed by what I have called the "post post-theory" stage. Those who have argued against what they have termed "totalizing" or "essentialist" epistemologies and ontologies have generally been concerned, at the very least, about the ways in which those views tie into male-dominated structures and masculinist arenas of thought. There also has been a concern, quite understandably, that such views lend themselves to a simplistic feminism, or that views that seem to be grounded on something demonstrably gynocentric and quite possibly cross-cultural will fail to take into account the nuances of various cultural traditions.

But many have argued against the current foregrounding of such concerns, because these too create their own sort of oppression. The clear fact of the immersion of women's lives—for the vast majority of women in the world—means that there is a strong political reality of oppressive structures that must be faced by almost all women. As Sabina Lovibond has argued, with respect to those who take the antitotalizing stance, "True, there is a risk that we may overestimate the value of order and so establish within ourselves the psychological equivalent of a dictatorship; but then there is a countervailing risk that we may romanticize the fragmented, decentred condition by representing it as a force for social change when, really, it would be more accurately regarded as a manifestation of post-political apathy."[41]

If, as many are now claiming, there is a tendency to settle for a depoliticized view in the name of saving theory or theorizing from "the psychological equivalent of a dictatorship," there is now a realization that "romanticiz[ing] the fragmented" has very little to do with the actual reality of women's lived lives. In this sense, Hildegard's work, which so greatly precedes chronologically our own time and is, therefore, removed from it in many ways, holds out hope that there are areas of commonality available for articulation if the thinker chooses to pursue them.

Hildegard points the way to demarcating some of those areas when she reminds us of the physical reality of our environment, our place in our environment, and our actual lives. Ironically, it is the very part of Hildegard's work that now relies on ancient and, some would claim, outmoded medical practices that provides the clearest indication of a way to go. *Causae* is, in a sense, for every human being. All human beings can benefit, even if only metaphorically, from Hildegard's analysis of our "humors" and steps to a healthier life, for what her prescriptions fail to achieve in actual practice is more than compensated for in, as her proponents have pointed out, her awareness of viriditas. We go against the force of viriditas when we ask women and children to undergo unhealthy rituals in the name of a patriarchal cleansing, for example. Thus Hildegard points the way to a realization of our place in the world, a realization that is greatly needed in the twenty-first century.

As was mentioned earlier with respect to the work of Patricia Hill Collins, many traditions that are now regarded as "indigenous" have within them components that are saner, healthier, and more eco-friendly than the highly intellectualized worldviews of the developed nations. Here again, Hildegard's work falls into the general area of articulation; the new interest in Native American philosophies, Asian philosophies, and those components of Latin American philosophy that are related to the *mestizaje* within Latin America is part of a trend toward naturalist conceptions that allow room for the development of metaphor. What some of these views refer to as the "spiritual" may have no literal basis, but many have found it helpful in guiding their own personal lives, hence the new interest in using these philosophies and overviews as tools for personal growth. Because the period in which Hildegard wrote was one of comparatively little development in Europe—because it precedes the period of European hegemony and colonizing, and the intellectual moves that accompanied it—Hildegard's work is much more amenable to the same sorts of conceptualizing, and is, as we might say, "user friendly."

Painting in broad strokes, we can see then that two major lines of influence in contemporary feminist thought seem to converge on a point: one is a response to the Continental theory that, as Lovibond has asserted, may tend to romanticize a decentering and/or fragmentation, and the other is a turn toward any type of view that originates, partially or wholly, in outlooks not dominated by European theory. It might naively be thought that these two lines do not really support each other—after all, the most common counter to poststructuralism on the theoretical level has been a return to theory that those in the English-speaking world are already familiar with, Anglo-American thought. But this is not necessarily the case.

After all, it could be argued, the voices of many who are speaking from non-Eurocentric points of view might readily be deemed more "authentic" voices than the voices allegedly or purportedly undermined by the destruction of the subject, which is, according to some, one of the accomplishments of portions of Continental theory. In any case, Hildegard's work has the advantage that it was composed far enough back in time that, except for the possible questions surrounding the notion of the authorial that were alluded to by the work of Catherine Villanueva Gardner, other sorts of concerns are unlikely to be raised. Thus this work pushes simultaneously in the two directions that now seem to be among those cherished by some feminists for their politically redeeming qualities.

Alice Jardine has asserted: "Seeing themselves as no longer isolated in a system of loans and debts to former master truths, these new discourses in formation have grounded a *physis,* a space no longer passive but both active and passive, undulating, folded over upon itself, permeable: the self-contained space of eroticism."[42]

What Jardine means here is something like the following: those discourses that no longer purport to be part of the "master discourse" self-consciously allow for multiple interpretations that divorce them from the phallocracy of the system of signs in which they are embedded. Leaving aside the difficulties of these strands of contemporary French thought, one thing can be said: Hildegard's work, both in its mode of composition and in its subject matter, is already divorced to a very great extent from the master discourse. This gives it its appeal, and this allows it, on almost any interpretation, to achieve the "permeable" quality that Jardine writes about. And, not so astonishingly when we consider the historical buildup of the master discourse, all of this was accomplished a very long time ago.

Those who have chosen to make use of Hildegard's thought—whether for ecofeminist purposes, or some other set of "contemporary" purposes—have already seen in her mode of knowing and composing the very sort of permeability of which Jardine writes. Hildegard's work, paradoxically, speaks to our time because it was composed so far before our time that the usual sorts of restrictions do not apply. In that sense, Hildegard is a very contemporary author indeed.

An Overview

As we have seen, Hildegard's oeuvre falls into two broad components: the visionary and the more empirical. Drawing on those strands of work that have been translated into English and thus are more readily available to scholars in the United States, Canada, and the Australasian region, I have been able to show how certain sorts of philosophical positions can be inferred from Hildegard's work, although she does not use the substance/accident language so common to eleventh-century philosophers. More important, I have tried to be more precise about what it is that lends itself to feminist theorizing in Hildegard, without being overly tendentious, since it is clear that these sorts of categories could not originally have meaningfully applied to her work.

In *Scivias* and the other visionary works, a Christian ontology is formed that permeates the rest of her writings, including *Causae et Curae.* One of my points has been that the notion of the divine light—which will, in a different way, remain important in philosophy and come to its chief fruition with the Rationalists—is crucial for Hildegard precisely because she regards the eye as the seat of the soul, and hence vision as the chief sense. This more metaphorical usage is exactly what led to the later notion of an "inner light"; stripped of some of its origins, the later version allows the would-be knower to see, for example, a mathematical truth. Although Hildegard's seeing is of a different type, it is not unrelated to this chronologically later sort of seeing.

Similarly, the notion of viriditas has the force that it does because it combines the metaphorical and the literal in new and unusual ways. The same system of humors—which, as the historians of philosophy mention, appears in the writings of Empedocles, Galen, and many others—employs notions of health and ill health, but Hildegard sees viriditas as something that infuses God's creation. Thus all of creation manifests this "greening," to varying degrees. Both of these sorts of epistemological and metaphysical moves, though couched in somewhat nonstandard language, allow us to proceed with a feminist analysis that is unforced. As we saw, ecofeminism does not even have to borrow Hildegard—she is already there. Analyses, such as Greta Gaard's, of controversies involving indigenous cultures and ecoactivists, who predominantly come from the very first-world cultures that have caused the ecological damage in the first place, tie directly to Hildegard's work.

If there are comparisons to be made, I have indicated that one such natural comparison with a thinker of her own time involved the work of Mechthild of Magdeburg, but in a sense Hildegard's work transcends, in scope and volume, the work of most other thinkers—male or female—of the period. During the twelfth century when scholarship was on the increase, and when translations of the work of the ancients were appearing with great regularity, Hildegard's prodigious output remains noteworthy. It is not so much the visionary origins of her work, but the uses to which those origins are put, that stun the reader. Copleston notes that the first translations of Aristotle made the impression they did because they seemed to divorce theology and philosophy: "The translation of works of Aristotle and his commentators, as well as of the Arabian thinkers, provided the Latin Scholastics with a great wealth of intellectual material. In particular they were provided with the knowledge of philosophical systems which were methodologically independent of theology and which were presented as the human mind's reflection on the universe."[43]

Hildegard's writings contain a great deal of the strength of such systems, but without the divorce. In other words, if part of the appeal of a system is its sheer breadth, Hildegard's has that quality in abundance, and all aspects of her work are tied together through what we might call, to borrow a phrase from Alan Watts, her "joyous cosmology."

It is this particular strong point that allows us to see Hildegard's work in a feminist vein without undue pushing or reshaping of the work, and without a sense that we are forcing categories. What is frequently referred to in feminist theory as the "view from everywhere" occurs in abundance in Hildegard, and at the same time her vitalism, if we may call it that, allows us to think of her as one who naturalizes before the intellectual split between the rational and other forms of categorization takes place. If, as those who have preferred forms of object relations theory to discuss gender matters frequently assume, thinking in the speculative and ratiocinative way is itself a form of "stylistic aggression,"[44] one of the reasons they are able to make that claim is that, historically, this form of thought was often divorced from the natural or, if empirical, employed naturalized categories in such a way as to objectify the items in those categories. Hildegard commits neither of these crimes: in general, she does not engage in the pure ratiocination of the conventional philosopher, nor does she employ the natural in an objectified way. Rather—to use a somewhat overemployed, but very apt, term—she weaves these ways of conceptualizing together in such a way as to achieve something that is simultaneously a unified whole and entirely new.

It is here that the work of contemporary feminist epistemology comes in, since there are already several ways of approaching thought that draw on the material world and human interaction with the material world for their strength. As we discussed at an earlier point, standpoint theory, since it is derived from Marx and Marxist-oriented views, allows us to take the notion of a woman's engaged labor with the world as a point of departure for theorizing about women's epistemological stance toward the world. Immersion in the realm of the senses is decidedly not the stance of the speculative male theorists, whose every attempt to divorce themselves from the senses is evident in most theoretical work, starting from the time of Plato and achieving its height in the work of, for example, Spinoza. What the standpoint theorists are indicating—and this can scarcely be overstated—is that women in most cultures have seldom had the luxury of engaging in ratiocination truncated from the senses, and, although there may be occasional women thinkers whose work falls under such a rubric, their numbers are few. Hildegard, certainly, was no such thinker. Our look at *Causae et Curae* reminds us of the extent to which all of her thinking was of a piece; the same deity who caused Adam's fall is also the one who shows Hildegard how, by employing an analysis based on the humors, the ills of Adam and Eve and their heirs may be remedied. As we noted, Hildegard is consistent in her metaphysical stance, so that even her letters bear witness to the unity of her beliefs. Baird and Ehrman claim that they have had to use the "pumice stone well to present a still-living Hildegard by treating her mysteries with respect,"[45] but a very great part of the reason that they have used the pumice is that Hildegard's mysteries are present, at least to some extent, in virtually every single piece of writing that we have from her.

Hildegard is, then, all of a whole. We do her a disservice when we try to make her work anything less than it is, but at the same time, upon closer examination, it becomes clear why her work is now so popular, and why new books about her and her writings appear on a regular basis.

The danger with a thinker of Hildegard's range of interests and overall breadth of work is oversimplification. *Scivias,* for example, when closely examined, is a work of hundreds of pages and of enormous complexity—the scope of the visions ranges, literally, over all of creation. Because of the difference in mind-set and worldview, it is almost impossible for us today to do justice to such a work, yet we cannot gloss over it lightly. It is perhaps easier to grasp *Causae,* since we are already familiar with the notion of a medical manual, and thus we have some rubric under which we can shove this particular piece of work. But we need to indicate the mistake that is made if we pay Hildegard the disservice of trying too easily to assimilate her or her material.

Just as Copleston indicated that we can scarcely conceive of the difference that translations of Aristotle made to the medieval worldview—or the difficulties of the labors of some of the translators—our appreciation of Hildegard should be enlivened by some knowledge of the intricacy of her work and of the sheer staggering brutality of life during her time. She was not simply a seer or visionary, nor does it make sense, clearly, to think of her as a philosopher in the traditional sense. But Hildegard speaks to us from a time in which most individuals, of whatever background, were much more in touch with the world in which they lived, and much less distanced from the growth patterns of the food that it produced, or the cycles of the seasons and the movements of the stars. It is for these reasons, surely, that it is accurate to say that she finds a new audience today. The philosophical mind of the twelfth century, constantly questing to find an answer to questions that was in harmony with revealed scripture and also in concert with the bare facts of the world around her, strikes us today as kin to the best part of what we would like to be.

ANNE CONWAY two

The world of Anne Conway (1631–79), although it may be easier for us to enter than was Hildegard's, is still remote in time and space. Seventeenth-century England was a cauldron of conflicting beliefs, many of which owed their origins to religious concerns that today's readers will find difficult to assimilate. In addition, although at least a few women—such as Mary Astell—seemed to be able to rise from comparatively impoverished backgrounds to a life of gentility, the class distinctions in English life are so marked during this time period that we may experience a failure of imagination in trying to grasp the life of this viscountess.

Some facts are clear at the outset: Anne Conway was indeed a philosopher, in the sense that Hildegard was not, and was recognized as a philosopher by other thinkers during her own lifetime.[1] This will make it much easier for us to examine her work, since it cannot be claimed that standard philosophical categories do not apply. Also, first and foremost, Anne Conway was a student. She was a pupil of Henry More, the celebrated Cambridge Platonist whom she appears to have met through her stepbrother, John Finch, a Cambridge undergraduate, although the exact circumstances of their meeting are unclear.[2]

What is clear is that she impressed More from the start, and his first letter to her is an attempt to explain the Cartesian system and to provide a short translation for her.

In this era of Dissenters, High Tories, and popish intrigue, questions that might have seemed to have an obvious resolution to Hildegard become perplexing for Conway and for others like her, whose quest is largely one of attempting to integrate the new sciences with established knowledge and with the Christian faith. Descartes's response of a strict dualism, which, of course, raises the troubling question of interaction—never satisfactorily solved—is but one attempt; Spinoza's system is another. (Intriguingly, Conway must have read Spinoza or had some acquaintance with his work, as she refers to it repeatedly.) Conway will, in full argument, set out the vitalism with its gradations of a monistic hierarchy that Hildegard may have intended but never developed. In so doing, she will achieve a genuine philosophical system of her own and will provide at least some response to thinkers of her own time.

Marjorie Hope Nicolson gives us a view of the intellectual spirit of Conway's time by delineating the effect that the new sciences had on the older, more Aristotelian thinking:

> When in 1687 More lay dying within the walls of the college he had served so long, he looked back over the greatest period of transformation the university ever was ever to know. The Commonwealth had flourished and fallen. Cambridge had weathered that storm, and the equally grave period of the Restoration. The Aristotelianism of his own student days had given place first to Neoplatonism, then to Cartesianism, finally to a fusion which was different from either. Science was taking the place of superstition; the Royal Society numbered among its members many of the masters and fellows; Isaac Newton was enthroned.[3]

The key sentence here, of course, is the last, and its final clause is paramount. The rise of the sciences could not help but cast doubt on an already shaken religious faith, all the more so since questions of faith had been among those that promulgated the Cromwellian period. Thus one question became overriding: was it possible to formulate a coherent metaphysics, and concomitant epistemology, that would answer the questions about the relationship of matter to the divine? How could matter be under divine authority when it appeared to be governed by its own immutable laws, laws that were there, so to speak, for the looking? Since Anne Conway was exposed to these debates by her brother, her other male relatives, and the general tenor of her time, the young intellectually oriented woman could not help but have become stimulated to begin the process of finding answers on her own.

In this, her correspondence with More must have been of inestimable help. Nicolson notes that he esteemed her so highly that he began to write her very shortly after meeting her; the sister virtually replaced the brother as the genuine pupil in almost every respect virtually immediately.[4] From the start, their correspondence is at once overtly philosophical and bordering on the intimate; the unusual combination of intense personal friendship and genuine desire to understand is one that impresses the reader even after an interval of centuries. Nicolson reminds us that some of More's letters to Conway were written in such haste that even the trained academic, familiar with the hand of the period, has difficulty deciphering their contents.

Henry More found a ready and apt pupil in Anne Conway for the same sorts of reasons—the chance mixtures of nature and nurture that affect us all—that are often cited in similar situations. Born into a well-off and semi-noble family, Anne Finch was reared, coincidentally enough, in the same Kensington Palace that we now see regularly mentioned in the media, for at least part of her childhood. From her earliest years, she impressed those around her as a studious and thoughtful child, and as one driven, by her own needs, to books and learning whether or not they were formally available to her. Nicolson indicates that there is no adequate record of her formal childhood education; this education may have consisted largely of her own attempts to read and understand, and she may have been essentially an autodidact.[5] In any case, it is certain that she mastered several languages, for we know that she could read and understand French and Latin, and that she had read Plato and Plotinus in Latin. Her studiousness and seriousness not only impressed those around her, but according to the medical thinking of the day were at least partially responsible for her many illnesses, for she was a lifelong sufferer from headaches so severe that it is by no means certain that they were classical migraines. Nicolson provides this poignant commentary on Anne's early life: "Even in youth her favorite reading was philosophy; so eagerly and constantly did she study that the members of her family always attributed her mysterious malady to overzealous reading. But until she was seventeen or eighteen, her study was without order or coherence, and her mind a storehouse of ideas and facts, jostling each other in increasing complexity. . . . Her sex forbade any organized education, which might have helped her to bring order out of this chaos."[6]

Given Anne's predilections, it is easy to see why the introduction by her brother to Henry More might have made the astounding difference that it did. But one also must take into account Anne's youthful marriage to Edward Conway, later Viscount Conway, and her attainment upon marriage of a house in Warwickshire that became a center for intellectual discussions and disputes.[7] Although at first her husband also joined in these lively conversations, his travels later took him away a great deal, and Anne was frequently left on her own. Since her only child died shortly after birth, and since she herself spent increasing amounts of time with books as a bedridden invalid, it is not difficult to see that the combination of inclination, marriage, and health pushed her surely and strongly in a philosophical direction.

The desire to bring some order and coherence to the variety of philosophical views to which she had been exposed led Anne to contemplate a number of systems in terms of their defects, and her other strong desire—to unite at least some form of religious belief with an adequate metaphysics—led her to the work of the Kabbalists of the time. Consequently, she began her philosophical work by rejecting the systems of most of those thinkers to whom she had already been exposed. Descartes's dualism she, like many others, found inadequate, and of Spinoza she was later to remark that he had confused various levels of being. Since her task was to provide for an ontology that would allow for gradations of beings—for like most of her day, she assumed that there was a strong ontological difference between, for example, a human being and a dog—she had to assume a notion of substance that would work for all of animal and human creation, but that could also be invoked for the mysterious entities that believing Christians also assumed inhabited the heavens. Thus her fully articulated monism of a vitalist stripe, that, as she herself maintained, allowed for "all creatures from the highest to the lowest [being] inseparably united with one another."[8] This rather intriguing attempt at accounting for a range of creatures is one of the remarkable features of Conway's philosophy that gives it its fresh and original air. It is one of the more interesting facts of philosophical history that this startling work was done by a woman living, much of the time, virtually alone.

Conway's Metaphysics

Developing her ideas in her one lengthy extant work, *Principles of the Most Ancient and Modern Philosophy,* Conway explicitly sets out a triad of substances, but her notion of the triad is different from what one might expect from more traditional ontologies. She sees all of creation—all matter, save Christ himself, and God, of course—as part of one substance, which she claims is composed of an infinite number of monads, themselves an interesting admixture of spirit and matter. God stands ontologically apart from this creation, obviously, and following Kabbalistic tradition of a third sort of entity known as "Adam Kadmon," she sees Christ as a figure metaphysically somewhere between God the creator and the rest of creation.

Conway is perhaps best known today for her use of the term "monad"—although it occurs only once or twice in the *Principles*—since there is genuine reason to think that Leibniz appropriated the term from her after having corresponded with her.[9] But more important for our purposes is the unpacking of Conway's conception of the monad, and its relationship to her account of the deity and the rest of creation. It is in the delineation of these areas that the originality of her work lies.

Coudert and others emphasize Conway's indebtedness to the Kabbala, and to its mystical tradition insofar as certain categorizations are employed.[10] Intriguing as this is, however, it would seem that the philosophically more interesting material lies in Conway's stated attacks on other thinkers, and the obvious fact that the opening sections are devised to construct an ontology that will be free of some of the pernicious influences of other seventeenth-century ontologies. Therefore, it would seem most illuminating to allude to the mystical material only when necessary.

In any case, the first two chapters of the *Principles* offer a closely reasoned view of God, time, and creation, and one which, as Loptson had mentioned in his commentary, contains a sophisticated use of the notion of essence. It is this use, which approximates today's technical use, that does most of the work for Conway in terms of establishing an innovative metaphysics.[11] Briefly, Conway holds that God is a creator *de re,* and that all of creation thus existed from the beginning of time with God, although its manifestation came later. Part of the argument is that it does not make sense to think that God, as a being omniscient, omnipotent, and omnipresent, made inferences about creation, so in a strict metaphysical sense what we, as humans, see as creation must always have existed with God. Conway makes these points in a number of different ways and in a number of different places, but they are crucial for the development of the rest of her argument; in the first chapter, for example, she writes: "In God there is an idea which is his image or the word existing within himself, which in substance or essence is one and the same with him, through which he knows himself and all other things and, indeed, all creatures were made or created according to this very idea and word."[12]

In this section, Conway establishes the beginning of what will become her metaphysical hierarchy, and does so by indicating how, in terms of substance, all of creation originates from God. This intriguing concept, which avoids the substance dualism of Cartesian thinking and some of the flaws of Spinoza's system as well, allows Conway to begin to establish the chain of being. She restates this point in the second chapter of the *Principles* when she writes: "Therefore the essential attribute of God is to be the creator. Consequently God was always a creator and will always be a creator because otherwise he would change. Therefore creatures always were and always will be."[13]

The importance of these opening sections lies in the work they will do later; Conway sees all creatures as related in a continuum. Aside from God, the only other being to manifest a different ontological status is Christ himself, whom Conway sees as an intermediary between God and creation. But the ultimate origin of creation in the substance of God means that creatures have the capacity to move along the hierarchy and to participate in the various gradations of beings, even if this is not immediately obvious.

What in other philosophers' systems is termed the difference between spirit and matter is for Conway a difference of mode, and not of essence. That Conway employs standard philosophical terminology not only makes it much easier for later philosophers to interpret her work, but it accomplishes something else simultaneously. It places her irrefutably in the canon of seventeenth-century philosophers, and does so in a way that admits of little dispute. It is clear that Conway makes this distinction—that spirit and matter are modes of the same substance, and not to be thought of as substances themselves—so that she can develop a system without the defects of those she had already encountered. She holds that "all creatures are mutable in respect to their natures," and, ultimately, this mutability will express itself, at least in the fullness of time. Since all creatures originally came from God, and since all of creation expresses the vitalist mixture of spirit and matter that she claims are modes, and not essences (although obviously some beings possess a greater degree of spirit than others), she is able to assert that the earth will change, and that, as she has it, horses and other animals will change their configurations along with the earth. Although it is unclear when this would occur, because of Conway's commitment to Christianity we can assume that part of her argument here is to establish a basis for apocalyptic revelation and its relationship to ontological status.

In any case, Conway's system saves her from the two sorts of errors to which, as she herself says, many metaphysicians of her time were prone. The difficulty of Cartesian interactionism occurs only if, as Descartes maintained, spirit and matter were clearly distinguishable from each other and possessed no admixture. On the other hand, to claim that all creatures are part of the same substance obviously does not allow for the types of distinctions among creatures with which our senses familiarize us. Thus, from the outset, Conway's thinking avoids the twin pitfalls of extreme dualism and extreme and pronounced monism.

Because of Conway's system of gradations, and her belief that ultimately spirit and matter are united in various degrees of admixture, she is able to posit a notion of perfectibility for beings that allows her to articulate a version of what will later become known as the Great Chain of Being. This gives her metaphysics a unique fluidity, and it is a factor that has struck virtually every serious student of her work. Writing of these relationships, in chapter 6, she notes: "We already see how the justice of God shines so gloriously in this transmutation of one species into another. For it is most certain that a kind of justice operates not only in human beings and angels but also in all creatures. Whoever does not see this must be called completely blind. This justice appears as much in the ascent of creatures as in their descent, that is, when they change for better or worse."[14]

Here Conway posits a notion of betterment for all creatures, and she fully explicates that notion, not only for the human world, but for animals as well. She indicates, for example, that a horse after death may "return[ ] to life and obtain the body of another horse, so that it becomes a horse as it was before, but stronger and more beautiful and with a better spirit than before."[15] Although her doctrine does not amount to a metempsychosis or doctrine of reincarnation, she sees the possibility for a number of creatures to obtain a greater admixture of spirit in a continual cycle of spirit/matter interminglings that go on as long as the earth abides and the New Jerusalem has not yet come.

Anne Conway had read, as I have indicated here, not only Descartes but also Spinoza and Hobbes. When we think of Spinoza's beautifully designed system, with its notion that God has an infinite number of essences, two of which we are familiar with in our everyday functioning (matter and extension), it may superficially appear that Conway has not thought through the implications of her ontological structure carefully. But here, at least to some extent, the situation is the other way around. Although there is no opening to Conway's work that parallels in structure the renowned opening of Spinoza's *Ethics* with its clearly deductive instantiations, Conway is concerned that the Spinozistic system does not leave enough room for distinctions between creatures, or more precisely, between God and creatures. (We might remember the Spinozistic dictum that "God has an infinite number of attributes.") Other than for various repetitions of the notion that "all things that are, are in God" Spinoza has no clear way to account for the various levels of being, with which we are already familiar. The later developments of science will, of course, allow us to distinguish between planaria and raccoons, or mountain gorillas and amoebae. But Anne Conway essays to do something similar within the framework of the philosophizing of her time when she tells us the reason we can make these distinctions is that some creatures are constituted so that they possess a greater admixture of spirit than others.

It is clear that Conway managed to strike a fairly even course between the rationalism of her time and the views of the church. In that era fraught with religious difficulties, Conway moved swiftly and surely in the *Principles* to try to show how it would be possible to retain a Christian worldview and still provide a philosophically accurate account of creation. That she was able to do this while seriously ill, with the plaguing headaches and other trials that wracked her throughout her life, is testimony to the endurance of her own spirit and to the strength of philosophical thought in the circles in which she moved during that perilous time.

The Axiological Anne Conway

"Wee fly!" "We die!" A wood engraving from 1665 shows Londoners moving under the aegis of the grim reaper, in his guise as a harbinger of the plague. Off to one side, the print shows the dead bodies of victims, while the living move to safe ground. The plague personified stands over the city, sickle in hand, ready to strike down anyone who happens to be nearby.[16]

Conway's brief treatise does not have a fully articulated ethics or theory of value that might address these London disasters, but a great deal can be extrapolated from what she has written, because it is clear that the notion of betterment and perfection that is entailed in her series of ontological gradations does indeed do ethical work. The example of the horse is but one example that shows her interest in the world around her, and her sensitivity to the lives of animals. In her time, many domesticated animals would have been abused in ways that we cannot understand or comprehend today—genuine work on the lives of animals and their protection did not become part of the English scene until the nineteenth century. But Conway was ahead of her time in using the somewhat homely example of the change in status of a horse over periods of rebirth and reentry into the world, because her allusion to the horse's spirit and beauty shows her awareness that other animals— above and beyond human beings—had traits worth protecting and developing. There is, in fact, a great deal in the *Principles* that speaks to these issues.

However quaint it may seem to us today, Conway is careful to provide a list of such entities as angels and other spiritual beings, simply to show the hierarchy that exists in traditional Christianity, and how that hierarchy might mirror or reflect the hierarchy of earthly creatures. One cannot say that what Anne Conway achieves has the force, for example, of Hildegard's viriditas— Conway is too much the careful philosopher who is trying to construct a system without ontological defects. But her philosophy is infused with a passion because she has spent time thinking about these issues, and also because she exhibits genuine caring about the world around her.

This caring—a sort of axiological sensitivity—manifests itself both in the *Principles* and in Conway's correspondence with Henry More. He, insofar as we may discern his personality and motivations, appears to have impressed everyone he met with his seriousness and dedication to all issues. In a volume on Ralph Cudworth, John Passmore notes of More that he was a "lover of ghosts and marvels," and that he is most likely the source for his character Bathynous, or "the deeply thoughtful [and] profoundly-thinking man" in his own *Divine Dialogues*.[17] What we can see from Passmore's brief contrast with the personality of the more painstaking Ralph Cudworth is a man whose temperament must have been a match for Anne Conway's, and who no doubt infused her with much of his passion and interest. In that sense, then, it is not difficult to distill from her writings and her correspondence with him a sense of value that is anti-utilitarian, for example, in the spirit of the narrow calculus that will later be developed, but much more deontological in its respect for persons and persons' lives.

A great deal has been written about the effect Descartes's belief that animals were mere machines had on later views of animals, the planet, humankind, and their relationship to each other. Descartes was, of course, simply trying to piece together as much as was known scientifically with a philosophical view that reflected his careful mathematical predilection for deduction. In the *Passions,* for example, Descartes tries to provide a strict account of how fear might operate within the body—and, as it happens, his account is generated by the example of seeing a tiger approaching. "Thus, for example, if we see some animal approach us, the light from its body reflects two images of it, one in each of our eyes, and these two images form two others, by means of the optic nerves, in the interior surface of the brain."[18]

This account, which is only accidentally about a wild animal, is selected here because it reminds us of the careful use of then-current knowledge about optic nerves and retinal reflection that Descartes has incorporated into his overall view of the functioning of the passions. But Conway is driven by no such scientific knowledge, and this may be beneficial to the overall pattern of her metaphysics. Descartes, who would provide a gloss on the tiger in the example above as nothing more than the sorts of parts that can be fashioned from fibers and nerves, has an intriguing counterpart in Viscountess Conway, who writes: "All creatures from the highest to the lowest are inseparably united by their subtler mediating parts, which come between them and which are emanations from one creature to another, through which they can act upon one another at the greatest distance. This is the basis of all the sympathy and antipathy which occurs in creatures."[19]

Conway is enabled to make this pronouncement by her radical doctrine that creatures possess a vitalist mixture of matter and spirit, and that this mixture is intermingled in various creatures in proportion so that some are largely matter and others have a much greater endowment of the spiritual. The "monads," in which Leibniz will later take at least a terminological interest, are in fact these subtle interceding parts, of which there are an infinite number and which are, so to speak, the building blocks of all creation. It might be objected that Conway shows only a slightly greater interest in this "sympathy" than Descartes does, but it is manifestly apparent in the text.

Anne Conway exhibited this same sort of care in her personal relationships, and the extant letters that we have from her to Henry More and to her husband exhibit a modesty and humility combined with a care for others that amounts, with hindsight, to what must have been an overvaluing of the others, but that provides us with an overview of her ethics, broadly construed. It is both touching and illuminating to examine these missives, as they provide insight into the care with which Anne Conway wrote, the feelings that she had for others, and the extent to which she tried to unite these passions with concern for philosophical issues. For example, in a letter to Henry More when she was still in her early twenties, she writes: "I see you are willing to have a good opinion of me, that can refute the plaine profession of my demeritt (which is a serious truth)."[20] And to her husband, stationed in Ireland, she writes, "I could not satisfy myselfe with writing seldome to you."[21] One might think that these are but the common courtesies of the time, and yet many other letters from this period are not infused with the same care. Anne Conway's modesty and gentleness, as manifested in her correspondence, seem completely genuine.

The extent to which the Conway ontology has something to do with notions of value cannot be overstated. If the vitalist conception is paramount—and it seems to point in the direction of a wholistic concern for beings—it is important to try to be precise about what it is that drives the wholism. One of Conway's greatest concerns is to refute the notion of "dead matter." Remembering that she strove to work within the framework of the Christianity of her time (a Christianity that was greatly influenced by the events around it), it is noteworthy how often in the *Principles* she takes the time to argue against the concept of matter as divorced from spirit. In chapter 7 of the *Principles,* she says: "[S]ince the goodness of God is a living goodness, . . . how can any dead thing proceed from him or be created by him, such as mere body or matter, according to the hypothesis of those who affirm that matter cannot be changed into any degree of life or perception? It has been truly said that God does not make death."[22]

Because Conway repeatedly says that the difference between spirit and body "is only one of degree not essence,"[23] and because she refuses to admit that there is matter devoid of spirit, the notion that humans, or other creatures, are entitled to be contemptuous of creation, in any sense, is unsupportable. The degree to which matter is penetrated by spirit is clearly, for Conway, a decision of God, and humans are simply one part of the chain of creation that is the result of divine decision.

Anne Conway's work does not have the explicit setting out of a theory of value that we have come to expect of later philosophers, or even of a few other philosophers from her period. But it is clear from what she has written in the *Principles* that all of creation is worthy of respect, and that the differences between creatures are, on her system, not nearly as great as the differences posited by Descartes. In this sense, Anne Conway has created an implicit ethics that merits the attention of every student of philosophy.

Her Correspondents

When we think of Anne Conway and her correspondents, literal or figurative, we have, of course, Nicolson's *Conway Letters* to serve as a basis for appraisal, and we have the enormous amount of work that has been done on thinkers of Conway's time with whom we know she was in contact.

It is most interesting to imagine the correspondences—again, in many cases more metaphorical than not—between Anne Conway and other thinkers of her time, at least one of whom was a woman. Although we can create a great deal of analysis about her relationship with Henry More, or with Francis Mercury van Helmont, since both are amply documented by Nicolson, a more intriguing area of inquiry revolves around Damaris Cudworth Masham. We have no evidence that the two women ever communicated directly, but they were certainly aware of each other, and, given the paucity of women thinkers of the time who would have had the substantial philosophical training required to correspond with either Leibniz or Locke (Lady Masham was a correspondent of

Locke's, and, apparently, at one point, a lover) it would seem to be worth inquiring into their relationship. It is also to the point to mention that many would argue that a more apt investigation would be to compare Conway and Margaret Cavendish; Cavendish's work, however, seems to be driven by more explicitly empirical concerns, and in any case such comparisons have been made before.

As it happens, Passmore notes Damaris Masham's awareness of the Cambridge Platonists and their circle in his work on Ralph Cudworth, Damaris Masham's father. He claims that "Damaris Cudworth . . . writing to Locke, speaks of 'my friends, the Cartesians and the Platonists,' meaning the group we now call 'the Cambridge Platonists.'"[24] Lois Frankel, in one of the few articles on the work of Masham extant in contemporary philosophical circles, notes that there is much reason to believe that Masham was at least aware of Anne Conway's status as a woman philosopher of the time: "Although there is no direct evidence that Conway's work was discussed in van Helmont's visit [to the Masham home], it is not unlikely that it was. Masham had at least a passing acquaintance with Conway's work through Leibniz, who mentions Conway in passing to Masham in a letter of December 14/25 1703. Additionally, Ralph Cudworth's fellow Cambridge Platonist Henry More was a close friend of Conway's."[25]

Although this particular incident occurs after Conway's death, it is nevertheless entirely possible that the young Damaris might have heard of Conway while she was alive, and it is even possible that they had some contact.

The fleshing out of these possibilities is intriguing because the concept of an actual philosophical correspondence here merely serves to highlight the differences in the views of the two women.[26] As we have seen, Conway's system is preeminently rationalist: a great deal of time is spent in the *Principles* arguing against the views of other thinkers because either their conceptions of substance, or of God, or of both, are flawed by inconsistency. Masham's work is comprised largely of two essays and a series of letters, but more to the point, she is, at least some of the time, concerned to defend Locke on a number of grounds having to do with religious concepts, and she is not preeminently interested in metaphysics or the construction of an ontology in the same way that Conway was. According to Frankel, Masham's writings emphasized "Christian theology, epistemology, and moral philosophy."[27] On at least one point, however, Masham and Conway do converge, even if they would not have been aware of it, and even if their articulations of the material would have been different. They both believe that there is no reason to think that the nature of God and human relationships to him cannot be thought through with the use of the human intellect. In other words, however infinite God may be in concept, we can use our God-given faculties of intelligence and will at least to begin to understand the divine nature. Frankel notes of Masham and her defense of Locke that: "Masham reiterates his [Locke's] claims that revelation may provide rational grounds for belief, but that reason must be employed in order to determine whether a revelation has indeed occurred. Absurdities must be denied the status of revelation, for no revelation could be contrary to reason."[28]

Although Damaris Masham does not attempt a system, as does Anne Conway, she does address philosophical issues of the day, and in that sense she serves as an apt person with whom a comparison can be made. What Conway and Masham may also have in common are tendencies that, in contemporary terms, might be thought to bespeak a gynocentric or female-patterned conceptual organization, a subject that I will address later.

Because so much of what has been written about Conway emphasizes her interest in the Kabbala, it does not do her justice as a thinker to fail to mention her actualized correspondence—and talks with—thinkers of the period who had read and studied this literature. Carolyn Merchant, whose work on Conway was catalytic in bringing her to the fore, spends a great deal of time on Conway's relationship to van Helmont, since he exposed her to the Kabbala and influenced her use of it as a starting point for at least some of her metaphysics. Although van Helmont has a somewhat intriguing reputation—Nicolson had written an article on him in the 1920s entitled "The Real Scholar Gipsy"—it is clear that he remains a person from whom Conway derived an enormous amount of influence, and that this influence cannot be minimized.[29]

Merchant describes the activity of van Helmont and the relationship of his writings to those of Conway in this way: "The word 'monad' had been utilized in the writings of Francis Mercury van Helmont and Lady Anne Conway and had appeared in the *Kabbala denudata,* published by Knorr von Rosenroth in 1677–78, to which van Helmont had contributed. . . . The sections of the Kabbala denudata referred to by Conway stated that matter had been made from a coalition of spiritual monads in a state of inactivity, or stupor, out of which is created the material world."[30]

Van Helmont was merely one of many visitors to Ragley Hall, the Conway seat in Warwickshire, but what almost all of these visitors had in common was a desire for philosophical conversation with Anne Conway. Although most commentators seem to feel that Leibniz and other thinkers who might have been in a position to judge were less than impressed by van Helmont—at least partially because of a reputation for flightiness—there is no question that this literary man, who also took an interest in medical matters, was a decided influence on her thought.[31] While the Kabbala has always been held to be a work derived from divine revelation—and its most important version, the Zohar, has usually been translated as the "Book of Divine Splendor"—the ontology set out by the Kabbala is one that also admits of gradations of being. It must have been this aspect of it that influenced Anne Conway the most, for we can see that one of her strongest motivations in the composition of her own philosophy was the desire to avoid either the stringent dualism or rigorous, dead monistic materialism of other thinkers of her time. Thus, although the work may have been presented to her as a work that was not composed on the basis of a thought-out, systematizing experience of matters philosophical, it is clear that the work must have been very attractive for other reasons, and van Helmont is, according to our available sources, the figure who acquainted Anne Conway with this mystical Judaic thought.[32]

Anne Conway, then, is one who has many correspondents in the metaphorical sense, some in the literal sense, and many others in a sense possibly less than metaphorical but perhaps best described as anticipatory. Because of her serious interest in philosophy, and commitment to it, everyone alive and working during her time would have been someone with whom, ideally, she would have liked an interchange.

It is worth remarking on the fact that Henry More and his circle—but especially More himself—filled the role of correspondent for Conway in almost every conceivable way. Not only was More her confidant and friend (and her lover, although we do not know the full nature of their relationship), he was also her instructor, tutor, and philosophical mentor. They were naturally suited to each other, in the fullest sense, because each of them was driven by a passionate commitment to the life of the mind and by a deep caring about obtaining an adequate account of the world. It is easy to say that such commitments form the basis for good philosophizing, but it is seldom that two individuals who are so complementary and, indeed, similar to each other are able to participate in such an extended relationship over a long period of time. In this sense, the relationship between Conway and More has few parallels—other relationships, such as that between Heloise and Abelard (to which we have already alluded) are more troubled from the outset, whereas this particular relationship, except for some quite understandable philosophical testiness from time to time, seems to have endured virtually trouble free for decades.

Conway may not have known Damaris Masham, may have been involved with van Helmont for a variety of reasons, and may have been chiefly concerned with More, but her passion made her one who was constantly referred to within the circle of Platonists. We find her mentioned in the actual correspondence because the remarkable freshness of her thought stood out, in her articulation of vitalism, as did her personal acuity and judgment, and her commitment. In this sense, she has few peers as a correspondent in her century, or in any other.

A Feminist Twist

There is a sense in which it has now become very easy to try to find feminist stirrings in women philosophers, regardless of the period in which they worked, and regardless of the plain fact that many women thinkers were driven not only primarily by their relationships with males, but by modes of conceptualization that might already be deemed to reflect male patterns.

Anne Conway is certainly a thinker who falls into the latter category. As I have repeated, she is one of the rare thinkers among the group of seventeenth-century women who are now cited with some regularity who actually is categorizable as a philosopher precisely because much of her work mimics or is in the style of the type of philosophical work customarily done by males. Unlike Hildegard, Conway does not write in a vein that forces us, at least on occasion, to guess at what she means. Rather, her precise alembication of many philosophical questions—especially those concerned with metaphysics, cosmology, and ontological gradations—places her firmly in the camp of one who has mastered all of the standard material of her day and who is ready to compose more such material, again in the same vein.

The question then arises whether it forces the issue to try to find tie-ins in Conway's work to feminist theorizing of the contemporary period. This is no small matter, for one does not want to be guilty of attempting to place square pegs in round holes, or of attempting to push material where it will not go. A preliminary answer to the question would seem to be this: Conway displays, particularly in her concern for metaphysical specificity, a number of tendencies that are allied with, if not precisely consonant with, some strands of current feminist thought. Yet there is no question that when we make this statement, we are at the same time constantly aware of the ways in which Conway fails to adhere to such categorization. It would behoove the discerning reader, then, to try with perhaps more than ordinary care to be precise about the ways in which Conway might be said to be consonant in her theorizing with contemporary feminist concerns.

The constantly cited work of Gilligan and Keller is beneficial here, because it allows us to begin a sort of bare-bones conceptualization with regard to what might count as gynocentric concerns.[33] When, for example, Gilligan opposes the "justice" voice to the "care" voice, she is speaking only of trends, and the trends do not necessarily—as she has repeatedly said—parallel gender links. Nevertheless, the preponderant majority of her respondents who chose to think in terms of connection rather than of abstract, person-independent rules were female. In the case of Keller, her notion of "dynamic objectivity" as applied to work in the sciences allowed her to use the Nobel Prize–winning thought of Barbara McClintock as an example of scientific work that was not predicated on complete objectification. Although she is careful to note that any investigator could employ this style, as it happens McClintock was a woman and one of the few women scientists of her era. The point is simply that Gilligan and Keller both push us in a certain direction; the dynamic of thought articulated by both authors (over a wide range of topics, both ethical and scientific) focuses on notions of interconnectedness, nonobjectification, identification with the other, and concern for one outside oneself. These are important, and striking, concepts.

As I have said, it might seem naive or misguided to attempt to see if we can locate hallmarks of this sort of thinking in Conway's work—except that, to some extent, this project has already been done. Almost all of her commentators, many of them by no means feminist, note the extent to which her work is focused, especially insofar as the ontological gradations proposed by her are concerned, on a number of areas that mesh well with at least crudely rendered constructs of nonidentification. For example, Richard Popkin, writing on the work of both Henry More and Anne Conway, makes the appeal of Conway's theorizing plain:

> Anne Conway laid out her case first by criticizing Descartes' conception of a body, "a mere dead Mass, not only devoid of all kind of Life and Sense, but utterly incapable of to all eternity." . . . Anne Conway pointed out that superficially her view looked like Hobbes' in that they both held that all creatures originally were of one substance, and hence can be transformed into one another. . . . [But a] . . . crucial difference is that for Hobbes and Descartes as well, matter and body have only extension and impenetrability. . . . As a result, they never understood that spirit, or life, or light . . . are quite distinct from extension and figure.[34]

It is precisely Conway's concern to avoid the "deadness" of matter under seventeenth-century conceptions of it that yields her overall metaphysics, and it is important to note again that the ramifications of her view extend to

animals and other aspects of creation. Although we can see purely intellectual merit to Conway's rebuttal (remembering that, according to her and
other thinkers who were in agreement, dead matter cannot move), it is not
difficult to see that Conway exhibits a sensitivity toward animals and the
world around her that is often missing from the work of other philosophers.

Again, her notion of "penetrability" is partly a simple response to Cartesian
sorts of objections about the separateness of matter and spirit, but the constant
objectification and desire to dominate and master, intellectually or otherwise,
signaled by Cartesian sorts of separations are completely missing in Conway's
work. Much of this can be said, of course, about More's work as well: it not only
reminds us of their collaboration, but also underscores Keller's point that what
is being described is a certain style. In any case, one inference can be made:
Conway's style is much closer to the fluid and dynamic style of a thinker like
McClintock, who felt an intimate involvement with her corn plants, than it is
to the static objectivity of a thinker like Descartes.

Ynestra King, in an important essay on ecofeminism, has claimed that
"[a]t the root of Western society exist both a deep ambivalence about life itself, our own fertility, and that of nonhuman nature, and a terrible confusion
about our place in nature. Nature did not declare war on humanity; patriarchal humanity declared war on women and on living nature."[35] In a manner
of speaking, then, Conway can be thought of in the same vein as Hildegard:
her ontology allows us to think of her as one who is environmentally sensitive, and who is ahead of her time. This probably is accurate in only the most
approximate sense, however; what motivates Conway, More, and others of
her circle is a desire to make the new scientific learning consistent or consonant with their understanding of revealed religion, and to do so in a way that
will alleviate some of the distress caused by Cromwellian tactics and the dis-
ruption leading up to the Restoration. (Indeed, Popkin notes that More believed "the Restoration of 1660 saved Christianity from a lot of madmen.")[36]
In any case, Conway's cosmology is so striking that the relevant features of
it move commentators from other centuries.

The acidulousness of debates about revealed truth is difficult for readers
in the twentieth and twenty-first centuries to assimilate, and Conway's turn
toward Quakerism at a later point in her life was the source of disparaging
commentary even from More. But the lack of certainty of our own time—signaled by the current mania for a sort of postmodern irony—misses the life-
and-death importance of disputes during the seventeenth century, a century
marked by fires, plagues, and bloodshed.[37] The desire to Get Things Right,

and to get them right in such a way as to alleviate the ever-present misery, which seemed a sort of punishment, must have been overwhelming. Conway's work was an attempt to provide an account of reality that allowed for motion, change, the (obvious to her) presence of spirit, and the existence of a Creator who had employed design and purpose in the original construction of that very creation.

The interest of the Cambridge Platonists in the Kabbala—an interest emphasized again and again by Merchant, Popkin, and others—is simply one more aspect of this same concern for a close approximation of how spirit drives the world. Those who have become enamored of Kabbalistic commentary often note its employment of the notion of *tikkun,* now widely cited in our own time. This concept, clearly, revolves around a notion of wholeness. All of these sorts of concerns indicate a desire to integrate a number of lines of argument, and to establish an overview that will allow for notions of interconnection and dynamism. It is not going too far to suggest that these notions bring us to a feminist place, as it were. As has been argued by feminists who have examined the thought of Descartes from the standpoint of object relations theory, few could have been more divorced from themselves and others than the thinker whom we frequently cite as the greatest philosopher of the seventeenth century.[38]

Theory of Knowledge and Anne Conway

Because I have articulated the point that it may appear presumptuous to attribute any views connected with feminist theory to Anne Conway (at least at first perusal), I need to be precise. At first glance, the more scintillating work in feminist theory of knowledge—and it has driven a great deal of gender-related commentary in philosophy in the past decade—may seem irrelevant to Conway's work.

Here one needs to tread with even greater care than in establishing a general line of argument about matters feminist, because a couple of points are immediately obvious. Conway was preeminently a rationalist; she worked in a time period that preceded, chronologically, the thinking of the empiricists, and, as we have seen, her philosophical desires have to do with consistency, and with establishing views related to an overweening conception of the deity. In Conway's case, it simply does not make sense to try to push lines of argument that, for other thinkers, seem to bolster an intersection with feminist epistemology; naturalized epistemology, for example, makes more sense in the context of thinkers who came later and whose work is, from the outset, more empirically derived. One might be inclined to throw in the towel at this point, for the androcentrism of traditions that espouse classic ratiocination is more or less beyond dispute; indeed, it is these traditions, with their notions of male authority and patriarchal sacredness, that gave rise to feminist responses in terms of theory in the first place. Again, Descartes remains the best exemplar; although he statedly pursues aims opposed to those of the Scholastics, he was reared in this tradition, and his concern for speculation in the classic vein is very much in the church mode.

What, then, can we retrieve from Conway, if anything, that is tied more closely to the intriguing work currently being done in feminist epistemology? It is important to note that traditional cultures, all over the world, often have domains of male sacredness and privileged thought, and these areas are often split off in the culture from areas deemed "female," since the latter will frequently revolve around rituals of menstruation, childbirth, lactation, and so on. In a way, we can glean more from a perusal of some of these areas, even if they are not located in European or European-derived cultures. Conway is placed in a position similar to that of the few rebellious women of whom we have record who wrote or spoke with authority in, for example, some Asian cultures or some early Mediterranean cultures. As a woman, she has chosen to write in a mode that is archetypically male, and before there is any well-established tradition of female thinkers or authorship, especially on matters philosophical.

Conway is, then, an appropriator of a male tradition, and although we cannot say—in terms other than the broadest—that she has tied gynocentric elements into her work, the one tradition that she is heir to is that of female appropriator. In this sense, she is like those in the Buddhist tradition, as articulated by Diana Paul, who courageously worked against the grain and gave us the concept of the female bodhisattva.[39] Although the tradition of pure ratiocinative speculation is, in almost any culture, paradigmatically a male tradition, Conway managed to become an exponent of it in her time, just as a few others became articulators of it in various other cultures and times. There are indeed some feminist-theory related elements of connection in her concepts of penetrability and of ontological gradation, but the most intriguing part of Conway's work is that she achieves those concepts through the male-sanctified method of philosophical thought divorced from the realm of the senses.

If it is accurate to say that the work of Anne Conway does not provide us with, for example, an intersection with today's feminist naturalized epistemology, with its emphasis on immersion in the realm of the material, then we can make some striking inferences from the extent to which Conway fails to fall within the scope of that thinking.[40] It is clear from her correspondence with Henry More, her husband, and others that the preeminent figures in her life were male. What her relations with other women (even women of her own social class) could have been we can only guess. And, of course, we must take into account the fact that, speaking in terms of both history and of Conway's own era, her only models for participants in the intellectual life would have been male.

Nevertheless, a fair statement seems to be that Conway appropriates a tradition that is largely masculinist and male-centered—the tradition of divorced and rarefied metaphysics—with a few twists that signal, at least to some extent, gynocentric strands in her thought. One of these seems to be her emphasis on interaction between the spirit and the body, in the vitalist sense, and the extent to which the phenomenon of pain signals to us this interaction; interestingly enough, at least some of this material seems to have come to her from a male thinker. Nicolson indicates that this particular strand of Conway's thought is due to van Helmont, and Nicolson finds van Helmont's own emphasis on the body and pain to be quite striking. As Nicolson notes, in one particular episode in his travels, Francis Mercury van Helmont found himself with a broken shoulder, but the intellectual inferences he made from this unpleasant experience were quite different from those that would have been made by most sufferers: "But all the while he had been suffering in body, his active mind had been developing from the experience one of his most characteristic theories—the *anatomy of pain*. 'The parts of the broken bones jarr'd against one another, which,' he truly declared, 'was a very sensible pain.' Yet though a pain, it had transmutative value. From the experience he developed a belief in the beneficent effect of pain upon the mind. . . . What a pupil he was to find in the gallant Anne Conway!"[41]

Here we can push a little further in our analysis than Nicolson herself does. It is clear that the emphasis on the value of pain hypothesized both by van Helmont and Conway allows Conway to make the philosophical moves in the *Principles* that specifically speak to Cartesian issues. At various points in that work, she announces that the mind and body cannot be completely distinct substances because of the obvious interaction afforded by the example of pain. Philosophically, of course, the Cartesians would have a series of replies, including occasionalist responses, but in any case this is one of the most powerful arguments marshaled by Conway in the *Principles*.[42]

More important, perhaps, the "beneficial" effects of pain also clearly involve some notion of moral growth. Insofar as we examined Conway on notions having to do with value, we can see that this awareness of pain might have led her to a greater empathy for God's creatures; as indicated, Conway's example of the horse is poignant in this regard. But what is genuinely singular about the use of the concept of pain here—whether by van Helmont or Conway herself—is that it is already somewhat gynocentric. It not only forces a focus on the body, and then posits that this experience is somehow beneficial, but it is within the tradition of women mystics and other thinkers whose experience of pain became iconic for following generations. Although there were, of course, male thinkers who fell into this category, female suffering has become paradigmatic of female experience, and in a number of cultures, not only those that fall within the Western tradition.[43]

Now we are in a position to better articulate an intersection for Anne Conway with contemporary feminist epistemology. In general, Conway's nonempirical epistemology, concern for consistency, and divorce from the senses place her firmly within the male-derived tradition, thereby making her work classically philosophical. But within her appropriation of that voice, Conway places emphasis on a number of areas that do, indeed, speak to concerns more gynocentric than not. Not only her concern for other creatures or her account of the connectedness of all creation are at stake; her use of the concept of pain (including, we can well hypothesize, her own pain; van Helmont was her physician) and her refusal to employ a gradation of natural kinds that easily cut each kind off from another tell of her female-centered awareness at various points.

John Morrill is explicit, as an historian, about the devastating effects of the religious disputes of the seventeenth century on the inhabitants of the British Isles. The Interregnum and the period immediately following it were intensely crisis-ridden, and the decline of the Church of England (and growth in "enthusiasms") quite pronounced. Anne Conway became a Quaker toward the end of her life, provoking one of her few disagreements with Henry More. But the Quakers urged "men to find the divine spark within themselves."[44] To a great extent, Conway had already found that spark. She had articulated it in the *Principles,* lived with it and through it in her bodily torment, and shared it, at least on some occasions, with some of her discussants. Her sense that this spark was also shared by other creatures, and not confined to the human world alone, led her to a complex set of arguments that survive to this day. In many ways, we find difficulty in placing Anne Conway in a tradition that will ultimately manifest itself in feminism, because her work so strongly embodies the traditions of those who preceded her. But in her humanitarianism, and her refusal to cut other living beings off, she shows herself to be full of that concern for interconnectedness that we have deemed one of the hallmarks of feminist epistemology.

Second and Third Waves

If the third wave of feminism is here, as has been said by many, then we need to inquire how feminisms of the future can interact with those of the past, and how, in turn, theory of the past can inform feminisms to come. In some cases, we can draw such linkages fairly easily, because the theorist in question has done work that lends itself to today's postmodern bricolage, with its emphasis on ecofeminism and the postcolonial. Hildegard, as we have seen, is one such thinker, and her work has already been appropriated—indeed, some would say that the appropriation has proceeded beyond the point that is useful or desirable.

The difficulty with a thinker like Anne Conway is precisely that which has already been articulated here. Conway is, indeed, a philosopher whose work deserves to be in textbooks that cover seventeenth-century or early modern philosophy; there is no question about whether she does or does not belong in the category "philosophers." In addition, there is also no question that her work follows standard lines of thought that might be deemed to be masculinist or androcentric, and that one has to do some work to find gynocentric tendencies in her writings.

What then, it might be inquired, does Anne Conway's work—even if seen in a feminist light—have to offer new generations of feminist thinkers, including many who might not be particularly interested in the ins-and-outs of substance and modality? Again, if we read her work carefully, and pay particular attention to some of the areas already mentioned, including notions of interpenetrability, gradations of ontology, and concern for other species, it can readily be argued that Conway's work is well worth pursuing for the feminist philosophy of the future.

Ecofeminist concerns and concerns for authoriality or "voice" are not the only areas of interest for third-wave feminists; another strong area of interest has been the postcolonial. Postcolonial theory has, of course, informed not only feminism but much contemporary literary theory; one has only to think, for example, of the body of work of Edward Said to see the impact that postcolonial thought has had on the academy in general.[45] But a crucial part of this thought that intersects heavily with feminist theory is the part that expresses European desires to see colonial or enslaved peoples not only as the "other," but also as somehow more "feminine" or "childlike" than their conquerors. An enormous amount of literature has been churned out on this topic, but it is worth noting that European colonizers ranging from those who first encountered indigenous Mexico in the sixteenth century to those who encountered Hindu India in the seventeenth, and finally those who imposed themselves on the cultures of Africa in the nineteenth, often wrote of the "female" qualities of the conquered peoples.[46]

Although the less inquiring reader might not notice it, Anne Viscountess Conway's philosophy is conceived so that differences among living things— including human beings—are accounted for in her metaphysics.[47] Because she is invoking a sort of Great Chain of Being, and because she sees all creatures as related to each other, she has more respect for each creature than did many other philosophers of her time. It would be simplistic to say that paying careful attention to the *Principles* rewards the feminist reader in some direct way that allows her to solve a number of conceptual riddles at once, just as it is a gross exaggeration to say that Hildegard's work undoes a number of intellectual tangles while simultaneously inspiring us to new heights. Nevertheless, Conway's notion of a vitalistic mixture of spirit and matter, while it in some ways buttresses colonial notions, also helps us in that it provides a ready explanation for how such notions arose.

It may, in fact, be the case that a number of thinkers among the colonists of several European nations, for several consecutive centuries, saw colonized peoples as comparatively devoid of spirit. In this sense, Conway's gradations are right on target for helping us to achieve an insight into their conceptual scheme. But more important, Conway's humanism—even, as we have seen, with respect to domesticated animals—probably would not have allowed her to place any human beings in the degraded categories that some colonists actually employed. Thus, when we are told, for example, that postcolonial readings of *The Tempest* are helpful in seeing why Caliban utters the lines that he does, we can think of Anne Conway as one who would have been concerned about the real-life Calibans whose rights were being taken away.

The newest wave of feminist theory has frequently focused on the intersection of disabled and gay rights, or on women of color who may possess other "debilitating" conditions in a society where to be a woman of color is already to experience overt hostility and discrimination. Susan Stocker, writing in *Hypatia,* notes that there are "two feminist accounts of human embodiment for Disability Studies. The contrast I draw is between two incommensurable accounts of the meaning of embodiment: the genetic and the genealogical approaches. The genetic approach to the human body emphasizes how our thinking is rooted in our biology. The genealogical approach emphasizes instead the social and discursive origins of what we think about the body."[48]

Conway is writing at a period far enough back in time that neither label is completely appropriate for her but she is closer, of course, to the genetic view. What is interesting about Conway's vitalism is how, nevertheless, it enlivens our own genetic view and alters our perceptions of the body and the ways in which the body's refusal to conform to our desires changes our lives. Even if we think of Conway's vitalism as no more than a metaphor—and for the centuries-later reader, it is difficult to think of it in any other way—her construal of the body as filled with spirit (and of some bodies as more filled with spirit than others) might prove helpful to those in disability studies who feel that the genealogical approach is less than whole, but who are disheartened by the flatness of the genetic approach.[49] Conway's emphasis on spirit can, without allusion to the sorts of seventeenth-century philosophical problems she attempted to solve, push us in the direction of valuing the extent to which "spirit" informs our own lives. Perhaps we all need an infusion of spirit. Reading Conway's *Principles* might have the beneficial effect, for many readers, of providing us with just that.

It is entirely possible that Anne Conway's philosophy represents, from the standpoint of the Cambridge Platonists, merely a happy convergence of a number of doctrines, and that it is only accidental that Leibniz and other thinkers later promulgated some of the same ideas. Stuart Brown, for one, forwards this thesis in his piece "Leibniz and More's Cabbalistic Circle."[50] Nevertheless, even Brown is struck by Conway's emphasis on interpenetration and on gradations. Although Brown's thesis is that the greatest single influence on Leibniz from this circle is probably van Helmont, Brown also notes that "[t]his belief [with respect to the interpenetrability of creatures] is also found in Anne Conway's *Principles of the Most Ancient and Modern Philosophy*. She not only argues for the same doctrine. . . . She even uses the Latin verb *'continere'* and the phrase *'creaturae infinitae.'*"[51] Almost all commentators have been moved by Conway's emphasis on all of creation and its interrelationships. Thus, Conway's work is very much a piece for our time, despite what we now think of—perhaps mistakenly—as a third-wave feminist emphasis on those who have not been acknowledged before.

As with work on ecofeminism, new work in feminist theory also draws on the thinking of indigenous women, or, insofar as the North American scene is concerned, the thought and work of those women of color whose theorizing has not often before been noticed. Much of this work, with its emphasis on oral traditions and alternate epistemologies and cosmologies, is infused with the notion that Western philosophy, traditionally, has too strongly bifurcated a split between mind and matter. The same cannot be said of the work of Anne Conway.

A Point of Departure

Much of the first scholarship done during the period of the retrieval of Conway emphasized her relationship to other thinkers. It seemed important to make this point, because it had the odd concomitant that well-known male philosophers of her time were actually more cognizant of the work and of the abilities of women thinkers of their time than many male philosophers have been of contemporary women thinkers.

Without much allusion to the continuing debate over Conway's influence on others, we can see that *Principles of the Most Ancient and Modern Philosophy* is a work of sufficient length and scope, not to say philosophic merit, that it should long since have been included in courses on seventeenth-century thought, and on the influence of the Rationalists in general. Anne Conway's desire to respond to the thought of others, to create an original system, and to deal with the philosophical conundra to which she had been exposed mark her as an original thinker.

In addition, as we have seen, Conway's thought is original in other ways; it is rationalist philosophy, with hallmarks of gynocentric concerns and patterns, and in that sense it may well be unique among seventeenth-century systems. Her positing of one substance for all of creation, save God and Christ, allows her to claim a relationship between creatures, and yet it allows her to account for the obvious distinctions that we see between creatures in a way that is not possible with the systems of Hobbes, or even of Spinoza.[52] And it does, of course, allow her to escape the Cartesian imputation that living creatures other than human beings are mere machines, devoid of important sensation or feeling.

To do justice to those who followed Conway, it is too easy to assume simply that the importance of her work was lost over time because she was a woman. For one thing, she was occasionally mentioned in philosophical tracts and articles; the frequency of citation to her in her own lifetime by crucial thinkers virtually assured that. For another, it is clear that one factor that may have had something to do with the decline in interest in Conway's work was her association with the Cambridge Platonists. All of these thinkers—including More, van Helmont, and Glanvill—suffered from a loss of reputation at a later point as their thinking became increasingly seen as irrational and, of course, anti-empiricist. Their relationship to the Kabbala, and their interest in it, so intriguing in our time, was thought by some to be a sign of lunacy at a point slightly after their own time. The circle also developed a reputation for interest in such phenomena as ghosts and apparitions, and this did not either sit well with a later, more empiricist temperament.[53]

It is difficult, as I have argued here, to attempt to appreciate the work of women thinkers of the past without making their work seem to anticipate feminist or gynocentric concerns in ways that simply were unlikely or virtually impossible. Anne Conway's work is indeed a special case, since, as is clear, it so much merits the appellation "philosophy," especially as philosophy was done in her time, but so obviously has features that mark it as differing significantly from the work of male thinkers. It is here that the commentary of Greenblatt may be helpful, at least insofar as sixteenth- and seventeenth-century uses of language are concerned. In his essay "Learning to Curse," Greenblatt points out that, often, Europeans encountering American Indians and Africans assumed that what they heard them utter was not actually speech. The assumption that learning to speak meant learning a European language was so rooted in many European cultures that travelers, explorers, and discoverers regularly failed to understand that "others" were indeed speaking. Greenblatt writes: "The unfamiliarity of their [American Indians'] speech is a recurrent motif in the early accounts of the New World's inhabitants, and it is paraded forth in the company of all their other strange and often repellent qualities. The chronicler Robert Fabian writes of three savages presented to henry Vii that they 'were clothed in beasts skins, & did eate raw flesh, and spake such speech that no man could understand them, and in their demeanour like to bruite beastes.'"[54]

We cannot confidently say that Anne Conway would have held a different opinion; she might very well, in fact, have held the same opinion. But she would have had a philosophical point of view to back her up and, more important, she would have been able to see at least some greater traces of humanity in the Indians, for there is no doubt that this woman philosopher was concerned about horses, domestic animals, and other living beings. Whereas at least some thinkers of the sixteenth and seventeenth centuries apparently placed the citizens of the New World in the ranks of animals—and if they held to the views of Descartes on animals, this cannot have been complimentary in any sense—Anne Conway would most likely have deemed them to be humans bereft of some degree of "spirit," but participants, nonetheless, in God's creation and entitled to a consideration of their own.

It is this aspect of Conway's philosophy that makes it attractive, and it is also this aspect that speaks to our time. We have seen the results of thinking that lacked respect for other creatures, for the environment, and for persons living in what we now refer to as third world countries, or the indigenous inhabitants of other regions. (Even in today's presumably more sophisticated global dialogue, some regions—Papua New Guinea, for example—are still singled out for their "wild" or "untamed" characteristics.) It is clear that Conway would probably not have put all human beings on a par with each other—it goes against the sense of her time to make this claim, and it does not square with the many pronouncements regarding gradations of spirit that are found throughout the *Principles*. Nevertheless, few thinkers of her time evinced as much concern for living creatures as Conway did; if domesticated animals are mentioned at all in the works of other thinkers, it is often in the most cursory fashion.

If there is a sense in which we must read into Conway, we are aided immensely by our knowledge of her correspondents and of the beliefs of those in whose circle she worked. Thus, when we come to know the importance not only of Kabbalistic beliefs, but of beliefs having to do with spirits and occult entities, for the Cambridge Platonists as a whole, it is not stretching the argument to say that a range of entities and modes of being was of interest to Conway. She herself mentions insects and other small creatures; the fact that she repeatedly mentions the notion of pure spirit means that she can at least conceive of such beings (and she does, of course, accord God and Christ a separate ontological status, as we have seen). Thus Conway's philosophy is more in tune with the "brave new world" encountered by the Europeans than much of what had preceded her, however difficult it might have been for her to confront the reality of the situations of indigenous persons.

The seventeenth century saw an outpouring of works by women in Great Britain, particularly in comparison with the centuries immediately preceding.[55] The free-for-all of the Interregnum, the religious disputes, the plague years, and the Great Fire seemed to generate a kind of ferment all their own; for the first time, large numbers of women—by no means all of them from aristocratic or even well-to-do backgrounds, as we shall see in the case of Mary Astell—contributed to the general culture and wrote and published in large numbers.

Whereas some, such as Damaris Masham, were more concerned with defending the views of favored male philosophers, Anne Conway was able to forge her own path, and the extent to which she takes other philosophers (again, male) to task is truly remarkable given her own comparative houseboundness and her inability to travel freely. The world of the imagination had always been important to her; to recapitulate, it was this same bookish Anne Conway who attracted the notice of Henry More after having been introduced to him by her stepbrother, John Finch. If More found her remarkable, it was because he recognized in her the spirit of a philosopher, even if it was housed in a female body. It speaks well of the Platonist circle that they were able to make these cognitive leaps, for despite the comparatively free spirit of the times, not everyone was so able. Conway's own husband had been initially interested in matters philosophical, but he later lost much of his interest and was content to leave philosophizing and speculative matters to her. This is unsurprising, but it must have been a rare household indeed, aristocratic or otherwise, where the woman engaged regularly in philosophical conversation that was at least somewhat over the head of the male householder.

Anne Conway's philosophy speaks to both her time and ours. The thinker who was so concerned to refute the "dead matter" hypothesis of Descartes and the "confusion" of Spinoza tried to clarify matters for herself and those around her. Because the *Principles* was published posthumously, she could not have predicted that it would still be read, at least by an admiring few, hundreds of years later. What we can glean from the *Principles* is a clearly argued concern for all of nature, and the place of humankind within that nature. The woman who asked us to consider "an Horse" was someone who often gave consideration to others. It seems very appropriate that we now engage in a genuine effort to appreciate her work and to give it the attention that it deserves.

MARY ASTELL three

Mary Astell's (1666–1731) life and work mirrored each other; she remains, even now, a contradictory and contentious figure, whose writings are an odd amalgam of Tory principles and far-seeing calls for reform and change. Although she is described as a "pamphleteer," the body of her work is sufficiently large, and her circle of acquaintances sufficiently vast, that she, like Anne Conway, is best thought of as a philosopher—although, in Astell's case, as one with a decidedly political bent.[1]

The statistical rarity of a woman from Astell's fairly humble background achieving acquaintance, and even intimacy, with well-born women, and a few aristocrats, is paralleled by the unusual flavor of Astell's arguments. Like many thinkers of her time—and here Locke, Shaftesbury, Masham, and many others can be named—she sees the contractarian nature of both home and state as fertile ground for theorizing and for speculation on the future of both. But unlike Locke, for example, she refuses to adhere to the notion that contractarianism may require a liberal attitude with respect to those who are most burdened by the contract; in her writings, Astell seems to argue in favor of a strict adherence to contracts, both civil and marital, and for the use of the terms of these contracts as stimuli to further growth. Thus she espouses a conservative line politically, and yet, in *Reflections upon Marriage,* for example, she creates arguments that are strongly feminist.

Because so much of Astell's early life is unclear, it is not obvious how she made the moves, literal and figurative, from coal carter's daughter to London author and celebrity. As Springborg says, in trying to portray the series of events that led to Mary's writing, "From her uncle [Ralph Astell, church curate] Mary Astell may also have learned her Tory politics. A Royalist family tradition had been attested in the epitaph for her grandfather, William Astell, which, after recounting his sufferings for Charles I, declared his reward union in death, not with his God, but with his master. . . . Mary Astell's mother, Mary Arrington, was from an old Catholic gentry family of Newcastle."[2]

In any case, Astell quickly came to represent a strident tone that simultaneously asked for adherence to Royalist doctrine while—at least insofar as women were concerned—promulgating new and even alarming views about the "fair sex" and their rights. In the late seventeenth and early eighteenth centuries (Astell was born in 1666, when Anne Conway was thirty-five) her writings became sufficiently well known that she was the object of satire in the *Tatler* and other publications, a sure sign of success, at least insofar as numbers of readers were concerned.[3]

Although the issues with which Mary Astell concerned herself were largely political, we need to remember that political issues during her time could not be separated from the larger metaphysical concerns of the church, which then issued in the various positions regarding the divine right of kings, toleration for dissent, the possibility (or desirability, for some) of Catholic rulers, and so forth. During a period in which debates were regularly held about the violence done to King Charles I and the damage caused by the Interregnum, the vast majority still adhered to some notion of a divine right of monarchy that entailed, of course, a strongly Christian notion of God, and, again, of a hierarchy of creation, with humankind's place one of obedience to divine rules.

In these matters, Astell was one to articulate the view (against, for example, Locke) that civil society ought to be strongly monarchical, and that any other sort of view went against divine law. But her views on marriage—which she did not disavow as an institution—made strong mention of the fact that the inferiority of women in marriage is assumed, not stated, and that marriage is a sort of test for women to see whether or not their Christian virtues can prevail over some of the unjust practices associated with this godly institution. As Springborg notes, part of the peculiarity of Astell's argument is that

Astell "reinstated the traditional interpretation of marriage" in order to undo a number of its concomitants.[4]

It may not be stretching things to posit as an explanation for Astell's seeming intransigence in matters political a sort of overcompensatory identification with Tories, while at the same time a sensitive awareness of the plight of women in, as she put it, "ship-wrack'd" marriages. Her origins, her friends, and her identification with those friends in high places may have, of necessity, created a Tory political sensibility, while other parts of her conscience were more than aware of damages accrued.

If, as I observed in turning to the work of Anne Conway, the vagaries of fortune suffered by those who lived through parts of the seventeenth century in England left them inclined toward peace, this still did little to alleviate the battles in print between Dissenters, friends of Dissenters, and those who favored the High Church or some form of it. Many of these debates became very arcane; in general, it is not necessary to go into all of the disputes in detail, but somewhat overlooked in Astell's work—above and beyond *Some Reflections upon Marriage, A Serious Proposal to the Ladies,* and *A Fair Way with the Dissenters*—are the pamphlets and letters specifically designed to deal with religious issues. Although Florence M. Smith's biography of Astell has the disadvantage of being out of date, it has the virtue of brevity, and she provides succinct commentary on the importance of matters religious for Astell.[5] She gives us an idea of the range of Astell's contacts when she writes: "Mary Astell proved a worthy defender of the Church in the discussion of the vexing religious problems of the day. Her first religious work as far as there is any record extant, consists of her letters to John Norris, afterwards published by him. These brought her into the philosophical discussions that were being carried on by John Norris, Lady Damaris Masham, and John Locke."[6]

Thus Astell the "pamphleteer" proves her mettle philosophically, and it is not difficult to see the motivation here; to be fair, the motivation must have been similar for almost all correspondents. Religious matters were so central to Britain at this time that almost all literate persons were involved in these disputes, if only to some extent.

Astell not only saw and heard a great deal of the religious controversies of the day, but she also witnessed a number of domestic disputes among those of the higher social classes, disputes that led, at least in part, to her work in *Reflections*. Almost all accounts agree that it is not obvious how the young Mary Astell managed a move from Newcastle to London and then, apparently fairly quickly, established herself in a wealthy Chelsea circle, but it is clear that this is what transpired.[7] Moving in these circles, she became acquainted with the Duchess of Mazarine, whose notoriously unhappy marriage provoked her to think about the plight of women in general. Here, as was the case with Anne Conway, we can guess that a fortunate combination of circumstance and serendipitous accident allowed Mary to come into contact with individuals whose levels of learning and access to power and wealth were very helpful to her. Conway's entrée into the net of acquaintances of Henry More was simply due to her having a stepbrother at Cambridge who introduced her; Mary Astell may have more or less introduced herself, so to speak, but she would not have been able to accomplish even this much had she not, by accident, moved into a neighborhood that allowed her such acquaintances.

In any case, as Smith remarks, "As an observer, Mary Astell saw the court life as it touched her Chelsea associates; the Duchess of Mazarine was her near neighbor, and she secured at first hand, her knowledge of the need of a change of the lives of women."[8] Like the other intellectually oriented women whose works and lives I will examine here, Astell created her own course based on her experience, knowledge, and—to employ a somewhat old-fashioned phrase— innate gifts. Her capacity to learn was quickly noticed, and she became something of a celebrity fairly shortly after moving to London. Pamphleteer, philosopher, and sometime theologian, Mary Astell was a formidable force in London literary circles in the late seventeenth and early eighteenth centuries.

Astell and Ontology

Astell may easily be categorized as a political philosopher, but with respect to other aspects of her philosophic thought some extrapolation is needed.[9] She left a number of pieces that touch on religious matters, and insofar as these works deal with the nature of the Deity, the place of humankind in creation, and so forth, they are inherently works that have some bearing on metaphysics, even if they are not as lengthy and developed as those of other thinkers.

It would appear that Astell adhered to a standard Christian belief in the Trinity, so it would not be presumptuous to assume at least a minimal spirit/ matter distinction in her work, although these sorts of questions are not addressed as specifically in her writings as they are, for example, in those of Anne Conway. But more important perhaps—and crucial, because of its relationship to other areas of metaphysics—Astell does develop a number of lines of argument about the nature of God, our duty to him, and how humans ought to think of the Deity and his works. In examining these strains of thought, we can see that Astell might well have written more on these topics at a later point.

As Ruth Perry says in her admirably clear biography of Astell, which does a superb job of situating Mary Astell in her time and place, "Religious writing had traditionally been an acceptable outlet for women's expressiveness."[10] Because of this, and because of Astell's own penchant for both writing and philosophical thought, her work ranges over a great deal more conceptual material than she is ordinarily given credit for. As Perry also goes on to say, "Astell found this a comfortable frame within which to ask the questions that interested her most, the questions posed by the new natural philosophy: the nature of thought, intelligence, God, the soul, the definition of a 'state of nature,' and the nature of proof."[11]

To this end, Astell wrote *Letters Concerning the Love of God,* and here we can see strands of what she aimed to accomplish with respect to metaphysics. Unlike the Lockeans, Astell wanted to divorce the notion of God's being the author of our sensations from his being the sole object of our love and devotion. For example, in letter I, Astell gives a complicated argument to the point that God is the author, according to that line of argument, of a number of sensations, both painful and pleasurable. If the argument that God is the direct author of our pleasure is used to buttress the notion that for this reason we should worship God, it falls flat at the consequence of the equally direct observation that God is the author of our pains. Surely, Astell continues, it would seem counterintuitive to suggest that we must love the author of our pains, so the argument cannot go through.[12]

In general, Astell's adherence to a Christian ontology commits her to the use of reason—which was given to us by the Deity—to defend that ontology, but she remonstrates with those who, by her lights, would abuse that reason to set forth specious or oversophisticated claims about the relationship between God and creation. She accepted the traditional argument for the existence of God that is sometimes cast in terms of the Unmoved Mover; she was not the least alarmed by Newton's new work in the sciences, for to her mind it simply underscored the unlikelihood that "Self-Moving Atoms and their lucky Jumble" could create a universe *ex nihilo.*[13]

Nevertheless, and despite a head for cosmology, as it were, Astell defended many of the more conservative beliefs of the Church of England, was against Dissenters and enthusiasts in general, and, as we know, held her feminism in the odd sense that she sustained notions of marriage even as she saw that marriage was often detrimental to women.

Astell's conservative nature led her to question how far reason could be useful in matters theological, and it is here that she parts company with Locke and to some extent those who were influenced with him or who agreed with him (Damaris Masham, again). Astell wants us to accept revealed scripture on the basis of faith alone, when it appears that reason might lead us astray, or if it appears that we are in some sense being confused by reason. Here Astell accepts a very traditional Christian account, and it is these sorts of moves in Astell's thinking that have led some to label her "odd."[14] But, as I have suggested, Astell was merely responding to her time in the way that someone of her (adopted) social class would ordinarily have done. As was the case for Anne Conway, the turmoil of the time created an atmosphere of chaos; it seemed necessary to try to get past it. Consider the following: "When in November 1688 William of Orange entered Exeter, the citizens were impressed by an exotic parade. After a squadron of expensively equipped cavalry in 'headpieces, back and breast, bright armour,' marched two hundred Negroes from the Dutch plantations in Central America in embroidered caps lined with white fur, to attend the horse. Then, by way of contrast, came two hundred Finns and Lapps in bearskins and black armour. After this prelude, came the prince's own banner, inscribed 'For God and the Protestant religion.'"[15]

It would seem that a thinker could be forgiven for becoming confused, especially when it is remembered that the previous ascendancy of Protestants had brought extensive bloodshed. We know that Astell came to London and began writing around this time, and that much of the extensive political debate, the formation of the Whig and Tory parties, and the exacerbated disputes in Parliament all revolved around religion, the question of the true manner in which God was to be worshiped, the importance of ascertaining credible arguments for the existence of God, and so forth.

It may very well be that we think of Astell as a largely political thinker precisely because a great deal of what she wrote was expressed in a manner designed to draw attention to it at the time, and that manner was, of course, related to civil society and its structure. But beneath much of this material a concern for ontological matters still abides, and we can see this in a number of works written by Astell.

If we have some difficulty deciphering these works, it is no doubt due to the arcane nature of the debates and the times. For example, the work *The Christian Religion as Profess'd by a Daughter of the Church of England,* usually referred to by shortened title, is one of those works that implicitly combines ontology, political advice, and a comment on the relations between the sexes all in one. Although this may well be said of most of Astell's works, it stands out in some pieces. In this work, she notes: "For what but the love of GOD can justly restrain Sovereign Princes from being Injurious, or excite them to be Just and Gracious to their people? Those who think the Awe of God's Sovereignty but a poor restraint, and are therefore for subjecting them to the Coercion of the People, against the Laws of this Nation as well as against the doctrine of the Church, . . . shew too little regard to any religion, whatever they may talk about it."[16]

This very short excision is an excellent example of Astell's ability to deal with a number of philosophical matters at once. She not only repeats a Christian metaphysics, but exhorts believers to hold it in mind, for bearing it in concentration will help them—rulers and subjects—adhere to what she deems to be appropriate relations between all. As God rules over us and has created us, as he is omnipotent, omnipresent, and omniscient, princes can rule over their subjects, but rule appropriately only if (as she explains) they have a sense of justice and of (divine) mercy. What she clearly is against—and this comes up as an issue time and time again in her works—is any application of the Lockean political philosophy in areas that, by her lights, are already covered by divine ordinance. It is, again, Astell's peculiarity that she is willing to countenance views that are conservative politically, progressive for women, and, simultaneously, very Christian, for she is making as close a reading of the Scriptures as she can.

Astell is perhaps not as overtly concerned with ontology as some thinkers were, so in that sense she does not come close to the levels of metaphysical astuteness displayed by Anne Conway, but we can be sure of her belief in a chain of being, and her further belief that humankind's place in this chain is demarcated by the Christian religion. At a later point in the same piece, Astell writes of the "Injury" one may suffer in "Temporal Affairs."[17] As one who had suffered many such injuries, from the various tempests created by her own involvements, Mary Astell was more aware than many people of the vagaries of time and fortune.

Astell is a careful reader of Scripture because she wants to save England from its former follies and at the same time invoke a sense of genuine Christianity to aid not only women, but all who would read Scripture carefully. She finds that life affords many opportunities for exercising one's charitable capacities—including, but not limited to, the matrimonial state—and she hopes that princes, subjects, men, women, and children will benefit from a close understanding of their duties. Part of that understanding will come about when they comprehend divine law, and when they understand that the origin of the universe is not accidental, but the product of design.

In the third of her *Letters Concerning the Love of God,* Astell actually notes that if members of her sex could be persuaded to a "higher Excellency than some well-chosen Pettycoat," they would be better off, and she directly links this grasping of excellencies and virtues to a proper understanding of the worship of the Deity.[18] But most of what Astell strives to achieve here is not easily attained. It may be for this very reason that her works are, in large, more overtly concerned with political matters. These matters, Astell no doubt thought, hit the reader more directly, are less abstruse, and are more susceptible of being understood.

The Place of Value

Stephen Coote recounts the circumstances under which Samuel Pepys first encountered Charles II:

> Once the convoy was under sail, Charles beguiled all around him with his charm of manner and his stories. Pepys watched him and listened with the most intense curiosity, almost certainly making there and then the shorthand notes that he would later transcribe into his *Diary*. . . . Incident followed incident as Charles felt free to tell the world of those brave and loyal people who had helped him in the days of his adversity. Pepys, the first to hear the story, noted it down assiduously as his new master told of his "travelling four days and three nights on foot, every step up to the knees in dirt, with nothing but a green coat and a pair of country breeches on . . ." Such pathos recalled in a moment of triumph was, to Pepys, almost unbearable and "made me ready to weep."[19]

Coote's account does a great deal to assist us in coming to understand Astell's views, because it is clear that Pepys's response to the king's travails is based largely on an enormous respect, bordering on the worshipful. Almost all citizens, we can surmise, would still have felt such respect for the sovereign in that time; the preceding years of beheadings, Puritans, odd parliaments, and rows between Dissenters and Anglicans had done little to establish the sense of harmony that most citizens required. Into this world of country-breeched royalty walking in the dirt to reclaim a crown came Mary Astell, ready to establish arguments about why it is that such overturnings amount to a grave injustice, and a danger to the nation.

In *A Serious Proposal, Some Reflections upon Marriage,* and *A Fair Way with the Dissenters,* Astell deals with important political issues that have extensive ethical ramifications. It is easy to say that hers is simply a Christian ethics (specifically, the Christianity of the Anglican Church, and no other), but it is something more than that. Astell exhibits a deep concern for the individual—and, as we know, for the rights of women—but she does so within the framework of a notion of caring based on a close Christian understanding.

Thus, Astell has no difficulty with supporting the right of kings or of the monarchy, because she believes that these rights stem from a correct under-standing of humankind's relationship with God. In the same way, Astell in-dicates that although there is much about women in the New Testament, none of it speaks to the inferiority of women vis-à-vis men. As she notes in *Some Reflections,* "The Apostle indeed adds, that *the Man is the Glory of God, and the Woman the Glory of the Man,* Etc. But what does he infer from hence? He says not a word of inequality or natural inferiority."[20]

In general, Astell's ethical stance amounts to a conservative Christian po-sition, with an emphasis on individual rights only when they may be achieved in the context of a well-ordered state, which she also sees as part of the rational Christian position. Her views on this are probably made most clear in *A Fair Way with the Dissenters,* since she was forced to go to some lengths to reply to Defoe's pamphlet *More Short-Ways with the Dissenters.*[21] Astell has no tolerance for the Dissenters because she sees them as the cause of most of the troubles of the preceding century, troubles that had an impact on her, her family, and their relations with others involved in the coal trade of Newcastle.[22] In addi-tion, of course, she can see that the entire nation had been done asunder, so to speak, by the efforts of the Dissenters and others of their ilk, and she views this as an intolerable abridgment of peace and freedom. She claims that reason is on her side, as she writes: "I shall frankly own with an Ingenuity they would do well to practise, that the *Total Destruction of Dissenters as a Party* (the Barbarous Usage that *More Short Ways* is so afraid of) is indeed our Design. 'Tis the Design of all honest Men and good Christians, even of the Dissenters themselves, if they may be believed, and if they are not notorious Hypocrites."[23]

In other words, the Dissenters do not (as they, of course, claim) represent a truer or more honest version of Christianity—the Anglican Church already practices that. Since the Dissenters have already been responsible for at least one royal death, and much strife, what they represent is the work of a band that must be put down at every opportunity.

Perry is adamant that a great deal of what drives Astell's conservative bent has to do with her own background. Although her family never belonged to the most wealthy class—let alone the aristocracy—until the death of Mary's father when Mary was twelve, they had been better off than many in New-castle, because the sale and transport of coal drove the town and its growth. According to Perry, then, Mary Astell identified with a social class that was probably always a step above the one to which her family had originally be-longed, and that was decidedly above the one to which her family sank when she was a teenager. As Perry notes, "her family's once proud position is reflected in how comfortably, without qualification, she held her opinions."[24] In any case, whether her identification with the Stuart cause is more a matter of personal feeling than it perhaps should be, given that she purports to present herself as a political thinker, she has a great deal of argument on her side, since it is obvious that the seventeenth century was devastating for much of England.

An emphasis on faith also drives Astell, and it is here that she parts company with many of the other thinkers of her time. Locke and his followers emphasized reason over faith; where they conflicted, reason had the upper hand. Astell is an astute observer of social mores, and her analysis of marriage is close, for example, to Hume's.[25] But her devout Christianity prevents her from being an empiricist in the full philosophical sense—although it certainly did not prevent Bishop Berkeley—and she shows the influence of the Cambridge Platonists as well, particularly since Ralph Astell, too, was an associate of this group.[26] Although Conway, for example, wanted to provide an argumentative analysis of the ways in which God's designs manifest themselves in the world, Astell is content to assume that this is evident to any thoughtful, believing Christian. What she does not think is evident is the necessity of stifling the voices of those whose disputes and contests are, she feels, detrimental to the order that would manifest God's creation, and the lives of those who might benefit from that order.

It is probably for these reasons that Bridget Hill, and others, have found it somewhat ironic—indeed, "unexplained"—that Astell now merits the title of "England's First Feminist."[27] What we fail to recognize when we problematize the issue of Astell's feminism is that there is no yoke that automatically unites this view to other views that are "progressive," especially if we consider time periods well before our own. We see Astell as an odd or unusual feminist because we assume that someone who would forward the views of women would be tolerant of Dissenters, nonsupportive of the establishment, and so forth.

But when we make these assumptions we are applying twenty-first-century standards to seventeenth-century discourse. (Indeed, these assumptions do not automatically hold for the twenty-first century, as many of us know from our own experience.) What enables Astell to hold views that we might find awkward or unusually juxtaposed is her assumption that they derive from divine law—an assumption that she makes manifest in her work, and that is, of course, supportive of her general stance with respect to Christian doctrine. We must remember that Astell is a "feminist" because she believes that such views are in accordance with the New Testament, not against it. As she says, she finds nothing in Scripture to bolster the notion of woman's "inferiority," and she spends much time arguing against such misinterpretations.

Astell has, then, a developed sense of value. It is in some ways similar to Anne Conway's, but we can hypothesize that Astell would not have been nearly so eager to countenance such notions as gradations of being, simply because her analytic and argumentative skills were much more devoted to political questions. If Astell claims that the Dissenters would just as soon be gone, she genuinely feels that this is what their beliefs compel them to accept. Astell is for all that Scripture says she should assert—the equality of persons before God, the relationship of humankind to God's creation, and the primacy of faith. In this regard, she is certainly not a philosopher of the Lockean stripe. But her iconoclastic qualities are what make her interesting—and of these, Astell has an abundance, more perhaps than we are ready to recognize or use.

The Acquaintances of Mary Astell

Astell had such a wide range of acquaintances, discussants, and correspondents that I will, of necessity, have to narrow my scope in my discussion of them. Unlike Hildegard, whose discussions took a largely epistolary form, or Anne Conway, whose circle was to some extent limited by her health, Astell knew many individuals, wrote to many, and saw many on a near daily basis.

This daughter of the formerly comfortable middle class was not well off when she moved from Newcastle to London, but she quickly made up for lost time.[28] Within a short period she made the acquaintance of Lady Catherine Jones and the Duchess of Mazarine, the latter's marriage furnishing fuel for *Reflections upon Marriage.*[29] More intriguing, perhaps, she quickly went to see the archbishop of Canterbury, William Sancroft.[30] Over a period of time, she was in regular correspondence with John Norris, and she became well acquainted with most of London's leading literary figures. The route that most of her social forays took her, however, was again to defend conservative points of view. After the initial arousal caused by her call for education for women, *A Serious Proposal to the Ladies,* she became "celebrated" and sought after. I will focus here on only a few of her acquaintances, and those chiefly whose work caused her to write or compose other tracts or responses.

Springborg comments on the fact that *A Fair Way* was prompted by Defoe's work, and this prompting is indeed an extremely interesting feature of Astell's oeuvre. As she notes, "Defoe's tone [later] became more serious. What he had originally painted as a possible scenario, the persecution of Dissenters and closure of the Dissenting academies, he now presented as Tory policy. It was in defence of Tory policy that Astell responded with her *Fair Way with the Dissenters,* in which she defends the positions of Leslie and Sacheverell, arguing that one does not have to be an extremist to hold that obedience to the English constitution required conformity to the Anglican church."[31]

When we think of Defoe's fame at this time, two points are immediately obvious. Astell was replying not only to one of the most well-known authors of the day, but to a male in a position of power. In addition, she was defending a position that was far from liberal and that was potentially damaging and injurious to a number of individuals. Although Perry sees Astell's political stance as due to her family's loss of status, and due to the social structure of Newcastle itself, it seems that something larger is at stake. It is clear that Astell sees an author like Defoe as a dangerous individual who needs to be stopped. The woman who has made her reputation writing about education for women intends to use her own education to try to derail those who are a danger to England and the fabric of society.

Astell was involved with so many individuals, their writings, and their various philosophies that it is difficult to narrow the field to one or two whose friendship might be thought to have been most important. I have already examined, to some extent, the thought of Damaris Masham, but it would seem to do an injustice to the spirit of the time not to include as outstandingly important in Astell's life John Norris. Norris, also identified with the Cambridge Platonists—at least insofar as we can discern their influence on him with respect to his disagreements with Locke—provided Astell with the impetus she needed to do the difficult ontological work with respect to the Deity that I discussed earlier.[32]

Letters Concerning the Love of God forces Astell to do some of her best work, if one is inclined to value grappling with the difficulties posed by definitions of God and their metaphysical concomitants over political thought. Although Astell might be thought to precede the empiricists with respect to her social observations—and this certainly seems to be the case with *Some Reflections upon Marriage*—her overall Christian beliefs with respect to the soul and knowledge are somewhat closer to the then-popular Cartesianism.[33] One must tread carefully here, as broad strokes are required to make any sort of argument for Descartes's doctrines to go through; it is simply the case that Astell's Christianity forced her, in some sense, to go against Locke.

But Norris's work inspired Astell to do a great deal of thinking at an early point. Norris and Astell share a belief in the importance of faith, the authority of the divine, and the extent to which arguments can be made that the visible world hinges upon the divine. Aside from *A Serious Proposal,* the *Letters* are among Astell's earliest known works. Perry indicates why Astell might have been sufficiently taken with Norris's work to want to respond to it immediately: "Norris acknowledged his debt to Plato, Plotinus, Proclus, and Marsilio Ficino—as well as to contemporary French and English Platonists—for the contrast between the ideal world of essences and eternal truths and the visible world of contingent sensory experience. . . . Astell and Norris wrote back and forth about the metaphysical properties of the soul, the possibility of higher and lower natures, the relation of the ideal to the material world."[34]

Locke's emphasis on sensory data in and of themselves was difficult for almost all thinkers of this period who identified themselves with the church, for it seemed to leave God out, and indeed the Lockean thought, with its forced empiricism, has little room for any account of immaterial substance. More important, the history of the century then concluding indicated that a failure to deal adequately with notions of the divine was the cause of a great deal of misery in England. Sensitive to these matters, Astell was more concerned than many newly arriving in London might have been to attempt to adjudicate them.

Norris's own thought, which espoused a line that ultimately proved to be somewhat similar to Berkeley's—we do not immediately perceive objects, but rather our perceptions are guided by God—attracted Astell because it seemed to address these issues without undue emphasis on the senses alone.[35] The extent to which some of Astell's most standardly philosophical thinking was influenced by Norris is difficult to overestimate.

At a much later point in her life (over a decade later), Astell made the acquaintance of Lady Mary Wortley Montagu, who had an enormous influence on a number of male thinkers of her time. Although this friendship and its products can be considered philosophical only in the broadest sense, it is noteworthy how many of the women, young and old, who came to read *A Serious Proposal* were strongly affected by it.[36] Commenting upon her relations to the well-known writers of her day, such as Pope and Gay, Perry notes that Lady Mary's published work, what little remains of it, reminds one of the debt that she owed to Mary Astell:

> Briefly, in 1737, she [Montagu] embarked upon publishing a fortnightly paper called *The Nonsense of Common-Sense* (to signal its contrariety to the leading Opposition paper of the day, *Common Sense*). Nine issues were put out at two- and three-week intervals before publication ceased. She sounds very much like Mary Astell in number 6, in which she proclaims herself a friend of the fair sex and "a protector of all the oppressed," and defends women's rationality. She

kept a printed copy of this single number, and scribbled on the top of it: "Wrote by me M.W.M."[37]

The combination of Astell's social contacts, those with whom she originally came into contact through correspondence, and direct replies to known literary figures with whom she had comparatively little contact is a forceful one and speaks to the extravagant nature of both her giftedness and her perseverance. Her biographers are amazed at her stamina, courage, and fortitude in making the move from Newcastle to London, but it would probably have taken more courage for her not to make the move. The world of letters called out to her as a haven from her earlier life.

Astell's talent for intellectual growth and personal change manifested itself most fully in her remarkable circle of women friends and acquaintances. Aside from Lady Mary Wortley Montagu, Astell knew Lady Catherine Jones, Lady Anne Coventry, and Lady Elizabeth Hastings and could count on their friendship.[38] The changes for women caused by growth in female occupations during the Interregnum—itself a product of males' going to war or leaving given geographical areas—lasted, and they greatly influenced Restoration society. A number of women became concerned about women's literacy, about freedom of choice with respect to marital issues, and other such topics. Astell simply tapped into what was available to her as she viewed London life around her. As Hill tells us, "One of the things that distinguished the post-Restoration period as far as women are concerned was the changed nature of the means by which articulate women expressed themselves."[39] Following Hill, the period of women's writing being confined largely to diaries and letters was now over, and a sea change in the status of women in English life had taken place. Astell moved swiftly and assuredly in this murky area, even if much of what drove her was an overidentification with a social class to which her family had never assuredly belonged, and to which she, in any case, did not belong as she made the physical move from Chelsea to London.

Astell's group of friends, correspondents, and acquaintances is large—but this is, of course, testimony to Astell's success. Unlike Anne Conway, Astell had a variety of companions from whom she could pick and choose.

Feminist Slants

Since Astell is regularly deemed one of England's first feminists, it would superficially not seem difficult to make tie-ins to contemporary feminist theory. But, as we have seen, there is little that is overtly feminist or even moderately progressive about Astell once one has stripped away the obvious material of *A Serious Proposal* and *Some Reflections*. In Astell's case, the conservative concern for state security shown in her insistence on divine right might, in a manner of speaking, be thought to trump many of her other concerns. Although Hill is careful to note that we overestimate the strength of a uniting link between feminism and progressive or even liberal politics much of the time, it is still difficult to see how the marriage/state model affected Astell's thought in the way that it did.[40]

Emphasis on this model, and its effect on women, has occurred throughout political philosophy, and many thinkers have been guilty, according to contemporary feminist analysis, of failing to be consistent with regard to these matters. Susan Moller Okin, writing about the position of women in the *Republic,* asserts that "Plato on the subject of women appears at first to present his reader with an unresolvable enigma, especially when his other dialogues are taken into account. . . . How can the claim that women are 'by nature' twice as bad as men be reconciled with the radical idea that they should be included among the exalted philosophic rulers of the ideal state?"[41]

A parallel dilemma appears in the case of Astell, according to much of the analysis. Since Astell accepts the common analogy between the state and the household, and since she indicates that there is no natural inferiority of women that might aptly justify their subordinate role in the household, by parity of argument she ought to espouse a Lockean position with regard to the state, or so one might argue. But to make this claim is to miss the larger point here: a strong rebuttal with respect to Astell is that part and parcel of her analysis of marriage is that it affords women the opportunity to test their virtues, even if it is a grave injustice that they should, in fact, be placed in a situation where such virtues as patience and charity are constantly tested. Astell then supports the notion that the king is head of the state by divine right in the same way in which the husband is the head of the household: continuation of the institution demands it. Although Astell does not go so far as to require of citizens that they exercise their Christian virtues in their participation in the polity, it is not difficult to extrapolate from Astell's overall position that this is indeed something like what she means.

Okin's concern about Plato is that there is a tension between the Philosopher Queen and his general construal of women. Part of the response here is that the Philosopher Queen is, of course, an extremely rare being. Concomitantly, with respect to Astell her feminism itself has two major foci: while strongly supporting the notion that women are not, by nature, inferior, she also does everything that she can to bolster the contention that the status quo demands that they use their capacities in a way that will allow for the most peaceful sort of kingdom.

Astell's feminism, then, is exactly what Hill and others have described it as: a conservative feminism, but one by no means out of step with her times.[42]

With the rich variety of feminist theory that now presents itself, it should come as no surprise that we also have available to us postmodern—or, at least, theory that for lack of a better term, we can subsume under the rubric of the postmodern—accounts of Plato, the female body, and the idealized state of the *Republic*. If anything, some of this work is even more helpful to us insofar as Astell's stance is concerned, since she herself violates so many seeming canons. Monique Canto has this to say about Plato seen in the light of contemporary French theory: "The city's only recourse is to politicize the emotions. . . . Women must know how to fight, because no human discourse has ever been conducted in the realm of the same. So much is stated in the manifesto. A politics of women's bodies gives rise to a politics of the real, precisely because only such a feminist politics can make reproduction—a major gamble in which a city can easily lose its model and its norm—one of the principles of the political."[43]

In a way, Canto is articulating points very much in congruence with Astell's main line, despite the chronological difference and Astell's pronouncedly Anglo-Saxon modes of thought. Canto is articulating the extent to which women are important in the *Republic,* regardless of whether or not an individual woman might be thought of as a Guardian, precisely because they are potential wives and mothers. This is, of course, the kernel of Plato's view, even if we are somewhat uncomfortable with a bare-bones summation of it. But it is also crucial to Astell's views. *A Serious Proposal* is written just because Astell knows that women are seen as potential bearers of children, and seldom more—and *Some Reflections* is generated almost solely because Astell has seen the place of women in the state to be one that revolves around a lower marital status, the consequences of it, and its parallel degradation. Poststructuralist twists aside, both Canto and Astell are simultaneously repelled and attracted to a view such as the one Plato espouses. Canto actually calls Plato's work a "feminist political manifesto."[44] Astell creates her own manifesto (or it is created for her) by viewing plights such as the Duchess of Mazarine's, a destiny brought on almost solely by the importance of marriage and childbearing for women in the society in which the duchess lived.

Astell fails to be a thoroughgoing feminist—in today's sense—because of her ontological commitments, but her recognition of the actual nature of women's degradation in society, and what might be required to overcome it, does indeed merit the appellation "feminist." On a more standard analysis of Plato, Okin continues to spell out how Plato understands the importance of women in society as a whole. She writes: "Women are classified by Plato, as they were by the culture in which he lived, as an important subsection of property. The very expression 'community (or common having) of women and children,' which he uses to denote his proposed system of temporary matings, is a further indication of this, since it could just as accurately be described as 'the community of men,' were it not for its inventor's customary way of thinking about such matters."[45]

In this line of thought, Canto, Astell, and Okin more or less meet. Plato sees that women are property, but the reproductive labor of the property is a sine qua non of the city's functioning. Because this is in some sense a politics of the body, Canto can see Plato's theorizing as a "feminist manifesto," particularly since he does, generously, allow for the possibility of women Guardians. Astell is only too aware of the possibility of such women; she herself might ordinarily be deemed to count as one. Her theorizing asks more about what should or could be done for the potential female Guardians, especially since the functioning of the city as a whole does indeed require the sacrifice of women for the greater good. That this is an inevitable consequence of social structure in any kind of state, whether realized or not, is not questioned by either Astell or Plato.

Although a different sort of ontological commitment from Astell might have precluded some of her views on marriage (and we have to remember that, given the time period in which she wrote, it is somewhat difficult to know how such a commitment could have come about), any society cannot continue without women's reproductive labor. Marx and Engels envisioned a society that recognized the rights of women and men to come together freely, without the bourgeois institution of marriage, but it is unclear what it is that they do when they get together. It is also unclear how domestic politics, in any society, could fail to replicate some other strands of political power.

Perhaps Astell deserves kudos for being enough of a realist to see that the harmonized social structure of England required a continuance of marriage as she had known it, but with more alert, better educated, and more charitable wives. What other sorts of social arrangements she could have envisioned remain to be seen.

We make a mistake when we construe Astell's feminism in such a way that we fail to do justice to the era in which she lived, or the constraints under which she wrote. This oversimplification is probably an inevitable consequence of our living in a time in which we hear such phrases as "postfeminist," or some synonym. But Astell's period so far precedes our own that we have difficulty imagining the mental set of this time when the New World still remained largely unexplored. Perhaps we can see Astell best when we allow ourselves to exercise historical imagination, and to come to the conclusion that Astell was, indeed, a feminist.

Astell's Feminist Epistemology

If we have some difficulties with the standard sorts of feminist labels with respect to Astell, we may well encounter more difficulties with the notion that any of the current work in feminist epistemology is genuinely applicable to Astell and her methods. As I noted when I examined part of her correspondence with Norris, she is a rationalist when it comes to matters metaphysical, and in that sense her epistemology, like Conway's, at first blush would appear to be one that would allow her to employ a nonempirical method to come to conclusions. Certainly, she was in disagreement with Locke on many of the most important matters of the day, and the intensely androcentric structure of rationalist thinking is a topic on which I have dwelt at an earlier point.

Nevertheless, my argument here will be that once we carefully examine Astell's work, we can see at least some intersection between it and some strands of contemporary work in feminist epistemology. It will also be important to distinguish between Astell the political and social thinker, and Astell the metaphysician. The two seem to be somewhat at odds, as is so frequently the case with Astell. It is clear that her observations of marriage form the basis of *Some Reflections,* and it is also clear that her social observations of the place of women in general buttress *A Serious Proposal.* With matters social and political, then, Astell is very much the empiricist, while trying to work within a Christian framework. All of this provides us with much food for thought.

In a stance that typifies some criticism, Kathleen Okruhlik has written, with regard to feminist thinking about the seventeenth century, that "[s]ome feminist theorists writing about the events of the scientific revolution have [not been] enthralled. Carolyn Merchant's 1980 book, *The Death of Nature: Women, Ecology, and the Scientific Revolution,* is an important example. She describes the period in question as profoundly gynophobic and argues that the mechanistic worldview developed at that time has led to ecological disaster and to a socioeconomic order that subjugates women."[46]

This concise summary of lines of argument that we have examined before both bolsters and draws attention to much of the work of Mary Astell. Her work was not, of course, in accord with the thinking that underlay the new science: if anything, it was antithetical to it. But if the new science was itself androcentric, then how much more the thought that chronologically precedes it. Astell's masculinism was of this more traditional stripe, insofar as it was anti-empirical and divorced from the evidence of the senses (here, of course, we are describing her metaphysics). So the pure argumentative rationality that underlay, for example, her objections to Norris's description of God does not, on the surface, lend itself to an analysis from the standpoint of feminist epistemics, although it is a type of thinking that is quite different from that cited by Okruhlik.

But there are at least two modes in which we can discern some of the sorts of thinking that have often been described as gynocentric, at least in the past two decades or so, in Astell's work. If we focus largely on *A Serious Proposal* and *Reflections,* we do, obviously, see the concern for women—and for relationships in general—that serves as the foundation for the authorship of these works. Drawing on Gilligan's work, for example, we can discern these stands readily enough, even if they are somewhat vague.

But more important, there are larger issues at stake in both of these works by Astell that speak, at least intermittently, to some of the issues in feminist epistemology. On the crudest level, Astell is a bit of what we now call a "feminist empiricist" in these works, since, with respect to anything having to do with the social scene, Astell is indeed concerned with numbers.[47] She feels that the lack of educational opportunities for women has meant that they are largely excluded. On a somewhat more sophisticated level, however, we can also discern in Astell a genuine concern for the development of all human personalities (including, perhaps somewhat naively, men's). Her emphasis on the virtues, their place in human functioning, and the lack of appreciation by all and sundry for opportunities to explore the virtues is something that—if only with respect to the two works in question—places her in the camp of the standpoint theorists. It is clear that Astell fully expects that women will continue to employ their virtues in enduring miserable marriages, even while most men will fail to benefit from the marital experience, except in the crudest way.

Contemporary philosophers sometimes divide over the role that reason should play in any account of feminist philosophy, or, indeed, even in feminist epistemology. A more traditionally minded camp reminds us that work originally done and deemed—at least in retrospect—to be feminist by women in the seventeenth and eighteenth centuries demanded that women be given the same rights to achieve a reason-based education as men. The argument, we are reminded, was that women only appeared to be weak, or even "foolish," because of their comparative lack of exposure to the so-called higher levels of education. Thus some feminists have experienced difficulty with the gender-derived arguments, alluded to here, that seem to place reason in the suspect corner of masculinism. Leaving aside for the moment the rebuttal that this sort of view greatly oversimplifies the claims that are being made, it is interesting to note that one of the women historians who has frequently cited Astell does so with respect to this very sort of argument:

> In tracing the development of rational thought in feminist writers of the seventeenth and eighteenth centuries, one is struck by their intense faith in the ability of reason to refute those who would define women's nature and restrict their lives through images of the "weaker vessel." . . .
> In the *Serious Proposal,* Astell presents the most systematic treatment of women's inferior education and its evil results during the seventeenth century. Strongly influenced by Descartes, she referred to his *Discourse on Method* in her marginalia throughout the *Serious Proposal.*[48]

Although there is no question that Smith is correct to place Astell on the "reason" side here, since, as she claims, this is the raison d'être for a work such as the *Proposal,* one must be careful to distinguish the claim that there might be modes of cognition that can be deemed to be gynocentric from any sort of general claim about rationality or reason in itself. Thus it would seem to be a mistake to assert that contemporary gender-based arguments are simply new ways of saying that women are irrational, although apparently some have misconstrued some of the arguments in this way. Original feminist arguments about education for women, or training of women's mental capacities, precede and are independent of most of the current gender-based material. Astell is most certainly on the side of reason, since as a philosopher she has ample place to use it. But the fact that we can see her employing reason and rationality in her construction of arguments does not mean that there may be no discernible gynocentric threads to such arguments. As we have seen with a philosopher such as Conway, such threads may be hard to make out and may, indeed, be smaller or less transparent than similar patterns in the work of some male philosophers (one thinks of Nietzsche, for example). But the task of pursuing these patterns is a valuable one, for it may show us where and why women's thought has been devalued.

Finally, pursuing work in feminist epistemology under its most broadly construed heading, it is worthwhile to note that some gynocentric templates appear in Astell's personal life. Almost all of her closest relationships appear to have been with other women, and among these the longest and most enduring one was with Lady Catherine Jones.[49] Although again one might be tempted to say that this fact does little more than to reflect the spirit of the times, Astell never, so far as we know, had a long-term or enduring relationship with a male. Thus, in this sense, her choice of companions and the styles of interaction between them—intense, affectional, and long term—speak to a certain sort of gynocentricity, and one that has been of special interest to twentieth-century feminists. Because at least some theory would claim that such relationships, on a Freudian analysis, recapitulate the intensity of the original mother-daughter bond, Astell's choices seem well worth remarking upon.[50]

Astell's overall epistemic bent is, then, complex. Although her writings on Christianity, the soul, and the love of God seem to assume a sort of Cartesian dualism, and although there is evidence of her influence by the Platonists, other parts of her work show a nascent political empiricism of the same sort that was put to use by Locke, even if she was not at all in agreement with Locke's views. In the same way that we noted that Anne Conway's rationalism allowed us to label her a philosopher without any difficulties, we can see that much of Astell's work is so classically philosophical (in the traditional, male sense) that one might naively think little intersection with the work of the contemporary feminist epistemologists could be found. But there are hints that there are such intersections and, as has been said, not merely in the comparatively easy sense in which it is clear that Astell is making a strong argument against female exclusion, as she does when she cites Scripture. Portions of her thought exhibit the same level of care and concern for others that Conway exhibits, although a striking difference is that, in Conway's work, this type of concern is much more exhaustively tied to her metaphysics. But we sell Astell short if we refuse to read her with two sets of eyes simultaneously, as it were. Both contemporary and historical vantage points are needed to get a full understanding of what she intended to accomplish.

A Look to the Future

It might seem naive to think that Astell would have much to offer women of color, or third-wave feminists who may believe that a number of battles have already been won. Nevertheless, we can extrapolate, at least to some extent, and indeed the situation demands that we do. For we must acknowledge the importance of work like Astell's, with respect not only to the women of her time, but to women of today, and we are now aware of the overriding necessity of speaking to a number of frameworks and issues.

If we recall what drove the creation of *A Serious Proposal,* we may begin to be able to do the necessary work to keep Astell's thought from being rendered nugatory. Astell was concerned, of course, about exclusion: we have mentioned this again and again. And yet it is clear, when *Proposal* is seen in the light of *Some Reflections,* that part of what moved Astell was a concern that women possessed virtues that might not be shared by men. Regardless of the controversial nature of such a stance, much can be said about how Astell's own thinking on this score is echoed again and again by women of color, even if, in many cases, it is a cultural viewpoint that they are attempting to espouse as their first line of attack, rather than a feminist one. For instance, when Astell writes in *Proposal* that in her "monastery" women will "suffer no other confinement, but to be kept out of the road of sin,"[51] we know that Astell believes that the compassion, courage, and charity that women frequently have to show in marriage can be harnessed to some other end.

Contemporary women of color who have written on educational issues have often said something remarkably similar, if perhaps not as essentialist as Astell's remarks might be taken to be. (I have addressed at an earlier point in the text lines of argument for asserting that at least some sort of mild essentialism is necessary, indeed, inescapable, if one is to address adequately women's issues across times and cultures.) For example, Beverly Daniel Tatum, in a *Harvard Educational Review* article entitled "Talking about Race," writes: "Unfortunately, less attention [than that given to content] has been given to the issues of process that inevitably emerge in the classroom when attention is focused on race, class, and/or gender. It is very difficult to talk about these concepts in a meaningful way without also talking about and learning about racism, classism and sexism. The introduction of these issues of oppression often generates powerful emotional responses in students that range from guilt and shame to anger and despair."[52]

It is clear that what Tatum proposes for the classroom with respect to race (and class and gender) is somewhat analogous to Astell's early proposal many decades ago. Astell's claim is that women's abilities will come to the fore in an environment that respects those abilities, and she takes it as implicit that at least the establishment of the centers of learning in itself makes note of the damage that has been done to women by their exclusion.

Analogously, Tatum is stating that raising issues—especially for women of color—of race, gender, and class in a course setting manifests a level of discourse that addresses previous lacunae and may (once energy has been channeled in an appropriate way) assist students in overcoming the obstacles in their path.

The conservative nature of Astell's overall views, plus the tenor of her time and its own treatment of persons of color in colonial situations, means that we can perform no more than a bare-bones extrapolation here. But the counter-argument to those who would claim that such a reading is misguided is to remind ourselves that this is what we do with all thinkers, especially those from the distant past. In many cases what they have to say, if read closely and at its most literal level, is scarcely relevant to today's concerns, or to the hurried and thoughtless nature of much of contemporary life. But if read broadly, and sympathetically, we often find that the work of a thinker of the past is much more relevant to what we have in mind as an intellectual goal than we might at first have thought.

Astell is such a thinker, and her lines of argument repay careful attention. Her political stance frequently prevents our seeing that concern for women and women's lives is at the forefront of her thinking, just as many current commentators want to address multicultural issues, or, as Tatum has said, issues of culture, gender, and social class simultaneously. It is a mistake to think that simply because Astell defended a number of conservative causes during her lifetime, she has nothing of relevance to say to us today.

Some Reflections, of course, pushes the line that women may indeed possess a number of properties that will allow them to learn from harsh experience and to use that learning in a way that men would not. Indeed, Astell urges her women readers to use "shipwrack'd" marriages as a point of departure for further growth. Seen superficially, one might wonder what the value of such advice could be in contemporary terms, since many individuals would not choose to make a relationship the testing ground of their own ability to sprout virtues. Yet seen through a different prism, Astell's advice is useful not only for marriages, but for all relationships. She was, of course, writing about a certain set of conventions of her day. Even with respect to that set of conventions, Astell was wise enough to see that some problems were more or less of a woman's own choosing. In a well-known passage that begins "But do the women never chuse amiss?" Astell acknowledges that some women fall into the category that she labels "Fool with a witness" for thinking that marriage can change qualities that might otherwise seem to be an intrinsic part of a person's character.[53] The broad aim of what Astell writes is to encourage both sexes to be more humane, more tolerant, and to exhibit greater forbearance—but she realizes that this goal is a lofty one, unlikely to be achieved. What she has seen in her life convinces her that the chances that women will benefit, morally, from marriage (largely because they are forced to) are greater than the chances that men will so benefit.[54]

The point is that, with a more broad-ranging view, we can read a work such as *Reflections* in such a way that its advice is helpful to all persons and applies broadly to all human relationships. In this sense, Astell's words are more than pertinent for our time, or any other. Astell is simply asking us to use human relationships, with all their flaws, as opportunities for growth, knowing full well that, frequently, one person is put more in the place of having to be the one who exhibits the growing, so to speak, than the other. This seems to be an inevitable quality of human relationships, and Astell, the political thinker, is more than ready to acknowledge it.

A great deal of what Astell wrote seems bound by time, particularly since the political tracts tend to address a narrow range of questions having to do with the church, the role of Dissenters, and so forth. *A Fair Way,* for example, is perhaps best seen as a document of its period, especially since its intended target is those who support the Dissenters. As has been argued here, however, other works—such as *Some Reflections* and *A Serious Proposal*—can be taken as broadly applicable to a number of situations. Since they deal with the large issues of human relationships and educational matters, it is much easier to try to discern a general point, and to move with it.

To end with a note on the educational concerns mentioned at an earlier point, the conservative Astell can be read as a champion of the underdog only if we read broadly. But there are a number of points in *A Serious Proposal* that encourage us to do just that if we are to make headway in attempting to use the insights of thinkers from previous generations for our own. The overall aim of the *Proposal* is to ensure that the reader recognizes that women, as a group, have never been fairly given a chance. As Astell herself remarks, the greater question is: "For since GOD has given Women as well as Men intelligent Souls, why should they be forbidden to improve them?"[55] Again, this general point can be taken so that we find it instructive for a number of groups, and in a number of locales. We need not look too closely to see that opportunity is the main theme here, and this is, of course, a theme that resonates today. As we saw earlier, Beverly Daniel Tatum has used this same broad theme to write about education for black students, and so has Geneva Smitherman. In still another piece on the education of black children, Smitherman writes: "The attitude of school officials [in a case involving an elementary school in Michigan] was that the school had done its job, and that perhaps the children were uneducable. Yet close scrutiny of the academic records and psychological and speech language evaluations failed to uncover any inherent limitation in the children's cognitive or language capacities."[56]

We may be tempted to say that what Astell has written in *A Serious Pro-*

posal has nothing to do with Smitherman's point, but if we make this claim we are failing to read in a way that will benefit us as women or, indeed, as progressive human beings. Astell's larger point is about the capacities for growth and change of persons who have always been excluded from educational circles. In that sense, what she has to say is relevant to a number of persons, and over long periods of time.

A Summation

As I examine the record of contemporary work on Astell, and interest in her, I am struck by the extent to which a great deal of the current work focuses on facts of her life and upbringing: Perry's noted biography, for example, devotes much of its first hundred pages to Astell's childhood and her crucial move to London at a very early age. All of this interest, of course, is despite the fact that we know comparatively little about these matters; the point is that what we do know excites our further interest, because Astell seemed to exhibit those traits of courage and farsightedness that we so frequently admire in individuals, and especially in women whose background has seemed in some way constricting.[57]

Folding our interest in Mary Astell's environment together with the broad sort of reading encouraged in the previous section assists us in coming to grips with her as a thinker. Astell strikes readers as filled with paradoxes and oddities because we often want to believe that someone's holding a "progressive" position on one issue means that the person will hold a similarly "progressive" position on most or all issues. Not only does this fail to allow for individual variation; it also fails to require us to do the necessary work on individual thinkers. If we are required merely to fill in the blanks, so to speak, we have to do little to try to see what it was that a thinker originally intended, especially if we talk ourselves into thinking that we can fill in those blanks in a way that makes us more comfortable, even if it does not correspond with what the writer in question originally had to say.

Astell's work is complex enough and covers a broad enough range of issues that it is difficult to do this with her, thus leaving many people frustrated and filled with a sense of bafflement. The "first English feminist" is a strong believer in the Anglican Church, so much so that she expends much energy in arguing against any generosity toward the Dissenters. She is also a strong believer in the institution of marriage, even as she writes of the difficulties, not to say dangers, that marriage imposes on women. In theory, at least, she believes that all could benefit from the exercise of their virtues and the more charitable aspects of their nature in human relationships, but insofar as marriage is concerned, she focuses almost solely on how women can use the institution to promote their own greater good.

Perhaps the current concentration on Astell's past is an effort to come to grips with the material at hand, and to try to make sense of her beliefs in a way that will allow us, as late twentieth- and early twenty-first-century readers, to understand her. Certainly this is what Perry seems to be doing, with her careful notation regarding Astell's family circumstances and the reduced straits that the Interregnum and general civil discontent of the seventeenth century brought to it. It also seems to be the case that there is a focus on Astell's personality and her own character traits—it seems helpful to examine these when we are faced with puzzlement about her various stances. Perry writes: "Astell's pride in self, her cool assurance, her public appreciation of other women's work, and her suggestions of an alternative female way-of-being-in-the-world, may seem obvious to modern feminists, but they created a sensation in London in the closing years of the seventeenth century."[58]

They also created a bit of a sensation at later points, for a perusal of the work done by nineteenth-century historians on such topics as women's education, learned women, and women authors finds that Mary Astell's name comes up with great frequency.[59] Because of the length and duration of her contacts with other women of her time—something remarked upon here at an earlier point—she is also often cited in works about those women; for example, even though there is over a twenty-year age difference between Astell and Lady Mary Wortley Montagu, Robert Halsband's life of Lady Mary devotes two or three pages to their relationship and its undoubted strong influence on Lady Mary's devotion to letters.[60]

I have been claiming that it is probably a mistake to read Astell so narrowly that we find ourselves put off by her obvious class interests, and unable to make use of a great deal of what she has to say. On the other hand, as Perry is at pains to point out, Astell would not have been the defender of High Tory principles that she was if she had not felt that the England of the Interregnum and its aftermath was, in general, a debacle. Perhaps it is more intriguing to try to ascertain why order was so important for Astell—order not only in the political sphere, and not only of property rights and Church rites, but order and harmony in the larger sense.

When we have made this sort of investigation of Astell's life, we will be onto something, for these concerns are at the core of Astell's being. We know her to have been of regular habits, and to have been personally courageous; all the accounts of her battle with breast cancer indicate her indefatigable spirit and strength in overcoming pain.[61] But since our concern is with Astell the philosopher, we can easily draw the lines necessary to connect points and establish an argument.

Astell the philosopher, whose ontology is closer to that of the Cambridge Platonists, and even to Conway, than might at first be obvious from her emphasis on political writings, needs order so that she can do the intellectual work that her very being requires. If Conway had the fortune to be able to live a life that sheltered her from a great deal of the stress and bustle of the outside world—even if it was purchased at the price of physical ill health—Astell was much more caught up in the world of daily turmoil than Conway ever was. Part of this, of course, was simply a result of living in London and being a regular confidante of a number of individuals. But part of it also devolved from their very different social situations—Anne Finch, later Conway, was a high-born woman to begin with, and this is not true of Mary Astell, however she might have liked to hold on to the notion that her Newcastle forbears constituted a better-off class. Whatever impetus pushed Astell toward London as she entered her early twenties, we can sense the desperation of her plight in her attempts to write to a number of figures soon after arrival, indicating material poverty and psychological and spiritual destitution.[62] Her work and her thought, then, are not the products of a woman whose stepbrother started off at Cambridge and was able to introduce her to a circle of intellectuals. Astell's work is entirely self-creation, and she must have sensed at an early point that the creative impulse in philosophical thought can come about only through peaceful external circumstances. If it is the case that a certain sort of scintillating animus has to be felt at the cognitive level, that mental excitement comes about most naturally when external circumstances are supportive rather than hindering.

Astell's emphasis on God, devotion to the concept of the divine, and an impulse away from this earthly life all point in the direction that we call broadly Platonic, and all of this effort on her part helps us to understand her personal adherence to the church and her aversion to Dissenters and radicals. Astell is at her best when, as is the case with these lines from *The Christian Religion,* she is able to show us as readers how she has woven all the threads of her thought together:

> A Woman may *put on the whole Armour of God* without degenerating into a Masculine Temper; she may *take the Shield of Faith, the Sword of the Spirit, the Helmet of Salvation, and the Breast-Plate of Righteousness,* without any offence to the Men, and they become her as well as they do the greatest Hero. I cou'd never understand why we are bred Cowards; sure it can never be because our Masters are afraid we shou'd Rebel, for Courage wou'd enable us to endure

their Injuries, to forgive and to despise them! It is indeed so necessary a Virtue that we can't be good Christians without it; for till we are got above the fear of Death, 'Tis in any bodies power to make us renounce our hopes of Heaven. And it can't be suppos'd that Men envy us our Portion there; since however desirous they are to engross *this* World, they do not seem so covetous of *the other* [emphasis in original].[63]

This paragraph goes a fair way to encompassing, in a few lines, a great deal of what Astell has to say. Christians agree that the other world is preferable to this one; and the exercise of the virtues not only assists us in getting to that other world, as it were—it also helps us to endure the present. Most important, it aids us in overcoming our fear of death and dying, for when we come to understand the falsity of this world and the reality of the other, we are reinfused with courage, a most necessary virtue. And, finally, it helps us to understand the behavior of males. Perhaps their tendency is to focus on material gain and comfort, competition and striving, to the exclusion of anything else.

The Astell who is so anxious to ensure passage to that other world—a realm of pure thought, to be sure, with no bodily admixture—is the same Astell who endeavors to put her kingdom aright, as it were, by making sure that no false religions are propagated, and by taking care to see that those who do promulgate such beliefs are defeated. If her overall emphasis on women, their capacities and strengths, harmony in the political sphere, and love of God perhaps elide more complex questions, such as how a just person might meet a Dissenter halfway, we can see that part of her instinctive response to these questions might have to do with the notion of "halfwayness." For Astell, as for many such believers, there can be no halfway, for halfway to meeting someone who errs is a long way down the path toward erring oneself.

The Dissenters, and anyone who comes to their defense, such as Defoe, place the polity in danger by failing to see how important a just and true worship is, and how that worship is tied to other political concerns—the divine right of the ruler, the ordinance from God that allows the ruler to reign in harmony and with sure sovereignty, and so forth. In *An Impartial Enquiry,* Astell notes that if a group of people move against the sovereign, "'tis all a case whether the *Dangers* are Real or Imaginary; if they happen to succeed, they will find Advocates enough to Justify them, Success will Crown the Work."[64] Here she warns us clearly that a justification can always be found for any rebellion, but the sort of rebellion that resulted in the execution of Charles I goes against God's established order, the very order that she finds necessary for the preservation of the kingdom, and for herself and her work.

We read Astell with some difficulty today because, in a very genuine sense, her side lost. The power and force of the Lockean political philosophy, and its ready application to the situation of the colonies, means that a contemporary reader instinctively moves toward the side of rebellion, and has great trouble assimilating Astell's point of view. But the young woman who moved from Newcastle to Chelsea knew whereof she spoke. Rebellions, however justified politically, cause chaos, confusion, and hurt. They impede the doing of philosophy, and for the philosophically minded, like Astell, the world of ideas always comes first.

MARY WOLLSTONECRAFT   four

Mary Wollstonecraft (1759–97), unlike Mary Astell or Anne Conway, is indisputably recognized as an important thinker of her time, and such recognition has in general not flagged since the early part of the nineteenth century. Unlike Hildegard, but perhaps like Anne Conway, Wollstonecraft is certainly recognized as a philosopher, for her works are lengthy enough and conceptually oriented enough that she is often included in anthologies of philosophical thought.[1] Thus, unlike Mary Astell—although both women are paradigmatically political thinkers—Wollstonecraft is not often labeled a "pamphleteer."

In the heady atmosphere of the French Revolution, Wollstonecraft, with the assistance of a circle of friends including many of England's most radical thinkers, wrote first *A Vindication of the Rights of Men* and then *A Vindication of the Rights of Woman*. If we think of Mary Astell as the "first feminist," then Wollstonecraft's name cannot be far behind, for her work on this topic is much longer and much more filled out in terms of argument, despite a somewhat emotional and strident style.

The same woman whose love affairs became well known in her time, and who for a long time was enamored of the Byronic painter Fuseli, wrote (against the concept of woman posed by Rousseau): "It does not require a lively pencil, or the discriminating outline of a caricature, to sketch the domestic miseries and petty vices which such a mistress of a family diffuses. Still she only acts as a woman ought to act, brought up according to Rousseau's system. . . . [I]n what respect can she be termed good? . . . [H]ow does she fulfill her duties? Duties!—in truth she has enough to think of to adorn her body and nurse a weak constitution."[2]

Mary Wollstonecraft's personal background, with its poverty and comparative degree of misfortune, may well have attuned her to the trials and misfortunes of others. In addition, her own acquaintance with male radicals who were already predisposed to see women in a light different from that of most contemporary Englishmen helped her to build a solid foundation upon which to write and compose. Her early London friendship with Joseph Johnson exposed her to a wide group; not only Fuseli, but Cowper, Thomas Christie, and others were the recipients of the generosity of this publisher who set Mary up, well before her relationship with Godwin, without any apparent expectation of sexual favors.[3] In the middle of all of this, Mary, the philosopher, replied to Burke's *Reflections on the Revolution in France* with one of the first printed responses. Mary's reply to Burke's cautious fears about beheadings and violence must have seemed quite an excited one: as Claire Tomalin says, "She was famous suddenly."[4] Mary, the daughter of the decidedly less than middle class, and the well-known "Amazon," became an even more celebrated woman warrior, who, according to a ballad of the day, had smote Edmund Burke.[5]

Wollstonecraft is revered today because we see her as preeminent among a line of thinkers who not only articulated what women deserved, but also spelled out at length the societal costs of the failure to give them what they deserved. We also see, with our contemporary eye, the merging of a life and philosophy: if we experience some difficulties with Mary Astell because of her paradoxical positions, as we are tempted to call them, Wollstonecraft calls out to us since it is clear that she lived a life completely in tune with her call for liberty and freedom. Finally, although it may seem peripheral, many of us know her and think of her as the mother of Mary Godwin Shelley, and the now recognized author of *Frankenstein* may seem to us the daughter, in flesh and in spirit, of that ardent feminist thinker.

Wollstonecraft's political philosophy, especially as spelled out with respect to property rights, makes it clear that the reliance of British thinkers on that right as paramount conceals a multitude of sins. Thus the very safety that Astell, for one, sought is dismissed by Wollstonecraft as unworthy of a genuine spirit; she and the other radicals of her time welcomed the French

Revolution for the confusion and stimulation that it caused, and its "ardour for liberty."[6] Few women can have lived as completely an embodied life of freedom as Wollstonecraft, whose ardent love letters are still stunning after the passage of time, and whose romantic attachments to men and women alike speak to her fiery nature. Perhaps part of what we admire in Wollstonecraft is a certain weaving—in some philosophers we are struck by the extent to which the life lived fails to match, in any way, shape, or form, the philosophical views. This is not the case with Wollstonecraft.

Catriona Mackenzie and others have argued that central to an understanding of Wollstonecraft is the importance of passion to her conception of a self, even a self that, at its highest levels, is governed by reason.[7] Both Mackenzie and Diana Coole, whose account of women political thinkers is standardly used, see Wollstonecraft as replying to Rousseau, but in a way that does a great deal more to salvage a notion of wholeness for women than almost any previous account of possibilities for women's lives has done.[8] Coole wants to emphasize the extent to which Wollstonecraft sees possibilities for women that are undemarcated by the standard binary oppositions, oppositions that Rousseau, of course, is more than willing to employ. Coole notes that Wollstonecraft is asserting that the female half of the human species should be "treated first as human rather than as sexed beings."[9] Somewhat in opposition to Coole, who chooses to emphasize Wollstonecraft's construction of rationality, Mackenzie claims:

> [T]he overriding preoccupations of Wollstonecraft's work, as well as of her life, were to articulate what it means for women to think and act as autonomous moral agents, and to envisage the kind of moral and political organization required for them to do so. Although at times she seemed to identify autonomy with reason, defining it in opposition to passion . . . Wollstonecraft also struggled to develop an account of women's moral agency that would incorporate not only a recognition of women's capacity to reason but also of their right to experience and give expression to passion, including sexual desire.[10]

One point on which almost all commentators agree is that Wollstonecraft is acutely aware of the roles into which women are usually cast—wife, mother, caring relation—and she is determined to make the case that, given the ubiquitousness of these roles, the well-educated woman with a formed mind is a better companion and parent than one who has never been allowed to learn.

Rousseau's Sophie seemed to Wollstonecraft to embody all of the qualities that made the woman of leisure, in either Britain or France, an insipid and

vain creature. In this she follows, although approximately a century later, Astell's concern about the occupations (choosing clothes, deciding on a hair-
style) that were to take up most of the time of any woman of the middle or
upper classes in a European society. As Astell was, Wollstonecraft is passion-
ately concerned that women be allowed the opportunity to make use of their
intelligence. But contra Astell, she cannot accept the more overtly distasteful
and discriminatory aspects of marriage, and she is not in the least prepared to
offer an argument that women should accept some of the more repellent features of marriage as a way in which to exercise their virtues. She is profoundly
aware of the physical limitations placed on women by the social demands of
marriage, and she is quick to point out that these are unhealthy. As Mackenzie writes, "she could not see a clear solution to the problem of women's sub-
ordination except the transformation of the family."[11]

Like Astell, Wollstonecraft has views on a number of topics, but unlike Astell, her stand on many sorts of questions not directly political is seldom as
well articulated as one might hope. Nevertheless, the fact that she is writing
so much later allows us to do the necessary extrapolative work with a greater
sense of ease, and her access to the thinkers of the London literary scene gives
us ample evidence for a number of conclusions.

Wollstonecraft's passion, which appears to have been evident from her
earliest years, allows us to place her as a thinker of her time, well in tune with
the sentiments of the French Revolution and the other cries for liberty heard
across the Continent and in Great Britain. The fact that she is mentioned in
the works of many thinkers of the day, and that Godwin wrote his own memoirs of his life with her, gives us reason to believe that we can have a certain
degree of success in reconstructing her thoughts. Wollstonecraft's life and
writings ask us to take her work with the utmost degree of seriousness.

Wollstonecraft and Standard Philosophy

Although Wollstonecraft seldom addressed the metaphysical and epistemological issues that we so intensely associate with philosophizing, she did at
least implicitly engage such issues, generally at the beginnings of her works,
or in any passages where she attempts an assay of the general lot of humankind. Wollstonecraft's overall position on the scheme of things and the
place of human beings in it reflects what has often been called perfectibilism:
she accepts God as divine creator, but argues that humans would not have received the gifts of reason and capacity for rationality that they have from God

if the maker had not intended their full use.[12] In a typical line of argument, Wollstonecraft notes, "When that wise Being who created us and placed us here, saw the fair idea, he willed . . . that the passions should unfold our reason, because he could see that present evil would produce future good."[13] Although she seldom takes a stance that would allow one to extrapolate an epistemology, Wollstonecraft seems to foresee the importance of empiricism, for she uses empirical arguments frequently in her citation of ills.

It is always tempting to assume a Christian ontology for a thinker who is writing in the eighteenth or seventeenth century and whose work refers to God, creation, and so forth. Yet it is interesting to note that Wollstonecraft does not employ a specifically Christian conception of God—indeed, her friendships with a number of freethinkers (some of whom were pronounced atheists) would seem to preclude that. Wollstonecraft's metaphysics seems to assume a general sort of Creator—the type of creator presumed or posited by many religious traditions—and a sense of duty that human beings owe to their Creator. But part and parcel of this is to make use of that most precious gift endowed upon human beings, "Reason," as Wollstonecraft refers to it, and to use it in a way that does not hinder the development of other humans.

Speaking to these issues in a section of the second *Vindication* called "The Rights and Involved Duties of Mankind Considered" (the only section of any length not specifically concerned with women's issues), Wollstonecraft notes:

> In what does man's preeminence over the brute creation consist? The answer is as clear as that a half is less than the whole; in Reason.
> What acquirement exalts one being above another? Virtue; we spontaneously reply.
> For what purpose were the passions implanted? That man by struggling with them might attain a degree of knowledge denied to the brutes; whispers Experience.
> Consequently the perfection of our nature and capability of happiness, must be estimated by the degree of reason, virtue, and knowledge that distinguish the individual, and direct the laws which bind society: and that from the exercise of reason, knowledge and virtue naturally flow, is equally undeniable, if mankind is viewed collectively.[14]

Here, in a nutshell, is much of what Wollstonecraft uses as a combined metaphysics and epistemology from which to develop her more salient political and moral views. Clearly, Wollstonecraft sees humans as above and beyond the rest of the created world in a way that will later come to characterize much of what is perceived to be Enlightenment thought (and that will anger many feminists, at later times). Equally perspicuously, she sees humans as having a moral duty to develop, as she puts it, "reason, virtue and knowledge," so as to reflect the gifts that our Creator has given us. Within this ontological framework, she uses both reason—in the sense of logical argument—and experience to come to certain conclusions about societies and about the place of women in those societies.

Part of what drives much of Wollstonecraft's theorizing about social development is not only a taken-for-grantedness with respect to the Judeo-Christian tradition, but a nascent Eurocentrism. Indeed, by the time Wollstonecraft wrote, Europeans had encountered enough of the rest of the planet, in Asia, Africa, and the Americas, that the superiority of European mores and ways of life seemed self-evident to many. Thus, in sections of the *Vindication* immediately after the paragraphs cited above, and before beginning her examination of the place of women, Mary Wollstonecraft explicitly mentions forms of government, some of which inhere in non-European societies, and many of which she finds abhorrent for their blatant injustice.[15]

Contra Rousseau, it is not "civilization" itself that she claims inhibits human growth, but rather a lack of respect for the growth of all humans within certain portions of what is called civilization. After inveighing against the aristocracy and its hereditary rights, she notes that failing to see that humans as a whole have a duty toward God to perfect themselves, insofar as they are able, is a flaw that is largely due to an overromanticization of a "state of nature."[16] The defects of civilization occur largely because privilege—especially that which is unearned—prevents individuals from developing their capacities, and allows them to sink into "vice."[17] If that liberty which is consistent with God's will for humans (and which she explicitly distinguishes from organized religion) were given to all, the development of virtue would proceed on a more or less natural course. Thus, within the limits of the time period in which she wrote, Wollstonecraft is indisputably a freethinker whose conception of God is one that might be a great deal more in harmony with an argument from design than it is with any particular religious institution.

Wollstonecraft's respect for humans as the crown of creation is not only in tune with a great deal of the Continental thinking of the time, to which she had already been exposed, but it does indeed precede, at least intellectually, the Romantic attachment to nature, and a sense that human beings derive their special place in nature from God's will. Thus Wordsworth's (and even Shelley's) ruminations on "sounding cataracts" seem very much in keeping with Wollstonecraft's intuitive sensation that human beings need to live up to the grace that was given them.

Mary Wollstonecraft's empiricism shows up in her careful cataloging of the ills that plague the women of her time. As we might expect, she is, of course, concerned that poorly educated women cannot be good mothers or adequate homemakers—or even adequate superiors of servants—but she is very specific about the ways in which a number of women of the upper and upper-middle classes fall short, through lack of education and through a lack of breadth of exposure. While attacking Rousseau's notion that civilization itself is at fault, Wollstonecraft makes careful note of the ways in which the general culture could be improved with attention to the lot of women: "Strengthen the female mind by enlarging it, and there will be an end to blind obedience; but, as blind obedience is ever sought for by power, tyrants and sensualists are in the right when they endeavor to keep women in the dark, because the former only want slaves, and the latter a play-thing. The sensualist, indeed, has been the most dangerous of tyrants, and women have been duped by their lovers, as princes by their ministers, whilst dreaming that they reigned over them."[18]

In other words, part of the problem is that women themselves do not know the difficulties that they are in, because their lack of education keeps them from seeing how they are being used. Surely God would not have granted women the rationality that had been granted to men unless it were intended to be used; common sense and justice, not to mention the demands of society, dictate that women be allowed to pursue educations worthy of their spirit and intellect.

If it is accurate to say that Wollstonecraft held to a freethinking sort of perfectibilism, compatible with at least a Unitarian outlook, if not any more formal sort of view, then her empiricism with regard to social relations was also bolstered by a desire to construct an argument that would back up her views. Although many faulted the second *Vindication* at the time of its publication for its somewhat strident tone, there is no question that it does indeed contain argument, and the amount of argumentation to be found on the pages is all the more remarkable when it is remembered that the work was written very rapidly.[19] We can hypothesize that the speed here was due partly simply to Wollstonecraft's impetuous nature, but also more reliably to the fact that the arguments presented were issues of long-standing interest to her. The difficulty that she had in her personal relationships, the general atmosphere, even among freethinkers, that derogated the rights of women, the attention among the *philosophes* to rights in general (but, in almost all cases, intended as those of males)—all of these factors must have propelled Wollstonecraft into a frenzy of activity.

Wollstonecraft's overall philosophical views, vaguely articulated though they may be, were sufficient enough to allow her to establish a notion of a just and perfectible social order. Her vision of the future was based on a be-lief that a Creator could not have intended for one-half of the human race to be bereft of social goods or a sense of equality. It speaks to the importance of this sort of issue for Wollstonecraft that she alludes to it throughout the first chapter of the second *Vindication.*

Society and the Concept of the Moral

We can argue that there are parts of Wollstonecraft's views that are implicitly utilitarian. She would already have been familiar with Jeremy Bentham, and Tomalin notes that three to four years before Wollstonecraft began the fem-inist *Vindication,* Bentham had published a tract on female suffrage that no-ticed inconsistencies in arguments put forward to try to stifle such rights (even though some of those arguments were indeed Bentham's own).[20]

If it pushes the claim too far to see Wollstonecraft as writing in the same vein that the Mills will later use, it is not too much of a stretch to note that the same perfectiblism to which I have already alluded is related to the later doc-trines. Taking the arguments at full value, the point is that society as a whole can function more efficiently—and make best use of the talents of its individ-ual members—if all are educated and taught to make good use of their personal characteristics and talents. According to Tomalin's analysis, part of the reason that Bentham came to at least a moderate sympathy with female suffrage was that, on the whole, the arguments against it were not a good deal stronger than those against working-class males' participating in government.[21]

What is intriguing about the growth in moral thought exemplified by Wollstonecraft's work is that preceding arguments, whether made by men or women, had generally relied on a much more strongly Christian under-standing of the nature of reality. We have seen that in the case of Astell, this involved her in genuine obstacles in trying to achieve a coherent and con-sistent view about what women could and could not accomplish.

It has been argued that, similarly to Astell, Wollstonecraft is caught in at least some contradictions and tensions. In a differing vein from Astell, how-ever, these airs of paradox do not arise because Wollstonecraft holds a very narrow and conservative political position with regard to a number of mat-ters that today might be deemed to be consistent with any straightforward feminism. Rather, the difficulty for Wollstonecraft, according to Moira Gatens, is that her straightforward application of a rights thesis with respect to women is a valorization of something that was intended, by most of its au-thors and proponents, as having to do only with men. Furthermore, Wollstonecraft does not (she cannot) divorce herself completely from the notion that women have obligations as mothers and wives. Gatens analyzes some of these rough areas for Wollstonecraft as follows:

> In her attempt to stretch liberal principles of equality to women she neglects to note that these principles were developed and formulated with men as their object. Her attempts to stretch these principles to include women results in both practical and conceptual difficulties. These principles were developed with an (implicitly) male person in mind, who is assumed to be a head of household (a husband/ father) and whose domestic needs are catered for (by his wife). . . . No matter how strong the power of reason, it cannot alter the fact that male and female embodiment . . . involved vastly different social and po-litical consequences.[22]

Reading Gatens's critique closely, it reminds us of the split in feminist theory that today might be labeled that between liberal and gender feminists: in other words, because what Wollstonecraft implicitly asks for women is so close to the male role, it tends to overlook a deeper and more profound fem-inism that might, in fact, use some of the notions tied to maternity and the "roles" of women for a purpose completely contrary to that of Rousseau.

Nevertheless, despite some wariness that we may have toward portions of Wollstonecraft's work, the tensions inherent in it are recognizable to us, and stem at least partially from Wollstonecraft's subsumption of a sort of conse-quentialism as her basic moral outlook. Since she is aiming at some greater good that is defined inherently in terms of its relationship to the social whole, she is also tied to those very views—especially in the Anglo-Saxon tra-dition—that are, at bottom, allied to some concept of property rights, liberty for the individual, and free thought, almost all of which (as Gatens claims) were originally developed for men.

As a bonus, a view such as Wollstonecraft's allows for a direct relationship between the social and the good, and it is not nearly as tied to devoutly reli-gious views as, for instance, the stands of either Conway or Astell. When we remember that *A Vindication of the Rights of Men* was a reply to Burke, we can get a fuller glance at what Wollstonecraft intended by reminding ourselves of Burke's classic conservative argument. This Gatens concedes: a look at Burke is a palliative in reading Wollstonecraft and makes her position appear scin-tillating. As Gatens herself admits, "Burke's lauding of tradition and heredi-tary rights and his dogmatic insistence on the conservation of existing rigid political relations are all treated by Wollstonecraft as evidence of his lack of reason."[23] Like other consequentialists, however, Wollstonecraft implicitly involves herself in some positions that prove dangerous if taken to their ex-treme. Because she is aiming at a better society, and because she is so divorced from any view that might be considered to be deontological, there is always a strong counterargument to be made that, at bottom, some such view might entail a denial of rights.

Like Astell, Mary Wollstonecraft was moved by the plight of women she saw around her, and the combination of abuses that she witnessed in a wide variety of social circles yields for her the concomitant treatment of entail-ments. Because she saw the despicable conduct of those in British society who had hereditary titles and privileges, she had no difficulty in supporting the French Revolution, and she was comfortable in the company of its most adamant English backers. Because she saw, as Astell did, the consequences of lack of female education—especially for those who might be thought to be the most privileged in terms of social class—she was able to make the intu-itive leap that women should, in almost all respects, be treated as were men with comparative ease. Nothing in Mary's background called out to her to at-tempt to represent a past, either actual or spurious, of privilege and wealth.

We can also hypothesize, with little difficulty, that some of Mary's per-sonal relationships with men may have influenced her views on rights and education. Her alliances with both Fuseli and Godwin are romanticized, and indeed she herself so romanticized them, but aspects of her personality—her fiery temper and general quickness of conduct—caused great consternation in both men. There is no doubt that Wollstonecraft realized at an early point that even the most stated admirers of the principle of equality for the female sex among the men that she knew experienced great hardship in living with this principle.

A recurring tension in moral thought, and one that thoroughly manifests itself in contemporary debates on ethics, is that between the deontological and consequentialist points of view. Part of the push behind the debate has to do with our post-Kantian "intuitions" that something like genuine moral thinking must reflect a notion of the ethical that is independent of ends. This, of course, is largely an artifact of comparatively recent ethical thought. The debates of the French Revolution—both within France itself and in Great Britain—are debates about how to form the best society. It is more or less as-sumed in these disputes that the goal of betterment for all (material, moral, and spiritual) is a worthy one, and that no set of means that fails to take the end in sight can aspire to the label "just." If we have some difficulty with Wollstonecraft's obviously perfectibilist, or perfectionist, consequentialism, it is probably because we see her as a forerunner of those other sorts of con-sequentialist views that will later, at least in some circles, come to be the ob-jects of ridicule.

Yet Wollstonecraft was simply writing within the framework of her time, and responding, as we have seen, to thinkers around her. The strength of the notion of divine right was still so great during Astell's time that she did not count as recalcitrant or as an outsider in arguing the High Tory case. A cen-tury later, in Wollstonecraft's time, this notion is much under attack; it is by no means moribund, however, for if it were, it would not have received the impassioned Burkean defense that it did.

Wollstonecraft's achievement in authoring the two *Vindications* is not an achievement simply because she was a woman. It is an achievement of im-passioned articulation, on behalf of all human beings. The spirit of the French Revolution, if taken straight, so to speak, would have empowered all and would have greatly enhanced the status of women. Those *poissardes des Halles* who refused to honor Marie Antoinette at the Feast of the Assumption in 1787 were women moved by the same spirit that Wollstonecraft herself expressed.[24] The best exponent of that spirit, at least insofar as women were concerned, was probably *une Anglaise*—Mary Wollstonecraft herself.

The London of Mary Wollstonecraft

Wollstonecraft's collection of friends, lovers, and acquaintances had a power-ful impact on her thinking and writing. Not merely Johnson and Godwin, but Imlay, Paine, Blake, and Priestly all influenced her and in turn were influenced by her. Although her relationship with Gilbert Imlay, who fathered her first child, may have caused her the greatest strain, and may have been the most profound relationship, Mary's passion-filled and tempestuous life is part of the reason that her works have been viewed on occasion with a jaundiced eye.[25]

In Wollstonecraft's case, comparisons on the basis of intellectual works or from the standpoint of philosophical thought can most easily be made with men, although there is some reason to think of her as forming a natural con-trast with, for example, Madame de Stael. Mary and Godwin were attracted to each other precisely for intellectual reasons, which in turn fueled the pas-sionate nature of the relationship. Although both were freethinkers, at least by the conventional standards of the time, and although both claimed to be against such conventions as marriage, they frequently found their stated views wavering under the virtual nonstop onslaught of attacks by others. Thus there is some reason to believe that their marriage was one that was made out of necessity, since both, at least on more than one occasion, had made several statements against the institution of marriage. In addition, Mary's belief in some sort of Creator (alluded to here at an earlier point) was at odds with Godwin's professed atheism. Tomalin writes: "In due course Godwin returned, . . . but there were still other problems. He wished Mary to give up all her religious ideas, she was unwilling. 'How can you blame me for taken [sic] refuge in the idea of God, when I despair of finding sincerity on earth?'"[26]

Atheism was a topic of the day, and Mary's attenuated cosmology, with its vague notion that humankind owed the force of reason and the ability to conceptualize to a divine Maker, was more than many of her companions could bring themselves to hold. More important, her social notions, instrumentalist though they were, ran into difficulties when the roles of the sexes were examined from the standpoint of their having been divinely ordained. We have already seen (as Gatens, for one, indicates) that Wollstonecraft's acceptance of the need for women to see themselves as mothers and hence as educators of children was at variance with the rights that she espoused, especially since such rights had originally been the prerogative of males. Wollstonecraft's central argument was that God had given reason equally to men and women, but the counterargument of those who had religious beliefs usually centered around the purpose for which women should employ their reason.

Among women thinkers of her time with whom comparison might aptly be made, Catherine Macaulay stands out. Although the French theorists Olympe de Gouges and Germaine de Stael also merit comparison, the demands of the Anglo-Saxon tradition push us into an examination of Macaulay's work in contrast to that of Wollstonecraft.

Macaulay is usually described as an historian, but her work may also be thought of as vaguely philosophical, at least in the political and moral sense, since she addressed the same issues with respect to women, their education, and their status in society that Wollstonecraft later took on. In her superb and lengthy biography of Wollstonecraft, Janet Todd remarks: "[Mary Wollstonecraft] was helped by Catherine Macaulay's recently published *Letters on Education*. This too was severely moral and religious, arguing against the present system of trivial female upbringing and for serious-minded co-education. There was no innate intellectual difference between the sexes: both could be taught to reason abstractly. . . . Wollstonecraft paid her predecessor a handsome tribute: 'the woman of the greatest abilities that this country has ever produced.'"[27]

Although Macaulay and Wollstonecraft are close in argument in many ways, two outstanding differences surface. Macaulay is more concerned to

make a catalog of social ills that have befallen women due to the fact of superior male physical strength, and she also has no difficulty in citing a number of societies, including Asian societies, the specifics of which seem to bear
out her case.[28] Wollstonecraft's arguments are simultaneously more general
and more passionate; it probably is accurate to say that the second *Vindication* is not as carefully constructed as *Letters on Education.* In addition, *Letters*
is at least implicitly tied to other social issues, such as slavery.[29] In any case,
that Macaulay's work made a lasting impression on Wollstonecraft is beyond
dispute; she is one of the few female figures of the period approximating her
own who receives a positive citation in her work, with the *Vindication*'s author characterizing her as a thinker who "possess[es] more penetration than
sagacity, more understanding than fancy, [and who] writes with sober energy
and argumentative closeness."[30]

Because it is clear that Wollstonecraft's time in France so deeply affected
her—she witnessed the march of Louis XVI on the way to his execution, and
it was in France that she met Gilbert Imlay—it can also be said that a natural
comparison occurs between the writings of Wollstonecraft and those of Edmund Burke.[31] Interestingly enough, although Burke had once been rather a
liberal, defending the American Revolution and from time to time attacking
the power of the British throne, the excesses of the French Revolution apparently caused a great change of heart. In any case, he is today largely remembered for his classic political work, *Reflections on the Revolution in France.*[32]

In a sense, both Burke and Wollstonecraft are consequentialists. Both are
concerned about the ends that certain social institutions will allow for; they
differ, of course, on what institutions will best attain those ends. Burke actually wrote his *Reflections* before the Reign of Terror, but the treatment accorded Louis XVI and Marie Antoinette he finds abhorrent, and he has no difficulty in articulating the point that it represents the worst excesses of a
society gone wild. Wollstonecraft's first *Vindication, A Vindication of the Rights
of Men* was, of course, a response to Burke's work. The tie-in between the two
Vindications is perhaps best expressed as having to do not only with rights but
with the uses that an individual makes of such rights. As she will later go on
to argue in the second *Vindication,* Wollstonecraft sees around her a number
of persons whose time, energy, and knowledge are spent on what she sees as
useless and frivolous pursuits, unproductive of the larger social good and in-
imical to society as a whole.

One of the best known passages from Burke's *Reflections* considers the
treatment accorded the hapless Marie Antoinette. He had written, "I thought
ten thousand swords must have leaped from their scabbards to avenge even a

look that threatened her with insult."[33] The implied status of women is easy to discern; upper-class and aristocratic women are there, so to speak, for the gratification of men, the occasional gallantry, and some sort of decoration. Other women—those too poor to have the requisite social standing, to have received any education, or to make their way in the world by any socially acceptable means—are beneath contempt. The same Burke who wanted to go to the defense of Marie Antoinette calls the women who marched en masse to Versailles in 1789 "the vilest of women."[34]

Burke's conception of a social structure rests on two important features that buttress and support each other: social class distinctions, hierarchically ordered from the aristocracy to a sort of unmentionable bottom, and gender distinctions that parallel the social ones, except for the fact that, at each notch on the ladder, women always take a second place to men. The "vilest of women" had no more say in their homes than Marie Antoinette and her peers had in theirs.

All that we know about the French Revolution strongly suggests that women were at the forefront of its key activities. The women who shouted "Du pain ou la mort" or "A bas à Monsieur le Véto" were expressing the desire for the kind of freedom that Wollstonecraft articulates in her work.[35] In Wollstonecraft's somewhat rarefied London world—at least insofar as her contacts were concerned—the initial concerns of the French must have seemed far away. But the response of someone like Burke indicated that the French Revolution had terrifying consequences: the possibility of a genuine leveling, the freeing of class strictures, and an overturning of the social structure. Wollstonecraft's work not only attacks Burke and furthers concerns that had originally been Macaulay's; it does so in a new way. The difference, as I have stated before, is in the passion. The *Vindications* were written before Mary went to France, but the fuel that fired them did indeed have revolutionary origins.

Wollstonecraft's work on women revolves around one contention, a contention that Burke would not have applauded. She sees women as possessing, by nature, the same sorts of intellectual capacities and strengths of reason that men have. Thus she cannot accept a social structure that will deny them access to the level of education to which men are entitled. Burke refuses to address the key question: what separates Marie Antoinette and the Princesse de Lamballe from the *poissardes* and the women who marched to Versailles? In a phrase, birth: social class and education are the barriers here, but in a society in which the privileges of birth are taken for granted, little movement can be made.

Burke is wrong, then, about the defense of Marie Antoinette. The "ten thousand swords" are not merited—not even so much because of any personal failings that the queen may have had, but because Burke and others like him see deference as owed to her because of her birth. In the new century, views such as Burke's would change throughout Europe.

Feminism and Politics

In Wollstonecraft's case, we have no difficulty drawing the tie to feminist theory; indeed, her work is a staple of women's studies courses and is regularly cited in any work on the history of women and women's thought.[36] Because her work so clearly forwards feminist concerns, it might naively be thought that there are few tensions within it, and that Wollstonecraft's work, at least, is comparatively unproblematized.

It is somewhat easier to write of Wollstonecraft and feminist theory than it has been to write of any of the other thinkers I have examined so far with respect to feminist thought. But there are at least two areas of tension in her work: she is a great proponent of rational control, an outstanding theme of the second *Vindication,* and she also is an acceptor of women's familial duties. Given the time period in which she wrote, the second of these gray areas is not such a problem—we can accept a certain necessity for theorizing within the context of domesticity, simply because she is writing at the start of the Industrial Revolution and before the enormous changes in women's social status and employment patterns that spring from it. The first area, however, remains a concern.

Catriona Mackenzie has extensively addressed the tension of passionate commitment, on the one hand, and rational control, on the other, in her essay on Wollstonecraft reprinted in *Hypatia's Daughters.*[37] It is not simply a question of the fact that Wollstonecraft frequently failed to exhibit such control in her personal life, her sad relationship with Imlay being a case in point. Rather, it is clear that in some sense Wollstonecraft sees that the passions do have a place in women's lived lives; she simply experiences tension in trying to establish what that place might rightfully be.

Mackenzie sees Wollstonecraft as moving back and forth on these issues in the second *Vindication.* While in general women ought to keep the passions and bodily desires under control, it is equally clear that the passionate attachments of women to home and family are the very emotional facts that yield much of Wollstonecraft's argument. As Mackenzie states, the complexity of the situation is such that every statement about Wollstonecraft's position on the passions must be at least qualified:

[There are indications] that Wollstonecraft's apparent devaluation of passion stems from a number of sources. As I argued above, it must be seen, in the context of Wollstonecraft's defense of equality and of women's capacity to reason, as a counter to the Rousseauian depiction of "feminine" virtue. But Wollstonecraft's anxiety about passion is also a response to a social situation that denied to women the scope for expressing desire and passion and hence gave rise to devastating conflicts between reason and sensibility.[38]

Here Mackenzie has spelled out the key problem: in a more just society, one that gives free rein to women's intellect, there might also be room for women's passion. And the emotional lives of women, at least with some moderate governance, are, in some sense, crucial aspects of women's being.

It is because her stance, even with its complexities, is so critical to future developments in feminism that Wollstonecraft is often cited, along with the Mills, as the forerunner of what today is known as "liberal feminism." Without making advertence to any of the lines of thought that will predominate in social philosophy during the nineteenth century—pre-Marxist lines, or even arguments echoing Saint-Simon—Wollstonecraft has caught on to a powerful issue: women have special capacities, at least to some extent, and we have seen these capacities used in their roles as wives and mothers. But what we have not seen, to date, according to Wollstonecraft's analysis, is an attempt at a level of education for women that would allow them to achieve any of their abilities to the fullest, even though it may well be conceded that some of these abilities will still revolve around gender-linked constructs. Alison Jaggar, for one, in her *Feminist Politics and Human Nature,* sees how special Wollstonecraft's place in the history of feminism truly is: "Systematic investigation of the effects of social influences on cognitive and emotional development has shown how well-founded were the speculations by Wollstonecraft and Mill on the way in which women's upbringing discouraged them from developing their full capacity for reason. . . . Wollstonecraft's vision still inspires many contemporary liberal feminists."[39]

If, as we have claimed, there remains a tension in Wollstonecraft with respect to the role of the passions, part of the historical record here may be relevant. Not only was Mary Wollstonecraft the self-made daughter of a father who lost a great deal of his own money, and not only was she tempestuous in her personal life; as we have said she lived through tempestuous times. Levy and Applewhite describe the activities of women in the French Revolution, activities that, of course, were reported in Great Britain and about which Wollstonecraft would have heard. According to Levy and Applewhite,

On October 5 [1789] many women gathered at the Hotel de Ville, armed themselves, and exhorted the National Guard to march with them to the king's
palace at Versailles. Seven thousand strong, the women, accompanied by a
contingent of guardsmen, marched to Versailles, confronted the National As-
sembly and the king with demands for bread and security for Paris. . . . After
some hours of hesitation, the king finally accepted the Declaration of Rights
and agreed to guarantee subsistence to Paris. . . . After a restless night, the
crowds invaded the Palace of Versailles and clashed with soldiers defending
the king. Both sides suffered casualties, and enraged crowds of Parisians de-
capitated two royal guardsmen and mounted their heads on pikes.[40]

We can see what drove Wollstonecraft—the same energy that the seven
thousand women who shouted for bread displayed in the Revolution (and
the same energy that countless women known to Wollstonecraft expended
on their toiletry) could be put to a social use, especially if it were channeled
and if at least some of it were tempered by formal education.

Thus the apparent paradox may be simply that: apparent. Wollstonecraft, like Rousseau, is willing to concede that, in general, roles for women
will be different than those for men. But what she is unwilling to see is an
abridgment of women's fundamental rights as human beings.

Although we can easily categorize Wollstonecraft as a precursor to today's
"liberal feminism," her work is more than that. With the current emphasis on
what Marks and De Courtivron have called the "new French feminisms," a
great deal of Wollstonecraft's passion-driven conceptualization meshes nicely
with, for example, the work of Cixous. In "The Laugh of the Medusa," Cixous
is trying to make the point that semiotics in general has excluded women because it is phallocentric. Women's writing, she declares, is "woman writing
herself"; Cixous claims that "[w]oman must put herself into the text—as into
the world and into history—by her own movement."[41] Not only has Wollstonecraft herself done this, in all of her texts, but she clearly is recommend-
ing a sort of eighteenth-century version of the same thing for women of her
time.

Although it is hard to make out the sorts of straightforward class concerns
in Wollstonecraft's work that will later dominate much of nineteenth-century
thought, there is no question that she is, indeed, sensitive to class. It is precisely for these reasons that she attacks Burke on his "vilest of women," and
that she is aware of the ludicrousness of attempting to vindicate the conduct,
in large, of Marie Antoinette and others of her class. Perhaps the clearest analysis here would be to say that Wollstonecraft needs to separate out gender, as
she is doing, before she can come to any other kind of analysis (and, of course,

she did not live to be able to do this). But her work paves the way for such an analysis, because she does understand the difference that class makes.

Feminists have little problem today accepting Wollstonecraft's work as one of the first extant pieces of feminist theory, especially in political thought, and the easy meshing of her work with the writing that comes later should be a cause for celebration. Chronology probably has a great deal to do with this—Wollstonecraft is writing at the very beginning of the Industrial Revolution, and she is certainly working during a period that is already beginning to be dominated by Enlightenment thought. But we can examine her work through a number of philosophical lenses. In the next section, I will look at her work through the time-honored prism of theory of knowledge.

Politics and Epistemology

Mary Wollstonecraft seems to write, as did Astell to some extent, with a rationalist bent toward metaphysics (insofar as we can make it out) and an empiricist bent toward social matters. She is an astute observer of the social situation, and it is her observations that drive her to her conclusions. In the second *Vindication,* for example, she notes: "Pleasure is the business of woman's life, according to the present modification of society, and while it continues to be so, little can be expected from such weak beings. Inheriting, in a lineal descent from the first fair defect in nature, the sovereignty of beauty, they have, to maintain their power, resigned the natural rights, which the exercise of reason might have procured them, and chosen rather to be short-lived queens than labour to obtain the sober pleasures that arise from equality."[42]

Remarks such as these spring directly from Wollstonecraft's experiences in London; she sees the problem as stemming from both the social structure that she has seen around her and women's responses to it.

In contemporary terms, as I have asserted earlier, a great deal of what Wollstonecraft wrote falls more under the rubric of "liberal feminism," or even "feminist empiricism," than it does any of the other labels that are often employed in feminist epistemology. But those thinkers who have pointed out the differences that advertence to Marxist theory makes in terms of theory of knowledge have hit at an important problem, and in Wollstonecraft's case it is intriguing to think what kinds of differences would have occurred in her thought if she had had some exposure to theory that came just a little bit later.

In her often-cited work on feminism and political theory, Alison Jaggar makes crucial distinctions between the types of feminism (nonsocialist) that do not allude to Marxist interpretations of class structure and those that do. The tie-in for epistemology, of course, is that a more strongly class-oriented theory would be one that would allow for the development of a standpoint epistemology. It would be unfair to say that Wollstonecraft is headed in this direction, for much of what she says (as can be seen from the quotation above) more properly applies to women of the upper social classes. Nevertheless, we can extrapolate from Wollstonecraft's note on Burke's "vilest of women": what becomes of theory when it is seen from the point of view of those women who are at the bottom?

Introducing the notion of a Marxist take on epistemology and what that might mean for feminist theory, Jaggar writes:

> Other versions of feminism do not claim to be more objective than liberal feminism in the liberal/positivist sense of objectivity. Instead, they challenge precisely the conception of objectivity that liberals take as a primary condition of theoretical adequacy. . . . The Marxist conception of knowledge challenges two basic assumptions of liberal epistemology. First, since praxis is necessarily a social activity, it challenges the view that knowledge can be the achievement of a single isolated individual. Instead, Marxism views knowledge as socially constructed and the expansion of knowledge as a social project.[43]

This take on what will be called by feminist epistemologists "standpoint theory" helps us get a handle on what Wollstonecraft could have done. "Pleasure is the business of woman's life," of course, only for those women who have the time and leisure to pursue such matters, as Wollstonecraft well knew.[44] The vile women who marched to Versailles did not have time for pleasure. Thus, a different sort of epistemological stance—one that could only have come later, in all fairness—would have Wollstonecraft focusing more on women at the bottom, and it would alter her rights-driven conception of what women can and cannot do. For such theorizing would push the second *Vindication* beyond its somewhat liberal bias into a more general, class-driven account of what was wrong with European societies, while at the same time it would give her greater insight into the kinds of work—messy work at that—generally performed by most women.

Wollstonecraft focuses comparatively little on caretaking, cleaning, and so forth, because she wants to develop a view that will not need to make use of those activities. But the concerns of hunger, shortages, and concomitant degradation that drove the women of France's lower classes to the palace must, in the clearest sort of analysis, come before a concern about liberal rights.

Virginia Muller is a theorist trained as a political scientist who is sympathetic to Wollstonecraft's attempts to deal with a number of issues, even if those attempts fall somewhat short. Like some of Wollstonecraft's other commentators, she sees a tension in the work, but Muller sees the tension as being located not so much in an account of reason versus the passions as in the matters I have been addressing here, the difference between an account that would take more note of social class, and hence be more tied to what will later be called standpoint theory, and one that does not. But Muller also agrees that the time simply was not right for any attempt at an account that would be more thoroughgoing; it would not have been possible for Wollstonecraft to write such an account.[45]

Muller's view can be instructive, for it assists us in coming to grips with what we may be tempted to see as flaws in Wollstonecraft's work. As I have indicated, Wollstonecraft does allude to social class—she simply does not do so very often, and most of the second *Vindication* relies for its account of woman's degradation on the victimization of middle-class women and women of leisure. Muller summarizes the force of Wollstonecraft's analysis, flawed though it may be, in the following: "Even a cursory reading of *Rights of Woman* shows a provocative recognition of class interests as one component of a revolutionary social theory. However, class warfare was not Wollstonecraft's goal; her self-chosen task was to encourage the emancipation of women. Hence, her analysis of economic forces on the status of women is more explicit than her treatment of class. In the end, she remained a classical liberal who championed and trusted individuals and individual virtue, not governments."[46]

Still, not all commentators are as pleased with Muller's moderate appraisal, and work continues to be done that faults Wollstonecraft for not developing a viewpoint that, cognizant of women's immersion in labor and of the ties between women and other oppressed groups, can be identified as standpoint work. Moira Ferguson has a sparkling piece on Wollstonecraft's notice of the slave trade and its relevance to work that she could have done, but again Ferguson is more critical than complimentary in her remarks, and at times she attacks Wollstonecraft with alacrity. She claims that Wollstonecraft's "bourgeois individualism" prevents certain insights; she also notes that at a point in the text where Wollstonecraft has written of women of more than one phenotype, "slippage and connection between black and white women reopen a fissure of sorts for comparing overlapping oppressions," a comparison that Wollstonecraft does not really make.[47]

If most of Wollstonecraft's work, in terms of contemporary feminist epistemology, is best described as a sort of liberal feminism/feminist empiricism with at least the potential for development along the lines of women's stand-point, it is important to see why Wollstonecraft's commentators sometimes become frustrated. At tantalizing points in the text, Wollstonecraft provides what appears to be a recension of important issues and then drops them. This occurs so frequently in the second *Vindication* that Ferguson writes of "tex-tual implosions."[48] The various chapters or sections of the second *Vindication* have provocative headings; chapter 4 is entitled "Observations on the state of degradation to which woman is reduced by various causes."[49] Toward the end of that chapter, after approximately twenty pages on the wasted time and effort of middle-class women who are concerned with their appearance, the creation of a sense of allure, and so forth, Wollstonecraft writes: "With re-spect to virtue, to use the word in a comprehensive sense, I have seen most in low life. Many poor women maintain their children by the sweat of their brow. . . . [G]entlewomen are too indolent to be actively virtuous, and are softened rather than refined by civilization."[50]

These are the sorts of lines that seem to cry out for further analysis, but in general that analysis does not appear. However, a generous assessment of what Wollstonecraft has done—such as the one made by Muller—shows her to be the forerunner of a number of other theoreticians who will push work in new directions. It is clear that Wollstonecraft does indeed believe that "virtue" has something to do with both mental and physical activity, and she can see that the "sweat of their brow" is directly related to the virtue of "poor women." But the time is not yet ripe for a fuller analysis, and, ultimately, this failure to push in a direction that will move beyond a sort of nascent liberal feminism may itself be related to the French Revolution. The same Mary Wollstonecraft who had originally, like many English radicals, been so en-amored of the changes in France was struck by the appearance of the king on his way to execution. The realities of revolution are never pleasant; Woll-stonecraft's time in France seemed to at least alter some of her stronger con-victions. The chaos and violence that she saw may have kept her from spend-ing more time in an analysis of the poverty-stricken classes, since they were clearly those who would benefit the most from revolution. Nevertheless, in her candid broaching of a number of difficult issues, Wollstonecraft shows herself to be far ahead of her time.

Projecting Forward

Superficially, Wollstonecraft seems like the ideal candidate for a woman thinker from the past whose work might be amenable to use by third-wave feminists, postfeminists, and post-postfeminists. Less facetiously, however, although it is probably accurate to say that we do not find the degree of tension in Wollstonecraft's work that we do, say, in Astell's, the problematic here is that which I have already alluded to: Wollstonecraft's feminism is a precursor of the liberal feminism of those whose desire is more for inclusion than for radical change.

As has been indicated in my work taken from Jaggar, many parts of more radical feminism owe a great debt to Marx: not only redistribution is at issue, but the notion of a division of labor, and the notion of reproductive labor as defining a space for epistemic stances. To recapitulate, Wollstonecraft wrote at a sufficiently early stage in the Industrial Revolution that these sorts of insights would scarcely have been available to her in any case, even if we can hypothesize that she might have been inclined to value them.

The question, then, is how much work we can still do with Wollstonecraft to push us in the direction of accepting her thinking in a less essentialist and more ironic time. The answer, it appears, is a great deal. As Moira Ferguson has noted, we can emphasize and valorize those portions of her work that speak to notions of slavery both actual and metaphorical, and that at least advert to the existence of women of color. Carol Poston has found still other areas in Wollstonecraft's work that speak to contemporary issues in a new-wave vein. Poston hears in the writings of Mary Wollstonecraft the voice of one who has been the victim of extensive childhood abuse, possibly even sexual abuse.[51] Poston writes: "I believe that Wollstonecraft is speaking [of abuse] . . . not necessarily sexual (although that is quite possible) but certainly emotional and physical. Childhood abuse is the text underlying the language that can seem so critical or confusing to readers who perhaps have not themselves been abused as children."[52]

Poston bases much of her insight that Wollstonecraft was a probable victim of abuse on what she knows of her family background (a brutally alcoholic father), the simultaneous interest in and divorcing from the passions that appears in the text—something noticed by many other commentators, including Mackenzie—and the evident concern in the text about "tyrants and sensualists."[53] Perhaps most important, and poignant, a great deal of the material that we have from either Godwin or Wollstonecraft about their brief marriage indicates that, pleasurable as Wollstonecraft found her relationship with Godwin, parts of it were unutterably painful for her because, as she said, "I am afraid to trace emotions to their source."[54]

If Poston's surmisals and argument are accurate, then Wollstonecraft's work, among that which we have examined so far, is probably the most *au courant* and constitutes the one body of work with which we have to struggle the least. Wollstonecraft is, without too much of the forcedness that we sometimes feel when dealing with Continental theory, actually concerned with the body politic, in the same sort of way that we saw earlier in Canto's commentary on Plato. Mary Wollstonecraft sees girls and women as victims of educational neglect, generally frivolous attitudes, and, most serious, brutal and tyrannical behavior. The decorated body—the body that serves simply as an adornment—is also the objectified body and later becomes the traumatized body. But if the body politic insists on neglecting or ignoring these bodies, it, too, becomes traumatized. It is injured in the sense that it cannot attain its highest level, or hope to flourish in the way that human societies can. Recognition of the rights of women means an alteration in the body politic, and, hopefully, in female bodies and female lives as they are actually lived.

Because of Wollstonecraft's awareness of what sexual pleasure could bring—an awareness that was probably heightened by the suddenness of her relationship with Godwin, coming as it did hard on the heels of her disastrous involvement with Imlay—she understands better than most women thinkers of her time that a certain health is the offshoot of a balanced life, one encompassing thought, the passions, and bodily pleasures. But it is precisely because so few women have been able to experience this health that a general illness pervades society as a whole, one that could be at least partially remedied by making use of the talents of healthy women. The objectification of women further encourages the worst passions of men and leads them to believe that, as a result of what they see around them, they are justified in the infliction of misery that they so readily pursue. A more just situation for women might possibly have the side benefit that it would alter the behavior of men.

A renewed awareness of and appreciation for Wollstonecraft's attitudes toward the body and bodily pleasures is brought to us in the opening chapters of Miranda Seymour's insightful biography of Mary Shelley.[55] Although Godwin's memoirs apparently did a great deal of harm to Wollstonecraft's reputation in the years immediately after her death, when read now they provide us with much information that speaks to contemporary issues. Because the changes that erotic love can bring are so important—and because they speak to issues of the body in ways that cannot be denied—it is worth citing Seymour at some length here:

> But under the spell of love [Godwin later wrote], her whole nature was transformed. In unmistakably sexual imagery, he compared her to a serpent on a rock which had sloughed its old skin to display the brilliant sleekness of youth.

Here, and in the description which follows, we are seeing not Imlay's Mary, but Godwin's.

> She was playful, full of confidence, kindness and sympathy. Her eyes as-
> sumed new lustre, and her cheeks new colour and smoothness. Her
> voice became chearful; her temper overflowing with universal kindness;
> and that smile of bewitching tenderness from day to day illuminating
> her countenance, which all who knew her will so well recollect, and
> which won, both heart and soul, the affection of almost everyone that
> beheld it.[56]

This change in Wollstonecraft represents a change that is based on the notion of a woman fulfilled—sexually, intellectually, emotionally, and in virtually every way that might be meaningful to categorize. It is not inappropriate to think that this was what Wollstonecraft had in mind for most women; the possibility of a satisfying life is almost always there but requires certain conditions in order to instantiate it. One of the requisite conditions is that sexuality cannot be impeded by a narrow view of women's functioning. And, of course, it goes without saying that the companionship that a woman might require for intellectual and emotional growth is not readily available in a society in which women are seen as less than fully human.

Wollstonecraft's vision of a society in which rights are accorded to women is in some ways substantially ahead of her time, and in other ways not. But the written work, the second *Vindication,* is, fortunately, only one of the many indications that we have of what Wollstonecraft felt and thought. It is not only her other written works that assist us here; as Seymour and others have shown, it is her life. Godwin, with his astonishing frankness, recounted these details in work published a comparatively short time after Wollstonecraft's death, and, unsurprisingly, they were met with scathing attacks on "wantonness."[57] But although we can surmise that some of these attacks were related to the recounting of the miserable Imlay affair, in which Wollstonecraft was regularly lied to over a course of months, after having borne Imlay a child, some of the rest of the commentary no doubt is intended to reflect on passages such as those cited above. Apparently a woman's growth, "sleekness," "confidence," and "bewitching tenderness" were unpalatable if it was believed that such alteration had anything to do with physical sex. But of course it did; as Seymour notes, when she quotes Godwin as having written of the beginning of his relationship with Wollstonecraft as "chez moi, toute," there was no harm in Godwin's having as many affairs as he could manage, given his schedule of literary productivity. The difficulty is in a woman's having had such a relationship.

It is perhaps the final irony, although a not altogether unfitting one, that in contemporary terms many know Wollstonecraft best as the mother of Mary Shelley, given the renewed interest in literary circles in *Frankenstein* and the multiple readings that have been given to the text. We cannot know what effect hearing of the death of her mother in childbirth had on the young Mary Shelley, and it is not easy to construct a relationship between that knowledge and portions of the novel she later wrote. But what the mother and daughter had in common was a passionate attachment to life. In commencing a relationship with Percy Shelley at a very early age, and leaving home to live abroad with him, Mary Shelley proved herself her mother's daughter. We can hazard the guess that a sort of bewitching temperament, fully capable of being realized, ran in the family.

The View from Somewhere

The particularity of Wollstonecraft's work, and the fact that it lends itself to readings that see it in terms of such rubrics as liberal feminism, means that we can place her work within the Enlightenment framework, even if we choose to make other interpretations of it. Wollstonecraft had the advantage, from our point of view, of writing approximately a hundred years later than Astell, and much later, of course, than either of the other two women thinkers whose work I have already examined. By the time she writes, the combination of philosophical and literary maneuvers that underlay the French Revolution (or the American Revolution) had already taken place.

Such changes of necessity led to powerful alterations in the lives of intellectuals in the major European capitals. We have seen how these changes affected Wollstonecraft and Godwin, and they had already affected Wollstonecraft's life well before she met Godwin, since it is clear that the overall direction of her thought—with its emphasis on individual liberties and its passion for experience—had a great deal to do with her pursuit of previous relationships, even if those relationships were ultimately unsuccessful. In a world of new slogans and new freedom (and a world that was unafraid to put to death powerful aristocrats) almost all could be questioned. Mary Wollstonecraft succeeded in doing just that.

Those who see her primarily as an Enlightenment thinker, however, miss a great deal of the point. Following along with Poston and Ferguson, we can see Wollstonecraft pointing in new directions. More important, perhaps, at least a few have read her in such a way that there is a refusal to employ Enlightenment rubrics at all for her work. Catherine Villanueva Gardner is one of those; in a chapter on Wollstonecraft in her *Rediscovering Women Philosophers,* she writes:[58]

> The most immediate point to notice is that the second *Vindication* contains what I shall call Wollstonecraft's "flights of imagination" as well as frequent bursts of dramatic—even apparently rambling—hyperbole. . . . The question of how to deal with this apparent problem no longer seems to be of importance to commentators. . . . Yet I think that if we choose to ignore these apparent problems of the style and form of the second *Vindication* . . . we are treating them as accidental to the content of Wollstonecraft's work. . . . Moreover, as we shall see, a neglect (no matter how well intentioned) of the stylistic characteristics peculiar to the second *Vindication* would prevent us from a potentially productive lens through which we can analyze Wollstonecraft's work, and in particular her moral thought.[59]

In other words, Gardner is arguing that the apparent "rambling" of the second *Vindication* is not accidental—it represents that uniting of passion and reason that Wollstonecraft herself wants to press upon us as some kind of goal. Threads of both reason and emotion, drawn from her own life and her observations of the lives of others, informed Wollstonecraft's work, and left us with writing that is peculiarly adaptable to our time and our concerns.

Perhaps the greatest tension in Wollstonecraft's work, and one that I have examined here at several points, is the extent to which the feminism that she espouses might best be thought of as simply a liberal feminism, without any admixture of more gendered or radicalized lines of thought. I have gone at this problem from two points: I have briefly discussed the sometimes hesitant sensitivity to social class that is nevertheless present in Wollstonecraft's work, and which might allow us to see her as a forerunner of thought that later becomes overtly socialist or even Marxist. But perhaps more crucial to feminist theory is the extent to which we can think of her feminism as gendered. As has been indicated in my citation of Poston, a concern for the body manifests itself at many points, and in ways that we might think of as contemporary, and, indeed, even postmodern. But intersecting Gardner and Poston, as it were, and bearing in mind that Mackenzie is also concerned about the extent of passion in both Wollstonecraft's life and thought, the most interesting assertion that I can make is that Mary Wollstonecraft seems indeed to be taking a gendered stance. In other words, contra the most fundamental lines of liberal feminism, Wollstonecraft appears to posit somewhat differing natures for male and female rationality, and even appears to be hopeful that, were her educational projects and hopes to come to fruition, they would manifest themselves in new styles of reasoning and growth for women that might affect women, men, and children alike.

Jaggar explicates the most basic sort of liberal feminism with the following gloss:

> [In the liberal feminist ideal society] there would not be the current extreme contrast between logical, independent, aggressive, courageous, insensitive and emotionally inexpressive men and intuitive, dependent, compassionate, nurturant, and emotional women. Boys and girls would receive the same educational opportunities and no attempt would be made to impose those character traits that are considered traditionally to be masculine or feminine. Instead, every individual would be free to develop, in any combination, any psychological qualities or virtues.[60]

But this view—the classic view, perhaps—runs contra contemporary views that either push in the direction of a Gilligan- or Chodorow-type of genderedness or, still more radically, opt for a separatist/lesbian feminism that sees the potential for groups that are extremely gynocentric in structure and style. It is important to note the contrast here: under the paradigmatic formulation of liberal feminism presented by Jaggar, it apparently would make no difference if a group, organization, or society were composed largely or even entirely of women, since women, with educational and other opportunities similar to those possessed by men, would not necessarily develop in different ways. Under a view such as those associated with Gilligan and her coworkers, it would make a difference, and it most certainly would make a difference to almost all of those who espouse separatism for "womyn," since presumably they would not espouse such separatism if they did not think that males, by and large, add something to societies or groups with their presence that women, in general, would not.

If it is going too far to see the beginnings of a gender-driven theoretical construct in Wollstonecraft, it is not going too far to point out the importance to her of passionate commitment, and I have examined this with the help of commentary from several authors. Wollstonecraft's point of departure, as I said at the outset, is that a divine being would not have created individuals with rationality if it was not intended that the capacity for rational thought be used. If such capacities were employed, one of the upshots would be that women would be better able to discharge their duties as wives and mothers. This point recurs throughout the second *Vindication;* Wollstonecraft says toward the end that "[a]s the rearing of children . . . has justly been insisted on as the peculiar destination of woman, the ignorance that incapacitates them must be contrary to the order of things."[61]

If that passionate commitment should unfortunately be put to base uses, then all sorts of wrongs arise—for the individual woman in question, and for society as a whole. In *Maria, or the Wrongs of Woman,* Wollstonecraft shows us that emotional attachment turned toward other objects, and deflected from its true course by male domination and circumstance: "How grateful was her attention to Maria! Oppressed by a dead weight of existence, or preyed on by the gnawing worm of discontent, with what eagerness did she endeavor to shorten the long days, which left no traces behind! She seemed to be sailing on the vast ocean of life, without seeing any land-mark to indicate the progress of time; to find employment was then to find variety, the animating principle of nature."[62]

Maria lacks the freedom, the education, and that important concomitant of education, direction, to alter her life. It is ironic, then, that Wollstonecraft's own life took its apparent shape and direction, at least insofar as personal relationships were concerned, shortly before she died. Whatever the defects of her life with Godwin, they apparently were few in comparison with the admittedly miserable circumstances of her previous affairs. Godwin displays an admirable ability to discern what is important in relations between men and women in the remarks that he composed as a preface to *Maria* once it was published posthumously. He claims that the sentiments of *Maria,* if instantiated, "would perhaps have given a new impulse to the manners of the world."[63]

Miranda Seymour closes the second chapter of her work on Mary Shelley, in which she describes Mary Wollstonecraft's death, by noting that young Mary knew nothing of hostility toward her mother: "Her mother was spoken of with a love amounting to veneration by her father."[64] In this relationship, then, Mary Wollstonecraft finally saw passion and intelligence united.

PART TWO Later Women Philosophers

HARRIET TAYLOR MILL five

In the process of beginning to work on Harriet Taylor Mill (1807–58) as a thinker, we need to remember not only the details of her personal life, but the time in which she lived and wrote. Insofar as political and social philosophy were concerned, this was a period dominated by Bentham's utilitarianism and the economics of Ricardo (the latter, work that John Stuart Mill [JSM] did a great deal to both promulgate and criticize).

The goal of the utilitarians was a simple one: to promote a better society. Although it might be objected that this had been the goal of almost all previous thinkers who troubled themselves with political and social questions, the followers of Bentham, at least, were much more specific about the instantiation of these goals than many other thinkers had been. At the same time, they were somewhat less utopian. Driven by the work of Adam Smith and by Britain's rise as an industrial and colonial power, they knew better than to theorize in Saint-Simonian terms.

Harriet Taylor Mill (HTM) was herself greatly affected by these thinkers, for their work was frequently discussed in intellectual circles, and even during her first marriage, to John Taylor, HTM must have encountered references to this sort of theory on more than one occasion.[1] From the start—and before she met JSM—HTM was concerned with individual liberty, the notion of a life well lived, and that concept that was to become central at a later point to the work they jointly produced, the idea of a life lived within the constraints of the greatest amount of personal liberty compatible with a similar amount of liberty for others.[2] Harriet was deeply concerned with these issues, and they appear in her earliest writings. Remembering that documents written during 1831–32 may or may not reflect the influence of JSM (she had just met him, and was pregnant with her third child, Helen, who was born in July 1831), we can assume that what they do represent is a chain of long-standing interests of Harriet's that came to the fore later in their relationship. For example, of this period Jo Ellen Jacobs writes:

> Number 2 [the second piece in the relevant Jacobs chapter, which Jacobs has called "Sources of Conformity"] is Harriet Taylor Mill's study of the source of intolerance, namely conformity, and the corresponding need for self-reliance. Harriet claims that conformity is the opposite of acting on principle (defined as the "accordance of a person's conduct with self-formed opinion") and that eccentricity is prima facie evidence of principle. Many will, no doubt, recognize in this second essay elements foreshadowing the discussion of eccentricity in *On Liberty,* written more than twenty years later.[3]

We can, of course, infer that this concern with "self-formed opinion" is a long-standing interest of Harriet's, and, more to the point, that it probably had something to do with her discomfort in her marriage. But in any case, a society that aimed at the best life for its citizens might well be more tolerant of such virtues as self-reliance and a certain sort of eccentricity, since they signal a well-planned and reflective life.

In a similar vein, HTM undertook a series of brief essays on marriage and women's rights, again in 1831 and again shortly after or around the time of her first acquaintance with JSM.[4] As she wrote in a piece that the editor refers to as "The Nature of the Marriage Contract," "I do not know what the *means* of advancing my opinions about 'marriage' should be— . . . how I should commence the steps which should prepare [society] to receive the ultimate opinion that all restraint or interference whatever with affection . . . is perfectly unwarrantable."[5]

The importance of the individual, the individual's thought processes, and the extent to which those processes shape a person's life—to some extent, independent of external circumstance—is a recurring theme in HTM's poetry, some of which was composed and submitted for publication before her relationship with JSM. A number of works ("The Seasons," "Daybreak") indicate that the importance of the emotional effect of the season in question is largely dictated by the individual's emotional response to it: autumn need not be a cause for sorrow, and so forth. Although we might be tempted to think that this kind of sentiment is commonplace, the first drafts of these poems were written when Harriet was in her late teens and early twenties. This work clearly represents her own thought, and the independence of the individual in a society not framed to value that independence, particularly for women, is of paramount concern to her.

What can be said, then, is that John Stuart Mill met a woman whose mind had long since begun to run in the same course. What transpired during the very earliest portion of their relationship we cannot know: as Jacobs has indicated, no letters from this period survive.[6] What we do know is that, in general, commentators until recently have placed a negative interpretation on the relationship and have felt that Mill greatly exaggerated Harriet Taylor's importance as an original thinker. The tide has begun to turn, however. Further scholarship has revealed the extent to which many important ideas did originate with Harriet, even if only in nascent form, and, perhaps more important, it has begun to reveal the extent to which hundreds of hours of devoted conversation can make a difference in anyone's thought patterns.

Alan Ryan, a commentator whom we can scarcely categorize as sympathetic to feminist lines of argument, devotes a section of his introduction to the Norton Critical Edition of Mill to Harriet Taylor Mill.[7] Although he feels, as many do, that Mill consistently overestimated Harriet Taylor's intellectual abilities, he has little doubt about the importance of their relationship to Mill. He writes:

> If Mill said too little about the effect on his mental development of his occupation at India House, he said perhaps too much about the greatest influence on his life—or perhaps the greatest after his father. He met Harriet Taylor in 1830; he was twenty-four and so was she. She had married young, found her husband dull, had found childbirth extremely unpleasant, and therefore found the rarified charms of Mill's intelligence irresistible. . . . What Mrs. Taylor got from Mill was not only adulation; she was a very intelligent and attractive woman and might have had any amount of adulation had she sought it.[8]

Although these comments might be thought to fall under the rubric "damning with faint praise," they are among the more charitable remarks that Mill commentators have made about Harriet Taylor Mill, and Ryan experiences no difficulty in admitting that HTM was "very intelligent." He also indicates that Harriet took the forefront with respect to women's rights and argued more straightforwardly for it, and that the texture of their relationship had a great deal to do with the sections of Mill's writings, *On Liberty* in particular, that strive for tolerance of individual deviation.[9]

Finally, the relationship between Harriet Taylor and John Stuart Mill, especially in its earliest years, might have been a source of gratification for them in more than one way. We know little about HTM's early years, but Mill himself, in striving to explain the coldness of family life that he, especially, experienced at an early age, cites the British family structure as often lacking in warmth and affection.[10] It does not take a pronouncedly Freudian outlook to guess that Harriet Taylor and John Stuart Mill were able to provide each other with an affection that not only had been lacking in their adult relationships, but that also was lacking in their childhoods, and in their relationship with their parents.

Thus the young woman who at an early point wrote a brief piece on "our faults of uncharitableness," whose poems showed an affection for what we bring to an event, rather than what we take from it, and who was driven by the idea that society, as a whole, was too intolerant of spirited and nonconforming individuals, made an apt companion for Mill.[11] Her ideas, energy, and spirit must have moved the relationship from an early point, and the constant output of drafts that we have from her indicate that she continued to write voluminously after meeting Mill. As is the case to some extent with Simone de Beauvoir—although certainly Beauvoir has long been better known in her own right—we have difficulty separating HTM from her male partner. In the past, such problematizing of the situation has been understandable, since we did not have an adequate amount of work authored by HTM herself upon which to make a judgment. That is no longer the case, however, and we are now in a position to attempt to see what positions HTM did, in fact, hold, and to be much more precise about the extent of her collaboration with JSM. The teen-aged poet who was interested in seasonal change continued to grow and change throughout her life.

Metaphysics and the Mills

Since so much of what was written by either HTM or JSM had to do with social thought, it is difficult to be precise about theorizing in more standard areas.

We do have in Harriet Taylor Mill's own hand a number of pieces on religious topics, and it is here that we can see the sort of argument against a conforming and rigorous Christianity that we might expect. It is difficult to discern whether HTM intended to be taken as an avowed atheist—probably not. Rather, she is concerned about the shoddiness and feebleness of a number of the standard sorts of arguments that are offered in defense of a Christian deity, particularly a deity possessing the three "omni's": omnipotence, omniscience, and omnipresence. Although Harriet does not specifically address a positive argument for another sort of deity, she is forthright in denouncing the conforming Christian ideas. Her arguments not only repeat more standard lines, such as the argument from the existence of evil, but do so in a novel and forceful way.

In a piece entitled "Enlightened Infidelity," Harriet (and possibly John) describes the following reaction to standard Christian attempts at ontology construction:[12]

> Any one [sic] who considers the course of nature, without the usual predetermination to find all excellent, must see that it has been made, if made at all, by an extremely imperfect being; that it can be accounted for on no theory of a just ruler, unless that ruler is of extremely limited power, and hemmed in by obstacles which he is unable to overcome. Mankind can scarcely chuse to themselves a worse model of conduct than the author of nature. None but a very bad man ever manifested in his conduct such disregards not only of suffering of sentient creatures, but of the commonest principles of justice in the treatment of them, as is manifested by the Creator of the World if we suppose him to be omnipotent.[13]

Here, and throughout this brief piece, two separate strands of argument are apparent: there is every reason to believe that the standard sort of Christian theologizing (the triune deity, the virgin birth, and so forth) is false—and not sustainable by reasoned debate—but there is no reason to think that some other account of the universe involving at least some conception of a deity could not be maintained. The piece, for example, describes the Christian religion as "superstition," but acknowledges the soundness of Hume's *Dialogues,* and also claims that "whether the world has had a creator, is a matter of hypothesis and conjecture."[14]

In other words, what is being attacked is largely the product of church-related doctrine; however, both HTM and, from his commentators and his own published work, JSM are probably best described as agnostics. All sorts of belief systems that might be compatible with a type of theistic belief, however attenuated, are far from being discarded by attacks on the specific beliefs and doctrines of Christianity.

What is also startling about the piece in question, assuming a large part of it to be Harriet's inspiration, is the very stated denunciation of that part of Christian doctrine that is sometimes referred to as "predestination." Shortly after the passage quoted above, the following lines occur: "setting forth the essential wickedness of the character of the Deity, as Christian writers have been forced, often against their own better feelings, to conceive it: the atrocious conception (for example) of a Being who creates on the one hand thousands of millions of sentient creatures foreknowing that they will be sinners, and on the other a hell to torture them eternally for being so."[15]

This specific attack suggests that these are matters about which Harriet had thought a great deal, and fortunately there is independent evidence, again dating from shortly before or around the time of her meeting with JSM, that underscores the nature of her thought. Around 1831, in jotting down a few notes on the subject of "Charlatanism," she had indicated that "the pseudo-religious instance" in its influence "rarely extends above the most fatuous minds";[16] in still another brief piece in her own hand, distinguishing some of the effects of Catholicism from Protestantism, she had noted that Catholicism appeals mainly to the "victims of society," and that "those classes are accordingly its nearly sole supporters and attendants."[17]

Because the beliefs of HTM and JSM are often so close, and because in some cases we have comparatively little in HTM's own hand—and that from a very early date—it is sometimes helpful to attend to commentary on John Stuart Mill for elucidation. Although Alan Millar is writing about JSM alone, he does indicate a set of beliefs that seems to be consistent with what I have just adumbrated here: "Mill [JSM, in 'Theism'] deals in turn with traditional arguments for the existence of God, the attributes of God, and considerations pertaining to immortality. Like Hume, Mill thinks that the best argument for the existence of God does not suffice to make it probable that there is a God as conceived by orthodox natural theology. Unlike Hume, he thinks that the marks of design constitute some, though not particularly strong, evidence that the universe in its present form is the work of an intelligent Creator."[18]

This seems very much consistent with what we can glean from a perusal of "Enlightened Infidelity" and the surrounding brief texts; at one point, Harriet Taylor Mill actually specifically mentions "St. Paul" as having done damage to the moral maxims of the Gospels such that, in the end, they wound up "very much worse than nothing."[19] This particular naming of St. Paul indicates, again, an attack on standard, church-organized theology and Christianity as ordinarily conceived. Although, as indicated, no forward argument is made for any other sort of view of the universe, both of the Mills are writing far enough back in time that the scientific thinking of the twenty-first century, with its notions of accidentality and random fluctuations of quarks, had, of course, not yet taken hold.

It is important to note that HTM apparently thinks that the damage done by standard theology is a good reason for abandoning it. She also has no hesitation in expressing a desire that, if we do indeed have a functioning Christian church, it ought to make inculcation of the virtues one of its tasks. In interesting short pieces, she makes it clear that she thinks that this can happen, but that frequently it does not. Here she goes a bit to the side of standard theological/ontological thinking and focuses mainly on the effects of Protestantism versus Catholicism, insofar as their effects on a community of believers are concerned. In a piece entitled by Jacobs "On Catholicism and Protestantism," HTM writes: "Equality as a principle & feeling can only come from the cultivation of spiritual ideas upon a different basis from what are now called religious doctrines. . . . The object both of Catholicism & of Protestantism is the elevation of the moral nature."[20]

In another brief paragraph, appearing in the text immediately after the section quoted above, she says: "England is the only country where it is universally felt to be an affront to doubt a person's word. I attribute this not so much to Protestantism wh[ich] for ought I know takes no particular note of this virtue, but to the accident of puritanism having adopted this fine principle, the purity and unselfishness of which suited well with the austerity of puritanism."[21]

Although these thoughts are clearly more related to a notion of the ethical, it is also obvious that, insofar as an ontology (especially a Christian ontology) might purport or allege to give us a Divine Instructor, HTM is making the claim that some accounts have succeeded in rendering their concept of such an Instructor more admirable than others. In this sense, and taking these remarks in the context of Harriet's earlier citation of the Argument from Evil, it is clear that her overall thesis is that the metaphysics presented to us by Christianity is, in general, neither coherent nor admirable—and, indeed, neither are its effects.

The style of argumentation here is very similar to some of that which later finds its way into JSM's work on metaphysics and religions. As Millar notes, some of what John Stuart Mill says in "Theism" is simply an argument about what should be the case, given that the Christian account of a Creator is one of omnipotence, omniscience, and omnipresence. Millar states, for example, that "Mill argues not just that the hypothesis of omnipotence is not well supported by evidence. He thinks it is actually inconsistent with known facts. The very marks of design which provide evidence of a Creator testify against the possibility that the Creator is omnipotent. Design is a contrivance."[22]

Analogously, HTM appears to be arguing that the disarray of the church, and its failure to find a unified voice, either with respect to the notion of a Maker, or with respect to moral teachings, tends to undercut any pretensions to a divine origin that the various voices of the Christian church might have.

As is the case with her writings in many areas of endeavor, we must extrapolate a bit in reading Harriet Taylor Mill on metaphysical, ontological, and religious issues because of the brevity of her writing and the fact that a great deal of it was not published in her lifetime. Nevertheless, a striking virtue of Harriet's work is its pithy quality. She is capable of saying a great deal in one sentence; we need to read her every sentence carefully, in order to give her work the justice that is its due.

Evaluating and Value

Harriet and her first husband, John Taylor, had already received a great deal of exposure to Benthamite utilitarian thought well before she met JSM. Thus the "greatest happiness" principle, and various concomitants of it, were already known to her. That she had spent much time thinking about these issues is apparent, again, not only from her early writings, but also from comments made at a much later point by her daughter, Helen Taylor. Addressing her mother's work after her death, Helen Taylor insisted that leading and central ideas of JSM's political and ethical thought, particularly those that appear in *On Liberty,* originated with Harriet Taylor Mill and had been expressed by her, at least in truncated fashion, at a comparatively early point in her life.

While assisting John in developing the variety of utilitarianism for which he is well known, Harriet continued to show an almost obsessive devotion to the concept of personal liberty and to the equally strongly held notion that some of the most virtuous or finely developed personalities were those that demonstrated a disregard for convention and that prized personal liberty above all. The extent to which HTM is, of course, writing about her own life and beliefs is obvious, but it is also clear that she maintained the utmost seriousness about the notion of a civil society learning how to restrain itself so as not to interfere with the liberty of its individual citizens.

The extent to which this is the case is best shown by attempting to draw a line between works done by Harriet early in her life and one of her strongest single accomplishments, the chapter of her own that was included in the later editions of *Principles of Political Economy.*[23] If we attempt to be precise about areas of commonality or golden threads, as it were, one of the strongest seems to be a striking emphasis on personal liberty and personal development throughout these works. Susan Moller Okin has noted, with respect to JSM, that there were times when he seemed to be a "natural rights theorist, rather than a simple utilitarian."[24] One is tempted to say this, of course, because of Mill's focus on the development of the individual, and her or his potential, a focus almost completely missing from the earlier Benthamite utilitarianism.

It is no exaggeration to say that these views are almost directly attributable to Harriet Taylor Mill. They are a persistent theme throughout her works, and they form the focus even of the relevant chapter from the *Principles,* in the sense that HTM is concerned that workers develop themselves as individuals. She sees the development of England in its industrial strength as necessarily giving rise to greater accumulations of capital, but unlike the stated socialists, she still sees room for competition, viewing many workers as functioning best in cooperatives. This spirit of entrepreneurship for the greater good she believes will arise from the larger education of workers, and from their concomitant growing freedom from "old custom" and "mental dullness."[25] To form a fair notion of the importance of this concept of individual growth/personal liberty in HTM's work, it is necessary only to look at one of her early pieces, "Sources of Conformity," and to compare it with the chapter in the *Principles.*[26] In "Sources," HTM notes: "Political conformity . . . [centers in] this one point. . . . [O]n all topics of importance a standard of conformity [is] raised by the indolent minded many and guarded by a fasces of opinion which, though composed individually of the weakest twigs, yet makes up collectively a mass which is not to be resisted with impunity."[27]

In "On the Probable Futurity of the Labouring Classes," chapter 7 of book 4 of the *Principles of Political Economy,* she says: "Whatever advice, exhortation or guidance is held out to the labouring classes, must henceforth be tendered to them as equals, and accepted with their eyes open. . . . There is no reason to believe that prospect as other than hopeful. . . . [T]here is a spontaneous education going on in the minds of the multitude, which may be greatly accelerated and improved by means of artificial aids."[28]

Both of the Mills believed strongly in the education of the individual not only for the improvement of society as a whole, but for the well-being of the individual herself. As a woman cut off from opportunities of formal education in her time, Harriet was keenly aware of how circumstances and public opinion—especially with respect to women, the working classes, and domestics—could combine to create what might at first appear to be an insurmountable set of obstacles, bound together in "fasces" even though composed of "weak twigs." But when other sorts of twigs and branches have been strengthened, they gain the power to throw off some of that stultifying force, and then have their "eyes open." Harriet Taylor Mill was acutely sensitive to the degree of difficulty in opening eyes, and a good deal of the chapter from the *Principles* is a detailed account of, for example, a group of French workingmen who struggled during the period circa 1848 to form a labor organization, to maintain it, and to nurture it to the point where it became profitable enough to support themselves and their families.[29]

Thus HTM felt, as did JSM, that different values could be assigned to different sorts of pleasures, and, of course, that the higher pleasures ought to take precedence in any fully developed human personality. Since these sorts of concerns have been the subject of extensive commentary on John Stuart Mill's own work—and since the "pushpin versus poetry" line is still regularly taught to undergraduates—it might seem unnecessary to belabor the point. But there is every reason to think that for both John Stuart Mill and Harriet Taylor Mill, personal circumstance had a great deal to do with this evaluation of different sorts of pleasures, and still more to do, at least in Harriet's case, with a firm desire to try to see to it that the opportunity to reach for the more elevated pleasure was given to everyone. Those who decry accounts of HTM's involvement in JSM's life and work regularly cite the extraordinarily laudatory passages on Harriet and her thought in Mill's *Autobiography*. Leaving aside spousal concerns (and some scholars seem to have written as if the Mills had never been married, or formally shared a life together), what is noteworthy about what John Stuart Mill does say about the Harriet Taylor whom he first encountered in the early 1830s is the following: "Up to the time when I first saw her, her rich and powerful nature had chiefly unfolded itself according to the received type of feminine genius."[30] Mill was more than cognizant of the truncated life that Harriet Taylor had lived as an intelligent woman in the Britain of her time. The lack of opportunities for her, or for any woman of talent, was due to a societal prejudice, and both Mills became strong advocates for a better society—one that would be comparatively devoid of that sort of prejudice.

Harriet Taylor Mill saw individual courage as a virtue that propelled social growth in more than one way. She first categorized such courage as that which made an individual stand out, so that the viewer or interlocutor would know that the person in question thought independently and had a developed inner life.[31] But in addition, HTM viewed personal courage and nonconformity as a social virtue, because the very presence of an individual with nonconforming traits in the social realm could not help but impress others, even if not always favorably. Finally—and this portion of her thought provides perhaps the greatest area of conceptual difficulty—Harriet believed that in general those who fell under the rubric of "eccentric" or "nonconforming" were indeed those who possessed a capacity for the higher pleasures; she felt this precisely because she saw the British society of her time as slavish to mediocrity, and she had no hesitation in saying so. Still another articulation of her beliefs on this score in "Sources of Conformity" manages to marry several concepts: "What is called the opinion of Society is a phantom power, yet as is often the case with phantoms, of more force over the minds of the unthinking than all the flesh and blood arguments which can be brought to bear against it. It is a combination of many weak, against the few strong; an association of the mentally listless to punish any manifestation of mental independence."[32]

This passage clearly demonstrates that HTM feels that personal courage is needed to go against "Society," that the general state of that society is low indeed, and (by implication) that those who possess the courage to stand against it are moving toward its better future.

The unusual combination of emphasis on personal liberty and social development that is a hallmark of John Stuart Mill's thought, and for which he is justly famous, is found at an early point in the writing of Harriet Taylor Mill. In her developed work, such as the chapter from *Principles of Political Economy,* she takes the qualities that she had already described years before and attributes them to a group of French workers who succeeded in forming a viable cooperative. In doing so, she provides us with a social model that, as she says, could indeed be the "futurity" of the laboring classes.

A Network of Thinkers

Before Harriet met John, and while she was still living with and very much involved with the activities of John Taylor, she was exposed to a number of groups that had already taken forceful social stands. Her husband and she were members of a Unitarian circle that met regularly, and the freethinking spirit of the Unitarians formed a core of belief for the very young (almost teenaged) Harriet Taylor. At a later point, she was exposed to individuals who were friends of Mill personally, and to acquaintances of the groups in which his father had participated. We know that her friendship with Eliza Flower was a particularly cherished one, and that she and John Stuart Mill conversed regularly with the Carlyles. Jane Carlyle had, indeed, been one of the women whose own thought had piqued John Stuart Mill's interest time and time again.

But in addition to the women and men who formed a social circle the acquaintanceship of which she regularly sought, a number of other thinkers and writers were present in Britain against whose work Harriet's may be compared. As was the case in my examination of Hildegard and Anne Conway, I have to extrapolate here: in some cases, there is no direct evidence that Harriet ever knew the persons in question, but because of overlapping chronologies and geographies, fruitful comparisons may be made. It is facile to attempt to compare the utilitarians one against the other, and, of course, if we examined Harriet's own work, we are, in many cases, examining work composed well before she became acquainted with much of standard utilitarian thought. Therefore it may be instructive to look at writers such as George Eliot, for example—she lived and composed at the same time as HTM, and, although we have no direct evidence of contact, there are intriguing areas of similarity. Furthermore, she is a woman thinker alive and working in Great Britain at that time whose work is now, at least according to one author, being accorded philosophical import.[33]

Intriguingly enough, one area of intersection for both Eliot and HTM is that, at various times, both wrote for the *Westminster Review* (it is in this periodical that one of Harriet's few published early pieces is found). Another intersection for these women thinkers is their interest in the work of Auguste Comte; this remarkably misogynistic Frenchman is the object of stated attack by both George Eliot and Harriet Taylor Mill.

More pertinent, however, the desire of some to categorize HTM's writings as too flimsy or too truncated to withstand inspection and count as philosophy is related, in an illuminating way, to some of the claims made about Eliot. What really does count as an area in common for both these women thinkers is that each is concerned about the range of emotion in a human life, and what humans can profitably do with that emotion. In other words, each is concerned, in a central way, with the human condition. Eliot chooses to demonstrate her concern largely through novels, although she also wrote poetry and published at least some nonfiction writing.[34] Her novels have frequently been referred to as having implicit philosophical content; it is clear that she regards the capacity of humans to develop both sympathy and empathy as central to an amelioration of the human state.

As we can see, HTM confined herself very largely to short essays or attempts at essays, in addition to some poetry written as a teenager. But what Harriet Taylor Mill has as a unifying link with George Eliot is a shared concern for human conduct; where they differ, however, is that Harriet Taylor Mill is much more concerned about the displays of courageousness and independence. These two sorts of concerns might be thought naively to have little to say to each other, were it not clear that, for Eliot at least, developing the capacity for sympathy requires an independence of spirit that may very well place one at odds with convention.

It is here that we can see the Harriet of "On the Probable Futurity" as being somewhat in the same vein as the Eliot of *Middlemarch* or *The Mill on the Floss*. I have already cited HTM's work that reminds us of the importance of personal courage, and that forwards a societal appreciation of uniqueness or even of eccentricity. In a parallel fashion, Gardner claims, a good deal of what Eliot has to say pushes the notion that nineteenth-century Britain is a hidebound place, the cruelty of which is often alleviated by the individual who takes the time and patience to go against the grain. Gardner writes:

> Eliot explains how art is to produce morality in the reader by comparing the good writer with the good teacher. The good teacher is one who does not merely dispense knowledge but aims at developing the skills whereby the students find learning easier. In the same way, the most effective writer is one who does not state right and wrong, but "who awakes men from their indifference to the right and the wrong, who nerves their energies to seek for the truth and live up to it at whatever the cost." Faced with such a role, the responsibilities of the artist are clear for Eliot.[35]

In other words, the unifying factor for these thinkers is clearly a concern about the individual in a cruel and uncaring world, and the notion that we all, as individuals, can help each other—we have the capacity to alleviate suffering.

English intellectual life in the early nineteenth century might have been a charmed circle, but it was also something of a closed circle. We have no direct evidence that Harriet Taylor Mill and George Eliot ever made each other's acquaintance, and yet, on the other hand, they may well have passed each other by literally and figuratively many a time. Eliot not only wrote for the *Westminster Review* but translated both Spinoza and Strauss. Although she was approximately a decade younger than HTM, they both would have been adults in the 1840s. By this time, the atmosphere of change had become palpable, and a general resentment against not only the aristocracy but the bourgeoisie had led to many reforms and attempts at reform. Oddly enough, both Eliot and JSM knew Frederic Harrison—he is mentioned in JSM's *Autobiography* and is cited by Gardner as having had definite influence on Eliot.[36] Different thinkers responded to this atmosphere in different ways, and the times might have demanded that a woman, were a woman to write at all, try her hand at the novel or at poetry. (We note, of course, that Mary Ann Evans felt constrained to use another name.) Although we can see that HTM began at least minimally to move in this direction, she retained a lifelong habit of writing down drafts and jottings, some of which are more or less completed essays and others of which are simply unfinished notes.

Both George Eliot and Harriet Taylor felt greatly stultified by the England in which they found themselves. Both felt that a great deal of the social misery they saw around them had to do with barriers of class and gender. Both felt that human beings owed it to each other to attempt to surmount those barriers, and both had at least some interest in women specifically making the effort—one has only to think of Maggie Tulliver or Dorothea Brooke to be able to make this claim with respect to Eliot. The very extent of women's oppression would probably make the more thoughtful or reflective woman aware of her own misfortune, and from that awareness might spring an awakening to the misfortunes of others. Thus, if we want to read Eliot philosophically, as Gardner and others think that we should, we find ourselves extrapolating, and that extrapolation leads to a familiar place, a place already visited by HTM.[37]

In addition to George Eliot, at least one other woman active in literary circles of the time bears comparison with Harriet Taylor Mill. Eliza Flower, later companion of the Unitarian minister W. J. Fox, is often mentioned in connection with the Mills, since she had known John Stuart Mill before he met Harriet, and since her own relation with Fox, married to another, bore a parallel to Harriet's relation to John. Eliza Flower also wrote poetry; like Harriet, she had a romantic imagination and impressed all who knew her. Josephine Kamm writes of Flower: "The enchanting Eliza, known to her friends as 'Ariel,' loved poetry and composed music even as a child. 'She worshipped Mozart, Shakespeare, Milton, Burns, Byron, but if these had never existed she would still have been Eliza Flower,' wrote Fox's biographer. Both sisters [she and her sister Sarah] contributed to Fox's *Monthly Repository*. Eliza won the adoring friendship of an incipient genius, Robert Browning, nine years her junior; but, although she appreciated poetry, music was her first love."[38]

Eliza Flower is primarily remembered today because of her friendship with the Mills, and because she, Fox, and the two Mills formed what Josephine Kamm calls a "quadrilateral."[39] It is clear, however, that she assists us in understanding HTM in that she provides another way of seeing her; the young Mrs. Taylor to whom Mill was introduced was not alone in her interests. It simply was very difficult for young women of the time, no matter what sort of formal education they had received, to be able to express themselves in other than a poetic and romantic vein. But the meeting with John Stuart Mill was, of course, to propel Harriet Taylor on a different path.

The Feminine and the Feminist

Kamm writes of the auspicious meeting of Harriet Taylor and John Stuart Mill: "Harriet Martineau was twenty-eight in the late summer or early autumn of

1830, when W. J. Fox escorted her to dinner at the house of a leading member of his flock, John Taylor: the other guests were John Mill, who had not yet met the Taylors, and his friends Roebuck and Graham."[40] This encounter was to reinforce for both Harriet and John most of their already formed and articulated opinions regarding the standing of women in society. Up until that time, as has been recounted here and was said by Mill himself, Harriet's talents and ambitions had been allowed only "the received type of feminine genius."[41] But it must have been clear from the outset that Harriet Taylor needed more ways in which to express herself, and the meeting opened the door to those ways.

As had Wollstonecraft before her, and Astell, HTM tried hard to make the point that women had been allowed only certain venues and that, in general, this set of circumstances had a great deal to do with what it was that women had and had not accomplished. As we know, she had written at an early point that "real lovers of justice will rather that their [women's] condition should get worse & worse rather than partially better—in as much as when a certain point of abuse is reached their [sic] comes from the nature of things a sweeping and large reform."[42] But what HTM also has in common with these thinkers is a view that women have something unique to offer, and that it cannot be offered without a change in their state. As we have indicated before, there are several ties between these views and contemporary feminist theory, whatever particular rubric is employed. In the case of HTM, she, like Astell, seems to be greatly concerned about the belief that women are "inferior"; and like Wollstonecraft, she seems also to feel that traits such as sympathy and generosity inhere more in women and could thus be harnessed to do the world a great deal of good.

Mill had already thought about these issues, and much as his *Autobiography* exhibits a dramatic devotion to Harriet, he is careful to state that his "convictions . . . on complete equality [between the sexes]" were "among the earliest results of the application of my mind to political subjects" and that his powerful belief in such equality was "the originating cause of the interest she [Harriet] felt in me."[43] But whereas JSM's beliefs were more wholistic in the sense that they were part of his program for the improvement of society as a whole—a program upon which he had, of course, been well embarked before meeting Harriet—Harriet's beliefs were initially focused upon women as a group, and were extremely radical for her time. She was, for example, much more of a champion of divorce, at least initially, than JSM. If we can hypothesize, with good reason, that most of what Harriet felt about these issues had to do with her own life and upbringing, it is remarkable that what she does say is not only in accord with a great deal of the feminist doctrine that preceded her, but also with contemporary work.

Harriet seemed to be firmly of the opinion that women possessed special virtues, that education could draw these virtues out and that what women had accomplished in the past had never been recognized. Although JSM was a longtime employee of the East India Company, and only slightly or somewhat more critical of British imperialism than even the most rabid Tories, both of the Mills, especially Harriet in her early work, exhibit a sensitivity to the plight of those who have been excluded. In her insistence that the actual "inferiority" of women is not sufficiently questioned, even by their champions, Harriet is ahead of many. She realizes, implicitly, the social construction of much of what is around her, even if the terms that we now use to describe such a construction are far removed from her context. In his *Pax Britannica*, James Morris notes that John Stuart Mill "once called the British Empire 'a vast system of outdoor relief for the British upper classes.'"[44] Regardless of what JSM did or did not think, HTM notices the extent to which social conditions create situations that then are turned against those who have been the victims of the conditions. As I noted at an earlier point, her section on the French piano factory workers in "On the Probable Futurity of the Labouring Classes" shows the extent to which she was aware of how those who have been disempowered can empower themselves.

In her writings on feminist thought and science, Sandra Harding has frequently challenged the original hegemony of white feminists in their quest to articulate a counter to standard philosophy of science or to standard scientific thinking. In the most narrow sense, HTM can scarcely be thought of as a forerunner of such views, since there is little in her work that displays an awareness of non-European cultures.[45] Nevertheless, there is a great deal in her work that displays an awareness of what we will later come to call social force and hegemony. Although she was apparently not as influenced or impressed by her travels as was, for example, Wollstonecraft, Harriet Taylor Mill was, if anything, more aware of social and economic oppression. In a contemporary vein, Harding writes of this particular social force and construction: "But then it is also necessary to decenter the preoccupations of white, economically advantaged, heterosexual and Western feminists in the thinking and politics of feminists with these characteristics. No longer should their needs, interests, desires and visions be permitted to set the standard for feminist visions of the human or to enjoy so much attention in feminist writings."[46]

When HTM writes, in "Oppression of Women," "People do not complain of their state being degraded at all—they complain only that it is *too much* degraded,"[47] she is setting out the tacit assumption that women are actually inferior, but should be treated with a greater kindness, that underlay a great deal of the thinking of her time. Just as Harding remarks on the agendas of white feminists, whether acknowledged or not, with respect to other women, Harriet Taylor Mill was acknowledging the agendas of the better-off males of her time, who, in pretending to be at least minimally progressive, thought that an ameliorative sop might be thrown to women as a group.

How to make sense of HTM's obvious commitment to virtues possessed by women is a different matter. Like Wollstonecraft, she of necessity draws on her exposure very largely to women of a certain class. When we think, for example, of other women in the circle of either HTM or JSM, we bring up names such as the Flower sisters, Jane Carlyle, and Harriet Martineau.[48] All of these women, well-off enough and privileged enough to spend their time attending lectures, reading, and, in some cases, writing, were scarcely representative of British women of their time. HTM says that "frankness" and "generosity" are intrinsic parts of woman's nature, and she also writes of woman's "fine nervous organization."[49] Leaving aside the latter remark, we can again try to draw a thread between this sort of claim and claims made by feminist thinkers closer to our own time. The stronger part of Harriet Taylor Mill's analysis, however, is that which focuses on the social structure of women's lives.

In "On the Probable Futurity," Harriet makes her strongest statement about the sort of improvement in social organization that benefits the top only without any beneficial consequences for the bottom (in contemporary terms, we might say that it violates the Rawlsian difference principle). She claims, "The observations in the preceding chapter [of *Principles of Political Economy*] had as their principal object to deprecate a false ideal of human society. Their applicability to the practical purposes of present times, consists in moderating the inordinate importance attached to the mere increase of production."[50] As she goes on to write, she is concerned about "improved distribution." This emphasis on maldistribution, increase without assistance for those at the bottom, and an awareness of living conditions of those at the bottom constitute perhaps salient instances of that "frankness" and "generosity" of spirit that HTM herself felt were characteristic of women as a whole.

Harriet Taylor Mill insists upon the education of women because she feels that women have much to contribute. Some of what they have to contribute could also be given to the social scene by interested males, but it is clear that some of what they possess (particularly in the moral sphere) is more or less theirs alone. Like Astell and Wollstonecraft before her, HTM sees women as having been shut out from the circumstances of their full growth. It is this sense of exclusion that drives Harriet Taylor Mill, and that leads her to antic-ipate, at least chronologically, ideas that were later expressed by John Stuart Mill in *The Subjection of Women.*

An Epistemic Feminism

Because Harriet's feminism is both so profoundly felt and so general in its scope, it is more difficult to attribute to her any notions in accord with what we might today call a full-blown feminist epistemology than it has been for some of our other thinkers. We can see traces of today's gender feminism, particularly in the notion that women might, as a group, possess special virtues, but this is probably not as great a theme for her as it is for Astell.

Perhaps the best exemplar of HTM on matters epistemic is not any partic-ular passage in her writings, but HTM herself, insofar as we can construct her from her works, her life as it is known to us, and the circumstances of her re-lationship with JSM. Her writings mingle concerns that might today be ex-pressed as feminist empiricism with other sorts of concerns. In her concern for the laboring classes and in her nascent interest in socialism, she precedes (as does Wollstonecraft) socialist feminism, Marxist feminism, and standpoint theory. In the care with which she attempted to live her life—the trouble she took, for example, to avoid obvious impropriety and to maintain at least pass-able relations with her husband—she is today's bourgeois, liberal feminist, more concerned with rights in a world where most "rights" are held by males.

H. O. Pappe, in a work that is very largely unsympathetic to HTM, says the following in an effort to debunk stories of HTM's possessing talent, or having had an intellectual influence on JSM: "Mill without Harriet would still have been Mill. Mill married to George Eliot (or to Mary Wollstonecraft—permitting the anachronism) might have been transformed. . . . Yet, considering [Eliot's] equality of stature, there would have been no need for him in masochistic guilt to magnify her contribution."[51]

But, of course, even if it is true that Mill magnified her contribution, there is no reason to think that he did so "masochistically." Part of Harriet's con-tribution was, quite simply, a new way of seeing, and that way of seeing is by no means unrelated to the fact that she was a woman.[52] Harding addresses some of these issues in *Whose Science?* when she attempts to defuse the time-worn assumptions that standpoint epistemologies require some commit-ment to the Enlightenment project in some way that is oppressive, essential-ist, or demeaning. She notes: "[M]ust standpoint theory make claims on behalf of a reasoning—a rationality—that is disembodied? On the contrary, it insists that reason is socially located. Our best beliefs as well as our worst ones have social causes, and it is better to begin from some social locations rather than others if one wants to generate less partial and distorted claims about nature and social relations."[53]

Harriet was not a member of an oppressed social class, to be sure, but she was a member of a group that gave John Stuart Mill a different perspective, one that he unfortunately received little exposure to in his youth, due to his abbreviated and truncated contact with his mother and other female figures in the family (this appears, according to most of his biographers, to be the result largely of his father's virtual complete usurpation of any parental role). This new way of seeing may well have encompassed aspects more expressive of the emotions, less replete with intellectual aggrandizement, and more in tune with the needs of others. In any case, it is clear that HTM at least pushed JSM further in the direction of recognizing emotional needs and divorcing himself from the Benthamite considerations that had already begun to trouble him.

As we know from his *Autobiography,* Mill had found Wordsworth a consolation during his emotional breakdown. But it is scarcely an exaggeration to say that that period of turmoil was due largely to what might be called an overexposure to one point of view, the male point of view (and a rarefied one at that). Mill himself admits as much when, again in his *Autobiography,* he faults his mother for not creating a warmer atmosphere in the family home, and for a lack of love.[54] In any case, part of what was missing for Mill was unquestionably a point of view that is ordinarily described as "female," in an entirely unproblematized way, and this is something that we can say, without difficulty, that HTM provided. If, at the same time, she encouraged other beliefs, it means that Mill had a new filter through which to see things.

A repeated theme for Harding, and for many feminist epistemologists, is that there are assumptions underlying all epistemologies, even if they are not fully articulated. The View from Nowhere assumptions are seldom explicitly set out; indeed, until the work of feminist epistemologists recently, little had been done to advert to the notion that males of European ancestry also had a point of view. We can move these arguments around, at least chronologically, to help us understand some of the underlying dynamic driving the collaboration of the Mills. JSM's modes of thinking were a product of his level of education, his social class, and the tutoring that he received from his father as a youngster.[55] It is not only the case that men from other social classes in Great Britain would not have had these opportunities; we can also generalize and note that, even in other European cultures—France, Italy, or Germany, for example—modes of inquiry would have been slightly or somewhat

different, because of different conceptualization patterns and language structures. All of these factors are important in the development of "epistemologies," and to fail to address these factors is to create a large gap in theory.

Harding ably explicates this important point when she writes: "It is easy
for conventional philosophers to overlook the fact that all epistemologies
make assumptions about how beliefs have in fact been generated and gained
legitimacy, even though few epistemologists discuss their psychological, so-
ciological and historical assumptions."[56]

Harriet's perspective, then, although it was English and from a similar social class, was different in two important ways: first of all, as a woman (and a
woman of a time when females still had extremely limited opportunities), she
had been brought up to see the world quite differently. Second, although in
theory some girls might have been the objects of experiments in education
similar to that to which James Mill subjected his son, she had less formal education than some other women of similar social classes.[57] A view of the world,
then, that would certainly have been at least somewhat different simply because of gender, was significantly different from John's because of both gender and self-education.

The latter was no doubt beneficial in discussions with John simply because it would have seemed to him that she was approaching problems from
a "fresh" perspective. He no doubt saw her approaches as more genuinely felt,
perhaps less carefully argued, but in any case quite original. He also, regardless of what he had previously thought about the subjection of women, had
probably never before been able to spend a length of time in firsthand conversation with a woman who was prepared to talk about her subjection specifically and the difficulties that it caused for her. (The assessment of JSM by
his friend John Roebuck around the time that he met Harriet is widely cited
and reprinted in Hayek: "[O]f the world, as it worked around him, he knew
nothing; and above all, of *woman* he was as a child.")[58] Thus almost anything
of substance said by HTM to JSM would probably have represented a different perspective, and if he himself could have been precise about the sorts of
perspectives he encountered from Harriet in a number of different situations,
he might well have been tempted to label them epistemic points of view or
epistemologies.

That we can make worthwhile comparisons between contemporary work
in feminist epistemology and Harriet's own work is underscored, again, by
"On the Probable Futurity of the Labouring Classes," her chapter in *Principles
of Political Economy*. After describing in detail the French cooperative whose
work she is examining, HTM notes: "It is painful to think that these bodies,

formed by the heroism and maintained by the public spirit and good sense of the working people of Paris, are in danger of being involved with the same ruin of everything free, popular or tending to improvement in French institutions. Before this calamity [alluding to the actions of Napoleon III] overtook France, the associations could be spoken of not with the hope merely, but with positive evidence, of their being able to compete successfully with individual capitalists."[59]

It is not simply that what Harriet Taylor Mill writes about here is a cooperative, and therefore represents a new way of doing things: it is clear that what she finds startling and worthy of emulation in the French groups is that they represent a group effort for the common good, instead of individual efforts based on competitive egoism. Because the decisions with respect to the cooperative had been made as a group, certain individuals, at certain times, had the intriguing experience of learning to subjugate their individual desire in the name of something else. This group orientation does indeed constitute a different epistemic point of view. And for HTM, that particular epistemics is a valuable contribution to nineteenth-century European culture.

Nouvelle Vague

The problem that occurs with HTM's work and the possible feminisms of the future is one that we have encountered now with other thinkers whose work we have examined: we can extrapolate, hoping to extract from the work indications of directions in which it might go (or might have gone, had the author lived longer), but when we do so extrapolate we engage in theoretically risky behavior.

Nevertheless, Harriet Taylor Mill's work is more susceptible to these lines of analysis for at least two reasons: the first is simply that, in contrast, for example, to Mary Astell, she lived much closer to our own time. By the end of her life, Marxism and the various forms of socialism had already made themselves known in Europe; indeed, this is how she was able to write "On the Probable Futurity of the Labouring Classes." Second, a great deal of HTM's work is much more overtly political and less concerned with other sorts of philosophical issues. Thus, although we might at first blush be tempted to subsume Harriet under the category of "liberal feminist," in a manner similar to the initial subsumption of Mary Wollstonecraft, HTM gives us enough to go on that other sorts of theoretical considerations can be brought to bear.

In a work that combines a look at Derrida with an analysis of the origin of the notion of sovereignty and of the state, the Italian theorist Giorgio Agamben notes how Foucault uses the notion of power: "One of the most persistent features of Foucault's work is its decisive abandonment of the traditional approach to the problem of power, which is based on juridico-institutional models (the definition of sovereignty, the theory of the State), in favor of an unprejudiced analysis of the concrete ways in which power penetrates subjects' very bodies and forms of life."[60]

Oddly enough, although she is writing well over a century ago, this is more or less what Harriet Taylor Mill accomplishes in some of her work. What makes her analysis of marriage so acute is that she sees that this is a form of power that is foisted on female citizens without their informed consent, and against their will. No young woman would intelligently or knowingly consent to a great deal of what she is asked to do when she enters a marriage, reasons HTM; the only way to get her to make the choices, so to speak, is to keep her in a state of ignorance with respect to the true nature of the situation and her role in it.

This sort of analysis precedes today's emphasis on the body and its status as victimized target of the civil and the political. One of her earliest analyses of marriage indicates that, although it would appear that civil marriage is a contract designed to encourage a certain sort of sensual enjoyment, it fails to do even that: "No institution that could possibly be devised, seems to be so entirely tending to encourage and create mere sensuality, as that of marriage. In the first place it makes some mere animal inclination respectable and recognized in itself. Then having encouraged this animal want to its utmost by the approval of opinion, it takes care to prevent all voluntariness, at least in the case of one party, by."[61]

Although the manuscript as cited by Jacobs breaks off here, it seems clear that Harriet Taylor Mill is attempting to address the fundamental coercive nature of marriage as an institution: it is a civil contract designed to ensure reproduction, and as such it is detrimental to the interests of women, because, as she indicates it encourages "animal wants." Since part of HTM's thesis is that it is the case that women have at least some special virtues that might plausibly be brought to bear on civil society, it does not make sense to invest marriage with any special status since it is often the very instrument of their downfall. In a sense, HTM precedes here the forward-looking post-theory feminist analyses of our time, since she has signaled out, by denigration of the body as an act of agency and political power, what it is that marriage actually amounts to.

Harriet has little hope for marriage because it is an institution ruled by men. She sees men, in general, as failing to possess those very virtues that she had already signaled as belonging to women, at least partly because society does not encourage them to inculcate these praiseworthy characteristics. But if men devise an institution to promote their animal wants, we must be very careful in our assessment of that institution. She goes on to note that part of what is wrong with marriage, as devised and constructed in the British society in which she lived, is that it lacked "in the case of one party all voluntariness."[62] What she means, of course, is that young women felt compelled to marry, and she is obviously thinking of her own case. But that compulsion would not exist were it not promulgated by the state—and Harriet Taylor Mill is very sensitive to this point.

Although there is little in Harriet's work that speaks to an awareness of colonialism, and although we know that JSM, in his capacity as a civil servant for the East India Company, took a dim view of early attempts at Indian rebellion, HTM's sensitivity to workers, as evidenced in "On the Probable Futurity," speaks well of her capacity to extrapolate from a set of circumstances. In one well-known quotation, JSM actually called the British rule in India "beneficent"; presumably, he meant in comparison to other colonial regimes.[63] But HTM constantly shows an awareness of the difference that is made in the lives of individuals if they are allowed their own organizations, their own polity—their own say. It is this spirit that motivates a great deal of her commentary in "On the Probable Futurity." Speaking of the difference that this type of independence makes, she writes:

> The capital of most of the associations was originally confined to the few tools belonging to the founders, and the small sums that could be collected from their savings, or which were lent to them by other work-people as poor as themselves. In some cases, however, loans of capital were made to them by the republican government: but the associations which obtained these advances, or at least which obtained them before they had already achieved success are, it appears, in general by no means the most prosperous. The most striking instances of prosperity are in the case of those who have had nothing to rely on but their own slender means and the small loans of fellow-workmen, and who lived on bread and water while they devoted the whole surplus of their gains to the formation of a capital.[64]

In this section, Harriet Taylor Mill is clearly saying that there is a spirit that endures when all else fails: the allusion to living on "bread and water" highlights that for us. If that spirit does endure, and if that spirit is what drives the cooperatives, their self-definition may enable them to prevail.

Although the poverty of French workmen is difficult to compare to colonial conditions, the analysis given by Harriet—that deeply penurious circum-

stances may call upon the strongest resources of the human will for survival—
may well be translatable into such conditions. There is little reason to believe
that HTM ever discussed colonial issues with JSM at any length, and in any
case, given conceptions of confidentiality, he would have had good reason for
not doing so. James Morris also reports that "John Stuart Mill and T. H. Hux-
ley were members of a committee that secured [Governor Eyre of Jamaica's]
prosecution for murder" for the "killing or executing [of] more than six hundred people," and other similar crimes, while putting down a rebellion in Jamaica.[65] Although there is no evidence of whether JSM and HTM discussed this
and other similar issues, we can have no doubt as to what HTM's opinion
would have been.

In general, HTM's emphasis on the importance of individuality and the
healthy functioning of the human, with all of her or his foibles, precludes the
sort of notion of hegemony that has driven most of the phenomena against
which "postmodern" commentary standardly positions itself. As we have
just articulated, this by no means necessarily implies that during her lifetime
Harriet Taylor Mill would have been in a position to recognize the force of
conceptual patterns that we would today label, for example, "Orientalist."
Like other thinkers of her time, the sort of construction of the East against
which Edward Said and other commentators have argued would most likely
not have been something she could question. But the seeds for such a questioning are sown not only in Harriet's insistence on the individual and her
rights, but in her notions of what drove the formation of a French cooperative, or what sort of deprivation actually furthered the cooperative's work.
We do damage to a thinker when we attempt to castigate him or her for failing to make conceptual moves that simply could not have been made during
the period in question. Harriet Taylor Mill was an extremely progressive political thinker. Her emphasis on women's rights is merely one arena in which
she forwards, in general, a strong notion of individual rights.

A Millian Set of Principles

Clearly, what is most important about the relationship between John Stuart
Mill and Harriet Taylor Mill is its strong collaboration, and it is comparatively
unimportant who wrote what. On the other hand, there is a lengthy history—part of which I have tried to recapitulate here—of women thinkers' not
having received their due. Thus the effort to resuscitate Harriet in the eyes of
scholars must take precedence over any other, given that so much of the

commentary on her and her effect on Mill is either studiously neutral or openly negative.[66]

I have noted that a great deal of what drove both Mills in the direction of forwarding individual "eccentricity" had much to do—as almost all commentators concede—with their relationship and the way in which it was perceived. The need to preserve appearances, the need for secrecy, and, apparently, a need to explain themselves to friends and acquaintances were paramount.

But much of what they did also assisted other individuals and spoke to a larger audience: the "quadrilateral" relationship alluded to by Kamm indicates that HTM and JSM both were aware that expanding the horizons of society as a whole required work on specific cases. When a scandal ensued because of the relationship of Eliza Flower and W. J. Fox—a scandal brought on partly, in this case, by the spouse's justified complaints, made public—the Mills were among the first to come to their aid. Kamm has described their foursome as she does because it was permeated by a sense of mutual recognition and obligation:

> In this dilemma [the open scandal of Fox's alleged adultery] he [W. J. Fox] turned to the Taylors and John Mill, who, despite their own dilemma, united to support him. They were firmly convinced, so Mill told Fox, that the attitude of a proportion of the congregation was caused by the erroneous belief that he and Eliza were lovers. Fox himself was partly responsible for the belief, for in the columns of the *Monthly Repository* he had openly advocated freedom for unhappily married couples to divorce, a subject he would have done well to avoid in the circumstances.[67]

That the topic was in the air is an indication not so much of an unprecedented increase in flirtations, altercations, and adulterous alliances, but of an increase in the awareness of different forms or "gradations" of happiness—and for this one must thank the Mills and Harriet Taylor Mill in particular. Her constant emphasis on higher pleasures, and her refusal to submit to what she deemed to be low or base—especially insofar as it involved a distinction between physical and mental pleasure—had a great deal to do with their joint contention that the conventional marriage might not be conducive to an individual's greatest happiness. As Harriet herself had written in the early piece that Jacobs refers to as "The Nature of the Marriage Contract," "For owing to the notion of chastity as the greatest virtue of women, the fact that a woman knew what she undertook would be considered just reason for preventing her undertaking it."[68]

What she is undertaking, of course, is obvious from the above description (at least insofar as we can infer the part of it that was especially bothersome to HTM). And then again there is the matter of who it is with whom one does the undertaking; after the contract is signed, one is not allowed to go back and rethink the decision. It is because of these sorts of inhibitions on personal freedom, particularly the freedom of women (remember that Harriet had also written about marriage's encouraging "mere sensuality") that she values the input of the individual so extraordinarily.

Harriet Taylor Mill not only valued individual freedom, higher pleasures, and the inculcation of individual virtue, but she encouraged the notion that education was related to a proper social response to these necessities. Lack of education, for everyone, but especially for women, led to abuses of personal freedom and injurious sorts of growth; as she also wrote, "holding the condition of slaves, they exercise retaliation by the vices of slaves."[69] Concern for the better sorts of feelings, sentiments, and sensations could be inculcated only by careful attention to childhood education. But such attention would be amply rewarded—it would yield someone who would not make the Benthamite error of equating pushpin and poetry; it would yield a person who could not only make informed judgments about her or his life, but who could assist others in making such judgments.

As even the comparatively unsympathetic Hayek has written of Harriet when she first met John,

> This delicate frame evidently harbored very strong convictions and emotions which during these early years however were still seeking an outlet and adequate means of expression. It is probable that from an early stage her character and outlook had been shaped by a violent revolt against the social conventions which not only, at the time of life when she did not comprehend what it meant, had placed her in permanent dependence on a man whom she regarded as her inferior in intellect and general culture, but which also excluded her from almost all of those activities for which she regarded herself fit.[70]

Harriet no doubt saw not only herself but myriad other young women as trapped in the same circumstances. To be bound for life to one with whom one could not discuss one's deepest pleasures and joys—this led her to a fuller articulation of her own values, values that she later shared with JSM, whose thinking, after the trauma of his youth, had pushed in the same direction.

HTM wrote on a number of topics, and some of what she has to say on what we might regard as extraneous issues sheds further light on her general outlook. She wrote on aesthetics and the arts in general: in a short piece entitled "The Unity of the Arts," she tries to establish what it is that gives each art, literary or visual, its intrinsic character.[71] She notes, for example, what it is that distinguishes sculpture from painting, and then goes on to make general points about drama based on her observations.[72] Analogously to some of the arguments that she makes about liberties, one's life, and the wholistic nature of one's construction of one's life, HTM sees the possible unity of drama as compromised by certain changes in its structure: "[W]hen a play is acted . . . [t]he endeavour is that the *external* sensations of the spectator shall be as nearly as possible the same as if he were actually witnessing the events: & *because* complete material resemce [*sic*] is attempted and to a great degree attained, therefore any great *absence* of material resemblance, in certain particulars while it is preserved in others is felt as a shock [emphasis in original]."[73]

HTM goes on to make several distinctions regarding the unity of place and the unity of time in drama, but we can see here a concern that, in a larger sense, is an overriding one for her: Harriet Taylor Mill is concerned with unity all the way around, so to speak. The work that she did on personal freedom, her writings on women's education, and her chapter in *Principles of Political Economy* all speak to another sort of unity, the unity of an individual's life. But it should come as no surprise that someone who has wholeness and integrity as a major area of interest would make similar remarks about the arts when the issue appears open for discussion.

In summarizing thought about HTM and her place, one finds oneself working within the framework of a circle. It is extremely difficult to write about Harriet Taylor Mill without writing about John Stuart Mill: part of the task, of course, is to correct the erroneous impression that Harriet had little or nothing to do with work that was published under his name. By the same token, we need to bear in mind that HTM had written hundreds of pages of manuscript, much of it unpublished, at the time of her death.

Why, then, is it so important to try to make the case for Harriet Taylor Mill as a philosopher in her own right? In her case, and to some extent in the case of Simone de Beauvoir, their accomplishments were immediately overshadowed by those of their spouses/companions, and for a long time the overshadowing kept observers from making an adequate assessment of their work. Perhaps the best indication of why it is crucial to try to give Harriet her due is found in the constant reference—no less so now than in previous times—to John Stuart Mill as the founder and architect of much of the liberties of civil government. Mill's stature is so much taken for granted that it may be invisible; we may have to push ourselves to see it.

A case in point is the work by Alan Dershowitz entitled *Shouting Fire*. This work, intended for popular consumption as a guide to civil liberties and to gaining a conception of the distinction between moral and legal thought, takes the legacy of JSM for granted. Precisely because he is intending to instruct, however, Dershowitz makes the legacy explicit at several points in the text: "Few principles of civic morality have had so profound an intellectual influence within Western democracies as John Stuart Mill's 'one very simple principle.' The principle, governing the proper allocation of state power and individual liberty, was articulated by Mill in his 1859 essay entitled 'On Liberty.'"[74]

Dershowitz's book is not intended for undergraduate instruction; that is what makes its general slant so remarkable. In a work intended for a general audience, more than one chapter revolves around the thought of John Stuart Mill. Perhaps this factor, more than any other, constitutes an argument for why it is time to recognize the life and work of Harriet Taylor Mill.

EDITH STEIN six

When we think of Edith Stein (1891–1942) today, more than one image comes to mind, but although she is by no means unknown, many of the images have little to do with philosophy. We may be tempted to think, for example, of the controversy surrounding her beatification and later canonization, or we may think of her as one of "three women in dark times," as the title of one book exhorts us to.[1] Then again, if we choose to focus on Stein's philosophical work—much of which, unfortunately, has not yet been translated into English—we will probably find ourselves thinking almost solely in phenomenological terms, since the work for which she is best known is her dissertation on empathy, completed while she was a student of Husserl's.[2]

What is not widely known or appreciated is that, after her conversion to Catholicism (1922), but before her time with the Carmelites, Stein wrote a number of philosophical essays that deal, to some extent, with problems such as empathy and the general human emotions, but from a Christian standpoint. In addition, she was by no means unaware of the need to make a linkage between the work that she had already completed in phenomenological terms, and the work that she began on, for example, St. Elizabeth of

Hungary, or the role of women. Part of the exciting task of uncovering Stein's philosophy is to attempt to unravel the moves that she made in an investigation of being-qua-being, à la Husserl, or more properly Heidegger, and her later work that borrows from such thinkers as Aquinas and St. John of the Cross. Sylvie Courtine-Denamy, for example, posits a direct line between the earlier phenomenological Stein and the later Christian thinker. This makes for some stimulating philosophical work.

One thing that is clear is that, like Simone Weil after her (Stein was born approximately eighteen years before Weil), Edith Stein was attracted to philosophical problems from an early age. Unlike Weil's family, Stein's was observant, and this was later to pose problems for her, since it made conversion all the more painful. An able student, Stein quickly displayed the acuity of thought that would later distinguish her work. Courtine-Denamy writes of her childhood: "Edith, who was highly gifted, also had an excellent memory: she could reel off Marie Stuart by heart and corrected her family when, trying to fool her, they suggested the play was by Goethe. She was nicknamed 'A Book with Seven Seals' while still quite young. She eagerly looked forward to growing up and going to school with her sister Erna and felt more at home there than in her own house."[3]

This scholarly side was to shine not only in the classroom, but in other ways. It is what led her to make the ultimate break with her Judaic past, and to go on to become cloistered. In making this move, she famously felt the pull of belief first simply from observing the devotions of others, and then from reading the life of Theresa of Avila. Her friendship with the Reinach family allowed her to witness the behavior of his widow after his death in World War I; this "calm, Stoic" attitude not only made a lasting impression on her, but led to the well-known episode in which she spent the night reading Theresa, and afterwards said that she had found the "truth."[4]

Speaking in broad general terms, the link between Stein's philosophical beliefs, both before and after conversion, is a concern with Being. The bracketing that Husserl taught her—summarized succinctly as "But how could we ever be aware of [the world's meaning] prior to the phenomenological reduction which first brings the transcendental subjectivity as our absolute Being into the focus of experience?"—was but one method of trying to get hold of being antecedent to categorization and conceptualization.[5] After taking the time to read some of the medieval thinkers, particularly St. Thomas, she was well able to see that similar metaphysical problems had vexed thinkers during that period, but that the language in which they were stated was the main obstacle to an immediate understanding of the conceptual process at hand.

Thus the link between the early Stein and the later Stein is not only a concern for such problems as empathy and human feeling; it is also a concern for the ways in which conceptual rubble may be cleared away to get to the phenomenon in its barest sense. Husserl's post-nineteenth-century method is one way; as Stein found out, there are other ways. What the Christian saints had in common with the later German thinker is an attempt to get at the immediacy of experience.

Stein spent a period of approximately a decade as a convert, but simply one who taught—she had not yet made the decision to enter a convent. The Christian conversion, however, did not yield for Stein the same sort of response to her Judaic background that apparently pervaded much of the life of, for example, Simone Weil. It is important to make this point, because it is related to the contiguity and sense of meshing that one gets from an examination of Stein's philosophical work. Husserl, a Jew who also later converted, was not only an instructor in phenomenology, but in some sense probably was an instructor in how to philosophize as a Jew. It is therefore important that Rachel Brenner, among others, wants to comment on Stein's retention of Jewish identity: "Stein did not see a contradiction between the Christian faith and identification with the Jewish people. Clearly, she felt Jewish when she denounced Nazi anti-Jewish policies, but at the same time her solidarity with the Jews was articulated through the Christian symbol of the Cross. . . . She wanted to emulate Christ's passion—his suffering—in her own experience of persecution."[6]

In other words, what we see with Stein is a powerful merging of at least three separate strands of thought: her training in phenomenology, which of course grounded her philosophical expertise; her later conversion to Christianity (and reading of Christian philosophy); and her identity as a Jew. If there is a concept that provides the leading tie-in here, it is probably that of empathy, but what Stein came to see later in life as a form of empathy—or even as a clear understanding of it—was probably fairly far removed from her work with Husserl.

Before we begin a precise examination of what we might characterize as Edith Stein's metaphysics, it helps to remember the underlying goal of phenomenology, at least as originally expounded. The point of the "bracketing" was to achieve a reduction that would allow the phenomenon in question to be examined in-itself. Whether or not it is even possible to accomplish such a reduction, the original project had a profound effect on the social sciences of its time, and it was originally described, according to at least one of Husserl's translators, as a "rigorous science."[7] Thus a comprehension of a psychological state such as empathy achieved under Husserl's method not only has little in common with the sort of description of such a phenomenon that might be given today (we could imagine today's account to be extremely reductivist), it has little in common with most descriptions that would have been given at that time. If a believing Christian may be said to feel empathy in reading of, for example, the Stations of the Cross and the journey of Jesus along the way, the kind of interiorized, descriptive, and ordinary language account that might be given would be virtually completely at variance with a phenomenological account.

Thus a driving question in examining Stein's philosophy becomes: why and how did she achieve the move from a phenomenological description of phenomena to a Christian one, given that she apparently believed she could, indeed, make a philosophical linkage? This question will guide our undertakings in attempting to come to grips with her work. To tie in the other thread of the argument already alluded to, if Stein does come to see the Christian mode of faith-based understanding as superior (and all evidence indicates that she did), how did she resolve that comprehension with her Judaism? To be fair, the latter is the easier of the two questions, and the fact that we can make this claim indicates just how difficult the first question really is.

One link to all of the foregoing is provided by Waltraut Stein, as quoted by Brenner. She said that Edith had "sought to fulfill the Biblical prophecy that the lion shall lie down with the lamb."[8] Brenner herself simply says, "She affirmed the Cross and wanted to carry it as a representation of Christ's Passion in her own suffering."[9] Empathy, identity, and Christian faith as a special form of knowledge: all of these elements are interwoven in the philosophy of Edith Stein.

Metaphysics, Ontology, and Stein

In one of the last sections of Stein's work *On the Problem of Empathy,* which seeks to move from the bracketing to an account of how to establish an empathic connection between persons, she writes as follows: "But if I get possession of it [the meaning context of an object as historical fact], I have an existing product and not a merely fantasized one. In empathic comprehension of the foreign spiritual individual, I also have the possibility of bringing his unverified behavior to givenness under certain circumstances. Such action is demanded by his personal structure of what I know."[10]

In this early philosophical work, Stein seems to have no difficulty positing the existence of a human soul or spirit, but still making the claim that

some of the actions of that human spirit could best be understood phenomenologically, since the idea here would be to try to get a "pure" account. Note
that from the outset she does not attempt to give what we would ordinarily
call a simple empirical description of the phenomenon of empathy (or of the
behavior of the other individual). Stein will retain her belief in the soul over
time, but other beliefs will change.

As near as I can make out from a perusal of Stein's later writings, from the
abbreviated commentary on her work that exists in English, and from the circumstances of her conversion, Stein later came to think that a form of Christian faith would do the philosophical work—in terms of getting to the core of
things—that she had originally hoped to do via the phenomenological method. Before I try to explicate precisely what this amounts to, it is important
both to examine the commentary on her work and to try to become clearer
about the Husserlian method.

The clearest assessment of Husserl's method, at least insofar as it applies to
Stein's attempts to deal with empathy, is probably given in Waltraut Stein's
special introduction to her aunt's work: "In the tradition of idealism, [Husserl]
takes consciousness as the area to be investigated. He posits nothing about the
natural world. He puts it in 'brackets,' as a portion of an algebraic formula is
put in brackets. . . . Answering the question of how knowledge is possible in
the most general sense, Husserl maintains that a reduction to phenomena in
an orderly manner is necessary. . . . When this reduction is made, the phe-
nomenologist is in a position to intuit the essence or eidos of phenomena."[11]

Here we have an adumbration of the original method by which Edith
Stein sought to distinguish the phenomenological "I" that was in a position
to establish an empathic connection with another being.[12] But if the point
of the reduction is to, as Waltraut Stein says, intuit the "essence" of a phenomenon, then it seems obvious from some of Edith Stein's later writings
that, although her philosophical training with Husserl had provided her with
excellent tools of analysis, she later came to think that there was another way
of getting at the essence of things (for purposes of what I do here, I will leave
aside entirely the objections of Anglo-Saxon twentieth-century philosophy
to the notion of "essence").

Although there is currently a dearth of philosophically sophisticated com-
mentary on Stein's work available in English, both Brenner and Courtine-
Denamy, writing about Stein as one of a number of women affected by the
Holocaust, provide some analysis of the theoretical moves that she made.
Brenner notes that "Stein's article on the Greek mystic theologian Dionysius
the Areopagite, as well as her . . . unfinished interpretation of St. John of the

Cross, shows that 'Stein was a contemplative, and [that] she necessarily tended to interpret her contemplative experience . . . as a phenomenological philosopher.'"[13] By this Brenner appears to mean that Stein hoped to accomplish, through Christian contemplative work, some of the same philosophical tasks that she had antecedently accomplished through phenomenology.

Courtine-Denamy provides us with perhaps our most valuable gloss on the changes that overcame Stein when she notes that, by 1932, Stein had come to query whether or not the Husserlian method was necessary to accomplish her goals. As Courtine-Denamy indicates, Stein had come to the conclusion that some of the methods appropriated by St. Thomas Aquinas were relevant to the task at hand. She writes: "[A] preoccupation with transcendental critique would have been foreign to Thomas, who interrogated reality 'naively.' If reason's path is endless for Thomas, as it is for Heidegger as well, it is also true that for Thomas, the philosopher can never reach his goal because there exists another road to knowledge, accessible to God alone. . . . This other road to knowledge is faith, 'foreign to all modern philosophies.'"[14]

In a series of essays written largely after she had taken her vows, Stein attempts to make clear precisely, in philosophical terms, what this road would amount to. It is this work—rather than her dissertation on empathy—that is Stein's most strikingly original philosophical work, for here she performs the difficult task of attempting to get clear on Christian concepts in more standard philosophical terms. We might say that Stein's work is also in the tradition of St. Augustine, who in "inquiring whence it was that [he] admired the beauty of bodies whether celestial or terrestrial," came to find "the unchangeable and true eternity of Truth."[15]

Stein sees believing Christians as all part of the mystical body of Christ, and although this type of conceptualization is common among Christian thinkers, Stein puts it to interesting use.[16] Specifically, Stein tries to be very clear about paths to knowledge of the divine. In simplistic terms, such as those used above, such paths have generally been reduced to faith, since it is clear that they have little to do with ordinary paths of knowledge appropriation. But in an essay entitled "The Knowledge of God," Stein draws careful distinctions: "What, then, is the foundation of this presupposed knowledge of God? There are several sources from which it may be drawn: natural knowledge of God; faith as the 'ordinary' way of supernatural knowledge of God, and finally a supernatural experience of God as the 'extraordinary' way of a supernatural knowledge of God."[17]

That Stein came to feel that there was this "extraordinary" path to knowledge is obvious from her own testimony with respect to her experiences, and as Courtine-Denamy says, it is clear that she ultimately believed that faith could perform many of the epistemological tasks that she had antecedently taken to be part and parcel of phenomenological analysis. But what precisely were those tasks? If we inquire as to why we might deem Stein's move from Husserlian phenomenology to faith a major one, we can scarcely do better than to cite Ricoeur on Husserl, since he was one of the early primary expositors of this somewhat recondite branch of Continental thought. As Ricoeur writes: "Husserl can thus maintain the transcendence of the perceived with respect to consciousness by a criticism of the critique of 'secondary qualities,' all the while denying the existence in-themselves of the things perceived. This difficult and original setting up of the problem of reality is phenomenology's essential philosophical contribution."[18]

With respect to the "bracketing," he notes that "placed in flux, the object is ready for the reduction to its successive appearances."[19] But this method of attempting to come to grips with essence, as opposed to appearance, has something oddly in common with faith. Both go beyond the appearances, although it may well be objected that religious faith seldom has so much as an appearance to go on. But the striking point here, philosophically, is that when we look more closely, we can see how, for Edith Stein, it may have been tempting to think—once she had become acquainted with the Christian mystical tradition—that certain aims she had possessed all the way along were finally being realized.

Eventually, even the specific phenomenological problems with respect to empathy that Stein had attempted to address began to appear to her as at least best approached through the Christian tradition. Since phenomenology is already complex with respect to the bracketing of, say, an appearance of red, the phenomenological investigation of another and another's experiences requires multiple levels of analysis, many of which are simply too arcane to bear repetition here, particularly since they are not as relevant to Stein's later thought as one might expect. (For example, the phenomenological account of empathy requires an awareness of some other "I," in the "psycho-physical body," and a development of that "I's" experiences through analogy.) But what Stein came to see through the writings of St. Theresa or St. John of the Cross employed a different approach: what might be intuited through faith, noting that believers are members of Christ's body, would perhaps be, if anything, a more accurate representation of the integrity of the "I" of the other than could be gotten at by a phenomeonlogical inquiry. Brenner, writing in a collection of essays on Stein's relationship to Catholicism, expresses this well when she says:

Let us recall that Stein's phenomenological investigation leads her to the conclusion that ethical social coexistence is predicated upon ethical wholeness of the individual. The wholeness of the individual is closely related to the "unchangeable kernel" of his or her personality. The "kernel" which contains "the true content of personality" is not subject to change; it is a given which contains all the distinctive qualities, values, and possibilities of the individual; it is the individual's "spiritual subject."[20]

Stein clearly came to believe that, through Christian faith, it was at least possible to develop empathy on the basis of acquaintance with an individual's soul.

Morality and Stein

Edith Stein's concern to provide an account of empathy is only one aspect of a lifelong quest for the moral and an adequate ethics. Once again, we can see how philosophical shifts moved her from Husserlianism with respect to these problems to a Christian account.

To emphasize for a moment only the later Christian portion of her work, the acquaintance with an individual in the full richness of his or her personhood—and assuming the individual to be part of God's plan—provides a springboard for Stein's assessment that we must respond to others fully and openly, and always in a spirit of love. That love is, of course, the agape or altruistic love that we expect of committed Christians; but what makes Stein's thinking here so remarkable is that she continues to rely on the notion that each individual has a special gift or heritage that we can cherish, and that we must fully investigate what gift it is that the individual possesses before we can adequately respond to the individual. Freda Mary Oben notes that Stein herself characterized this as a "self-bestowing goodness," and that we can see how this goodness was, in her case, manifested in her response to her sentence to Auschwitz.[21]

Stein's attention to matters ethical flows directly not only from her original work with Husserl on empathy but from her general conception of the person. As we have seen, part of the difficulty with a phenomenological account of interpersonal relations is that it becomes increasingly complex as one moves from the initial bracketings performed to attempt to make statements about the primordial "I" and the "I's" relationship to the world, to the "I" of the other, and the primordial relationship of the "I" to that other.[22] Christian thought was only a partial success in removing some of these difficulties, since the existence of the Other is, in any case, a difficult philosophical problem for any system.[23]

But the shift in Stein's perspective to the mystical body of Christ in the sense of a community of believers constitutive of this body, as the language of the New Testament suggests, moves the burden more successfully to the moral agent, since the agent no longer has to respond to complex philosophical questions about whether or not reasoning by analogy helps us to understand the "I" of another at anything like the level that we understand the primordial ego. Instead, we can respond to the Other as another believer in the faith, and also take as a guide to behavior Christ's injunction that when we assist others, we assist him. This allowed Stein to develop a concept of the importance of altruism that, while not nearly as recondite as her work in phenomenology, was sustained by her in a series of essays.

Stein's work on the moral then encompassed several notions as foci. Perhaps most controversially for contemporary thought, she drew on notions of God's choice to further distinctions between the sexes, but nevertheless—as had Astell centuries before her—her views sustained women's rights. Stein argues that what believers refer to as the Fall "restricted" the "powers" of women.[24] More important, she expands her ontology to include in the largest sense all persons in Christ's body, and thus she finds it a moral duty to interact with others in a way that mirrors divine love and grace. As Oben notes: "Edith Stein writes that she cannot believe that any human being is excluded from redemption by the visible limits of the Catholic church. Rather, she believes that Christ lives constantly in his members and continues to suffer in them. Hence Jews are also part of the mystical body of Christ, and the persecution of the Jews is a continuation of Christ's crucifixion in time, a continuation of his crucified humanity."[25]

This particular point of view allowed Stein to respond to the Holocaust in a manner completely different from the mode employed by Simone Weil, for example. At a later point I will discuss the controversy surrounding Weil's difficulties with her Judaic history, but it is noteworthy that, although it is Stein who actually makes the conversion to Christianity (and then to the convent), Stein refuses to turn away from Judaism. Rather, in her extrapolating point of view, she sees the trials of the Holocaust as part of the Jews' participating in a Christological suffering.[26] It also allows her to pray for the Nazis, being constantly aware of their humanity and the possibility of their moral redemption.

If Stein has a strong Christian morality that manifests much of the concern that drove her original philosophical work, she also incorporates into her ethical views strands of mysticism, which given her previously articulated epistemology (in which the highest form of knowing was reserved for a supernatural experience of God) drive the substantive portion of her moral reasoning. According to Oben,

> [Stein] writes of the being of the three divine Persons. She defines the divine spirit as the utterly "selfless" which is made manifest, rather than lost, in the surrender of each divine Person to the other. Creatures' spirituality, though different, must enter into this realm of generous love. And the three fundamental forms of the human being are related to the triune Being: psychical being to God the father, corporal being to God the Son, and spiritual being to God the Holy Spirit.[27]

Thus, as Oben notes, each of us, in a bestowal of the self to another, participates in this form of divine love. This account of empathy, to be sure, is on a completely different footing from that which Stein had given in her dissertation, but what is remarkable about the continuity of Stein's thought is that it is clearly the problem of Empathy, writ large or small, that motivates much of her work. How can we as humans in our world interact with others so as to accomplish a good, rather than yield a harm? This age-old question of ethics—not to be confused with such twenty-first-century variants as "why be ethical?"—can be viewed deontologically, consequentially, phenomenologically, or Christologically. That Stein, in the course of her work, chose the latter two paths (certainly the least frequently explicated in the literature) is testimony to both an original mind and a refusal to lose sight of a goal simply because of shifting frameworks. It is no doubt this amalgamation of a variety of takes on Judaism, Christianity, and morality as a whole that has a great deal to do with the response to Stein's canonization.[28] Although some of this response (as mentioned in the Cargas anthology, and as detailed in the media) is doubtless related to the fact that objections have been raised to the church's appropriation of a Jew for Christian purposes, a larger emphasis must be placed on the fact that Stein was ultimately ecumenical herself. In other words, it can be said, and quite accurately, that Stein created, through her writings and her life, the conditions for the response that the church gave.

Whatever merit can be attached to Stein's philosophical shift from a phenomenological account to one based on a Christian metaphysics, it certainly alleviated much of the profound difficulty attached to providing an accurate overview of a complex topic such as empathy. As we have said, and as Ricoeur and others have mentioned, an account of the Other in phenomenological terms is intensely difficult because of the privileged epistemic status of the primordial "I." But a Christian account, particularly one that draws on the writings of St. Theresa or St. John of the Cross, allows one to make the move toward intuiting the other's sensations, feelings, emotions, and so forth simply on the basis that the other is also one of God's creatures, and hence must possess the characteristics that are possessed by the agent.

In a sense, then, Stein is right in thinking that a Christian account is a much clearer account. If I can accept what a Christian account has to offer—and if I can accept it on faith, which is, of course, of crucial importance here—then I no longer have the whole range of philosophical problems that I once had. Philosophers, of course, are inclined by training to question any religious stance. But it is an intriguing coda to Stein's life that the religious stance was adopted by her after she had already undertaken rigorous philosophical training—training that had only recently become available to women at that time. It is by no means a stretch to hypothesize that Stein was, in some way, dissatisfied by the results of her philosophical training. It may be that it did not speak to core parts of her that intended to reach out, both intellectually and in other ways. Whatever the case, with a Christian ethics, the problem of empathy insofar as construction of the Other was concerned was solved.

Edith Stein and Friends

Although we have records of Stein's friendships with Max Scheler and others, and although we have at least some account, available in English, of her relationship with Husserl, once again we are struck by the parallels between Stein's life and the lives of other women thinkers of her time, even if she was not personally acquainted with such thinkers. Both Rachel Brenner and Sylvie Courtine-Denamy, in their works with similar titles, have wanted to compare Stein to Simone Weil, and Courtine-Denamy has also made the comparison to Arendt.

Since we will shortly be investigating in some depth the work of Simone Weil, a comparison with Hannah Arendt might be most fruitful. Both women were Jews, and both women were students in Germany at a time when it was comparatively unusual for women to pursue advanced degrees in philosophy. Both women studied with male thinkers who are now renowned, and who have a secure place in the history of twentieth-century philosophy: in Stein's case, it was with Husserl; in Arendt's case, it was with Heidegger.

A great deal of the similarity stops with an adumbration of these points however. Arendt's family was more assimilated, and her mother has been described as essentially nonobservant.[29] More important, perhaps, are internal differences—differences of psychological temperament—that led them along dissimilar philosophical paths. The spirituality that had always been a strong element in Stein's personality (and this is obvious both from accounts of her family life, and from the very fact that she chose, for phenomenological investigation, such a difficult topic) was absent in Arendt. Hannah Arendt (1906–75) was quintessentially a political thinker, and in her response to the Holocaust (and the general problem of totalitarian twentieth-century societies) she provides analyses that are devoid of inquiry into the sorts of questions that normally involve metaphysics. Indeed, Arendt's work, where it is taught in the United States, is most frequently taught in departments of politics or political science.

Courtine-Denamy captures some of the differences manifested by Arendt when she writes:

> Heidegger and Jaspers were to remain Arendt's "friends for life," Jonas says. Yet Heidegger's Nazi "episode" is no secret ("ten short hectic months," as Arendt put it): he conscientiously paid his Party dues down to 1945. Without going back over the details of this involvement yet again, let us nevertheless note that Arendt was a Jew; that she would face Nazi persecution; that attacked "as a Jew," she would react by counter-attacking and assuming an active role in a Zionist organization; that she would be forced to become a stateless person, go into exile and switch languages . . . [and that she would finally] win recognition in her adopted land, the United States.[30]

In addition to questions having to do with identity, of course, we can see more fruitful comparisons—and more significant ones—between Stein and Arendt in the ways in which their intellectual lives responded to the times. For Stein, the turning inward that is required of Christian metaphysics, particularly that which is derived from the mystical tradition, resulted in a pulling away from any kind of philosophizing that had an emphasis on the social, even if she had been so inclined. (And it might well be objected that Husserlian training is one of the least likely paths for pursuing such ends, in any case.) Arendt, on the other hand, in a secularized manner of confronting the world that was not divorced from its Judaic roots, but that did not push specifically toward any other religious traditions, established a large body of work that dealt with the concept of *homo faber,* and, as she titled one such work, *The Human Condition.*[31] Arendt is a thinker who is thoroughly at home in the world, and her thought is not only decidedly political, but decidedly worldly, in the nineteenth-century social and philosophical tradition of which Marx is also a part.

Whereas we can well imagine, given her Christian writings and her thoughts on topics such as St. Elizabeth, the differences between men and women, and knowledge of the divine, how Edith Stein might have confronted the existence of someone like Adolf Eichmann, Arendt is perhaps best known, at least in the United States, for her work on this individual and his trial in the Israel of the early 1960s. Not only does Arendt fail to make use of any sacred tradition in her analysis of Eichmann, but, at least according to some, she did not make adequate use of a number of political traditions. As Baehr notes, the originality of Arendt's work on the concept of banality in connection with the Holocaust caused enormous personal pain for her and resulted in extensive condemnation: "Soon after Hannah Arendt's report on the 'word-and-thought defying *banality of evil*' was published in February and March of 1963, it became the subject of a venomous campaign. Both the phrase 'banality of evil' and Arendt's comments on the complicity of the Jewish Councils (*Judenrate*) in the deportation of their own people drew angry recrimination."[32]

Far from attempting to encompass Eichmann under some demonic guise, Arendt saw his behavior as symptomatic of a disturbing ordinariness, that very ordinariness that we encounter daily which refuses to take into consideration the existence or feelings of others. Whereas we can imagine the early Stein analyzing such behavior in phenomenological terms, and the later Stein in Christian terms, it is not difficult to make the assertion that Stein would almost certainly not have used a concept such as "banality." What is noteworthy is that both thinkers might well have employed some derivative of the concept of empathy, since a complete failure of empathy is what is at stake here.

Ever the metaphysician and epistemologist, Stein retains an emphasis in her philosophical work on the importance of ontological and epistemological categorizing. It is for these reasons that we are struck by one of her most salient moves, that from an Husserlian account of knowledge of mental states of the other to an account that relies on faith and awareness of the other's membership in the body of Christ. But, conversely, Arendt is never the metaphysician or epistemologist—she is always the social thinker, in the same way that the Marx of *Economic and Philosophical Manuscripts of 1844* was. Arendt is concerned with human functioning in this world, and this allows us to see Arendt as having more in common, intellectually, with Simone de Beauvoir, perhaps, than with either Edith Stein or Simone Weil.

David Woodruff Smith sees Stein as part of a tradition of commentators who were influenced by Husserl to take on that most challenging—and as Woodruff claims, most interesting—of tasks, attempting to use phenomenology to apprehend interpersonal action.[33] One of those commentators whose influence on Stein is well known was Max Scheler.[34] As Smith sees it,

> Empathy is not only the way we understand the actions of our fellow human beings in the life-world or "spiritual" world. It is also the way we understand the movements of other animate beings as living bodily movements. Husserl's conception . . . influenced . . . some of the most interesting phenomenological work of the century. Edith Stein extended Husserl's rudimentary account . . . [it is also related to] Sartre's description of the "look of the other" [and] Merleau-Ponty's understanding of the other's body.[35]

In that sense, then, Stein has a number of extended friends and correspondents, because it is clear that she was working in an area, originally, that was to become one of the focal points for the development of twentieth-century Continental philosophy. Sartre's work, especially, since it resulted in a spate of novels and plays that achieved great popularity, did much to familiarize the intellectual world with these concepts originally developed by Husserl and Stein.

If providing an account of the Other is always difficult in phenomenological terms, it is worthwhile to explore briefly some of these extensions of the account that, while begun by Husserl, Stein, and others, were to become more important at later points in the twentieth century. Stein was originally concerned to develop an account of empathy; but as Smith notes, many of our interactions with others are not empathetic. The cultural climate of the later part of the twentieth century, especially in France, seemed to foster attitudes of alienation that (as we will see in examining the work of Simone de Beauvoir) had a number of philosophical implications. But among them are the notions that the Other defines me by her/his gaze, or that I am objectified by the look of the Other. A curious sort of understanding of the Other is engendered by these accounts; in order to comprehend what it is that the objectification amounts to, I may need to attempt to enter the Other's state of mind. But this, of course, is precisely what is meant by the original project that Stein had in mind, even if her purposes were contrary to those developed by later Continental thinkers. Of one thing we can be certain: the projects begun and promulgated by those who had studied with Husserl or who had become familiar with phenomenology were of long-lasting import, and they had powerful ramifications throughout the rest of Continental philosophy and for the rest of the century. As we have seen, Edith Stein was at the center of this work, and her contributions are receiving wider recognition (several recent works on Husserl cite Stein frequently in the text, among them the

Cambridge Companion).[36] It may be said that Stein was a powerful figure in the development of this important strand of philosophical analysis.

Feminist Thought and Stein

There is no question that Stein wrote on a number of issues that intersect strongly with feminist theory and practice, and also no question that, cast in today's terms, Stein's thought cannot truly be considered feminist and is, in many ways, antithetical to a developed feminism because of her reliance on Christian categorization. Stein has a collection of pieces entitled *Essays on Woman* available in translation, and several of the essays available in other places also touch on issues having to do with women and the status of women in contemporary society.[37]

We may expect Stein to address these questions because she must have been acutely aware of her status as that rarity of rarities, a woman attempting to obtain an advanced degree in philosophy at a German university during the World War I period. (Academic positions were still not available to women at German universities at this time; we are often told by those who write on Stein that Husserl had said he would recommend her most warmly for an academic position should it ever become possible for women to obtain such positions.) Nevertheless, it is also the case that for many women intellectuals of this time, identification with women and with a general cause that might be thought of as female was simply not possible. Part of this is because the very project in which they were engaged required that they identify with the male intellectuals who were training them; part of it is no doubt also due to the social-class structure of early twentieth-century Europe, a class structure with which women intellectuals could have been all too familiar. In any case, it is important to examine Stein's work on women because of the light it sheds on her thinking as a whole. We could, of course, attempt to argue that an interest in the concept of empathy itself is somewhat gynocentric; it may very well be the case that Stein's charitable interest in an account of interactions with the Other is related in some sense to her identity as a woman.

But Stein wrote specific essays—such as "The Vocation of Man and Woman"[38]—that address issues we ordinarily categorize as feminist issues in Christian terms, and we cannot afford to fail to take into account these writings. The writings show a gift for threading through complicated layers of argument about gender, Christian ontology, and the place of humans in a chaotic world. Remembering that Stein also held, by the time she engaged in her Christian work, that an epistemology for the human condition would be one that privileged knowledge of God, as found through faith and "supernatural acquaintance" with God, we can guess at how she might have arrived at some of her conclusions.

Knowledge of the divine and of the created order, and acquaintance with the fact that we are all members of Christ's body, helps us accept the differing vocations of men and women, according to Stein's essay on the topic. Remembering that Stein would claim a faith-based epistemology as the support for many of her statements, it is interesting to note how she categorizes gender relations: "Owing to the fall the destiny of woman has changed. First, her powers were largely restricted by the difficulties of providing for even the most primitive needs of life. . . . Moreover, the harmony between the sexes being disturbed by the fall and both male and female natures corrupted, the subjection necessarily became the occasion for a struggle to be given opportunities for action."[39]

Although we may find the language of the "fall" problematic, what Stein is attempting to say here is that, clearly, men and women have differing styles that can be offered to the world, and, insofar as those styles interact with accomplishments, they have different accomplishments. Although it is tempting here to think in terms of Gilligan, Chodorow, and Dinnerstein, and of the differing types of conceptualization that have been employed to deal with gender, there are other gender-related issues that may help us in coming to grips with what Stein has written.

In an essay published in 1995 in *Philosophy and Public Affairs,* Martha Nussbaum attempted to address the concept of objectification, and to present new arguments with respect to it within the context of gender relations.[40] Although much of what she has to say might be regarded as ameliorative, and in that sense has little to do with Stein's work, what she says about "objectification" at the outset is instructive:

> Sexual objectification is a familiar concept. Once a relatively technical term in feminist theory, associated in particular with the work of Catharine MacKinnon and Andrea Dworkin, the word "objectifiction" has by now passed into many people's daily lives. It is common to hear it used to criticize advertisements, films, and other representations, and also to express skepticism about the attitude and intentions of one person to another, or of oneself to someone else. Generally it is used as a pejorative term, connoting a way of speaking, thinking, and acting that the speaker finds morally or socially objectionable.[41]

What Nussbaum means, of course, is that objectification has become a common term because the behavior it refers to is all too familiar to us, even if it is the case that the current usage of the term originated with the notion of gender relations. Briefly, the term is being used to describe behavior (usually from men toward women) that typifies the person as less than a human being. In some cases, especially where sexual objectification is concerned, the term may be used to express the androcentric mode in which women are categorized as body parts—this usage is familiar to us from the work on pornography to which Nussbaum alludes. In other contexts, it may simply refer to using a person in a particularly manipulative and harmful way. We can hypothesize, without difficulty, that even though this term was not available or in common use during the periods of slavery in the New World, it would have been an apt term to describe some of the behavior toward slaves of African ancestry.

The point of this brief quotation from Nussbaum's article is that the attitude that it describes (and which she goes on to analyze) is completely antithetical to the attitudes that Stein is espousing. Seeing all human beings as related to each other in Christ, and seeing special roles chosen for the two genders, Stein would probably not only have difficulty in accepting the extent to which objectification occurs, she would find herself incredulous that such a concept could be the focus of intense philosophical scrutiny. For the entire project in which Stein had originally been engaged—the inquiry into empathy, and the concomitant inquiries, which, as we have seen, are related even if conceptualized in Christian terms—is one that admits of no "objectification." It is not only morally reprehensible in the terms that Stein originally sought to establish; phrasing it more bluntly, it is unthinkable.

The seeing of each person as a member of the mystical body of Christ prevents objectification and leaves each individual as the object of love and regard. Stein's original work, the dissertation done under Husserl, is such an important piece on the concept in question that it is even cited in general clinical works on empathy (many of them with a Freudian or straightforwardly psychoanalytic bent).[42] More important, and with emphasis on the aspects of the unfolding of the person that Stein might well hypothesize to take place in a Christian context, is her concept of the "kernel." As Brenner writes, "It follows that the personality which obliterates the past cannot unfold completely either and, therefore, cannot realize its kernel and fulfill itself as a 'total person.' Stein defines 'the meaning of life' as 'the complete unfolding of the person.'"[43]

The tie-in here to some concept of feminism is clearly that, although much of what Stein writes is so avowedly Christian that it seems not to be consonant with today's feminist concerns, the core of her work is feminist in the best and fullest sense, in that it promulgates a notion of growth for all human beings, one that she clearly feels could be aided by the work of women, with their differing capacities. We do not need contemporary gender theory to see that Stein is taking roles that have already been assigned to women—nurturer, helpmate—and trying to make the fullest use of them. If everyone can benefit from the seeing of another as a "total person," then Stein has, without knowing it, shed some light on a topic that is related to current concerns about objectification, for her work allows for no such concept and no such behavior.

Both Courtine-Denamy and Brenner, in their works in which Stein is compared with other women thinkers of her time, attempt to remind the reader of the constraints that women faced in World War I Germany, and the period immediately before and after. Much of what Stein writes is itself constrained not only by her Christian beliefs, but by the prevailing mind-set. In that sense, the fact that Stein even worked on these problems is already a step in the right direction. If it cannot be said that what Stein wrote was liberating, or even feminist, in the sense in which the term is now used, what can be said is that Stein's life provides us with many lessons in women's achievement and liberation.

Knowledge and Stein

One of the facts about Edith Stein's life that immediately strikes the reader or observer is the large move made from a formal philosophical system like phenomenology to a belief set such as Christian mysticism, even if part of it is philosophically articulated. One might wonder how the well-trained philosopher could so easily give up a sophisticated and recondite system, and move toward an acceptance of faith.

Even with the comparative paucity of philosophical commentary on Stein in English, this particular issue has come up again and again. It is all the more remarkable that it has surfaced, as it is clear that much of the available commentary, even where it has some philosophical origins, is essentially Carmelite.[44] It has not been difficult for commentators to address the issue, because it is obvious. As Graef herself writes:

> She starts with the difficulty of finding a way from the intellectual world of
> Husserl to that of St. Thomas, a difficulty which she herself had experienced to
> the full. Yet there is a *philosophia perennis* not only in the sense of the
> Aristotelian-Thomist system, but in the sense of "the spirit of genuine philos-

ophizing which is alive in every true philosopher," that is to say in everyone who, by an interior necessity, is irresistibly drawn to investigate the *logos* or the *ratio* (as St. Thomas translated it) of this world. . . . By excluding the supernatural factor from their thought, modern philosophers have intolerably limited their field of knowledge.[45]

Here, in one paragraph, we can see a great deal of what was motivating Stein. She sees St. Thomas and Husserl as pursuing similar goals, but feels that the phenomenological method limits its investigators to, as she phrases it in still another sentence, "natural reason."[46] One might naively want to investigate or inquire into how it is that Edith Stein became interested in, as she phrases it, "supernatural reason," except that the answer is clear. She herself experienced something like this supernatural reason when, upon reading the life of St. Theresa—in an experience that amounts to perhaps the best-known episode of her life, and one that is cited by nearly all commentators—she came to feel that she had found "Truth."[47] Another way of articulating this shift in terms that are familiar to us, and that have a philosophical basis, is that these projects also have a great deal in common with the quest of Descartes, at least in the first part of the *Meditations*. All three quests are ways of using interiority to try to address accounts of knowledge. Can we know? If knowledge is possible, what, if anything, can we know with certainty? It is clear that, after years of rigorous training using a method that is itself related to the original Cartesian quest, Stein had a personal experience that for her was a great deal more certain than any of her other previous life experiences.

Having said so much, and having tried to establish the philosophical links between a phenomenological endeavor and one that accords faith a privileged epistemic status, we might inquire as to how all of the foregoing is related to the feminist concerns, however nonstandard, that clearly appear in Stein's work.

The short answer is that the relationship is as has already been adumbrated here: Stein uses her faith to try to demarcate areas of female endeavor, and to try to be specific about what gifts women can bring to the world. But, other than with respect to the specific theory of knowledge issues that we have already attempted to address, there does not appear to be an overt intersection between her work and the various strands of thought that compose today's feminist epistemologies. In a sense—and this is part of what drives contemporary feminist commentary on the church fathers—faith-based rationality is already highly androcentric, since the religious quest has always been defined in male terms, and has been quintessentially a male endeavor (witness the still-present controversy over women priests). Because this sort of thought is so speculative and so detached, it does not mesh readily with the types of feminist epistemologies that might be deemed to be standpoint epistemologies, or any varietal of them.

There is, however, at least some small intersection with current gender thinking. The reason that object relations theory has had the force that it has had in the development of contemporary feminism is at least partly related to a certain commonsensicality that it possesses. Almost all of us have had the archetypical experience that is at the bottom of such theory: the experience of having been cared for during our early lives by one or more primary female caretakers. Almost all of us can, however truncatedly, recall episodes from early childhood that spoke to the establishment of gender roles along the lines alluded to by object-relations theory.

When working with the material that is clearly more psychoanalytic in orientation, many theorists have not done all of the conceptual work necessary to articulate what the tie-in actually is. Although she does not seem to be cited as frequently as either Chodorow or Gilligan, Dorothy Dinnerstein has apt and concise descriptions of how it is, in terms of Freudian-derived theory, that gender personalities arise:

> Early rage at the first parent, in other words, is typically used by the "masculine" boy during the Oedipal period to *consolidate* his tie with his own sex by establishing a principled independence, a more or less derogatory distance, from women. . . .
>   In sum, then: Unilateral male sexual possessiveness rests on strong old feelings, both in men and in women. And so long as the care of the very young remains in female hands these feelings—in which echoes of infancy and of early childhood are fused—will persist [emphasis in original].[48]

The key, of course, is the "principled independence"—the "derogatory distance." This distance does not merely manifest itself as making fun of girls, or refusing to join in games such as jumping rope and playing store. Much more important for feminist theory—and it is this point that is at the core of work by Gilligan, Keller, Chodorow, and others—the distancing also manifests itself, usually at a later point, in the stylistic aggression employed in theorizing and thinking about the world. This theorizing gives us the alembicated thought that attempts—whether in physics or in philosophy—to provide a complete account of the world. Theorizing becomes a form of male competition.

It would be pleasing to be able to say that in moving from a Husserlian phenomenology to a faith-based epistemology, similar not only to that of

Thomas but also Augustine, Stein had exchanged an example of this mas-
culinized and independent thought for one more wholistic or less distanced.
This is certainly not the case. As has just been indicated, the entire history of
the church—and of the lives of those who composed the works that are, in
general, considered to be Christianity's greatest examples of thought—repli-
cates all of the androcentric structures to which I have alluded.

What Stein does accomplish is perhaps best related not so much to any
sort of feminist epistemology with which we are familiar as to the work of
some women living in indigenous or at least non-European traditions. A
great deal of contemporary scholarship has been done on several traditions
in which contemporary women activists have simply appropriated parts of
the male tradition for their own purposes, thereby at least partially creating
a sort of feminist epistemology. Obviously, when appropriated, these traditions had to be modified, but this is the point. When the activist work of Ela
Bhatt in India is cited, she is sometimes spoken of as having participated in
the "renouncer" tradition of classical Hinduism. Although there is little in
the tradition that speaks to women (and although it is assumed that the
householder who, progressing through stages, will become the renouncer, is
male), Bhatt has become her own sort of renouncer.[49]

This is what Stein has done. To be fair, as we can see from the lives of
Theresa, Joan, and a number of other women mystics and saints—a tradition
of which Stein herself is to become a part—there is a much stronger heritage
in the Christian corpus than in some others of women's achieving knowledge through the supernatural and mystical leaps employed by believing
Christians. Nevertheless, here we must say that it is not so much the methods
employed by Stein as what she does with them that speak to feminist concerns, let alone feminist epistemologies. Stein almost certainly would not
have been comfortable with anything like Dinnerstein's explanations, yet in
moving toward a tradition that itself was part of the distancing described,
Stein must forge her own path.

In writing about Edith Stein's ultimate canonization, Kenneth Woodward is concerned, as many have been, by the dispute between believing Jews
and Catholics over who ought most worthily to claim Stein, and the result-
ant confusion about whether or not there could justifiably be a Catholic
place of worship or convent on the grounds of Auschwitz.[50] He also is at pains
to show that a great deal of what motivated at least some in the Catholic hierarchy to take an interest in Stein's case had to do with the intriguing similarities in philosophical interests between the early Stein and Pope John Paul

II. As Woodward notes, "For his own thesis, [the former] Wojtyla had chosen to write on the phenomenology of Max Scheler and its relation to Thomistic thought."[51] But Woodward unwittingly pushes us still further here—at least those of us with feminist inclinations. Stein had already taken the somewhat unusual, although not unheard of, path of meshing two disparate traditions separated in time and space. Her final move is to take a still decidedly andro-centric pattern, that of the Christian mystics, with its removal from worldly cares and gritty reality, and to use it in a way that at least addresses issues having to do with women's lives. We cannot accurately say that her work has much to do with contemporary feminism, because neither in the articulation of its concerns for women's roles, nor in its thought models, do we see such an intersection. But what we see, instead, is a woman thinker at work. That may well be enough.

Stein and the Future

As we have seen in preceding sections, almost every thinker can be said to provide food for thought with respect to second- and third-wave feminist theorizing if a genuine effort is made to work with what the theorist has to offer. Stein is no exception, although a special effort must be made in her case, because unlike Astell, for example, she is more or less our contemporary, and unlike the two other twentieth-century thinkers whose work we will examine, she is decidedly conservative insofar as she also has a strong religious orientation.

Perhaps most instructive in examining Stein's work is the line that we can construct on the basis of contemporary examination by feminists of Christian artifacts. In a spirit of serendipitous juxtaposition, one of the influential volumes on women and the body that I have used here at an earlier point has work that is centered on images of Mary, and that also cites the commentary of Hilda Graef, one of Stein's chief English-language exponents.[52] More important, perhaps, what Margaret Miles has to say is relevant not only to Stein, but to a general line of argument that asks us to examine artifacts revolving around the female and the feminine and to make of them what we can, given extant feminist critique.

In a piece entitled "The Virgin's One Bare Breast," Miles notes:

> On the side of the viewer, an interest determined by life situation and the need for meaning directs the viewer's unconscious or conscious choice of messages. In uncritical or nonreflective viewers, this "choice" determines that

those aspects of the painting congruent with their interests will be seen, and those aspects unrelated to understanding and coping with their lives will be ignored or, more precisely, not seen. . . .

The medieval viewer was likely to associate the sight of an exposed breast not with soft pornography, but with an everyday scene in which a child was being nursed. The similarity of the Virgin and actual women was one of the immediate visual associations of the image.[53]

In this passage, Miles makes some important points that, although they are constructed around visual images of the Virgin, tell us a great deal about how it is that Edith Stein comes to the conclusions that she does about women's roles. For believing Christians, especially Catholics with the Marian tradition of Catholicism, images of Mary and ideals with respect to Mary's life can have a powerful impact. It is for these reasons, no doubt, that much of what Stein writes about women not only reflects a Christian outlook, but is imbued with the spirit of Mary—notions of sanctity, devotion, and altruism are closest to those that guide Stein in her adumbration of female roles.

Thus, we are better off as readers when we take Stein's writing on women's roles as "polysemic," to use a term that Miles and others associate with Barthes.[54] Mary has many roles for the believer, some of them more metaphorical, some less so. Although portions of the beliefs about Mary that appear to have sprung up at least partly out of a felt need for a feminine influence in the church became established dogma, such as the Immaculate Conception, we can hypothesize that at least some scholars will take these Marianistic beliefs as striking metaphors. We are better off when we think of Stein's comments on women's roles in this way.

It is Graef's translation of the fifteenth-century Franciscan monk Bernardino of Siena that provides a focal point for some of Miles's commentary, and part of that translation notes that "God fashioned us from the soil, but Mary formed him from her pure blood."[55] The point is that, following church beliefs, it is Mary who provided the humanity from which the son of God is formed. More centrally—and here even believers would concede the strength of metaphor and image—Mary's own maternal qualities provided the nurturing and care that gave rise to the teacher later revered by Christians.

It is clear that Stein sees women as all possessing, at least in potential form, the sort of role with respect to others that Mary herself had. In other words, each woman has the potential, as a mother, caretaker, or simply friend or assistant, to nurture another. What we today see as the sexism of these roles is a concomitant not only of obvious fact, as espoused in Christian theology, but also of the deeper levels of doctrine, those, for example, that indicate that certain sorts of bodies have become demarcated by God for certain sorts of roles. Just as the priesthood is then defined as male because of Jesus's male body, nurturing qualities and caregiving activities are defined as female because of the special status of the first Mother, Mary.[56] Thus, Stein is simply attempting to rephrase and rearticulate a standard Christian line, but we do not give her full credit for ingenuity when we leave the analysis at that. We must remember that Stein has arrived at her conclusions, as we have said, after careful study—phenomenological study, at that.

It might seem that in these times when the "body" has become the focal point of extensive commentary—much of it of a metaphorical, ironic, or post-modern stripe—focus on the body in the sense that Stein's work would give us is outdated. A strong counterargument can be made, however, because if Stein came to at least some of her conclusions on the basis of the sort of Catholic imagery to which Miles refers, she is in some sense thinking of the body much as we do now. We all come packaged in bodies, and our various phenotypes are perceived by others in certain sorts of culturally constructed ways. For persons of color in white America, we often think of being "trapped" in a black or brown body—and of that housing as having particular importance for our relations with our fellow human beings. Stein is saying something similar with respect to gender, yet she is, of course, promulgating conservative views. Nevertheless, the views that she chooses are views that enjoin us to make the best of the bodies in which we find ourselves. Until recently, we had little choice with respect to gender. Stein's emphasis on body-as-gender-laden construct is one that forces us to think about the historical choices that women have had, and how these might have been dealt with at an earlier point. To be sure, we may be inclined to valorize the views of Wollstonecraft or Harriet Taylor Mill: these women seemed ill-inclined to accept the roles that their sex and gender assigned them. Yet their moves against such assignments were fraught with danger, misfortune, and ill health. Working under the guidance of what she takes to be the transcendent, Edith Stein is asking women to choose a careful and perfected assumption of the roles that they would be given in a Christian society, and then to work within that framework.

As I have argued at an earlier point, there is at least some connection between these sorts of views and other contemporary lines of thought that focus on nurture. Not only the so-called gender feminists have engaged in this sort of thought; other thinkers, of a variety of feminist slants, have said much the same thing. The philosopher of education Jane Roland Martin, in a variety of works, has enjoined us to reconceptualize our old ideas of what might be called education with respect to homemaking and caregiving activities—Martin thinks that these areas are important for all humans, and that they have wound up historically devalued because of their association with women. She does not believe, of course (since she does hold that they are valuable areas of endeavor), that no women should ever pay attention to them.[57] Similarly, in the material that I cited earlier by Dinnerstein, the culmination of the careful lines of argument is that nurture is a task in which all human beings should participate—not that nurture is not a worthy and important task.

For Stein, then, every woman is a replication of Mary, and every woman has the capacity for important nurturance and sustenance that fuels her own spiritual life and the lives of others. When Miles writes that "[t]he similarity of the Virgin and actual women was one of the immediate visual associations of the image," she makes a crucial statement that indicates how deeply ingrained in the Catholic tradition Stein's sort of thinking was. Nurturing, both literal and metaphorical, provides the food for the believer, food that the faithful may use to help them grow toward a stronger degree of transcending. The push away from the material world, as the New Testament reminds us, is a push away from that which is devoid of meaning toward our highest ground. Stein had originally studied with Husserl because she thought that such study would enable her to see into the core of things. That seeing-at-the-heart turned out, for Stein, to be achieved best through Christian faith. But once Stein was able to achieve it, the core she sought became manifest to her. This ability to articulate a core, work with it, and achieve its ends is the center of Stein's philosophy.

A Fuller View

Naively, one might be tempted to ask, "Why Stein now?" As I have said, the interest in her life and work comes at least in part because of her canonization, but the beatification took place over a decade ago and she was canonized in 1998. Still, the interest has not abated. Nor can such interest be perceived as being largely related to the general interest in women writers of the Holocaust—as we have seen, there are at least two contemporary books in English on this topic. Etty Hillesum, for example, although her writing is much more easily understood than Stein's, has not been the focus of as much work.

A guess might be that the level of interest is almost directly concomitant to the degree of statistical rarity inherent in her thinking—Arendt, for example, was much better known for a good while, and her work is much more easily assimilated, but it does not have the same appeal. Stein is most readily compared with Simone Weil. Both felt a call toward the more traditional philosophy from the start, and both were driven toward what the popularizers refer to as mysticism. Although the similarity breaks down to some extent with Weil's lack of interest in her Judaic roots and with Stein's actual conversion, we sense that they were aiming in the same direction.

Interestingly enough, one might state that there was more interest in Stein at a much earlier point. Due to the efforts of the Carmelites, and some few other Catholic scholars who were aware of her life and work, a fair amount of material on Edith Stein appeared in English in the early 1950s. Some of the books are still available today; they may be found on the back shelves of libraries, tending to be the sorts of items not checked out on a regular basis.[58] One can hazard the guess that in a less ecumenical time, a number of Catholics were driven to work on Stein for precisely the reasons that now are deemed to be problematic; she represented a martyr among those who had converted from Judaism to Christianity, and indeed this is how she is described in some of these earlier works. The introduction to a work by Henry Bordeaux, translated from the French and published in English shortly after the war by a Catholic publishing house, notes: "Edith Stein is eminently a 'saint' for our time, and this for several reasons. She represents all of those converts from Judaism who freely accepted martyrdom and thus became a bridge between Christians and Jews. She is the type of Christian scholar who was willing to give up the life of learning along with everything else for the sake of Christ."[59]

What was once acceptable in the realm of religious publishing is no longer, and it is, of course, this kind of statement that precipitated the crises of the late 1980s and early 1990s with respect to Stein's work.

But in addition to an appeal that has been there all along, based on her stunning reversal of scholarship, and on the plain fact that at least some believing Christians are impressed by converts, there is probably still another reason that moves to the fore when we try to articulate Stein's appeal. Oddly—or not so oddly—that reason likely has a great deal to do with the very sorts of attachments possessed by the iconography of St. Theresa, and it is in its own way bound to the postmodern and Continental exegesis of the Marian iconography by Margaret Miles that we have examined. In a way, Edith Stein is our nearest living embodiment of the range of emotions expressed by St. Theresa. For nonbelievers, Bernini's *St. Theresa in Ecstasy* may present a more familiar icon, but it is precisely this aspect of Theresa's belief that almost all commentators find in Stein. This union of body and mind and ecstatic and contemplative devotion is apparently one to which Stein herself had access; it is one point on which almost all authors of commentary on her life and work agree.

A work published on Stein in 1952 by still another Carmelite contains rec-
ollections of her that read as follows: "[Maria Schafer, a contemporary, wrote
about going over proofs of Thomas' De Veritate with her], 'She would go very
gladly into the questions which occurred to me during the reading; and how
clear her answers were. An old carved crucifix which lay on the table kept
catching my eye, or were they [sic] drawn to it by the loving glances which
Edith Stein would give it from time to time?' "[60]

It is this relationship between Stein and belief—completely unforced, apparently spontaneous in origin, and manifestly all the more genuine because
of its historical rarity—that has driven commentary on her and her life all the
way along.

As noted earlier, even commentators on Husserl now are much more willing to at least mention Stein. Given Husserl's obvious respect for her intellectual ability, one might find the recalcitrance of this recognition somewhat
unusual were it not simply another instance of failure to recognize a woman
philosopher. But new work on Husserl routinely mentions Stein, even if only
in passing.[61]

Because it is now much easier than it was to make philosophical moves
that might seem to be category errors, it is also much easier to recognize at
least the general aim of Stein's epistemological task: as I have said, Edith Stein
saw the "knowledge" of faith, especially that achieved through what she herself termed supernatural means, as akin to—and more important, and more
certain than—anything that could be achieved through phenomenological
reduction. It is not accidental that this is the case; the parallels between the
"essence" allegedly attained or grasped through the reduction and the core
gotten at by faith are great, and since Husserlian phenomenology is at best a
Cartesian sort of endeavor, asking for a temporary suspension of all else, it is
not going too far astray to say that it is, in itself, a sort of faith. This was Stein's
insight, and for this insight we owe her a debt of gratitude, since it remains a
strikingly original philosophical effort.

Courtine-Denamy and Brenner, our contemporary authors who write of
Stein under the rubric of Jewish women authors of the Holocaust, so to speak,
also see Stein as someone driven largely by faith. What they want to emphasize, however, are the Judaic origins of that faith. It is interesting to note that
there is, in the popular culture, now a much larger recognition of some elements of commonality among Judaism, Christianity, and Islam. Such recognition has been fueled not only by recent terrorist events, but by the hard
work of such thinkers as Michael Lerner and Cornel West who have striven
to find points of intersection between the major Western faiths.[62]

The Judaic tradition of devotion was, then, a springboard for Edith Stein, and one that she took seriously. If here I have emphasized the strength of her original commitment to Husserlian method, this does not detract from what all accounts mention as the devout nature of the household in which she grew up. Two factors, then, collided to make Stein's conversion to Christianity an intellectual one and at the same time an importantly faith-demarcated one: her original Jewish observance and the inward and Cartesian nature of the phenomenological system itself.

The difficulties posed by Stein's beatification and canonization are, if not philosophical difficulties, thought-provoking ones, for surviving members of her family by no means agreed on the importance of the ceremonies, or what to do about them. Susanne Batzdorff, Stein's niece, writes: "Choral singing and short speeches heighten the joyous mood that pervades this audience of about 70,000 [in a stadium], as they await the arrival of Pope John Paul II. I sit between my son and my husband, and suddenly it hits me: all these people are gathered here to witness my aunt Edith Stein declared a blessed martyr of the Catholic church. Yet in August 1942, when a freight train carried her to her death in a gas chamber, no one would help or cry out to stop the horror that snuffed out her life."[63]

The problem for surviving family members had been not only the plain fact of Stein's conversion, but what we now know as the refusal of many believing Catholics and high-ranking members of the Catholic bishopric to make statements or to intervene in the killings, about which they knew. But intriguingly enough it was the very efforts of Dutch Catholic prelates to make a statement against the deportations of the Jews in Nazi-occupied Holland (the same wave of deportations that ultimately led to the death of Anne Frank) that led, historically, to Edith Stein's execution, since it is known that the order for her arrest and the arrests of other Catholic religious who had converted from Judaism came immediately on the heels of such a statement.[64]

So conundrum follows on conundrum, as the very circumstances of Stein's death baffle, both in what they say about worshipful communities at large, and in what they say about Stein herself. As Woodward notes, she is supposed to have remarked, "Come, let us go for the people," when told that she would have to go to the camps. This remark has been interpreted as having referred to nonconverted Jews, but a more generous interpretation—one that Stein herself might have employed—is that she went for all people.

Edith Stein's life is indeed the life of a woman in dark times. From Simone Weil's questioning of Vichy authorities as to who or what is a Jew, to Arendt's more politicized response to the Holocaust, Jewish women intellectuals left a mark that stands through the decades and certainly will continue. Stein's life and work stand out as marked by their interiority and their incessant devotion. Since the next chapter will address the thought of Simone Weil, it is perhaps fitting that I close with these remarks by Sylvie Courtine-Denamy: "The destinies of these women cross, even if we do not always find all three at the same moment. We shall be following them from 1933 to 1943. None of them can leave us indifferent; all three are compelling figures who move us with their fierce desire to understand a world out of joint, reconcile it with itself, and, despite everything, love it—*amor fati, amor mundi.*"[65]

SIMONE WEIL   seven

Simone Weil (1909–43) is widely regarded as one of the outstanding thinkers of twentieth-century France, and over a period of time her work has gained in importance. It is cited in a number of areas of endeavor and disciplines. Far from being regarded merely as a philosopher, Weil is frequently thought of in other terms, as a religious thinker or, as some would have it, a mystic. Her work has in common with the thought of Edith Stein a devotion to belief and an attempt to get to the core of things, while with that other Simone, Simone de Beauvoir, she shares the elite philosophical training and bent of the Normaliens of pre–World War II France.

It is a truism that Weil's work is difficult to categorize. In part, this is due to its aphoristic nature. Because her work was discovered and disseminated after the war by friends who had access to notebooks that she had left with them for safekeeping, it was published initially in a piecemeal fashion, and in any case was often composed aphoristically.[1] It is not that Weil fails to address philosophical topics—it is that the manner in which she addresses them is so highly original, pithy, and category-crossing that those with traditional philosophical training usually have difficulty in discerning the point of her remarks. These facts about her work, taken together with the extraordinary facts about her life—her death at the comparatively early age of thirty-four from what most have surmised was at least a partially self-inflicted condition (based on a refusal to eat)—have made her perhaps the most difficult to discuss of the women thinkers whose lives and work I am attempting to address.

Weil was the deracinated child of assimilated bourgeois French Jews—her brother, André Weil, became a noted mathematician, and for the earlier years of her life she had to contend with his undoubted giftedness and her femaleness. Unlike Stein, or even Arendt, Weil at a later point came not only to divorce herself from her Jewish background, but to write about Jewish history in a way that some have interpreted as anti-Semitic. In any case, her early and astonishing intellectual gifts led to her entry into the Ecole Normale Supérieure at a time when women had just been given admittance. (She did, in fact, famously encounter Simone de Beauvoir there.)

Perhaps most poignantly, her history of failed lycée teaching, miserable factory jobs, and experiences of religious insight in a number of Christian settings has been documented and has added to the atmosphere of mystery and incomprehension surrounding her work. One fact stands out: her original interest in matters philosophical had been prompted largely by an interest in ancient philosophy, particularly Plato and the Hellenistic schools, and an interest in the sorts of questions associated with Greek thought later manifested itself in her work on labor, faith, and love.

Although her writings fall into areas that might be generally demarcated by the three topics just listed, a more obvious overview of her thought is that Weil was obsessed by what it is that humans really need, and what can be done socially to try to arrange things so that their needs are met. This, tersely, is what drove her work, and it constitutes the central point of her work. It also constitutes, according to her biographers, the point of her death. While gravely ill with tuberculosis, she began to refuse food, and efforts by friends and staff at a number of medical sites did little to alleviate her ill health, or her own efforts to persevere in ill health. But it is also agreed by all that the reasons for her refusal were humanitarian, indeed, political reasons—her death occurred in England in 1943, when the war was at its height. Here is Francine du Plessix Gray on the circumstances surrounding her death:

> Throughout these last weeks in the hospital and the sanatorium, however, she continued to write in her journal, forcing herself to maintain a clear, strong hand. . . .

"The eternal part of the soul feeds on hunger," she also wrote during her last weeks. "When we do not eat, our organism consumes its own flesh and transforms it into energy." . . .

Her vital signs remained fairly good on her last Sunday and Monday, but weakened greatly thereafter. Tuesday, August 24, was a warm summer's day. At half past five in the afternoon she suddenly fell into a coma. Her heart stopped beating at half past ten that evening.[2]

As Gray goes on to note, the coroner's report claims that "the deceased did kill and slay herself by refusing to eat," but this culmination of Simone's life scarcely illumines or underlines the totality of her life's work.[3] Labels such as "anorexic," although they may well in some sense be applicable, clearly are of little help, since the motivation behind Simone Weil's anorexia is hardly a statistically common one.

Weil's refusal to eat, or her insistence on eating very little, her penchant for sleeping on hard floors, and her general insistence on self-abnegation are all related to a desire to experience the sufferings of others. Such desires are not, of course, uncommon, and many thinkers of the past have exhibited such traits. What is unusual in the case of Simone Weil, perhaps, is the steadfastness with which she pursues her goals, and her thoroughly intellectualized way of achieving an overarching view of the situation. It was not enough for Weil to take little nourishment, to have an unusual sleeping arrangement, and then to write essays on oppression: her essays are extraordinarily well thought out, and bring together lines of thought seldom juxtaposed. In some cases they are almost too original; most commentators have experienced a difficulty with her insistence that the Judaic culture of ancient times had a great deal in common with the Roman. But at other times her insistent originality and knowledge of a great many languages and cultures (she was famous among her friends for her ability to teach herself a number of ancient languages well enough to be able to read texts in the original) help to shed light on a subject in a way that goes beyond mere novelty.[4]

Simone Weil's commentary on the political events of her time is instructive for its refusal to conform, even to leftist ideas, and for its striking amalgamation of a number of lines of thought. Developing ideas that she will, in later notebooks, bring to a full fruition with respect to more religiously oriented thought, she still shows in some of her early essays the same penchant for wholeness. In the collection of essays entitled in English *Oppression and Liberty*, for example, we find a number of pieces written well before the beginning of World War II.[5] It is worth remarking that Weil was still in her early twenties when she wrote many of these penetrating essays. A brief piece published in the periodical *Révolution Prolétarienne* in 1933 claims: "Throughout history men have struggled, suffered and died to free the oppressed. Their efforts, when they did not remain sterile, have never led to anything except the replacing of one oppressive régime by another. . . . The Paris Commune was an example not only of the creative power of the working-class masses in movement, but also of the fundamental impotence of a spontaneous movement when it comes to fighting against organized forces of repression."[6]

One can only guess at what the editors genuinely thought of this piece, which seems not at all hopeful about escaping oppression and which, at least obliquely, attacks that sacred cow of the Left, the Paris Commune. But such a startling ability to penetrate is typical of her work: it is not merely the intellectual giftedness that awakens us, but the emotional depth concomitant to it. These qualities resonate throughout her work and make it difficult to comprehend, but, once the difficulties have been worked through, it is extremely valuable to read.

To give an idea of the course of Weil's thought, Sian Miles includes in her excellent anthology a piece written approximately a decade later, shortly before Weil died. By this time, Weil's concerns were no longer political in the ordinary sense. But the passion for justice that is obvious in the piece just quoted now carries one along with much more force: "There is a reality outside the world, that is to say, outside space and time, outside man's mental universe, outside any sphere whatsoever that is accessible to human faculties. Corresponding to this reality, at the centre of the human heart, is the longing for an absolute good, a longing which is always there and which is never appeased by any object in this world."[7]

Now the quest is not merely for human political liberty; it is as if one could not appreciate political liberty without something more, that something being the ultimate goal of most human endeavors in the first place. Although we may not agree with the emphasis that Weil places on these aspects of the human condition, it is clear that reading the work as a trajectory tells us much about the circumstances in which she died. Her work was nothing if not concentrated, and it will be my task here to try to tease out important elements of her thought.

The Ontological Weil

Most of those who have attempted to obtain a perspective on her thought begin with the later work, for it is here that key concepts such as *décreation* make their appearance. After a number of experiences usually described as "mystical," and well documented in the Weil literature, the last five or six years of her life saw an enormous increase in writing that attempted to unify her original interest in the suffering of the oppressed with a greater interest in the metaphysical origins of the human plight in general. It is difficult to know how to account for her religious experiences, although they are, of course, by no means unknown in a wide variety of literatures, and still more perplexing to attempt to account for them when her adamant refusal to take notice of her Judaic heritage is brought to bear on the question.

It would appear, then, that insofar as ontology is concerned, we can split the adult Weil's life into two parts. In her earlier, more overtly politicized part (roughly until 1938), she appears—at least on the basis of her adamantly political writing, and her antireligious statements to friends—to have been a materialist whose main concern was alleviation of the suffering of the working classes. It is for this reason that she began the factory work for which she is now noted, although to be sure she was by no means the first twentieth-century intellectual who undertook such employment, and it was in the spirit of previous Marxist analysis that she wrote such works as *Oppression and Liberty*. Gray notes that Camus, in the French edition of this piece, had claimed that "western political and social thought has not produced anything more valuable since Marx."[8]

But the turn in Weil's thought after a number of religious and/or mystical experiences, well documented, is remarkable. It seems to have altered her belief about the reality of something above and beyond the material realm: given her level of formal education, her philosophical background, and her self-description at an earlier point in her life of "atheist," this is indeed a noteworthy alteration. After the late thirties, it seems fair to say, without exaggeration, that Weil's ontology became very similar to that of Edith Stein, even if Weil refused, for a variety of reasons, to undergo formal conversion or baptism.[9] She came, then, to believe not only in a God, but in the personal presence of a God, and she came to believe in Christ. She also, as near as one can make out from reading what she said, and reading it with care, believed that on at least one occasion she had had a personal encounter with Christ. Robert Coles finds this particular experience, related to an encounter with a stranger at Solesmes who showed her a copy of the seventeenth-century poet George Herbert's poem "Love," so unusual that he describes it in detail: "Once Simone Weil met Christ, her life began anew, a slave, now, to a particular master. I think it fair to say that she fell in love with Jesus, writing about him, praying to him, fitting him into her social and economic and political scheme of things. She was a nun of sorts, following her vocation alone."[10]

Thus, Weil became a standard metaphysical dualist, despite the fact that she was quintessentially a twentieth-century thinker. More important, however, than the mere fact of Weil's unusual ontology are the purposes to which it was put. Concern for the poor had always been a driving force with her: Gray, who does not hesitate to use the label "anorexic" with regard to her eating habits—even at a fairly early point in her life—feels that at least parts of her eating pattern were guided by a genuine concern for the poverty stricken. She also, for example, frequently refused the offer of a bed, even when she was a guest in someone's home or flat and there happened to be a perfectly good unused bed nearby. Simone's choice was most often the floor. So there is ample evidence that at least part of her personal life, from an early age, was dictated by a desire to not possess more than the least well off possessed, as interpreted by her understanding of what they did in fact have.

After her religious conversion, however, not only did such habits increase, but she began to develop a stated rationale for them that, in many instances, encompassed the new spirituality that she had found. Robert Coles discussed her writings with Anna Freud; Francine du Plessix Gray has no hesitation in indicating that at least some of what she wrote is open to psychiatric interpretation and probably best interpreted as evidence of some sort of pathology. Nevertheless, her concern for the poor grew, since she could claim to be emulating Christ, and some of her behavior—again, that revolving around food is most remarkable—began to be linked to Christianity. Her work comes to be filled with metaphors of food and hunger, the believer's hunger for God, and God's "hunger" for the believer.[11]

All of this changed, and deepened, her social beliefs. Although she was one of the first to denounce the more heinous aspects of Communism, as it appeared in the Soviet Union, and at a time when many leftists argued that the Soviet Union was a light in a world filled with fascism, her later social writings emphasize spiritual sustenance for the world's population even above and beyond mere material needs. Thus her last notebooks, left in the hands of Gustave Thibon and later published as *Gravity and Grace* and *The Need for Roots,* all emphasize the lack of contact with the spiritual in a world entirely given over to material concerns. Weil sees these needs as akin to a kind of homesickness, a longing for wholeness on the part of humanity that cannot be assuaged by the accumulation of material possessions—or degrees, or different sorts of employment—and that is perhaps the regnant ill of our time. For example, to quote again from "Draft for a Statement of Human Obligations," she writes: "The needs of a human being are sacred. Their satisfaction cannot be subordinated either to reasons of state, or to any consideration of money, nationality, race, or colour, or to the moral or other value attributed to the human being in question, or to any consideration whatsoever."[12]

Even given the admitted importance of Weil's religious experiences, one might legitimately wonder how such startling changes in her views about reality and the salience of the material world came about in such a comparatively short period of time. Although it can only provide a clue, one might want to look more closely at her political views; in a sense, they were always more than political.

Although Weil had been called the "Red Virgin" by her contemporaries at the Normale,[13] she did not remain Red in any true way for a very long period of time. Very shortly after completing her studies and beginning her lycée teaching, Simone Weil began to come to the conclusion that many differing political views, when instantiated, bore a startling similarity. Thus she began to make the assertion, for example, that Communism and the various varieties of fascism that she was seeing spread across Europe amounted to the same thing. This realization on her part, insofar as it became a powerfully important intuition for her, is much more in tune with her later beliefs than with anything approaching an analysis of political power. She came to this equation because of what she took to be the denial by each group of basic human needs, and the failure on the part of each system to recognize the importance of human life.

In "Are We Heading for the Proletarian Revolution?" she gives us an unusual juxtaposition of the two opposing forces that she saw in the late twenties and early thirties, a juxtaposition that most would not have made: "The other outstanding phenomenon of our time, that is to say fascism, fits no more easily into the categories of classical Marxism than does the Russian State. On this subject, too, there are clichés serving as an escape from the painful obligation of having to think. Just as the U.S.S.R. is a 'workers' State' more or less 'deformed,' so fascism is a movement of the lower-middle classes, based on demagogy, and constitutes 'the bourgeoisie's last card before the triumph of the Revolution.'"[14]

What Weil argues in piece after piece is that both of these systems—whose proponents would have said that they were in diametrical opposition to each other—amount to something very similar. Her fairly early political pieces that denounce what appear to be political "solutions" of the time merely pave the way for a change in viewpoint that, at a later place, will amount to a complete revamping of ontology.

Much has been made of the place that Weil's early life and habits had in her later beliefs. Interestingly enough, the one among her major biographers who has the most analytic training (Robert Coles, a psychiatrist) is probably the least likely to want to ascribe much of her thought to any sort of pathology, or to inquire too deeply into its origins in her childhood. All seem to agree that Weil showed an aversion to having more than others from an early point in her life, all the more ironic since her family was quite well off and since, of course, it would have been very difficult, if not impossible, for the daughter of a working-class family—no matter how gifted—to have gone on to the lycée in early twentieth-century France. But whatever the origins (whether, for example, childhood eating and cleanliness habits are related to adult abstemiousness, and hence to theorizing that emphasizes suffering), we can be sure about one thing—Simone Weil's beliefs were deeply held, and all of a piece.

Weil and Theory of Value

The changes in thought that Simone Weil underwent toward the end of her life deeply affected, as one would expect, her concepts of value. The easy distinction between ethical theories that we might expect to be able to make for a thinker of her time period simply does not apply. She is neither a consequentialist nor a deontologist; toward the end she is, quite simply, a religious thinker who sees each human being as something sacred.

Again, this shift parallels the other, perhaps larger shift that I have just articulated. It also led to some remarkably prescient but jarring work toward the end of her life. Because she believes in something beyond this world by 1942, the first part of *The Need for Roots* makes repeated reference to a system of obligations that partakes of that realm beyond: "The men of 1789 did not recognize the existence of such a realm [above this world]. All they recognized was the one on the human plane. That is why they started off with the idea of rights. But at the same time they wanted to postulate absolute principles. This contradiction caused them to tumble into a confusion of language and ideas which is largely responsible for the present political and social confusion. The realm of what is eternal, universal, unconditioned is other than the one conditioned by facts."[15]

These are, obviously, not the words of a thinker who is genuinely concerned about the ethical or political in straightforward terms. The shift that we will later see overtly in the work of Simone Weil is there, in nongerminated form, so to speak, all the way along, and it may be seen in some of her earlier work.

The lack of standard ethical or political analysis all stems from Weil's intense desire to focus on the individual human and her or his needs. When we conceptualize ethically or politically, we often do so with an implicit group emphasis; politics is, of course, the study of human social formations and their power, and in standard ethics we would like to be able to generalize over cases. Weil refuses to do this. Even her early work is infused with a concern for the individual human being, and because of this she finds almost all conventional analyses lacking.

The reader is frequently struck by her style, and part of the striking quality is the unconventionality of her thought patterns. A common response to Weil on first reading is that she has misunderstood the thinker to whom she is responding; in her early work on Marx, for example, it might forcefully be argued that Weil misappropriates Marxian categories, or that she has not really presented an adequate analysis of Marx's own empirically driven studies of the stages of history. Although there may well be some merit to these claims, a fuller analysis of Weil reveals that she misunderstands, in a manner of speaking, for a purpose: Weil refuses to go where Marx ordinarily leads because she wants to provide an analysis of oppression in general, rather than oppression as attached to any social phenomenon. It is this "oppression in general," which she clearly feels is a nearly inescapable part of the human condition, that she wants to analyze.

Thus a more careful reading of the essays in *Oppression and Liberty* (pieces that, as is the case with almost all of Weil's work, were composed over a period of time and placed together for editorial reasons) reveals how the work of Simone Weil took the overtly spiritual and religious focus that it eventually did. She finds human relations, in general, the source of oppression, rather than human relations tied to any particular set of forces of production or social institutions, feudal, bourgeois, capitalist, or otherwise. For example, in her analysis of Marx, she writes:

> [Marx] . . . while believing that he was limiting himself to describing a system, . . . probably more than once seized upon the hidden nature of oppression itself.
>
> Among all the forms of social organization which history has to show, there are very few which appear to be really free from oppression; and these few are not very well known. All of them correspond to an extremely low level of production. . . .
>
> What is surprising is not that oppression should make its appearance only after higher forms of economy have been reached, but that it should always accompany them.[16]

The reader who has read a great deal of Marx may be tempted to interrupt that Marx took himself to be going into what Weil is surprised to see, that is, the "hidden nature of oppression." But Weil and Marx are not, obviously, talking about the same thing. It is this startling nature of Weil's analysis that prompts the discerning reader to another level of inquiry and demonstrates a firm grasp not only of history but of human need. What is all the more remarkable is that this particular essay—a lengthy one—was written when Simone Weil was only twenty-four or twenty-five years old. It is the maturity of the thought pattern that is difficult to assimilate, and no amount of intellectual training, at a lycée or elsewhere, can account for such a staggering reach in someone so young.

Later, Simone Weil will take this initial interest in attempting to get to the heart of Marx's work and to the notion of oppression to a new level. It is here that we find the leap toward the sort of material that is in *The Need for Roots*. The human desire for dignity, and to escape the oppression that Weil sees as an inevitable part of the human condition, can be turned toward other matters. To some extent the later work certainly loses touch with political realities, and remains visionary in the extreme. But this is precisely what Weil wants. The impulse behind what she is saying is that we need to step outside of political realities to get a grasp of what it is that humans require.

Robert Coles provides us with a similar analysis when, remarkably, he refuses to yield to the temptation to categorize Weil's later thinking, including work written right up to the time of her death, as primarily symptomatic of a sort of pathology. His work includes a chapter entitled "Her Moral Loneliness," and he makes it clear that he feels that we have missed something crucial in the thought of Simone Weil if we cannot accept the extent to which she moves outside categorization. (Indeed, almost all commentators on Weil insist on this, yet few are able to maintain the stance for any length of time. It is difficult to adopt precisely because her work, drawing on such a rich understanding of intellectual history, first appears headed in conventional directions and then derails the reader, as it were, leaving the reader stunned and disoriented.) Coles notes, with respect to her attack on journalism in *The Need for Roots* ("We all know that when journalism becomes indistinguishable from organized lying, it constitutes a crime")[17] that an appropriate question might be, "What in *God's* name was going on?"[18]

Toward the end of her life, Weil realized, most assuredly, that the combination of wartime circumstance, her own ill health, and the unknowns of the future would make it very difficult, once having left France, to return to old friends and acquaintances. Thus she left with Gustave Thibon the notebooks that were later published, after careful editing, as *Gravity and Grace*. These aphoristic remarks seem to be taken by many to be the quintessence of her final thought; in any case, portions of that work are quoted at length by Miles in her anthology, for example, and interspersed with the longer essays that were written earlier. For contrast, the juxtaposition is quite effective: the new, later voice of *Gravity and Grace* is no longer particularly interested in such problems as how Marx failed to give an adequate account of oppression *simpliciter*. It is this voice that, as Coles notes, puts us in the frame of mind where we want to ask "What in *God's* name . . . ?" For instance, in the section that has been entitled "Detachment," Weil writes: "Affliction in itself is not enough for the attainment of total detachment. Unconsoled affliction is necessary. There must be no consolation—no apparent consolation. Ineffable consolation then comes down. To detach our desire from all good things and to wait. Experience proves that this waiting is satisfied. It is then we touch the absolute good."[19]

Here the oppression that Weil had originally tried to analyze at least in a semipolitical fashion now takes on a life of its own, as a concept that leads to a union with God, at least under some circumstances. Although much has been written about décreation, it seems that its core meaning is directly related to the passages just cited. The "ineffable consolation" and "absolute good" come to us when we have withdrawn ourselves from existence, and despaired. God has had to withdraw himself from us in order to create us—or so Weil came to hold toward the end of her life. As Gray notes, this somewhat Kabbalistic doctrine is something that apparently came to Simone Weil spontaneously, based on her religious experiences. But more important, she came to hold that that particular wanting, that hoping, that striving for consolation that we feel in our most desolate hour was, in fact, the absolute good making itself manifest to us. Thus the withdrawal of the creating process for that good is reversed—hence the term décreation.[20]

We cannot categorize Simone Weil's work along standard lines of theory of value, but that does not mean that she does not possess such an outlook. It is simply the case that her view is such that, in its complexity and originality, we cannot adequately do it justice.

Europe in the 1940s

Unlike either Simone de Beauvoir or Hannah Arendt, Simone Weil worked in an intellectual milieu without, perhaps, making as much use of the various contacts and acquaintanceships that she made as she could have. Her penchant for independent work, her general solitariness and even dislike of interpersonal contact, and her somewhat obstreperous personal character are well documented and no doubt had a great deal to do with some of the social embarrassments that she suffered.[21] Although it is tempting to think of comparisons with the work of persons she directly knew—and she at least met Simone de Beauvoir, as we know—it is probably again the case with respect to her work that some of the best comparisons can be made to persons no doubt unknown to her, but who were her contemporaries and who responded to events in a similar way.[22] As Ruth Brenner has pointed out, even women who approached the Holocaust from a nonphilosophical and overtly personal perspective, such as Anne Frank and Etty Hillesum, have something to tell us not only about that experience, but about the work of women philosophers such as Stein, Arendt, and Weil who were writing at the time and chose to philosophize.[23]

Etty Hillesum presents an interesting figure for contrast, since she, like Stein, has no difficulty in avowing her Jewish identity, but unlike Arendt, for example, she does not purport to write philosophically. Perhaps most poignant, she (also like Stein and certainly like Weil) finds that the experience of spending a year in the camp at Westerbork, from where she saw many taken to Auschwitz, altered her thinking sufficiently that over a course of time her letters and diary become much more overtly spiritual and religious in tone. Thus Hillesum provides us with the example of an intellectually oriented, thoughtful woman whose work appears to be a simple journal, but which reveals unexpected depths simply because of the experience through which she lived.

Brenner is at pains to note the extent to which Hillesum tries to respond adequately to an overwhelming experience. In her writing we find echoes of both Stein and Weil. (Interestingly enough, despite her youth, we can also make a comparison with Anne Frank.) Brenner quotes Hillesum on the experience of watching dozens or hundreds per day being taken to the trains with their inevitable departure to Auschwitz, and the trip to inescapable death.[24] Because of the differences in their temperaments and outlooks, Hillesum and Weil make excellent contrasts to each other, since Hillesum's perhaps somewhat more standard way of conceptualizing the religious leads us into familiar territory. Brenner indicates the extent to which Hillesum was drawn to a straightforward worship of God when she writes: "The notions of God, as they emerge in both Frank and Hillesum, are instrumental to their resistance of terror. God reveals himself in the motivation to construct a self potent enough to transcend the inner imprisonment of fear and despair, to break away from self-concern. This ability emerges in Hillesum's realization of her inner self as the refuge of the defenseless God."[25]

Several points come to the fore as I attempt to broaden the comparison. To be sure, Weil's concepts are driven essentially by her own personal experience, and they have comparatively little to do with any concern about the Holocaust itself—to reiterate, almost all commentators have been struck by Weil's lack of identification with the Jews, and, again, almost all commentators have found this problematic. No matter how assimilated her family may have been—or so the argument goes—one could reasonably expect Weil to have taken a new interest in her own roots as she saw the chaos around her. This, however, did not happen, and as we know from the historical record, during this period Weil wrote a number of letters and other short pieces in which she continued to express puzzlement and dismay at the use of the term "Jew" to describe assimilated Jews who no longer had any interest in or identification with their origins.[26]

So we cannot claim that the Holocaust is a direct precursor—except in the sense that a general time of war and unease almost certainly made a contribution—to Weil's thought, although we can make such a claim for Hillesum. But more important, part of what we try to articulate in looking at the two women thinkers is what it is that a notion of God amounts to for each of them. For Weil, as we have seen, part of the articulation revolves around the notion of décreation. Our hunger for God, and even our disbelief, creates a space in which God comes to us—this is at the heart and core of her explication. The scope of her thought reminds us of the New Testament's "seek and ye shall find." Hillesum, in a more standard conceptualization, saw God in the natural world around her, a world that was being destroyed by the Nazi onslaught and the general horrors of war. She also, again more standardly, saw an image of God in other human beings and was moved to attempt to help them. She wrote of prayer as a "convent cell," a way to escape the ceaseless torture caused her by what she saw.[27] Once again, Brenner notes: "It is significant that at a time when [her] own [life was] in constant danger [this] assimilated Jew, who spoke neither Hebrew nor Yiddish, spoke unknowingly in the old Jewish tradition of *tikkun olam,* mending the world, combining its universal message with [her] Enlightenment heritage."[28]

Finally, in addition to what we might deem beliefs, opinions, or professions, one other point of comparison emerges between Weil and Hillesum: that of the mode or format of the written word itself. Here, oddly, they seem to coalesce. Brenner comments that Elie Wiesel has said, "There is no such thing as a literature of the Holocaust, nor can there be."[29] But what we do have is literary evidence and testimony, much of it composed as a way of coping with the madness. Weil writes tersely, especially later in life. *Gravity and Grace,* as has been stated, is an example of a work that is a compilation from the notebooks given to Thibon, and it was pieced together well after Weil's death. Although Hillesum's style is not a series of comments, the area of intersection here is the journal: both writers have left us extensive journals, and for both it may be said that the journal is one of the most, if not the most, important aspects of their work.

The journal is obviously an instrument of personal testimony, but that is far from being central to the assertion that Weil and Hillesum come together on mode of exposition. The journal also has an immediacy—it bears witness to the thoughts of the individual at any given moment, allows for access to the person's innermost feelings, and demonstrates, at least to some extent, the process of piecing together that goes into any thoughtful work. Whether that work remains completely in a mental format and is never put to paper, or whether that work later itself is written down, or even subsequently published is rather unimportant. That both Hillesum and Weil chose to keep extensive journals during the war tells us that they themselves valued a record of what they were witnessing and thinking, and that they felt that a spontaneous report was the most valuable form of all. As Brenner says, "Anticipating the predicament of the post-Holocaust writer, the artist in the Holocaust contended with conflicting emotions: on the one hand, the frustration of the futile search for an adequate language of representation, and on the other hand, the irreducible need to express the horror."[30]

We frequently speak now of the need to remember the Holocaust, and of its importance as perhaps the paradigmatic event of oppression of the twentieth century. Yet, despite Wiesel's pronouncement, much of what we have now is literature that was created after the war—or literature that speaks to general themes, without the degree of personal involvement that we might ideally wish had been present. The testimony of Weil and Hillesum is of a different sort; it cries out to us over the passage of time, and alters our conceptions of daily events. What if we were to live in a set of circumstances where the deportation of individuals to a death camp on a regular basis was signaled by the sound of a train? The irrevocable intertwining of the tedium of the mundane with death is a feature of these testimonies, and it is one of the facets of the journal literature that adds to its compelling nature.

Hillesum and Weil lived through the time of the Holocaust and responded to it with similarities and differences. Both were moved to a religious response, although, understandably, Weil's is much more theoretical and clearly formulated. Both were moved to an examination of their roots, but Weil is alone among women intellectuals whose testimony we have from that time, and whose roots were Jewish, in her complete denial of her roots. (Of course, as we know, this denial is already predicated upon a highly intellectualized stance.) Both were women from assimilated families who might never have had to address these questions if the Holocaust had not occurred.

Weil's independence in word, thought, deed, and lived life place her in a category apart from other thinkers of her time, without regard for issues confronted. She remains a highly individualistic figure of the war period.

Woman in Dark Times

Because of our response to the Holocaust today, it is easy to take a naive view and suspect that everyone tends to see the situation in similar terms. Thus Rachel Brenner and Sylvie Courtine-Denamy have no difficulty in writing about four women, or three women, and finding the parallels in their responses.

We forget, however, that the Holocaust, and the war in general, are phenomena through which generations of non-Jewish Germans lived, and that it might be possible to categorize their reaction separately. Gitta Sereny, an Austrian whose childhood was marked by the war and who has written a number of historical works, has addressed this issue in a work entitled *The Healing Wound*.[31] Her take on the war, Hitler's rise to power, and the impressions that it left on Germany as a whole does damage to any all-inclusive claim that might be made about general responses to the catastrophe, let alone responses by women. Nevertheless, it will be instructive to compare what she has to say to Weil's work, and then draw some conclusions.

It is easy to recall Weil's striking appropriation of the notion that fascism and Communism were at bottom similar, since all of her biographers and commentators are at pains to make the point that this sort of claim on her part was one of the first that caused problems for her in intellectual circles, and also in her lycée employment. Weil was, of course, concerned with the general degradation of the human spirit, and of the ritualistic organizational pressures to which it must be said that both fascists and Communists tended to subject their followers.

But in making these assessments, we forget how it was that fascism came to power in Germany, and what it may have represented for many Germans (men, women, and children). Far from an oppression—however accurate we may be now in making that claim—many apparently initially experienced fascism as it came to notice in Germany as a genuine triumph of the will. Without advertence to Heidegger or any material as philosophically sophisticated as some of his early apparent attempts to discern in fascism some notion of "being," we can give an account of how the Nuremberg rally of 1934, for example, was seen by one child. Sereny is very candid in her assessment of how she came to attend this rally and what it meant to her:

> And so it happened that in 1934 I was travelling back to my boarding school in England from my home in Vienna when the train broke down in Nuremberg. I was an eleven-year-old girl, on my own, wearing my English school uniform—brown, as it happened, though I don't really think it influenced subsequent events. The German Red Cross, or its equivalent Nazi organization, quickly took charge of me; within an hour, to my amazement, and it must be said, pleasure, I found myself in a spectator's seat at the Nazi Party Congress.
>
> I was overcome by the symmetry of the marchers, many of them children like me; . . . the rhythm of the sounds; the solemnity of the silences. . . . One moment I was enraptured, glued to my seat; the next, I was standing up, shouting with joy along with thousands of others.[32]

This somewhat lengthy quote gives us an unparalleled view of a child's—girl's—introduction to fascism. It is immediately apparent that, like it or not, her response is probably not what we would expect. But this merely signals to us the complexity of the topic.

If, as I have said with respect to some other thinkers, it is crucial to remember the variety of women's experiences, it is probably even more urgent to do so in the case of Simone Weil, since we know that as an adolescent she frequently identified with males, and since she never evinced any interest in what we would now call feminism. In addressing the issue of what it is, especially in developed countries, that might be thought to be common to women's growth and personality structure, one can hardly do better than to return to some of the original writings on this topic by Nancy Chodorow. In an influential early piece, Chodorow discusses female personality formation: "The care and socialization of girls by women ensures the production of feminine personalities founded on relation and connection, with flexible rather than rigid ego boundaries, and with a comparatively secure sense of gender identity. This is one explanation. . . . More specific investigation of different social contexts suggests, however, that there are variations in the kind of relationship that can exist between women's role performance and feminine personality."[33]

Taking these few sentences as a point of departure, Weil's personality development certainly might be thought in many ways to be more characteristic of males, and it is no doubt part and parcel of the influence that was exerted over her in the home by her brother André, and by the family's response to his precociousness. But, as Chodorow suggests, there are "variations," and the fact that both Weils—who might, under some characterization, be thought to be equally gifted—manifested their giftedness through voluminous output, but in completely different ways, has not been lost on most observers.[34] The Simone who had actually gone so far as to sign some letters to her parents "Your son, Simon," during her teens, manifests female personality development—if we may be allowed to say that—most thoroughly in her appropriation of personalized relationships with the divine, and in her theorizing about the nature of such relationships, what they represent with respect to an overview of cosmology, and so forth.

Although such an assertion may appear naive, there is reason to believe that it can, at least to some extent, be substantiated. As we have noted, the later part of Weil's thinking revolves around a series of experiences that she had while visiting various religious sites, and these episodes were, of course, intensely personal. More important, her writings reflect the personal nature of both the experience and the thought derived from it. The notions of décreation, affliction, and suffering, and the manner in which, according to Weil, God fills up the space or void created by our doubt, are all testimony to a personalizing of religious experience that one seldom encounters, especially among thinkers who have been subjected to philosophical training.

An example of this is the frequently cited brief piece "Prologue," composed in the last few months of Weil's life. Commentators have been much perplexed by it, but it is clearly a fine exemplar of the strong level of intimate involvement that Weil brings to her thought.[35] Aside from Kierkegaard, it is difficult to think of another writer within the European tradition who might attempt to address such a subject in a similar way. The opening few sentences of "Prologue" read as follows: "He entered my room and said, 'You miserable creature, you who understand nothing and know nothing. Come with me and I'll teach you of things you cannot even imagine.' I followed him. He led me into a church. It was new and ugly. He brought me before the altar and said, 'Kneel down.' I said to him, 'I haven't been baptized.' He told me, 'Fall down on your knees before this place with love, as before the place where truth is to be found.' I obeyed."[36]

Given what we know of Weil's experiences at Solesmes and in the Portuguese village cited as the focal point of her first deeply moving religious experience, the wording and tone of "Prologue" do not surprise. But "Prologue" is clearly intended to be just that—it is the introduction, obviously, to some longer written work that Weil did not have the chance to complete, or possibly even the introduction to something that she had completed, but which we are unable to identify as the material that ought to follow "Prologue." In any case, its striking tone is reminiscent of, if anything, passages from Kierkegaard's *Philosophical Fragments*. Regardless of what we might say about personality development, there is no doubt that Weil used her intellectual gifts to establish a new context: a context of individualized religious and moral thought that transcended the usual boundaries for such subjects. As Springsted notes, Simone's genius was "very different" from that of her brother. Whether, in the end, this is related to gender is moot, but it is a striking difference, and despite the initial attempts of the "son Simon" to conceal a feminine persona, Simone's manifestation of her talents may, on some level, be read as a feminine development.

Irrespective of how we see gender on a standard analysis, we also have another area of interest with respect to Simone Weil's work that cuts across contemporary feminist theory. Like Edith Stein before her, it might be thought that Weil is developing a notion of knowledge that could be used in new ways. Both thinkers share, especially toward the end of their lives, a concern for extraordinary experience, and for the articulation of that experience as a form of knowing. Weil is, of course, less explicit than Stein on this account—Weil does not, in most cases, advert to anything like standard philosophical theorizing in her later work. Nevertheless, Weil's writing has an epistemic thread, and also possesses a specific social filament that may be related to epistemic notions.

Knowledge

In Weil's early work, more standard philosophical categories—at least social philosophical categories, having to do with exploitation and oppression—are used to get across the point, for example, that instantiated Communism may be no more liberatory than instantiated fascism. In this sense, and in pursuing her analysis of Marx, Weil writes in terms with which we are familiar, even if we have some trouble following her argument.

But in her later work—*Gravity and Grace* and *The Need for Roots*—Weil is thinking not only aphoristically, but in terms so unusual that there is no argument to which one can point (or with which one might claim to be having difficulty). What, then, does one get from Weil's later work? And if Weil may be said to be employing any knowledge categories to make her claims, what might those categories be?

In an important essay, Staughton Lynd argues that Weil is part of what he calls the "first New Left."[37] He sees these precursors of the radicals of the 1960s (and they are indeed precursors, because the writing that he cites, by Simone Weil, Ignazio Silone, and A. J. Muste was generally done in the thirties and forties) as defining themselves by making a great distinction between what Marxists and/or Communists actually do, and what they were, at least according to theory, supposed to do.

Thus Silone, Muste, and Weil have no qualms about pointing out that the Stalinist purges of the thirties left Russia in ruins, and that in no sense of the word "liberatory" can that period be said to have accomplished anything. The crucial question here is how these authors came to these conclusions. Although Muste's work, at least according to Lynd, is comprised to some extent of straightforward analysis, there is an interesting parallel between Weil and Silone.

Silone is well known for *Bread and Wine,* a novel that sets out his point of view. According to Lynd, Silone writes about a dedicated Communist who has to take on a role disguised as a priest in Mussolini's Italy. His "clandestine" experience "takes him from person to person—old comrades, a Catholic monk who was his teacher in high school, a young woman preparing to enter a convent—[and] the disguise becomes something more than that. Spina comes to feel that the Marxist abstractions he brought with him from exile do not describe the elemental realities of peasant life in Southern Italy. He also comes to feel that Christianity, provided his tenets are fully acted out, can give him a new place to begin."[38]

Although it might seem that the important approximation here is some appropriation of Christianity, especially since it is this sort of move that we associate with Weil's experiences in Solesmes and Assisi, a still more crucial appropriation appears to be that of the notion of "elemental realities." For it is here, as well as in the citation of Christianity, that Silone and Weil seem to converge. In other words, Simone Weil had already come to a concept of elemental needs well before her religious experiences; these are the needs that she argues fascism and Communism fail to meet when she is writing the opening essays of *Oppression and Liberty* during the early thirties.[39] So, one wonders, how did she come to these conclusions?

A bent for the altruistic, the "saintly," and the transcendental appears to have been a feature of Simone Weil's life from her earliest childhood, and it was remarked upon by her brother at an academic conference on her life that took place during the 1970s.[40] Although Weil and her many admirers would no doubt eschew any sort of conceptualization for this thinking that employed epistemic categories, or even the term "epistemic," there is no question that such terms are relevant. What Weil did throughout her life was to arrive at conclusions on the basis of a strong intuition that at a later time apparently gave rise to the "special," or as Stein would say, "supernatural," knowledge of religious experience. André Weil says as much when he states that she had a "certain kind of inclination" from childhood for the avocation of "saint."[41]

It is by no means entirely amiss to parallel this sort of thought to that of

Edith Stein. Interiority, and a quest for the transcendental, as I have said, mark both kinds of thought. But although Weil's commentators seem somewhat struck by the manner in which she moved away from a strictly philosophic tradition, they also admit that she was very much a part of that tradition—especially insofar as she studied with Alain. Thus we can see that Stein made a move from her focus on phenomenology (itself, admittedly, influenced by Cartesian thinking, at least in its overview) to a sort of Christian interiority. At least some writers on Weil have wanted to discuss not only the extraordinary anticategory moves that she made, but the part of Weil that is a student of the Ecole. J. M. Cameron has written: "Her education with Alain and at the Ecole Normale was one which was occupied with *texts*—Plato, Descartes, Racine, Kant et al. There they lie in front of one, complex, finely articulated, but in the end available to the attentive reader, especially one who has mastered that great French discipline, *explication de texte.* They are not looked at historically, and they are not seen to have many layers of meaning, layers that perhaps are not so logically harmonious as the surface suggests."[42]

Here Cameron seems to be making a valuable, and somewhat radical, suggestion. Far from buttressing the assertion that Weil's thought fails to make uses of, or entirely pushes past, her more formal training, Cameron seems to be suggesting that at least some of what we see in her thought is the result of a very special sort of training (one that has become outmoded).

Juxtaposing these two lines of thought, we are left with the inference that, for Weil, knowledge arrives in at least two ways: one is clearly, toward the end of her life, through that supernatural level of experience that she, Theresa of Avila, Edith Stein, John of the Cross, and others value. But the part of what she has written that does rely to some extent on the work of other thinkers may seem to us to be almost supernatural in its origins partly because she is given to her own, idiosyncratic interpretations, independent of the interpretations of others. As Cameron has suggested, these may well be independent of history or of any other factors. Thus her Marx is, in many ways, not the Marx of Marxist thinkers or of social historians. It is instead the Marx of someone who has looked at Marx, read him carefully, and decided—with a great deal of academic brilliance and intellectual insouciance—that he is an open book to her and that what she claims he has said is, in fact, what he has said. It is the meshing of these two tendencies in Weil (aptly seen, in at least one guise, by Cameron) that no doubt accounts for much of Weil's apparent independence of style, an independence that many have found impenetrable.

Still other takes on what has been dubbed a mystical, saintly, or Gnostic streak are found in the secondary literature on Weil, and many of these are valuable for the insight that they produce. Excellent work on Weil has been done by the late Michele Murray, two of whose essays are available in *Simone Weil: Interpretations of a Life,* edited by George Abbott White. Refreshingly, Murray does not attempt to label Weil's death something other than a suicide, nor does she deny that Weil's behavior most properly falls under the rubric of anorexia, even if it is an unusual anorexia. It is easy to simply make the assertion that Weil acted toward the end under a "saintly" tradition, and to leave it at that. Murray, however, pushes the analysis further. Following my analysis of modes of knowledge acquisition, Murray is more specific about a certain type of Gnostic tradition of both knowledge acquisition and overt behavior. Murray elucidates the connection to the Cathars, an heretical group related to the doctrine more commonly known as Albigensian, and frequently cited in the Weil literature. Murray writes:

> Simone Weil chose her death from the model proposed by those Cathari who had achieved the highest mystical experience and passed the most secret initiation tests to become the Perfecta, the leaders of the community. Steven Runciman explained: "There was one other ceremony or rather practice in which the Perfect indulged, though its importance and frequency has probably been exaggerated by horrified Orthodox writers. This was the Endura. Certain of the Perfect carried out their doctrines to the logical end and deliberately committed suicide by self-starvation. The whole process was undertaken with the observance of a ritual . . . the dying man or woman being regarded with deep reverential admiration."[43]

The tie-in to knowledge is, of course, related to that supernatural form to which I have already alluded, although this act represents the culminating point for the believer. As Weil herself had written, at that point "the very mind which conceives finds itself degraded to being one out of the number of appearances."[44] It is there that supercognitive or superrational knowledge begins—and it cannot properly begin until the more rational, more lucid, more logical parts of the mind have been turned off. Presumably, if adequately nourished, they will still remain in control. Part of the apparatus of their destruction is the withholding of nourishment.

Weil Again and Again

In reading the commentators on Weil, one is surprised by the number of times that one sees remarks to the effect that "Weil's thought is for all time," or "We can easily make use of Weil's thoughts on war today." This somewhat simplistic account seems to assume naively that everything that Weil wrote was of equal value, or that Weil herself was not a human being on the face of this earth, like any other, and like all human beings, prone to error.

It is difficult to remember that a great deal of the work for which Simone Weil was most noted was never intended by her for publication, and is the result of efforts by Gustave Thibon and others.[45] The work that was published, even before the war, is scarcely of uniform quality. One of the most interesting compilations is infrequently cited: Dorothy Tuck McFarland and Wilhelmina Van Ness edited an anthology entitled *Formative Writings: 1929–1941,* and it contains a number of pieces actually published before the war and during the early years of it that are not normally cited in overviews of Weil's work.[46] Lost by many writers in the desire to glorify all things written by Weil is the plain fact that much of the early pacifist writing, as Weil later herself admitted, was wrong-headed: it failed to understand adequately the special and peculiar menace posed by the Nazis and the terrible risks to all posed by their collaborators.

For example, Weil published a brief piece entitled "Do We Have to Grease Our Combat Boots?" in a leftist periodical called *Vigilance* in 1936. In it, Weil writes:

> It's said that fascism is war. What does that mean, if not that the fascist states will not shrink from the unspeakable disasters a war would bring about? Whereas we—we do shrink from them. Yes, we do and we will shrink from the prospect of war. But not because we are cowards. I repeat, all those who are afraid of looking like cowards in their own eyes are free to go and get themselves killed in Spain. . . . It is not a matter of courage or cowardice; it is a matter of weighing one's responsibilities and not taking on responsibility for a disaster of incomparable magnitude.[47]

Weil, of course, is well known for having attempted to participate in the Spanish civil war herself.

Because of the alterations in her position over time, Simone Weil is not easily categorizable in any sense—as McFarland and Van Ness claim, some of her work is recognizably philosophical (they have taken the trouble to include her thesis on perception in Descartes in their compilation), and insofar as it is recognizably philosophical, much of it runs counter to standard commentary.

It is a mistake, then, to think of Weil's work as all of a piece, or even as all equally valuable. But this is perhaps why we do value Weil. In an unusual sort of way, she bears a parallel to Mary Astell. Like Astell, she treads many paths, and we are drawn to her because of one apparent position, only to find other threads in her work that seemingly contradict it or that do not engage us in the same kind of way. But this, paradoxically, may represent what is most worthwhile in her and her work. It is easy to value the Weil of *Gravity and Grace* or *The Need for Roots*. It is much more difficult to value the works that seem to ask for peace at any cost, when it was obvious to many what the cost would entail. What drives our interest in Weil is that we can see that, at each turn, she herself is genuinely interested in what she is saying, and that what she has to say is motivated by intense personal conviction at that moment, even if the conviction later changes.

In that sense, Weil is indeed a thinker for our time. What we can place in opposition to Weil—and here there is little chance of error or moving in the wrong direction—is that sort of formulaic writing that is now not only the norm in academic circles, but, unfortunately, even in journals of dissent or leftist reviews. Weil is nothing if not unformulaic. Every piece is composed in the same passionate spirit, and she seems, in some cases, to be unable to let go of the passion even briefly, regardless of whether it pushes in an irrational direction. For a movement long associated with the phrase "the personal is political," Weil is the right sort of thinker. There is nothing that is not personal for Simone Weil, from the sensation of the absurdity of existence that was to drive postwar commentary to the arguments about right and wrong in the Spanish civil war.

Coles and other commentators seem to want to protect Weil from a certain sort of analysis that would tie together the obvious facts of her illnesses, both physical and psychological, and her work. There seems to be little doubt that a great deal of what Weil wrote was a desperate attempt at escape from a world filled with unthinking human noise in which she was terribly ill at ease.[48] Her writings simply reflect her general withdrawal.

Whatever the motives behind her work, however (and they seem far too complex to explicate in any one-sided manner), it is her very confusion, attempts at self-correction, and even her anorexia that call out to us. In previous centuries, intellectual confusion may not necessarily have been related to any conscious attempt on the part of the individual to come to grips with his or her personal problems. Or, to phrase the matter more carefully, if it was so related, it is most likely the case that the individual in question was not aware of it. Although none of us can be as certain as we would like to be about the motivations behind what we do, Simone Weil is a precursor of that more contemporary line of thought that asks us to see connections between our unconscious, our everyday activities, and our long-term goals. Thus when

Weil becomes concerned about the hungry, she becomes concerned in a way that leads to new thinking on her part and on the parts of those who read about her—her own concern may lead her (as it ultimately did) to the Upanishads or to the Albigensians, whereas our interest in her concern leads us not only to this material, but to—at least in some cases—a psychological explanation of it. Thus, on whatever construal we choose, Simone Weil is a contemporary thinker, and a thinker whose appeal will lead us into the future.

One aspect of her work may trouble many, and that is (despite a title that alludes to roots) its deracination with respect to both Jews and women as a whole. Although we can categorize her relationship to the Jewish community as one of an assimilated Jew who chose not to identify—even if we find this quite disturbing, in the context of World War II—many of us will feel that her lack of gender identification is an obstacle to our contemporary understanding of her.

What we need, here, of course, is the large view. Like many women intellectuals of her time, Weil was convinced (and this was also said by Sylvia Plath, among others) that she would have been much better off had she been born male. The combination of this belief—which, insofar as education is concerned, is indisputable in that time period—with her own sense of inferiority vis-à-vis her brother André is completely understandable when we think that Weil was, in all actuality, one of the first women to be admitted to the Normale. We may wish that she had taken a more feminist stance, but that path was not open to her, precisely because of the psychological turmoil in which she found herself with respect to the foregoing issues. Thus, again, if we take the broad view, we can see that even some of the problematic areas for Weil are signs of serious engagement and psychological struggle, and those markers of that engagement are themselves items that we can file away and store for our own future use.

McFarland and Van Ness are on to a special feature of Weil's thought when they tell us that "[p]enetrating to the full wisdom and beauty of her writings . . . may always be . . . extremely difficult" since, as they claim, "something like her own intelligence and genius is needed to understand and assess them."[49] McFarland and Van Ness weave a careful spell around the material and insist that, whatever epoch we find ourselves in, we have to go at Weil carefully: "A phenomenal amount of work remains to be done on all Weil's writings, on their content as well as on the linkages and continuities that underlie them. Because both her thought and her psychology were concrete responses to concrete conditions, it may be necessary to wait until a view of them can be had from a perspective of real elapsed time—perhaps from some point in the next century."[50]

Weil speaks, as the editors indicate, to real conditions. That is the part of Weil that speaks to us, and we do not have to guess to suppose that Weil will continue to be relevant for a long time to come.

Weil in Toto

To see the entire Weil means, perforce, to be able to assess Weil's philosophical antecedents and intersections, and to be able to assess them alongside of that part of her that seems to move far beyond philosophy as we know it. As I have indicated, it is no doubt a mistake to think of Weil solely as a "mystical" thinker—that is to miss a great part of what she wrote. Once we see Weil in her various guises, we can more carefully piece her together, and at the same time do justice to each guise. The philosophical Weil precedes, but is still attached to, the mystical Weil.

As a child, Weil claimed to be an atheist. That she had a position on this philosophical topic from an early point is something that many of us might find intriguing, but it ties beautifully into her later work. We have to ask what motivated the change—and we have to wonder how that change is related to philosophy as a whole.

Part and parcel of what drives Weil from her earliest work is a desire to go deeper than the existing theory allows. When I say "go deeper," I do not mean, of course, deeper in the sense of more recondite and arcane permutations on a certain batch of thought. What I mean is that Weil almost always drives to a point that is the core of the theoretical view, expands on it, makes it bigger, and then tries to move on from it, using her alterations as a platform. Thus in her original work that used Marxist thought, she notices a general concept of "oppression," but she pushes it in a much broader direction than Marx himself is able to. Whereas Marx might have theorized the workers on arable land to be less oppressed than the proletariat, through some notion of "species being," Weil asserts another level of oppression and then places much human misery under this rubric.

This is what makes Weil's thought so intriguing. At first, as I have said before, a reader might be tempted to think, for example, that Weil did not understand Marx, or that there was something else going on—a misconstrual of terms, perhaps. Eventually, the reader comes to see that Weil does understand Marx, completely. But Weil pushes a general Marxist concept in a direction that, although technically in error, is probably very much along the lines of what Marx originally had in mind.

All of the foregoing is what makes Weil so frustrating but attractive to read. We find ourselves stimulated by the moves in her thought, and by her willingness to play with concepts. It is this sort of structure to her work that makes someone like Robert Coles reluctant to grant that Weil had very serious mental problems—it seems that Coles, although a trained psychiatrist, wants himself to view Weil through a lens that is less narrow.

For example, Coles writes: "In trying to understand the life of someone whom doctors declared a young suicide, a psychiatrist finds it all too tempting to scrutinize her childhood, especially when she had no later family life—she never married or had children—and especially, too, when she herself made references to her family that sound a note of pain."[51]

Here we can see Coles employing a certain sort of hesitation—he writes of it being "all too tempting" to scrutinize parts of her life that, in all fairness, psychiatrists traditionally do scrutinize. It is perhaps the ultimate compliment to Weil that the reason Coles withdraws from viewing these areas is that they might tend to diminish the importance of, motivation for, or originality of her thought.

So far I have categorized the appeal of Weil under a number of rubrics. It is clear that part of her appeal is her intense focus on what was the here-and-now of her time, and another part of her appeal is her renunciation. As I have also said, a third part of her appeal is her refusal to adhere to standard categories (although admittedly, this is frustrating, particularly for someone with philosophical training). Given all of this, why was Weil so unappealing to so many during her life? It is clear that, of the thinkers we have examined here, perhaps only Mary Astell (or Harriet Taylor Mill, and even then largely through her relationship with John Stuart Mill) suffered as greatly from personal rejection as did Weil during her lifetime. Fired or asked to resign from many a job, Weil began to take it for granted that what ordinary mortals found in adult life was to be denied her—and we cannot be sure that she did not, on some level, want at least part of what ordinary mortals usually want. With the possible exception of some sort of relationship with Boris Souvarine—and commentators seem to disagree on what this might have amounted to, since Weil's journals are impenetrable on the subject (in any case, it clearly was not sexual)—Weil's adult life seems to have been comprised largely of political contacts and an intense reliance on her parents. Indeed, this reliance was so strong that, characteristically, Weil hid from her parents the truth of her final illness, and all but concealed her tubercular state, and her impending death, until the very end.

Her life was, then, a catalog of efforts to live up to the demands that she made on herself, a failed series of jobs (by any standard), and an unusually childlike attachment to her own aged parents, who then spent a number of years after her death working daily on her manuscripts.[52] In short, as is so often the case, Weil had the virtues of her defects and the defects of her virtues. The very facts of her life that make her so extraordinarily appealing today are facts that speak to a marked strain of unconventionality and a lack of care about mores and traditions. We may admire, from afar, someone who exhibits these traits, and we may well enjoy reading about her life or thought. But to know such a person is, of course, another matter—particularly when it comes to daily contact. Unlike, for example, Anne Conway or Edith Stein, there is little that we know of Weil's life that inclines us to think that we would actually enjoy having known her during her own time on earth. Rather, it is the reverse—we may see Edith Stein, for example, as more conventional in her later thought but also someone whom it would have been pleasant to know. Nothing written by any of her biographers indicates that it would have been particularly pleasant to know Simone Weil or to have had regular encounters with her. Her abruptness, single-mindedness, and lack of conventionality with respect even to dress and appearance make her unique among twentieth-century female thinkers of whose work I am aware.

The most confusing feature of Weil's existence, to many, was her refusal to identify with her Jewish background, or to address any of the issues posed by the forced removals of Jews from areas occupied by the Nazis. This refusal is in part related to her degree of assimilation and her family's bourgeois background. It has troubled those who have written on her not only because it seems to display a lack of humanitarianism, but, also on another level of analysis, because it seems to betray a lack of interest in a culture that has played a critical role among human cultures with written languages of whom we have a lengthy record. Commentators have been puzzled, for example, by the fact that Weil seems to identify the development of Christianity, with which she identifies more and more as she ages, with Greece, and for some reason has a great deal of trouble discerning, intellectually or in any other way, the plain Judaic origin of Christianity. She also seems to want to create an identity between Judaism and Rome, and she then castigates both for their failure to take the "big view."

Even Robert Coles has a very difficult time understanding what motivates Weil on this score, or why she is plainly unable to see that, although portions of the New Testament may owe a great deal to the Greek tradition, we may think of Jesus primarily as a Jew and even a radical rabbi of his time. Coles writes: "What lay behind her deep antagonism to Jewish tradition? Why was she determined to believe that the ancient Jews were especially brutal and mean-spirited? Why did she expend so much of her intelligence and compassion on the Greeks, on the New Testament, and so little on the people who gave the world the rabbi Jesus Christ?"[53]

Coles finds it hard to answer these questions. On an intellectual level, the entire matter plainly has something to do with parallels between Judaic and Roman law, or between what Weil sees as the angry God of the Old Testament and a general anger in Roman culture. But finally, as if completely perplexed, Coles opts for something deeper, that Weil needed to feel herself a sacrificial transgressor and heretic of her past, even if this is largely unconscious. She is able to do this by stepping outside of her heritage. Summarizing his view, Coles writes: "For Simone Weil her Jewishness became a cross, perhaps an unintended instrument in her repeated attempts to follow Jesus by finding herself wrongly judged."[54]

Iconoclast, anorexic, intellectual supreme, betrayer of heritage—Simone Weil was all of these things. Perhaps the greatest part of her appeal goes back to that word that has come up more than once in this context, "saintly." We expect individuals to fail to live up to their commitments, to fall short of standards (even self-imposed standards), and to let us down. As we grow older, we frequently become so jaded that we are quite surprised when these things do not happen; and indeed, experience teaches us that it is all too infrequent that they do fail to happen.

Weil does none of these things, or at least not in the ordinary way. Her last and greatest disappointments—suffered only a few months before her death—had to do with the refusal of the Free French to allow her to parachute into France. Her constant self-abnegation (never an easy task) would have been made more difficult, one would have thought, by health problems. And yet in Weil's case, her frail health only seemed to make it easier for her to deny herself anything and everything. There is, then, a sense in which the label "mystic" is an appropriate one for her. It is a label that we often apply when completely baffled. As I have said, Weil is a religious thinker, as was Kierkegaard, and a philosopher, as was also Simone de Beauvoir. But we would not call either of these individuals "mystics." We perhaps apply this label to the extraordinary Simone Weil because, to be blunt, all else fails.

SIMONE DE BEAUVOIR eight

Of all of the women whose work I have investigated here, Simone de Beauvoir (1908–86) is by far the best known and, with the possible exception of Simone Weil, the only one whose work has already more or less passed into the pantheon of philosophy. Indeed, there is enough contemporary debate about her work and commentary on it that it does not seem necessary to reinvent the wheel; we can count Simone de Beauvoir as a philosopher, and as one whose work has been recognized.[1]

There are several facts that go a long way toward explaining why it is that Beauvoir, much more so than many of our other thinkers—including Conway, Stein, or even Weil—has received a high level of recognition. One might naively think that it has a great deal to do with her twentieth-century philosophical training, but, as we have seen, Weil and Stein both had formal training in philosophy, and in recognizably modern times. There is no question that it may very well be related to the fact that Beauvoir early on became celebrated for her friendship with Sartre and then, of course, for her own work, including novels such as *The Mandarins* and, obviously, *The Second Sex,* but not even the latter of these is particularly philosophical in the overt sense. Trying to take the broadest view of the matter, what her recognition qua philosopher is probably most closely related to is the strength and readability of her work. Unlike Stein, she has a body of work that is obviously philosophical, has been translated into English, and is more readily comprehensible than some philosophical work that has been done. Unlike Weil, her work does not fall so much outside of any categorizable tradition as to startle us with its difficulty and originality. And, unlike Conway or even Wollstonecraft, she is close enough to our own time so that, given even a moderate build-up of a philosophical reputation, so to speak, there simply has not been time for that reputation to dissipate (which appears to be an accurate description of what happened to Anne Conway, over a period of time).

Given all of the foregoing, and given the preeminence of commentary on *Second Sex,* it might be asked in what it is that Beauvoir's philosophical reputation now consists. In general, lines of argument are being promulgated to the effect that Simone de Beauvoir is the originator of the use of the concept of the "Other," at least in the sense in which Sartre himself later used it, and that her work *The Ethics of Ambiguity* is crucial for its establishment of the notion that overriding ethical theories, whether teleological or deontological, are useless in an attempt to come to grips with the contingency of our lives and our constructed natures.[2]

Although I will be concerned to forward these arguments, there are at least two other crucial areas in which it appears that a strong argument can be made about Beauvoir's philosophical originality: the first is the way in which she ties analyses of literature to philosophical themes (a move with which many of us have been made more comfortable by the work in philosophy of the last two decades or so), and the second is her developed ontology. In works such as *A Very Easy Death* and *Old Age,* Beauvoir continues to do important philosophical work, even though these pieces might not be thought to be as overtly philosophical as, for instance, *The Ethics of Ambiguity.* Beauvoir has extended analyses of French classics in *The Second Sex* that pave the way for other, more overtly ontological and ethical works. Her analysis of Stendhal alone is worth reading not only for the light that it sheds on that very important nineteenth-century author, but also for the extent to which it underlines important themes in her other works. *A Very Easy Death,* about the death of her mother, contains important arguments and analyses of bodiliness, death, and decay that are directly related to our conceptions of interpersonal relations, and the recognition of what is referred to as the "for-itselfness" of others.

In all of these areas, Beauvoir has shown herself to be an original thinker, and one whose work will stand. This is all the more remarkable given that she, like Simone Weil, began life in the comfortable circles of the French bourgeoisie of the late nineteenth and early twentieth centuries, with an ease of life that could not, in and of itself, have encouraged philosophical reflection. The temperamental differences between the two Simones are obvious from the directions that their work took, and from the recurring stories about their one (or possibly more than one) encounter at the Normale.[3] In general, Beauvoir was a person much more socially at ease than Simone Weil, and much more comfortable with relationships in general and with at least some social conventions. Although much is made of the fact that she and Sartre ceased to have a sexual relationship after the first few years of their acquaintance, they did begin their relationship as lovers, and we have absolutely no evidence that Simone Weil ever experienced a sexual relationship with anyone at any time.

A great deal of the impetus that drove Simone de Beauvoir in her philosophical work, and in her life, had to do with the complex concept of "freedom," as espoused by her and Sartre. That this young woman, a self-described bourgeoise, should find the concept of freedom so appealing, philosophically and otherwise, tells us a great deal about the spirit of the times and, insofar as philosophy is concerned, the rebellion against the dead weight of the Continental past.

A universe with no God holds no meaning for some—Beauvoir addressed this issue in the opening of *Ethics of Ambiguity*. But whereas Simone Weil used this phenomenological experience of the absurdity and facticity of our existence as a springboard for concepts such as décreation and the experience of the "descending" aspect of the divine, Beauvoir uses it as a platform from which to address how we form our own lives. At the beginning of the work, she notes: "Does not Sartre declare, in effect, that man is a 'useless passion,' that he tries in vain to realize the synthesis of the for-oneself and the in-oneself, to make himself a God? It is true. But it is also true that the most optimistic ethics have all begun by emphasizing the element of failure involved in the condition of man; without failure, no ethics; . . . One does not offer an ethics to a God."[4] The conception here is one of a meaningful ethics that is not imposed from without, but is rather the product of human construction. Although it is perhaps easier for us today to admit that any ethics is itself such a product, decades ago there were still—and to be fair, still are—some thinkers who apparently believed in divine manifestations, and certainly some Catholic thinkers who would not have been able to countenance the notion that all is human.

In any case, Beauvoir begins this important philosophical work from a point of departure that, as she herself notes, leads to differing ends for different sorts of thinkers. Comparing her thought to Marxism, for example, she notes that Marxism also finds man in an unfree situation, because the classic Marxist analysis places man as the object of a necessary historical unfolding.[5] But Beauvoir will use the analysis that she has already given to show how a nondeontological, nonteleological ethics can be constructed: one that admits the contingency of the human place in the universe, and that is prepared to work from it.

The weaving together of philosophical themes across works of literature, overt philosophy, and essays of general intellectual interest and orientation is one of the features of Beauvoir's work. Some of the material in *Second Sex* that has proven most perplexing for contemporary feminists is perhaps best understood as a response to and development of previous work. As would have been the case for any thinker writing in her time, Beauvoir's paradigmatic "human" for philosophical purposes was, of course, male. Thus when she begins the development of the position of women in her most noted work, she has to start from a stance that has already allowed for the male as the definer of the "for-itself," and woman must be opposed to it. This may explain why some of the most compelling parts of this work are those that have to do with literature and literary analyses. It is in the work of a number of nineteenth- and twentieth-century French authors that Beauvoir seems best able to make statements about the relations of men to women and the philosophical significance of those relationships.

Beauvoir's work is all of a piece, perhaps to an extent that has not been recognized by many of her commentators. The Beauvoir who sees Gina Sanseverina of *The Charterhouse of Parma* as a woman who has succeeded in casting off much of female "immanence" is also the thinker who wrote the opening pages of *Ethics of Ambiguity*. We must inquire into the sources of Beauvoir's thought.

The Ontology of Simone de Beauvoir

Beauvoir's materialist ontology is set out flat-footedly in *Ethics,* but it comes across perhaps more clearly—and certainly with more verve—in some of her other works. *A Very Easy Death,* a work written after she had experienced the death of her mother from cancer, is a somewhat neglected piece of her corpus. If it is always somewhat difficult for us to experience the Other in the Other's for-itselfness, one might be somewhat surprised by the paradoxical notion that it would be possible to experience the Other more genuinely when that

Other has, in fact, been reduced to a heap of the in-itself. But this is precisely what moves Beauvoir in this work, and in this analysis of her mother's death we find a moving account of how coming to grips with mortality, facticity, and the sheer corruptibility of human flesh makes one perceive the other parts of human existence—constructions though they are—more fully.

Beauvoir had to suffer through some of the difficulties attendant upon any caregiver of the terminally ill. Her experience in caring for her mother was defined by sights, sounds, and odors that left a shattering mark, and she employs these sensations to give us philosophical perspective. Combining this material with some thoughts taken from *Old Age,* we are easily able to get a new perspective on the importance of materialism as a bare-bones address-ing of ontological issues for Beauvoir, and on the uses to which it may be put.

A central insight taken from *A Very Easy Death* has to do with the impor-tance of frailty and vulnerability in our construction of the human and in our ability to guess at another's existence as a for-itself. Simone's somewhat frag-ile relationship with her mother has been well documented in *Memoirs of a Dutiful Daughter,* and it is clear from a great deal of what she wrote that she was often unable to see her mother as anything more than a bourgeoise, and one who did not understand her—Simone's—own aims. But as her mother lies dying, the bare fact of her soon-to-be-death and the corporeality with which she finds herself faced are overwhelming: "Poupette [her sister Hélène] had suffered from the smell, but for my part I was aware of almost nothing, except for the scent of the eau de cologne that I often put on Maman's fore-head and cheeks, and that seemed to me sweetish and sickening: I shall never be able to use that brand again. . . . I was calmer than before Prague. The tran-sition from my mother to a living corpse had been definitively accom-plished."[6]

This seeing of her mother has an effect on Beauvoir that is somewhat un-settling: for the first time, she is able to experience her mother more fully as a person. As Elaine Marks writes, "The image of a human being agonizing on a bed . . . is forced on her by the event."[7] One way of articulating how this al-teration in point of view changes Beauvoir's perspective is to notice that our perception of the Other is related closely to the mirroring phenomenon that the Other forces upon us. The stern *maman* in black silk is the *maman* whom Simone has always known; the actual corporeal *maman* of decay and death is new to her, and oddly, more fully human. Her dying also causes some small alterations in her mother's beliefs: when she is first admitted to the hospital, she is quite upset to be placed near some working-class women whose behavior bothers her. Toward the end, she begins to be able to speak to everyone in the hospital as an equal, regardless of social class.[8]

A concomitant theme of the human-as-trapped-in-a-contingent viscosity is also part of *Old Age*. Here the importance of memory is elucidated; memory serves to bind us to our previous projects—our ways of overcoming, at least insofar as is possible, our materiality—but memory can play the older person false. The phenomenological accounts of memory delineated by Beauvoir are quite striking, and portions of this particular work serve as the exemplary material on Beauvoir for Mary Warnock's *Women Philosophers*.[9] One of the reasons that memory becomes more alive for the elderly individual has, of course, not only to do with the pull of the past in its vivacity but with the lack of projects of current compelling interest for those who are older. Then, of course, there is the obvious phenomenon that the experience of time when one is older renders each moment less valuable, simply because more moments have been lived. As Beauvoir writes:

> It is his childhood above all that returns to haunt the aged man. . . . The reason why [old men] turn so readily to their childhood is clear—they are possessed by it. Since it has never ceased to dwell in them they recognize themselves in their childhood, even though for a while, they may have chosen to ignore it. And there is another reason: life bases itself upon self-transcendence. But this transcendence comes up against death, particularly when a very great age has been reached. The old person attempts to give his existence a foundation by taking over his birth, or at least his earliest years.[10]

In other words, at least two things happen simultaneously: the possibility of projects is more or less lost, at the same time that the future is foreshortened. Thus to recapture the notion of a project, or self-transcendence, as Beauvoir has it here, it is necessary to recapitulate the past. This is not only not difficult, it is forced upon us. The past clamps down upon us, simply because each year was experienced much more vividly and of longer duration at that time, and the memories take on an overwhelming life of their own. As Beauvoir herself writes of childhood, "And above all, the world is then so new, and the impressions it makes upon us so fresh and lively . . . that we think it far greater than it comes to appear when familiarity has impoverished us."[11]

Putting all of these works together sheds new light on the greater Beauvoirian aim, and it does a great deal simultaneously to underscore some of the concerns of the *Ethics* while making clear why these concerns are important. If the individual described at the beginning of the *Ethics* is trapped in his or her body, then that universe devoid of a deity who will provide a set of ethical principles for the individual is at hand. Navigating in that universe, the individual must confront contingency, old age, and death. It is in that confrontation that the individual finds a number of modes of transcendence, depending upon personality, stage of life, and a variety of other factors.

Although it is always easy, and sometimes superficial, to attempt to get hold of the conceptualization patterns of a thinker by alluding to events in the individual's life, at least two points stand out as salient in retracing the steps of Beauvoir's construction of a metaphysics. One is obviously her relationship with Sartre; the mutual influence that they had on each other's work is so profound that one must advert to it on a regular basis if one is to attempt to do justice to the work of either. But sometimes left out of the equation is the effect of World War II, and the fact that Beauvoir and others remained in Paris throughout the war.

Without entering into the debates regarding "collabos" and resistance fighters, we can be certain of one thing: the deprivations, humiliations, and sheer dangers of life in Occupied France from roughly 1940 to 1944 cannot be overestimated. The psychological toll on the individual was high, and the atmosphere of frustration, impotence, and the sense of being doomed or trapped was hard to describe. Many street signs were in German, everything was carefully rationed, censors abounded, and many people were executed by the Germans for whatever reasons the occupiers felt to be reasons at that time. On top of the daily insults, from time to time German troops marched around the city and paraded down the Champs Elysées in a show of strength. If, as Camus was to write later, life is the plague, life is also a state of war. Beauvoir wrote *She Came to Stay,* the novel based on her triadic relationship with Sartre and Olga Kolzakiewiecz, during this period. As Annie Cohen-Solal indicates in her biography of Sartre, superb in its evocation of historical detail, the period immediately before the liberation in 1944 saw "[t]he last German parades in Paris: The Champs-Elysées once again witnesses the passage of one of the most famous SS armored divisions under the proud eyes of Generalfeldmarschall von Runstedt, and of the 'Kommandant von Gross Paris,' von Boineburg-Lengsfeld."[12] Perhaps recent events in the United States can help us to understand better the psychological devastation and displacement caused by scenes such as those described by Cohen-Solal. One cannot help but think that a materialist ontology is reinforced and buttressed by the apparent random cruelty of fate and the overwhelming sense of oppression.

If Beauvoir and Sartre may be thought of as conspirators in the formulation of a philosophy that would address contemporary times, it is Beauvoir who much more clearly—and in much more lucid prose—moved toward a resolution of a number of issues having to do with the ethics of everyday life. Camus's work consisted almost entirely of novels, plays, and essays; except in looser terms, we do not think of him as a philosopher. Sartre left us *Search for a Method* and, later, *Notebook for an Ethics;* neither is easy to read, and, like *Being and Nothingness,* movement through them remains a trial.

Beauvoir's *Ethics of Ambiguity* spells out for us what is needed for an individual to come to grips with her or his freedom, and to try to construct a life that does not engage in the self-deception of pretending that that freedom does not exist. In language that is readily understandable to anyone with minimal training in Continental thought, Beauvoir describes those who hide in "seriousness," and those who accept their freedom and try to define their lives. One cannot help but feel that, as was said by many of the French during the war, the Occupation reinforced a great many of the lines of thought by essayists, novelists, and philosophers that might, in any case, have been articulated at some point, but that now came out more strongly. *The Ethics of Ambiguity,* insofar as we think of works as standardly philosophical, is perhaps Beauvoir's greatest philosophical work.

Ambiguous Ethics

How does one, in the course of life, come to a realization of her or his freedom? Does everyone come to the same realization? Will some escape, so to speak, this realization?

Beauvoir's remarks on adolescence and the transition from childhood to the world of the soon-to-be young adult are among the most interesting passages in the early sections of *Ethics.*[13] We think of childhood as a time of safety; in Freudian terms, we see our parents as gods, in control of a universe in which we are key players. In Beauvoir's philosophical terms, we find ourselves in a universe in which all is "given" and in which all is "real." The trials of adolescence, especially for the thoughtful child, begin when the facticity and accidentality of that world are finally disclosed to us. She writes: "[E]very man was first a child. After having lived under the eyes of gods, having been given the promise of divinity, one does not readily accept becoming simply a man with all his anxiety and doubt. What is to be done? What is to be believed? Often the young man . . . is . . . frightened at having to answer [these questions]."[14]

This is, of course, the path of the individual who has enough reflectivity and intelligence to question the world as it is. But Beauvoir makes it clear that the young person is right to be frightened: there simply are too many decisions to be made. One's parents are disclosed as, after all, only human—they have their frailties, and all too frequently, more than a few.

How does an individual resolve this crisis? Employing some categories from the past, and some of her own creation, Beauvoir makes it clear that what the individual chooses to do with his or her life is of paramount importance—but there must be a conscious choice, otherwise the individual remains trapped at a level that is little better than an in-itself. Indeed, the world of objects is continuously juxtaposed by Simone de Beauvoir to the world of human activity to help us understand just precisely what our choices amount to. As she says: "Today must also exist before being confirmed in its existence: it exists only as an engagement and a commitment. If we first considered the world only as an object to be manifested, . . . then there would also be nothing to say about it, no form would take shape in it; . . . But at the heart of existence he [the struggling individual] finds the exigence which is common to all men. . . . [I]n the light of this project situations are graded and reasons for acting are made manifest."[15]

By struggling against the world and its facticity, human freedom is revealed to us, and we define ourselves. But some definitions are worth more than others, and some choices are not genuine choices, so to speak. The crucial part of Beauvoir's doctrine on this score is revealed by what she calls the "serious" attitude, or what in Sartrean terms is usually called "bad faith." We can pretend that we have discovered that the universe has a design and that all things have been disclosed to us for all time. But if we persist in this belief, or in acting as if we believed this apparent fact, we are guilty of "seriousness," of hiding behind a label or a discovery and failing to come to terms with our own freedom. For Beauvoir, this is the great moral failing, and all else comes second. It is this part of her theorizing (as well, to be sure, as the thinking of most of the French theorists who have come to this point of view) that causes the greatest amount of difficulty for readers, as she appears to be more concerned with how the choices are made than what the choices are.

Although it is always dangerous to attempt to push Sartre and Beauvoir too closely together, literary works by Sartre in general bear careful testimony to this core of the doctrine of human freedom, and it seems fair to say that this central concept is held in common by both thinkers. *The Flies,* for example, was one of Sartre's first plays to receive a public performance, and the theme of human freedom is the theme of the play. Without recapitulating the plot of this work, in which the tragedy of the Oresteia is given existential dimensions by Sartre, it is worth noting that the idea, at least, for the work came to him in a German prisoner of war camp, and that the play had its rudimentary beginnings as a Christmas vehicle (initially entitled *Bariona*) performed in that camp. The circumstances here are more important than the play itself: Sartre later said that he was never so free as in the prison camp.[16]

What he meant, of course, was that the perfect imprisonment of the sur-roundings—and the time to be filled—gave his mind complete freedom, and in that complete freedom he experienced most fully the notion of self-defini-tion. This is the crucial existentialist notion. What Beauvoir says in *The Ethics of Ambiguity,* somewhat unkindly, according to today's thinking, is that those who do not experience their own freedom and grapple with these is-sues are "sub-humans." But insofar as a for-itself cannot be fully constructed without experiencing these problems, she is, of course, correct.

In order to explain more fully what she means, an important section of the *Ethics* speaks of "perpetuating itself" and "surpassing itself," given that the crucial notion here is one of a human life. Again the human who has not confronted her or his life is simply perpetuating human life or conditions of living. There is much more to be done in human terms than that. Beauvoir's explication of this section is as follows: "Life is occupied both in perpetuating itself and in surpassing itself; if all it does is maintain itself, then living is only not dying, and human existence is indistinguishable from an absurd vegeta-tion; a life justifies itself only if its effort to perpetuate itself is integrated into its surpassing and if this surpassing has no other limits than those which the subject assigns himself."[17]

The latter phrase here does a great deal to explain the parts of this doc-trine that many have found difficult: if an individual sets the limit of his or her project, then it is difficult to see how external factors—such as a conven-tional morality—can come into play. But the point here, surely, is that they do not come into play unless they are so accepted by the individual in ques-tion. And genuine acceptance cannot be had on this score unless those fac-tors are fully thought out; it must spring from part of the individual's sur-passing. If I come to the notion that taking something that does not belong to me is morally wrong, I genuinely acquiesce in this construction of moral-ity only if I have thought about the issue myself. My accepting this as a given because it has been transmitted to me socially or by approved others is of no assistance here.

Although, along with *Pyrrhus et Cineas*—which achieved an English trans-lation only in 2004—*Ethics* is, in a genuine sense, Beauvoir's most overtly philosophical work, contemporary commentators have viewed it with a somewhat jaundiced eye. Beauvoir herself tended to underplay its importance in later interviews and essays, and some have seen it as simply an exercise in expounding Sartre.[18] Nevertheless, its salience has at least been reiterated in some contexts: Nancy Bauer, for instance, in her *Simone de Beauvoir, Philosophy and Feminism,* sees the *Ethics* as important because it develops the notion of the Other in new and striking ways: "There is a sense, then, in which Beauvoir wants to say that genuine love is an expression of the highest moral laws: when I love another person genuinely, I both exercise my existential freedom and evince the highest respect for the freedom of the Other, on which, I understand, my own freedom rests."[19]

This focus on the possibility of transcending the mere "Look" of the other with its objectification is an important feature of *The Ethics of Ambiguity,* and one that is almost entirely absent from Sartre's own work. As Bauer notes, there is a certain respect in which this feature is Hegelian, but whatever its origins, it is as important for the full understanding of the notion of freedom at work as one's own project is, or one's assumption of a certain mode. Margaret Simons has also written of the influence of Richard Wright on Beauvoir around the time that these works were undertaken.[20] Certainly, what Wright and Beauvoir do have in common is a need to articulate how it is that the assumption of one's freedom alters one's outlook. Just as Wright does not want to rest content simply with an analysis of the situation of blacks that uses Du Bois's "double consciousness," there is a great deal in *The Ethics of Ambiguity* that goes well beyond Sartre (aside from its having the simple virtue of being very clearly written). One is tempted to say that, whatever Beauvoir may have felt toward it at the end of her life, it remains a very important work.

Simone and Iris and Others

Although the "family" that Beauvoir and Sartre composed contained a number of women—Olga, Wanda (Olga's sister), and later the actress Evelyne Rey—it is difficult to pinpoint women thinkers of Beauvoir's time with whom she was in regular contact, or who might have had an influence on her work. Unlike Stein, Weil, or Arendt, Beauvoir was not Jewish, and hence the same sorts of concerns do not arise for her on a personalized basis.

Interestingly enough, some of the most intriguing commentary about her and her work to be done by another woman thinker (at least one whom we can readily identify as a contemporary) was written by Iris Murdoch. Superficially, the two appear to have had several key points in common: both are women whom we can identify as having done philosophical work and as also having written novels, although, to be sure, it may well be the case that

Murdoch is now thought of primarily as a novelist. Both have an interest in metaphysics as one their chief areas of philosophical endeavor. Both had long-standing and important relationships with well-known male thinkers, whose work is also the subject of extensive comment (in Iris's case, this is, of course, John Bayley).

But perhaps the most intriguing fact about Beauvoir and Murdoch is that Murdoch did comment directly on Beauvoir—and on the project of "existentialism" in general—and one is tempted to say, sadly, that much of what is written by her on either head is dead wrong. Peter Conradi's edited collection of some of Murdoch's short pieces, *Existentialists and Mystics,* contains several relevant articles, including a review of *The Ethics of Ambiguity.*[21] To be fair, in general Murdoch has an interest in these matters, insofar as can be made out, largely because she wants to make what she herself admits is a "ramshackle" distinction between the "existential" novel and the "mystical" novel of the nineteenth century.[22] A general philosophical attack on—or engagement with—what she terms "existentialism" does not seem to interest her. But in her characterization of the *Ethics,* Murdoch writes:

> She [Beauvoir] presupposes, rather than argues, Sartre's view of the self, and produces her imperatives therefrom without discussion. Freedom is the foundation of all value, man founds and maintains all the values he recognizes. The existentialist lesson is that, since he is the sort of being that he is, he ought to do this in "anguish.". . . This position, as held by Miss de Beauvoir and other popular existentialist writers such as Camus, defines itself as a polemical attack on the esprit de sérieux . . . [rather] than as an attempt to work out a philosophical view of moral action.[23]

Although it might be tempting for someone seriously interested in Beauvoir's work simply to dismiss the foregoing, it might prove more instructive to attempt an investigation of it. It is not difficult to say that Murdoch engages in gross oversimplification, but the motive behind her generalizations is, of course, a philosophical one.

Murdoch, as we know, was a thinker quintessentially driven by Plato. Not only do her philosophical works show us her own conception of the Good, but we can see similar sorts of conceptions sprinkled throughout her novels.[24] If Murdoch insists on reading Beauvoir and others as lacking any conception of the Good—and in this sense, she is quite right to do so—then it is perhaps not so unforgivable that her characterizations of the project, for example, of the *Ethics* seem so far off base. But Murdoch seems to be either unable, or unwilling, to read a thinker such as Beauvoir carefully enough to be able to discern that there are smaller "goods" at which an individual might aim, once the individual has assumed her or his freedom and begun the task of coming to grips with the surrounding universe. (It is interesting to note at this juncture that parts of *The Second Sex* make it clear, à la Lacan, that this is a task that begins at infancy.)[25]

In a striking series of generalizations odd for one trained in philosophy, Murdoch seems determined to understand Beauvoir—or any thinker whom she labels an "existentialist"—as someone who is without any sort of ethical view, and for whom anything goes in a universe devoid of meaning or reason. This somewhat adolescent response is frequently encountered in secondary school students, but it is puzzling in one schooled in the careful reading of texts. To be fair, it may simply be the case that the greatest difficulty here is the well-known antipathy of British and Continental thinkers toward each other's work. In her essay "Existentialists and Mystics," which becomes the title-bearing text in Conradi's collection, Murdoch writes, of her original distinction, "I now want to suggest, for purposes of diagnosis, a distinction between two types of recent novel. . . . [E]ven a ramshackle classification may be instructive and set the imagination in motion."[26]

Although Murdoch may also be said to be responding to her time, and to the travails of war, there is a sense in which Beauvoir is a much better and more careful thinker, even given the limitations of the comparison that can inevitably be made between the two traditions. In most of her works, Murdoch never gives what might be termed today a precise philosophical argument for why we should buy her definition of the Good, or even believe in its existence. Although her work may be emotionally moving and inspirational, it is probably no accident (and not necessarily a claim driven by page count) that she is known primarily as a novelist. The complexity of a work such as *The Ethics of Ambiguity* appears to be somewhat beyond her, at least insofar as one can make a statement based on what she wrote.

Beauvoir interacted with an enormous number of the thinkers of her time, mostly male, of course, who lived or worked in France. And yet, save for Sartre, there is no one thinker with whom she might easily be compared, even though it is clear that Merleau-Ponty, Aron, and Lacan were her contemporaries, and that she was influenced to some extent by all of them. If we are tempted to compare her to Simone Weil—simply, perhaps, because both were women, both were French, and both were associated with the Ecole—the comparison is scarcely more satisfactory than that with Murdoch, as they move in completely different directions from an initial conceptualization of the void.[27]

If we compare Beauvoir's use of the concept of Otherness to the ideas of at least one other thinker of her period, according to Margaret Simons she might profitably be compared to Richard Wright. All of Wright's early works, even before his move to France in the late 1940s, manifest a conscious awareness of himself as man trapped in a black skin, and hence subject to extreme objectification from white Americans. We know that Beauvoir and Wright met at an early point, and there are photos and other documents that attest to their friendship. We also know that both Beauvoir and Sartre, in their various trips to the United States, evidenced a strong interest in what was then called the "Negro problem." But Simons, for one, believes that a certain politicization of problems occurs for Beauvoir after the war and marks a shift in thought from the *Ethics* to *The Second Sex*. She sees one important aspect of this shift as a frequent reference to the situation of blacks in America, and a referencing of the parallels between, as she sees it, the plights of blacks and women.[28] Simons writes: "How can we account for this radical shift in Beauvoir's frame of reference? . . . Beauvoir had not been actively involved in any feminist organizations; nor had she been in a Marxist organization where she might have gained a firsthand understanding of its problems. One clue to Beauvoir's innovation might be a reliance in *The Second Sex* on an analogy with racism."[29]

Both Beauvoir and Wright see individuals as trapped-in-bodies and as victimized by a society that sees them as Others-by-virtue-of-their-bodies. The conceptual distinction here is important, for this is a level of trappedness, so to speak, that goes beyond the mere "Otherness" that is created by being under the gaze or "look" of another. Here Otherness and social structure combine to give back a redoubled sense of oppression.[30] As Simons notes, Beauvoir's analysis—at least insofar as the parallel between women and blacks is concerned—goes beyond anything that is to be found in Sartre's "Anti-Semite and Jew," and it does indeed represent a new level of thinking.[31]

Maybe one of the reasons that it is difficult to compare Beauvoir with other thinkers of her time is that the "natural" comparison to Sartre seems obviously to beg the question, and other comparisons find us somewhat at a loss, since Beauvoir wrote a great deal more, and is much better known, than almost all other women thinkers of the twentieth century. But, in addition to these rather humdrum facts, the noteworthy aspect here is Beauvoir's originality. While Weil's work is stunningly original in the sense that we have seldom encountered anything like it, and also in the sense that it is extremely difficult to grasp, Beauvoir's work, at least superficially, seems much more readily placed in the philosophical tradition, and it is something with which we can more easily grapple. Once we do begin to grapple with it, however, we notice that it makes moves that we have not seen before. *The Second Sex* alone often strikes readers in just this way; but precisely because that work has received so much comment, many have not taken the time to examine more carefully others of Beauvoir's works. *Old Age, A Very Easy Death,* and *Adieux,* in addition to *The Ethics of Ambiguity,* all provide outlines of philosophical moves that repay close examination. Beauvoir's work has yet to receive a full and clear analysis.

Feminism

At this point, one senses a weariness or a tendency to shrug the shoulders when thinking about the intersection between the work of Simone de Beauvoir and feminism as we know it today. Most recent commentators on Beauvoir have wanted to move beyond the obvious: the debates about the difficulties of *The Second Sex,* its contradictions, and the extent to which it may, in some sense, push an "essentialist" view of woman are now so old and tired that it would seem to be unnecessary, and even harmful, to recapitulate them.

To cite just one example, Elizabeth Spelman's attack on the alleged essentialism of *Second Sex* and Beauvoir's failure to see beyond the position of European bourgeois women of her circle or acquaintance is now so well known that Nancy Bauer began a passage on the difficulties of analyzing *The Second Sex* in this manner: "A particularly negative version of this view [essentialist, contradictory] is memorably expressed in Elizabeth Spelman's merciless attack on *The Second Sex* in her book *Inessential Woman.* Beauvoir, Spelman claims, runs roughshod over 'the populations she contrasts to "women."' "[32]

In other words, this is far from uncharted territory. Rather than remining some of the territory—apparently so familiar to many that Bauer feels free to use the phrase "memorably expressed"—what I propose to do here is to look at ways in which some elements of contemporary feminist theory might be pulled from sections of *The Second Sex* that do not ordinarily elicit so much commentary. A good deal of the written response to the work has always focused on its intersections with biology (notoriously, the translator of the original English edition was an individual with medical training who, it seems agreed by all, cut out significant portions of the text and failed to translate adequately other portions).[33]

But a great deal of this work shows off, to full advantage, Beauvoir's complete command of French literature, and some of the most resonant points about the possibilities of escaping the realm of immanence for women are actually made with reference to specific works of literature. Like many with a broad view of the nineteenth-century canon, Beauvoir is entranced with

Stendhal, that author whose works are still so valued that a retranslation of *La Chartreuse de Parme* was reviewed widely in numerous American periodicals when it appeared in 1999. Even brief excisions from these sections are helpful in providing specific examples not of women's oppression, but of the type of transcendence available to women. Why these sections have not received the commentary that is so obviously their due remains a mystery, unless it could be that many with philosophical training simply are unwilling to plunge into French literature of the preceding century. But in any case, Beauvoir begins a section that makes extended reference to *The Charterhouse of Parma* with the following: "If I leave the present epoch and go back now to Stendhal, it is because, in emerging from this Carnival atmosphere where Woman is disguised variously as fury, nymph, morning star, siren, I find it a relief to come upon a man who lives among women of flesh and blood."[34]

Gina Sanseverina, the female protagonist of Stendhal's classic, must be one of the few romantic heroines in nineteenth-century literature to have her age mentioned specifically in a text—we are told that she is thirty-six. The relationships between her and Comte Mosca, and between her and Fabrizio del Dongo, her nephew, are depicted as human relationships in which Gina has, in a rare twist for the time of the novel, the decisive role. Stendhal is justly famed for the combination of romanticism and prescient realism of his novels, and for the complex interiors that he assigns to his major characters—interiors that seem more apt to the twentieth century. But what Beauvoir seems to be doing in these passages is providing us with a view of the possibility of female transcendence. This is important not simply because we need such view, but because many other portions of *The Second Sex* do not develop this possibility, or speak of female immanence in such a way as to leave us with the impression that this possibility has been abrogated.

Toril Moi's superb *Simone de Beauvoir: The Making of an Intellectual Woman* provides us with a detailed analysis of some of the tensions, philosophical and otherwise, that arise in portions of Beauvoir's text having to do with the problem of transcendence.[35] A large part of Moi's argument has to do with notions of metaphor: Moi claims, correctly insofar as the structure of the argument is concerned, that Beauvoir proceeds by metaphor and, specifically, metonymy. According to her analysis, woman is to man as the in-itself is to the for-itself, since metonymic association assists Beauvoir in building a case for immanence for the female. Moi's point, of course, is that both men and women are humans, and the overall existential analysis of the for-itself holds, in general, for women as much as it does for men. Tersely, Moi claims that Beauvoir goes much too far in promulgating a notion of immanence for women, and that any clear analysis of what she does would show that the sections of *Second Sex* that revolve around the female body are overwritten and poorly argued. (Moi is writing of such passages as "All voluntary effort prevents the feminine flesh from being 'taken'; this is why woman spontaneously declines the forms of coition which demand effort and tension on her part.")[36]

Whatever the problems with the text (and in a work this long, there will, inevitably, be many difficulties), most commentators seem to have chosen to focus on the sections that address issues of biology and sexuality, and to ignore or pay little attention to the sections involving literature and myth. But Beauvoir cites authors such as Stendhal for a reason.[37] "La Sanseverina," as she is referred to at various points throughout *Charterhouse,* is a woman of resources and intelligence. She easily gets the better of her lover, the comte, is able to navigate her way through court intrigues and remain unfazed, and is idolized by her young nephew, who, at least nominally, is the protagonist and hero of the work. This must be one of the few novels written during this period with such a structure. Beauvoir's point is that Stendhal saw women, as she has said, not as "furies," "nymphs," or "sirens," but as human beings—and in seeing them in their human fullness, he paves the way for an articulation of projects that might allow a woman an escape from immanence. (In her level of activity and thought, Sanseverina is male; Fabrizio, young and confused, finds that fighting with Napoleon is not to his taste, and has to withdraw.)

Contemporary feminists who have seen *The Second Sex* only as a flawed precursor to later work are failing to view the work in its entirety; for every transgression, there is a redeeming feature at some other point. Reyes Lazaro, for example, writes that Beauvoir "makes openly deterministic statements" and that she "claims explicitly that biology by itself is not a sufficient factor to explain the domination of women under patriarchy, [but] other passages belie that assertion."[38] There is no question, as Moi also argues, that there is a slippage in the text between male perception of women and the way that women actually are, but other passages seem to show us an opening. Needless to say, the situation is much more complex than is apparent in the work of some who have written—at length—on *The Second Sex.*

Still another problematic area with regard to the text was briefly alluded to in a quotation at an earlier point from Bauer. When Bauer quoted Spelman's work on Beauvoir's allegedly essentialist tendencies, she was simply recapitulating a point that has been made again and again. Moi spends a great deal of time in her work assessing the exact problematic posed by the level of education that Beauvoir achieved in her time; although she was not the first female *agregée* in philosophy, she was, precisely, the ninth. Although she met

Sartre, Nizan, and others at the Ecole Normale, and although she took the *agregation* exams there, she was not, officially, a student there; rather, she was a student at the Sorbonne who pursued an unusual and independent course in obtaining her various certificates and degrees.[39] Moi's point in recounting this material is that Beauvoir in some sense failed to see how exceptional she was for her time; because of this, she may have thought that her own case— even insofar as her social class and other conditions were concerned—was more typical than it was.

With all of the ink that has been spilled over *The Second Sex,* it would be wonderful if some actual conclusions regarding the text had been reached by even a slender majority. But even today there is scarcely a unanimity on any aspect of the work, save that it is a work of the utmost importance. Current commentators seem reduced to citing the review produced by Elizabeth Hardwick when it was first translated into English—the book is "madly sensible and brilliantly confused," with an emphasis, in each case, on the more positive of the contrasting terms.[40] However one wants to append "brilliant," there can be little doubt that this word is applicable to this startling and resounding work.

The Alterity of the Known

Beauvoir seldom addresses questions having to do with knowledge or modes of knowing in any straightforward way. It is obvious that the Husserlian-Heideggerian-Hegelian project that she completed with Sartre forces some sort of epistemic stance on her, but it must be pulled out of her texts. Nevertheless, if we recall that for Stein an epistemology (this time in the more formal sense) having to do with the Other and the Other's mentality was a difficult project in Husserlian terms, we can see some of the directions in which we might head if we want to move Beauvoir's ethical work toward an epistemics.

Simply put, the objectification of the Other that seems to be a concomitant to much human functioning makes it difficult to recognize the Other as another for-itself. This much is patent, but there are ways around this difficulty. Moments of transcendence may lead to moments of insight that change the status of what has been objectified, and, paradoxically, other sorts of encounters may lead to similar moments of insight. Although it is clear from her relationship with Nelson Algren, written about in detail in *The Mandarins,* that Beauvoir lived through an intense erotic love that altered her personal life, it is not clear that she was able to express philosophically such an encounter, at least not in clear terms.[41]

Her new knowledge of her mother as a functioning human being is one of the most moving aspects of *A Very Easy Death,* and from this work and what she wrote about her mother it is straightforward enough to draw some conclusions. Here the catalyst for change toward the Other is not so much the intensity of the focused love that one finds in romantic relationships but, oddly, the intense realization of corporeality that is involved in watching someone die. Françoise, her mother, had always represented for Simone a world that she was against; it was difficult for her to see her mother as another person, in any case. The fact that her mother maintained many classically bourgeois attitudes and disapproved of Simone's adult life did not help matters any, of course.[42]

But her mother's illness was a particularly striking and graphic instance of infirmity and decline, with the attendant problems. This set of changes seemed to prompt in Simone de Beauvoir a new awareness of human frailty, and that awareness allowed her to see her mother as a human being (in philosophical terms, as another for-itself) for perhaps the first time. Thus, in epistemic terms, it seems that some radical change is often required before the pattern of objectification of the Other can be broken and before the Other can become more fully known. As Elaine Marks has said of the importance of this work, "[The change] . . . is forced upon her by the event."[43]

One of the most striking aspects of *A Very Easy Death* is that it seems that it is the very awareness of bodily decay that signals a change, in Beauvoir's case, in her realization of the status of the Other. This is part of what Marks means, but it is articulated most carefully in the passages where Beauvoir is very explicit about the nature of her mother's illness and the changes that it wrought. As she said, "During the dressing of the wound I turned my face to the wall, thanking my good fortune that I had a cold that was blocking my nose."[44]

This "corpse" is, in fact, seen by Beauvoir almost for the first time. She now sees how she, in objectifying her mother, had failed to come to know her as a person. She also sees her mother as capable of growth and change; she begins to understand her mother's fears. The very materiality with which she is faced alters her conception of her mother and has the effect of making her mother's physical vulnerability provide her with, in Simone's eyes, a more human appearance. It alters what it is that she knows. As Dawn Rae Davis has written in a piece that employs epistemic language in the now-common poststructuralist manner, "In epistemological terms, the relation [of subject to object] takes this formulation: what knowledge discloses is simultaneously an effect of what it inevitably conceals. This deconstructionist approach not only makes knowledge its object but challenges notions of certainty by acknowledging the continuous action of deferral and displacement."[45]

Throughout Beauvoir's work, from *The Second Sex* to *The Mandarins* to *A Very Easy Death,* matters epistemic can be read in this move to attempt to cease the objectification of the Other. Here I write only of knowing another human being, of course, but some of the concerns that Beauvoir raises are even applicable to ordinary situations, in the sense that there are strong hints throughout her work that we know most certainly only when we have had an altered state of consciousness. Paradoxically, this change, which in ordinary epistemic terms might signal a loss of certainty, is for many in the Continental tradition precisely what gives rise to a raised attention and a new form of attentiveness. But because knowing the Other as another for-itself is such a crucial issue for Beauvoir, it is important to try to become clear about what it is that this amounts to.

The same dialectic that in *A Very Easy Death* allows Simone to see the real Françoise for the first time is also found in the opening sections of the "Dreams, Fears, Idols" chapter of *The Second Sex.*[46] At least two things are accomplished here: in being precise about the mythological aspect of Otherness that woman has always had for the male, the difficulties of communication, and hence, of knowledge, are treated. For example, Beauvoir writes: "This dream incarnated is precisely woman. . . . She opposes him with neither the hostile silence of nature nor the hard requirement of a reciprocal relation; through a unique privilege she is a conscious being, and yet it seems possible to possess her in the flesh."[47]

Insofar as man tries to "possess her in the flesh," he fails to see her as a conscious being, and hence fails to be able to make the move that might enable him to communicate with another for-itself. On the other hand, the possibility of such communication is always there, insofar as man does realize that he is meeting "a conscious being." At still another point in the same section, Beauvoir notes that what is utopian about a Marxist society, at least according to the original theorizing, is that "in the authentically democratic society . . . there is no place for the Other."[48]

Knowledge of another person then, requires a move of reciprocity that at least temporarily slows or puts a halt to the game of mirrors and objectification—the game that for Sartre is discussed in his well-known section entitled "The Look" in *Being and Nothingness*—between two individuals. The difficulty of this achievement is underscored by the usual Husserlian difficulties of knowing another that I have already articulated in working with Edith Stein. Interestingly enough, however, there is reason to believe that, following along with this perspective, knowledge in a more mundane aspect—my knowledge of what I do at this moment, or my assessment of a door frame or the clouds in the sky—also has something to do with my positioning myself in the world in a certain way, and my response to it.

These less arcane aspects of what we might ordinarily classify as epistemology are not really addressed in Beauvoir's work, but they recur at various intervals when she discusses situations that might be thought of in an epistemic context. The opening scenes in *The Mandarins,* for example, are replete with sensual description. At a Christmas party to celebrate France's new freedom and the coming end of the war, the protagonist, Anne Dubreuilh, is made more aware of what is going on around her by her own internal quandary and her sense of the passing of time and the lack of meaning in her personal life. Her heightened awareness—a heightened existential awareness, one might say—makes her more sensitive to sights, sounds, and smells: she is more alive and aware, precisely because she has stepped outside of the realm of the daily for just a few minutes. She has been thinking of matters of life and death, and of the murder by the Nazis of her daughter's young lover, Diego. Immediately after her reverie on life's impermanence, reality pulls her back to an encounter with her hostess, Paula: "I went over to Paula. The war had not affected her aggressive elegance. She was wearing a long, silk, violet-colored gown, and from her ears hung clusters of amethysts."[49]

Shortly after, in another effort to stave off feelings of mortality, and aging, she begins an affair with Scriassine. Although she feels little for him, the oddity of her personal situation and her ruminations makes her more sharply aware of what is going on around her. "I was the first to arrive at the café, a small place, painted bright red, with highly polished tables. I had often bought cigarettes there, but I had never sat down. Couples were sitting in booths and talking quietly. A waiter appeared and I ordered a glass of ersatz port. I felt as if I were in a strange city; I no longer seemed to know what I was waiting for. Suddenly Scriassine burst into the café and walked hurriedly over to my table."[50]

Nonobjectification is the key to knowledge for Beauvoir, and although she is chiefly concerned with interpersonal relations, we experience life more fully—and know more and more certainly—when we are more fully aware of our freedom, and the freedom of others. There is nothing about this awareness, however, that is less than very painful.

New Shocks

It is precisely third-wave feminism that has been so critical of Beauvoir; often, it seems, little of merit can be found. Her work, it is claimed, is essentialist; she did a poor job of recognizing the existence of women of non-European cultures, she did not deal properly with material having to do with lesbians or lesbian interests, and so on. Although, from the vantage point of more than fifty years, some or even most of these claims may be accurate, it is also helpful to turn the situation on its head, so to speak. If it is clear that there is much in *The Second Sex* that is difficult to read today because of the movements that have been made since then, we can also use these difficulties as catalysts to further growth. Seen in this light, the work in question (or even the body of work) is still richly stimulating.

Consider, as we have noted, the "Dreams, Fears, Idols" section at the opening of part 3, "Myths." Material that was once new is by now shopworn; almost all who are interested in feminism, and many who are not particularly interested, are familiar with the recitation of the symbols associated with woman throughout most human cultures, of the taboos surrounding menstrual blood, and so forth. But looked at in another way, Beauvoir is the precursor of a great deal that is now part of the newer feminism—the emphasis on the goddess, the now more standard (but for a long time stunningly new) ways of regarding patriarchal religion, and on and on.

Rosemary Radford Ruether is one whose work has often been cited in this regard, and it is startling to read some of her work in conjunction with the appropriate sections of *The Second Sex*. Here is an extract from some of Ruether's work on the maleness of the Redeemer: "What, if anything, is the theological significance of the maleness of the savior? . . . Christology is compounded of two theological symbols: the dying and rising god who symbolizes the conquest of sin and death and manifest Wisdom of God through whom the world is created, guided, and restored and who is the presence of god/ess in all revelatory disclosures."[51]

What we forget when we read passages such as these—written in the mid-1980s—is that they were preceded, by over thirty years and then some, by similar passages in *The Second Sex*. Ruether goes on to say that "both these ideas existed first in female form."[52] But Beauvoir had written in the late 1940s, "Woman thus seems to be the inessential. . . . This conviction is dear to the male, and every creation myth has expressed it, among others the legend of Genesis, which through Christianity has been kept alive in Western civilization."[53]

In other words, it is clear that what Simone de Beauvoir accomplished in writing *The Second Sex*—among other things—was to pull together a rich compendium of material that later served as a catalyst for feminist work, even if it is sometimes unacknowledged, or even if the debt to it may be more or less unconscious. The slide and slippage that Moi writes about in the work (that between Beauvoir's asserting that some sorts of claims have been made about women by others, and Beauvoir's seeming to assert, at least on occasion, those same claims herself) cuts across a number of issues, and the controversy it generates is itself a stimulus to feminist reflections.[54] Several sections of the work lend themselves to this "new" sort of reading, wherein we can see the influence that they have had, direct or indirect, by comparing them with more contemporary work that we take for granted, and then asking what some of the possible origins of this "contemporary" work are, especially given what we know about Beauvoir's influence, and about the lapse of time between the writing of the book and the second and third wave of the feminist movements.

Not only the material on myth, the sacred, and things religious in general serves this purpose, but also any of the material on development. In addition—and despite the controversy it has raised—the very inclusion of material on lesbianism in a book published in 1949 signals to us an enormous shift in thinking that eventually gives rise to still other movements. Beauvoir's chapters on development can also sound refreshingly new: the work of Gilligan, Dinnerstein, Chodorow, and others can be seen as a direct link to her thought. In the chapter entitled "The Young Girl," after noting parallels between the situation of blacks in the United States and France under the Occupation, Beauvoir writes: "The other [the adolescent girl] simply submits; the world is defined without reference to her, and its aspect is immutable as far as she is concerned."[55] Contemporary work on the adolescent girl, including the work of popularizers, owes a great deal to these lines and to the thinking that produced it; without articulation of the world of the adolescent male as one that allows him to give notice of his existence, no conceptualization process highlighting the taken-for-grantedness of these artifacts could have begun. When we read Gilligan in *In a Different Voice,* for example, we are reading work that bears out, to a great extent, exactly the sorts of distinctions that Beauvoir originally made. The world of imperious notice is very similar to the justice voice, and the care voice is one that may very well be said to be related to the young girl's attempts to cope with that world to which she must submit. If Beauvoir was not the first to make these points in this way, she must have been one of the first, simply because so little had been done on gender differences at the time that she was writing. That is why Deirdre Bair is more than justified in saying, in her introduction to the work specifically prepared for the Vintage edition, "I believe we would do well to start with *The Second Sex.*"[56] Assessing a future for women cannot meaningfully proceed without cognizance of this work.

In a review of a work on Beauvoir's sexuality, the reviewer notes that there is a tendency to see "Beauvoir as not choosing her relationships with women, as being responsible only for relationships with men, or as participating in a voyeuristic relationship with Jean-Paul Sartre in which her relationships with women were just escapades that she would later recount to him."[57] There is no question that one of the major social changes of the latter part of the twentieth century in developed countries has been the lesbian/gay/bisexual/transgender movement, and also no question that the emergence of this movement certainly makes the portions of Beauvoir's work that deal with lesbianism among the weakest and least relevant today. In addition, as the reviewer asserts, many have tried to argue that there is an enormous amount at stake in attempting to cover up or minimize Beauvoir's obvious—by today's standards—bisexuality, and there also appears to be some motivation having to do with that particular stance that is at least minimally philosophical, since one gets the impression that acknowledging the importance of relationships with women for Beauvoir would somehow be seen by many to undercut the importance of her relationship to Sartre.

Nevertheless, at least two points are salient here. First, the relationships with women are widely acknowledged in much of the more contemporary work on her and her life, and her relationship with Sylvie Le Bon de Beauvoir has been spoken of with complete frankness.[58] Candor about relationships is, of course, different from an assessment of Beauvoir's work on lesbian relations. If this work strikes many as useless today, it is important to remember that Beauvoir was writing in an era immediately succeeding the salons of Natalie Barney and Gertrude Stein in Paris, and that the descriptions that she gave are completely consonant with the construction of lesbian sexual identity in the circles in which she moved in France at that time. It might even be deemed to be progressive for its time. Her opening paragraph in the relevant chapter reads: "We commonly think of the lesbian as a woman wearing a plain felt hat, short hair, and a necktie; her mannish appearance would seem to indicate some abnormality of the hormones. Nothing could be more erroneous than this confounding of the invert with the 'viriloid' woman. There are many homosexuals among harem inmates, prostitutes, among most intentionally 'feminine' women."[59]

Certainly the wording of the paragraph appears to be, as it is, approximately fifty years out of date. But the very first move made by Beauvoir here is to attempt to refute stereotypes—this is why she takes the trouble to say that "homosexuality" is also to be found among "feminine" women. Perhaps the most accurate remark about the chapter is simply that its appearance, at that time, is a step forward. That is a remark that could be made about almost any chapter in the book.

Woman of the Twentieth Century

I began by noting that the sheer amount of material about Beauvoir makes it, in some sense, extremely difficult to write about her. It is not simply a case of its being difficult to say anything new; the problem is more than demonstrated by some of the material that I have already covered. One can say something new by looking at her work from the standpoint of the later poststructuralist French philosophy that seemed to bypass her, or by looking at her writings from the standpoint of today's work on gender, race, and class. But none of this really does Beauvoir or her writings justice, because they were so startlingly fresh at the time that she composed them, and because to fail to recognize this seems to diminish the importance of her work.

Outside academic circles, it took approximately a decade for the importance of what Simone de Beauvoir had done to filter into the general culture. Existentialism had already become a part of the popular culture at an earlier point—so, as has been said frequently, Beauvoir's association with Sartre was a help in drawing attention to her. But insofar as *The Second Sex* is concerned, it remained for the second wave of feminism in the United States, in particular, to bring it to a full light.

Ironically, as so frequently happens, the initial responses (at least those in primarily feminist, rather than primarily academic, circles) were more positive than some later responses. Popular women's magazines and other venues in the late sixties and early seventies were more than willing to accord Beauvoir a special place as one of the "founders," along with Betty Friedan, of the burgeoning awareness. It was only at a later point (perhaps something like a decade later), once departments of women's studies had been initiated, and once some of the difficulties with respect to theorizing about "women" had been articulated, that it was possible to see that Beauvoir might have been off the mark.

In any case, scholarship of the type that I have examined in this chapter became possible only after two or three intellectual moves had been made: it was necessary to have a formal investigation of women, and of gender; it was necessary to have the poststructuralist "turn" that later took over scholarship, and both of these together probably had a great deal to do with more recent investigations, such as those with respect to race, that have proven germane to Beauvoir scholarship. At the same time, at least some of the hostility associated with such questions as "essentialism" has been defused, at least partly because Beauvoir is now seen as a philosopher whose work is much more of a piece than some had originally thought.

So if it is clear that Beauvoir scholarship has come full circle, so to speak, it is also obvious that parts of her work have never received sufficient attention. Her own novels, for example, are wonderful testimony to the wholeness of her thought. *The Mandarins* is filled not only with insights into women's condition, but with commentary on time, the sense of oneself among others, the fragility of interpersonal relations, and so forth. The plot, since it involves the resuscitation of France after World War II and after an interval of Occupation, makes it easy to draw contrasts that have to do with both the passage of time and the mark that that passage makes on a person's interior. Anne Dubreuilh's monologue to herself as she recounts the origins of her relationship with Robert at the beginning of the book reflects these themes: "Thanks to Robert, ideas were brought down to earth, and the earth became coherent, like a book, a book that begins badly but will finish well. Humanity was going somewhere; history had meaning, and so did my own existence."[60]

It is not possible to read work by Simone de Beauvoir that does not speak to these issues, which are at bottom ontological and metaphysical issues: humanity's place in the world, the lack of an absolute (in terms of, for example, conventional religion or former philosophical theory), and the difficulty of one's relations with others. *A Very Easy Death* is moving precisely because it is, by some miracle, a sort of combination of personal testament with the same theoretical issues, and it is written so fluidly that the reader can easily move from one to the other: "I looked at her. She was there, present, conscious, and completely unaware of what she was living through. Not to know what is happening underneath one's skin is normal enough. But for her the outside of her body was unknown—her wounded abdomen, the fistula, the filth that issued from it. . . . She rested and dreamed, infinitely far removed from her rotting flesh, her ears filled with the sound of our lies."[61]

The writing has a highly unusual quality; each time that the reader is taken in by the bare account of the facticity of Maman, the reader also becomes aware that this person is, in actuality, the author's mother. As Beauvoir notes throughout the text, the severity of her mother's illness made her too unwell to indulge in the usual conventions. This stripping away of conventions, literally and figuratively, reveals her mother to her and allows for at least some moments of genuine communication between the French Catholic mother—who says to her at one point, "You frighten me, you do"—and the unconventional existentialist philosopher who long ago broke with all the standard forms of bourgeois life.[62] The author of *She Came to Stay* is also someone's daughter, a plain fact of existence that cannot be denied.

If there is now more recognition of what it is that Beauvoir brought, philosophically, to her relationship with Sartre, and how this view informed her other works, we must guard against a tendency to overestimate either the one or the other, insofar as this unique collaboration is concerned. Among the women whose work I have examined here, there are at least three other collaborations: Anne Conway and Henry More, Mary Wollstonecraft and William Godwin, Harriet Taylor Mill and John Stuart Mill. The Beauvoir-Sartre collaboration is, however, probably the longest lasting, most intense, and most fruitful for both parties. It is difficult to overstate the strength of their work together, and its unity, because it is made plain in everything that Beauvoir wrote. It also accounts for her falling out with Nelson Algren—he could not understand that an intellectual relationship could have such intensity. The relationship became exactly what Sartre had initially prophesied; it was a relationship of "necessity," not of "contingency." It is also clear that an enormous reservoir of profound affection remained in the relationship, even if it was largely intellectualized and perhaps not demonstrated so often as might have been the case in more conventional arrangements.

If it has been difficult for many to give Simone de Beauvoir her due, it is probably because we now have difficulty conceiving life before her writings. A completely taken-for-granted view of women, their lives, and their place in the surrounding culture preceded her, and its strength is at least partially attested to by the fact that Beauvoir herself indicates that she experienced problems, at least initially, in realizing that the fact that she was a woman could mean anything to her. Moi and others have been careful to note how her social class privileged her and shielded her from some of the facts of life for other French women of her era.

But the fact that a conceptual world before *The Second Sex* is inconceivable is testimony to the book's importance and to its endurance. Beauvoir articulated "woman" in a number of ways, and each of these articulations cut through the accompanying swathing. The section on myths and literature was crucial in opening up for further view the metaphorical import of these icons on society as a whole, and on the formation of beliefs. The sections on biology, and on psychological growth and development, though now outdated, are just as important, because the tendency in the past had been to be unable to separate these components adequately. The scope of *The Second Sex* was—and probably is—unparalleled. The fact that we may now say that it essayed to do too much is simply a tribute to what it actually did accomplish.

After her mother died, Simone de Beauvoir found some newspaper clippings saved by her that indicated that Maman had never fully been able to accept Simone's life. As she recounts in *A Very Easy Death,* some family members had told her mother that "Simone is the family's disgrace."[63] Her mother had apparently taken seriously a report written up in a French paper claiming that the performance of Sartre's first play, in the German prisoner of war camp, at Christmas, had "saved a soul."[64] This erroneous report, somewhat laughable, implying that an individual had been converted because of seeing the play *Bariona* at holiday time, was something that Simone de Beauvoir's mother felt she had to hold on to, in the midst of life as the parent of a wildly—and scandalously—successful daughter. When recounting this incident toward the end of her work on her mother's death, Beauvoir writes: "I know very well what she wanted from these pieces—it was to be reassured about me; but she would never have felt the need if she had not been intensely anxious as to my salvation."[65]

In this closing portion, Beauvoir is able for the first time to see her mother as another individual, one victimized by the beliefs of her class, station, and age just as much as anyone else.

We need to do the same for Simone de Beauvoir herself. The inconsistencies, inappropriate uses of essentialist conceptualization patterns, and awkwardnesses of her writing and thought will always be there. But without her writing, the level of work in the second and, indeed, the third waves of feminism is unthinkable. It is the case, as Deirdre Bair remarked, that women "owe her everything."[66]

Conclusion

An historical endeavor across a long span of time, by its very nature, is fraught with difficulties. I have assumed that it is possible to make a comparative analysis of the work of eight women thinkers whose lives range from the eleventh to the twentieth centuries and who, although they are all European in the broad sense, encompass cultures ranging from the Teutonic to the Anglo-Saxon to the French. If it is difficult to compare the lives of women cross-culturally, it is also difficult to compare the lives of women across time—we know so little about the eleventh century, or even the seventeenth century, that much of what we write can be no more than informed guesswork.

There is one fact that assists us however: it is indisputable that each of these women felt herself to be following a tradition that was broadly philosophical, and a tradition that, at least in moderated form, would have been recognized by the other theorists. Thus Hildegard, especially in *Causae et Curae,* followed a tradition first set down by Galen and others, and these names were, of course, already well known to the churched of her time. Anne Conway, and the other Cambridge Platonists for that matter, expressly took themselves not only to be interested in the work of Descartes, but to be commenting upon it, and Descartes was preeminently and self-consciously philosophical.[1] Both Mary Astell and Mary Wollstonecraft either described themselves or were described by others as "philosophers" during their time—indeed, Mary Astell was satirized as such. Although few, other than John Stuart Mill, recognized Harriet Taylor Mill's talents while she was alive, there is no question that she worked directly in the tradition of political philosophy that preceded her. With Edith Stein, Simone Weil, and Simone de Beauvoir we have the good fortune of being able to address issues formulated by women who were trained as preparatory-school or university instructors in philosophy.

Having said this much, however, it still remains to cope with other issues inevitably posed by a project that encompasses so much space and time. Conway, Wollstonecraft, Harriet Taylor Mill, and Beauvoir all lived with or were married to male thinkers whose own work was philosophical, meaning that their work was almost of necessity in some sense collaborative. Hildegard, Astell, and certainly Edith Stein and Simone Weil worked alone or had, at best, correspondents and small numbers of discussants. Two of our thinkers come from the French tradition, three from the Anglo-Saxon tradition, and two from the Germanic tradition—what counts as philosophy or the posing of a philosophical problem varies enormously, of course, from tradition to tradition. Although almost all lived through some political and social turmoil, three lived through a world war and two through a civil disturbance so important that it is the subject of many history courses hundreds of years later. Finally, although it is particularly difficult to make comparisons across time for social class, at least three thinkers came from backgrounds that would best be described as well-to-do (in one case, aristocratic) and at least one or two thinkers remained in such close touch with her family of birth that her parents and nuclear family might have been thought to have had a great deal of influence upon her.

Perhaps most important ultimately—and certainly crucial for the framing of this project—has been the grounding fact that philosophy is a quintessentially male endeavor, and that women thinkers have been thrown up against it, as it were. The demiurge that drives philosophical thought may drive both men and women in roughly equal ratios, but our difficulty is that the historical record for women is small, especially since, until recently, the compilers of that record have almost always been male. Thus we do not have lengthy written records of the work of other women philosophers with which to compare, at least not in easily accessible form, or compiled over a long length of time.[2] As one might expect, at least a few of the thinkers here seem not to have been particularly consciously aware of their status as female philosophers, and, notably, at least two seem to have had a great deal of difficulty even addressing the issue.

I have also tried to assess the work of these thinkers along lines both traditional and innovative. For each woman, I have tried to provide an alembicated analysis of questions surrounding metaphysics, theory of value, and to some extent epistemology. But precisely because the thinkers were female, and because there has been so much recent work on the possibility of gender-linked thought patterns that might tie into questions surrounding the formulation of problems in these areas, I have also tried to ask whether or not what the thinkers have written has any bearing on contemporary feminist theory, regardless of whether or not the thinker in question took herself to be addressing such issues. (It is, of course, clear that some of the thinkers did not take themselves to have even examined feminist topics.) And, finally, with feminism itself in a state of flux insofar as theory is concerned, and with much current discussion about a "third wave," I have also tried to explicate how feminists of the future might envision the work of these women scholars.

Perhaps, then, what is needed is an analysis of many of the foregoing areas and problematic foci, with a goal of trying to make as many ties between thinkers as possible. For, as many have argued, without a search for areas of commonality it is difficult, if not impossible, to make an argument for women as a group, and without such an argument it is difficult for progress to be made toward remedying the obstacles facing women, particularly women thinkers. In the following sections, I will attempt reconstructive work in four broad areas, each of which represents a conundrum when viewed from the point of our eight women thinkers as a collectivity. I will examine areas of cross-cultural comparison and take a special look at intracultural comparisons. Fortunately, this is not nearly as difficult for thinkers all of whom are of European origin as it would be if some of our thinkers represented other cultures.[3]

I will also examine the notion of collaboration. Luckily, a great deal of new work has been done in this area, and some of it does examine the specific sorts of female/male collaborations that have borne fruit here. Collaboration was until recently an under-investigated area of intellectual endeavor, particularly when we take into account our historical awareness of the frequency of such work. The blurring of boundaries is part of collaborative work, and this is what makes it so appealing and also difficult to analyze. Because each individual might be thought to bring something unique to a collaborative relationship, it could be argued that it is important to try to untangle the various skeins and to come to some conclusions about who has brought what to the endeavor. In the sort of intense collaboration with which we will be concerned, here, however, it may be futile or impossible to separate the skeins, and perhaps unnecessary. Certainly even the historical record is often of little help in such cases.

Another tack on the products that I have examined is to look at them with an eye to the intellectual development, over a period of time, of European cultures as a whole. In other words, from the standpoint of intellectual history and philosophy in general, some of the questions that motivated the thinkers from earlier periods would not necessarily motivate later thinkers. The nature of the investigations changed, the nature and scope of the questions changed, and the surrounding historical circumstances (which cannot be divorced from the intellectual work of the time) yield different responses even to similar questions. Hildegard's work of the twelfth century examines issues that are no longer relevant by the seventeenth; the thought of the seventeenth century, particularly in Great Britain, is so entangled with the Interregnum, and, later, with the Glorious Revolution, that it is difficult to make a separation.[4]

The long historical view enables us to see how philosophical questions have changed over the course of time, and it gives us a particularly rich slant on how it is that the rise of the sciences changed what counted as a philosophical question. All of the examination of the past, however, also pushes us in still another direction: an examination of the future. In each chapter, I have tried to assess how an individual woman thinker's work might be viewed at a later point in time. This is difficult; even now, some of what has been written by individual thinkers may seem irrelevant, or hopelessly androcentric and class-biased. (There was, for example, the particular difficulty in addressing the work of Mary Astell, whose arguments in favor of High Toryism sounded outdated even fifty or a hundred years later.) Inevitably, some work is of historical interest only—but if this were a general point of departure, it would be very difficult to make a case for most of the classics today. Indeed, some of the best recent work in classical philosophy has insisted, rather pointedly, on the continuing relevance of the thought of the ancients.[5]

We can look to the future most assuredly if we address the work of the past somewhat in counterpoint to the historical view: for future purposes, we need to pull out generalities, instead of focusing on issues that were of particular interest only to a given time. Fortunately, this is not difficult to do: although Simone Weil, for example, and Mary Wollstonecraft might be thought to be offering more easily usable material for the future, a case can be made for each thinker, and that case almost must be made for the usefulness of the rubric "woman thinker" as a whole. Clearly, some of the goals of those who have decried gender constructs have had to do with their eventual elimination. Whether it is at all likely that this will come to pass is somewhat beside the point; it could be argued that we ought to write and think as if its coming to pass were part of our goals. Hence, in assessing the work of these thinkers, we must once again address the question of a general assessment along gender lines.

In the opening chapter, arguments were made for the use of material in a New Historical vein, and also for the contemporary "post" material that recurs so frequently.[6] We need now to examine our thinkers in a different light.

Collaborators

Those who work and write intensely in dyads—or even larger groupings—are already pursuing modes of inquiry that are different from those pursued by the standard, individual investigator. For one thing, the psychodynamics of collaboration are obvious: in a desire to continue a fruitful relationship, collaborators may be given to acquiesce in a number of matters that they would not choose to assent to on their own. Even more important, perhaps, are levels of interaction best explored under the rubrics of sociolinguistics, or even conversation analysis. Collaborators tend to communicate in a dense verbal shorthand, and they tend to do "repairs" on each other's phrases. They may speak with an inordinate number of tag endings, understood best by themselves alone. They may develop something akin to an idioglossia.[7]

Because of all of these factors, the four thinkers whose work I have examined who wrote and thought more or less independently—Hildegard, Mary Astell, Edith Stein, and Simone Weil—are in a category significantly different from that of Anne Conway, Mary Wollstonecraft, Harriet Taylor Mill, and Simone de Beauvoir. And even with respect to the latter quartet, there is an important distinction: Conway and Wollstonecraft had either briefer or less intense relationships than Mill or Beauvoir. The last two are more or less on a par with each other, since it is no exaggeration to say that Beauvoir's relationship with Sartre had the intensity of a marriage.

In any case, with all four of our collaborators, there is ample evidence that their thought was affected by their work and interaction with, in each case, a male philosophical figure. Because of Conway's isolation and later illness, there is ample reason to believe that she would scarcely have been able to pursue philosophy had it not been for her relationship with Henry More.[8] Although Wollstonecraft had done most of her work before her relationship to Godwin came about, her letters indicate his extensive influence on her in the last year of her life, and in her case some other male figures—such as Imlay and Fuseli—might at least minimally be thought to have functioned as collaborators. In the cases of Mill and Beauvoir, we are left with the classic dilemma: we literally cannot tell who had the greater influence upon whom, insofar as their relationships with their male co-conceptualizers are concerned. In my work here, I have been concerned to forward the cases, made strongly only in the most recent literature, that Harriet Taylor Mill did have something like the impact on John Stuart Mill that he himself credited her with, and that a great deal of what later came to be called "Sartrean existentialism" originated with Simone de Beauvoir. But even in these cases, we cannot deny influence the other way around—no one would strongly suggest, for instance, that *The Ethics of Ambiguity* is not a working out of many of the ideas in *Being and Nothingness* or even *The Flies,* in ethical terms, regardless of which thinker is most responsible for the origination of the ideas. Harriet Taylor Mill's case remains, at bottom, the most difficult, because the sheer bulk of work published in John Stuart Mill's name alone is so much greater than the few publications actually done by Harriet that there is an inevitable tendency to believe that the influence must have been largely one-sided. Although we may strongly suspect that this was not the case, and although we have Harriet's unpublished work, a remaining problem is the somewhat unfinished nature of much of the work.

We know more about the psychodynamics of collaboration than we did in the past, and at least two points are clear: not only does the collaboration involve the obvious intellectual exchanges—exchanges that, for Beauvoir and Sartre, clearly became the most important parts of their lives—but the intriguing emotional exchanges, however small and muted, feed into the more overtly theoretical exchanges in interesting ways. Here, of course, we can only speculate, but some speculation does seem to be merited. In the case of Anne Conway and Henry More, the intense nature of their correspondence and the necessarily somewhat muted nature of their personal relationship (More was a friend of Conway's husband, the viscount) may have affected the content of their philosophizing. All of the Cambridge Platonists were noted for their departure from doctrines that they took to involve "dead matter." They were distraught by some of the implications of the new science, and part of the point of their thinking was to attempt to account for causality in ways that would allow for the interaction of spirit and matter. Intriguingly, Conway argues for the interpenetrability of the "subtler mediating parts" of spirits. This, in some way, is a metaphor for her relationship with More.

Jacobs compares the relationship of the Mills with that of Sidney and Beatrice Webb, and again we have to assume that style is part and parcel of what makes the comparison a viable one.[9] If it becomes commonplace for individuals to finish each other's sentences, then body language, gestures, and facial expressions may, in some way, also become part of the thought process.

The emotional closeness of collaboration may, in itself, lead to leaps in conceptualization that cannot otherwise be accounted for. Almost all commentators on the life of Mary Wollstonecraft note the change in emotionality and content of her thought after the beginning of her relationship with Godwin.

Although poetry is the subject, and not philosophical thought, Diane Middlebrook remarks on a brief collaboration between Linda Gray Sexton and her mother, the poet Anne Sexton: "As Linda's skill developed, her mother began making her a sounding board for new work, trying out *Transformations* and then other new poems on her."[10] This short sentence encompasses a great deal—we can imagine not only verbal criticisms, but facial expressions, shrugs, and quizzical looks. These exchanges may alter (especially where poetry is concerned) content and the emotional rapport of the two collaborators, which itself feeds back into a never-ending cycle of intellectual and emotional reverberation.

Because both of the Mills and Sartre and Beauvoir saw each other nearly every day for years (and, in general, for hours a day) their collaborations may be deemed to be the most intense. Insofar as content is concerned, it is clear that, for the Mills, changes in theory and concern for others went hand-in-hand. Their biographers have no difficulty discerning the attention to the plight of the downtrodden that no doubt was heightened by their awareness of the precariousness of their own social state. For Beauvoir and Sartre, an odd sort of mirroring seemed to allow for objectification of others. The Olga-Sartre-Simone triangle, well documented in *She Came to Stay,* and the subject of many analyses, seemed to bring to the fore an already intense desire to intellectualize at the expense of the emotions.

Among the elements of collaboration that may not have received as much analysis in the literature as the situation warrants are those that have to do with the linguistic distinction between orality and literacy. It might naively be thought that this has little to do with our collaborative dyads, since all of the authors were, of course, literate. But this is not to the point. What is striking about so much of collaborative activity is that it has to do with face-to-face interaction, and that these verbal exchanges are spontaneous and immediate.[11] This sort of spontaneity allows for its own type of conceptualization; thinkers may move in loose, associational ways, perhaps more evocative of the arts or of poetry or drama than of straight philosophical thought. Then the insights gleaned from these interactions weave together, and at a later point are written down, rehashed, and in some cases made a great deal more linear in their structure than they originally were.

When a linguist such as Robin Lakoff notes the spontaneity of orality, she is not alluding merely to its instantaneity or the rapidity of exchanges. Rather, the point is that orality allows for a type of thought in which "catches," as it were (one can almost think of Wittgenstein's "singing catches"), pass back and forth between members of a dyad, and in which the associational thinking brings to bear insights that are at a more intuitive, less highly theoretical level than might be obtained if writing were the only mode. As indicated earlier, because all four of the collaborative dyads that I investigate here consisted of pairs having a great deal of interpersonal contact, I have to hypothesize that these sorts of thought patterns emerged on a regular basis. Again, Beauvoir and Sartre and the two Mills are the best candidates for exemplifying these interactions, since they saw each other the most frequently.

One exchange that probably took place would involve extensive reconceptualization of the notion of the "Other" on the part of Beauvoir and Sartre. We can imagine that, for each of them, travel in the United States heightened their awareness of differing constructions of "Otherness" based on the interior core of a given society. But Beauvoir's associations with Nelson Algren and Richard Wright probably had a great deal to do with altering Sartre's thought, in this instance. Who altered whose thought is not of paramount importance here—we can imagine conversations in which a range of "Others" come up, and associational slippage calls for new candidates for alterity, and so forth. A concept as open to interpretation as this particular concept is a likely candidate for exactly the sort of amelioration that we have described with respect to oral processes and thought patterns.

In excluding Hildegard, Mary Astell, Edith Stein, and Simone Weil from our group of collaborators, I do not mean to imply that no collaboration took place. (To be fair, in the case of Simone Weil, especially toward the end of her life, it appears that she worked almost entirely alone.) But we have no record of regular, intense collaboration of the type that we have for the other four thinkers, especially since—as the social structure makes obvious—the most profitable type of collaboration, from the standpoint of publishing and making one's work available to the public, would be with a male thinker. It would help enormously, of course, if that male thinker were himself already well known, and this is the case, in varying degrees, with the male collaborators whom I have described as working with four women philosophers.

Commonalities and Differences

Perhaps the most striking similarities across the thinkers I have examined have to do with developed areas of metaphysics and ontology. At first glance, it may seem as if we assume too much when we indicate that there are such areas of commonality, but closer examination will reveal a care for particulars that, taken on the whole, is a striking characteristic of the eight women theorists.

It is probably easiest to note these similarities when we go back further chronologically and examine systems that are closer to the classical tradition. Hildegard's viriditas, which fleshes out the views that she has announced mystically in her visionary work, is but one such example. More to the point—and apropos with respect to the thesis at hand—is Anne Conway's vitalist metaphysics. It will be recalled that part of the motivation behind Conway's work was a desire to avoid the "dead matter" thesis of the new science, and simultaneously to move away from a Cartesian dualism that provided no explanation for movement or change. Conway's ontology of monadic entities, composed of vitalist mixtures of spirit and matter, provided her with an explanation for motion while at the same time allowing her to develop a graded hierarchy of particulars. What is so noteworthy about Conway's work is not merely that she attempts to solve some of the problems inherent in other philosophies of the time, but that the manner in which she does so is consistent with a great deal of the contemporary work in feminist theory that has noted a gynocentric attention to particulars. This is, of course, something that simply springs from Conway's work, rather than being part of the motivation behind it. It is also noteworthy that a good many parts of the *Principles* contain specific allusions to living beings—horses and other creatures—and that Conway is clearly concerned about the world around her in a way that is different from the concerns of the more purely deductive thinkers.

Likewise, although the thought of Mary Astell and Mary Wollstonecraft might be deemed to be overwhelmingly political, each woman has at least some reference to Christian ontology in her works, and each finds her particular political stance (especially with respect to women) to be completely consistent with that Christian ontology. Again, although their work does not represent a major achievement in metaphysics, what is noteworthy about Astell and Wollstonecraft is that they have taken seriously the injunction to respect humans as part of God's handiwork, including the female members of the species.

The quartet of thinkers closer to our own time all deal with these questions, even if their varying styles make it more difficult to be precise about their responses. Harriet Taylor Mill is enough of an empiricist to be very concerned, epistemically, about evidence for the ills that she sees around her.[12] Edith Stein takes her very precise phenomenological training—as difficult to

explain as it is to comprehend, even for those with a philosophical background—and moves in a new direction with it, holding the notion that faith
involves a special kind of "bracketing" and a special sort of knowledge. She
then uses that knowledge to forward concerns for others. Simone Weil makes
a very personal move from simply reading about hunger and trouble to leading a life, again on the basis of faith, dominated to some extent by both. Simone de Beauvoir tells us, throughout her work, that an account of the self
and others is one of the chief tasks of philosophy.

We can also, of course, examine the work of the thinkers in question with
an eye toward the other traditional area delineated here, value in general and
ethics in particular. Here we find much similarity, particularly among the theorists of our first quartet. Hildegard and Anne Conway clearly value life, and
the value that they place on life is demonstrated by their metaphysics and the
desire to provide a vitalist explanation for much of what exists. It is also noteworthy that, despite the lapse of centuries, Hildegard and Conway share a respect for nature and life that is manifested in their constant use of natural examples, examples taken from animal and plant life. Although Mary Astell and
Mary Wollstonecraft cannot, obviously, be said to be vitalists, their traditional
semi-Christian viewpoint (much more Christian, it must be said, in the case
of Mary Astell) again manifests a distinct respect for life, and for the various
forms life may take. This ties directly into their feminist stance—it is especially
remarkable that Mary Astell, despite her Toryism, is able to write astutely on
the plight of women, for she sees women as God's creatures no less than men.
As she often says, scripture says nothing about the inferiority of woman.

Insofar as our second foursome of thinkers is concerned, Harriet Taylor
Mill's thought is, as we would expect, much closer to that of Wollstonecraft,
especially since they are both working in the same Anglo-Saxon tradition. Despite Mill's concerns about a too-literal Christian interpretation of various biblical stories, it is clear that she does stay within the broad framework of the tradition. Edith Stein and Simone Weil both evince, insofar as interpersonal
relations are concerned, a focus on value that can be articulated as stemming
from empathy or notions of personal respect. Although neither of them wrote
on questions of value in a much larger sense (they both were more overtly
concerned about political, social, and simply human concerns), their concerns are similar, at least with respect to the period before Weil's thought becomes more overtly mystical.[13] Simone de Beauvoir stands apart here, since
she has written a work that overtly addresses ethical questions. But her concerns are also, at least initially, motivated by the kind of intense interpersonal
mirroring that causes humans to be categorized as "Other." It is probably

going too far to use the term "empathy" in connection with Beauvoir's work, but since she is aware of the difficulties encountered by those who face a negative mirroring, the word is not entirely inappropriate to capture some of her thinking.

As I have said repeatedly throughout this work, it is facile to attempt to claim that either the metaphysical thinking or the work in ethics of the various thinkers examined here consistently shows strands of gynocentrism, or is devoid of the aggrandizement of theory so common among male thinkers. Anne Conway, again, writes completely in the tradition of her time, and it is clear that her work is intended as a response to the work of well-known male philosophers. Edith Stein's initial work—at least in her dissertation—is, of course, an application of Husserlian theory, and not a departure from it. The interweaving between Beauvoir and Sartre is so intense that, even if it were completely the case that Sartre received most of his most important concepts from Beauvoir, her work must inevitably reflect her ongoing relationship with him and, plainly, their numerous and lengthy conversations. Nevertheless, each thinker does, in general, reflect some gynocentic thought patterns at some point in her work.

If we are thinking in terms of care for particulars, then it is comparatively easy to pick out at least some gynocentric theorizing. Here, we move to the level of counterpoint and counterargument: Conway writes in a tradition that is almost completely male (especially insofar as she is aware of it), but her graded ontology and her awareness of life around her speak to gynocentric concerns. Again, these concerns, as we know, have been most clearly delineated in contemporary theory by Chodorow, Dinnerstein, and Gilligan. The same can be said of Hildegard, and Astell and Wollstonecraft, of course, had overtly feminist concerns, although their political thought, especially in the case of Astell, was decidedly conventional and in tune with the masculine political thought of the day.

Harriet Taylor Mill's thought is so closely tied to John Stuart Mill's that the gynocentricity of her thought emerges most fully, as it does for the two preceding thinkers, in terms of her political stance. But as we have seen, the experiences of her life were such that she became acutely aware of the limitations placed on women. Edith Stein's initial work is decidedly without a gynocentric focal point, but as her thought becomes more Christian, concern for others—and empathy developed in a Christian sense—manifests itself. With Weil and Beauvoir we must tread carefully. If we insist on the label "mystic" for Weil, we remember that the tradition of male mystics within the church is even larger than the tradition of female mystics, and in any case some of what Weil read that made an impression on her in this regard was derived from male thinkers, for instance St. John of the Cross. With Beauvoir, the relations between the self and others are of the utmost importance, and this, of course, may be construed as a nonmasculinist awareness.[14]

To reiterate a point made in the introduction to this book, a project that inquires into the status of women philosophers must be conceptualized on at least two fronts. The first and most obvious way of addressing the problems is to think of the exclusion of women from the academy, and from male intellectual endeavors, until the latter portion of the twentieth century. But this exclusion is itself woven into still another strand. Women have been excluded, and the exclusion itself may have a great deal to do with why they have developed, according to some, a different voice. That, and the sort of thinking that is derived from feminist standpoint theory, help us to understand why a concern for androcentrism versus gynocentrism might be powerful here. Exclusion creates its own parameters, and if exclusion is tied to the sheer reality of the sorts of tasks performed by most women historically over a period of time—including at least some of our thinkers, for they did not all come from the same social class—then the upshot is that there is a powerful reason for believing that at least some of the theoretical work of women scholars will bear hallmarks that will separate it, stylistically and otherwise, from the work of male thinkers.

How powerfully this argument can be made is simply related to the desire to construct it. We can look for evidence, but at the same time we want to be sensitive to the lack of evidence. As we have seen—and common sense would bear this out—such evidence varies from thinker to thinker. But our project is made more exciting by the awareness of the fact that exclusion, in terms of numbers and activity, is not the only force driving the categorization "women." There is ample reason to believe that there are differences in thought patterns, and the work that we have done here tends to bear this out.

The Old Historicism

In the past, philosophers and even those who wrote in the area of history of philosophy might have been reluctant to employ as much information about various historical strands and trends—intellectual or otherwise—as I have employed here. There has always been the feeling, rightly or wrongly, that the positions that a philosopher held on such matters as metaphysics and epistemology should be viewed as independent of the intellectual currents of the time, and should be evaluated on their own merits. In addition, those few philosophers who themselves seemed to allude to the learning of the period in their work (in a way that might today be viewed as "naturalization") were also often suspect, even though we know, for instance, that such motives drove the empiricists.

Among the various turns that have taken place in philosophy, at least as done in the United States, in the past two decades or so is the historical turn. It is now much more accepted than it had been previously that philosophical work and the articulation of philosophical positions may require allusion to history and matters of historical record. In the present project, it has been obvious from the start that the women philosophers whose work I have investigated were vulnerable to the currents of their times—partly simply because they were women functioning in a male world, and partly because all human beings are so vulnerable.

It would not have been possible, for example, to understand Anne Conway's work without knowing that the rise in science, as exemplified by the work of Newton and others, drove much of the response of the Cambridge Platonists to the philosophical thinking around them. Both Mary Astell and Mary Wollstonecraft—the latter in particular—were responding to the events of their era. When we read Todd's description of Wollstonecraft's view of the execution of "Louis Capet," we gain insight into the shifting currents of her own political philosophy, and to changes in the attitudes that greeted the French Revolution throughout Europe and especially in Great Britain.

It simply is not possible to read the work of our two women thinkers whose Jewishness affected their position during World War II without advertence to the events of that time. (And it is worthwhile pointing out that the newer, more contemporary response to the debate about the relevance of historical matters to philosophy has now made it imperative that someone like Heidegger be viewed in the totality of his beliefs, and not without reference, for example, to his Nazism.) Historians such as Ruth Brenner have greatly assisted us, because the necessary work that needs to be done to understand the importance, for example, of Edith Stein's conversion cannot be done without a knowledge of what drove her to that conversion, and what it would have meant for a Jewish woman from an Orthodox family to convert during that period.

It probably has never made sense to attempt to understand the work of a philosopher as unrelated to the events of her or his time. Nevertheless, we can comprehend how such views came about, especially when we think of the fact that the beginnings of our tradition, as we are so frequently told, revolve around Platonic theory and its divorce from the material world. The concept that even the explication of a philosophical view should have little to do with context, historical circumstances, or the general intellectual tenor of the times not only is derived at least in part from the thought of the ancients, but has a great deal to do with seventeenth-century thought, because the type of conceptualizing indulged in by the rationalists was decidedly divorced from any allusion to the material.

One way of examining the difference between the sort of approach that I have taken here and the type of approach that might have been taken in times past is to look at an exemplary thinker. For Anne Conway, the seventeenth-century style is an explicit point of embarkation, and it is, of course, possible to examine her philosophy almost solely in terms of its consistency, the development of her notion of a graded hierarchy, and so forth.[15] One could proceed slightly further and compare her work with that of the other thinkers whom she explicitly cites, such as Descartes and Spinoza, and still remain comparatively ahistorical with respect to any of these thinkers.

The difficulty is that not only does one lose any believable account of the motivation behind the construction of such systems of metaphysics, but one also loses any overview of what drove the construction of systems in the first place. In other words, philosophical style is also partly a matter of the time, and there are reasons—reasons that themselves are a matter of historical record—why the eighteenth century produced a burst of empiricism, why empiricism took hold first in Great Britain, and so forth. Without an historical overview, one has no access to these facts or their relevance to the production of philosophy.

Thus, to continue with Conway as an exemplar, Marjorie Hope Nicolson's work does much to fill in the blanks on how it is that Conway came to be acquainted with matters philosophical, and why it was (through her friendship with More) that Descartes became such an important thinker for her, but without still further explication we remain lost. When, however, we know more about the Interregnum, the effect of the Reformation and the counterreformation on philosophy, the importance of the disputes concerning the rights of the monarch, and the rise of science during the same period, we are in a much better position to understand why the issues of matter versus the immaterial, the status of humans in the Great Chain of Being, an ontological account of Christ for Christians, and so forth, became of paramount importance. The old historicism might point us in a certain direction—the new historicism invites us to look at Pepys's diary, Newton's science, the outbreaks of the Black Death, and the London fire as all relevant to the lives of philosophers and their production of philosophy.

Interest in Judaica may not take us far in an examination of the content of Simone Weil's work, to employ still another case as exemplary, but knowledge of Judaica may help us understand why Weil may have unconsciously bent her work in a certain direction. And once we understand how Weil consciously read her Jewish past (even if her reading of it was largely uncharitable and possibly incorrect) we can understand more fully how various Christian beliefs, including heretical ones, might have initially looked more promising, and how it was that—again, perhaps unconsciously—some of Weil's Christian ruminations began to look somewhat like portions of Judaism.[16] Likewise, both Edith Stein and Simone de Beauvoir cannot properly be understood without direct reference to their time.

Attention to context is, of course, associated with lines of endeavor in philosophy that have currently drawn much attention. Although what is meant by "context" is by no means always historical, it is of interest to try to find the intersection between this newer look at context and the sort of historical framing I describe here. Feminists are interested in context, by and large, and one feature of their interest has been that philosophy has frequently cast itself in an ahistorical and acontextual mode. (I have already examined this line of argument here to some extent in noting that the origins of Western philosophy, particularly insofar as they may be categorized as classical Greek thought, characterize themselves as acontextual.) But other contemporary lines of work in philosophy also take context into account: the newer work on race and ethnicity asks whether or not indigenous cultures, or cultural points of view derived from indigenous cultures, can have "philosophies." These inquirers ask these questions because indigenous cultures themselves seldom would characterize their own chronologies, myths, creation tales, and so forth as acontextual, whether or not we are entitled to think of them as philosophy.[17]

Interest in American philosophy—by this is usually meant pragmatism and its offshoots, although it may also encompass older thought, such as transcendentalism—frequently notes the extent to which Dewey and other thinkers, far from pretending to divorce themselves from context, reveled in it. Dewey is seen as an important thinker now (in contradistinction to his status in many philosophical circles three decades ago) because it is recognized that Dewey pointed us in a certain direction that was completely separated from the a priori tradition that preceded it.

In sum, the time is right for historical work that is philosophical, and for at least some work, overtly philosophical, that has an historical twist. Thus what I have set out to do here with this compendium of the work of eight women thinkers helps in establishing not only a record of philosophical work by women but in clarifying the origins of many of the philosophical issues of given time periods. It should be unnecessary to attempt to defend such areas of interest, but unfortunately it is not. Stein, Conway, and Beauvoir will be characterized by some as "not philosophers" because their work was too much the product of its time, too driven by nonphilosophical concerns, too little a priori in spirit, and so forth.

Perhaps one of the greatest virtues of contemporary feminist theory has been to give the lie to the idea that there is a "view from nowhere." The combination of recent work in the social sciences that details the origins of much of what is deemed to be "hard science," and the feminist attacks on this work, has been of great import for the development of philosophical theory in areas such as epistemology and philosophy of science.[18] It is not possible to divorce any view from its point of origin, and points of origin, in general, have a great deal more to do with the contents of views than some would have us believe. (This includes, again, work in areas such as physics and chemistry.)

Harriet Taylor Mill's "On the Probable Futurity of the Labouring Classes" is a product of its time and of her relationship with John Stuart Mill. Insofar as chronological context is concerned, the same may be said of Hildegard's *Causae et Curae,* or of Simone Weil's *Oppression and Liberty*. Nothing that can be said about history, context, or relationships prevents these works by women thinkers from being regarded as works of philosophy.

Now and Forever

I have already addressed, more than once, the question of whether the rubric "woman" merits the attention that it has received here and in other places where the work of women thinkers has been examined. My take on this set of problems has been both historical and driven by contemporary work in gender; my conclusion has been that we are, indeed, warranted and even obligated to examine the work of women theorists qua women.

It could be argued, however, that the future to which I have turned so often here in my examination of the work of women philosophers will make employment of gender-laden categorizations unnecessary and even harmful. If—as I very well might hope—gender continues to be of less significance insofar as the professions are concerned, I could hazard the guess that at some later point in time much less will be made of whether or not a given philosopher, mathematician, or historian was a woman.

Sadly, this may be nothing more than a guess or a hope. The progress of women in many disciplines has not been as rapid as one might have expected, based on projections and prognostications from the 1970s and 80s. More poignantly, worldwide the problems remain tremendous—the vast majority of the world's illiterates are women, and in most traditional societies it remains unusual for girls in villages to receive any sort of formal education.[19] In any case, there would still remain one other area to be examined in connection with this large question, even if numbers ceased to remain a problem. At the outset, I had asked whether or not there was evidence that women thinkers might conceptualize sufficiently differently from male thinkers, for their conceptualization patterns to themselves constitute areas of interest. I have implicitly and explicitly answered this question in the affirmative, since a great deal of the material that I have covered here indicates a tendency (nothing more than a tendency, obviously) for women to categorize in ways that emphasize relationships and particularity, and I have been fairly precise about how such tendencies have affected the ontologies and ethics of various women thinkers.

Although one might easily imagine a future in which numbers are no longer as problematic as they are today, and although one could hazard a guess that in India or Mexico a century from now a much higher proportion of women will have received formal education, the gender-driven conceptualization question is something of an altogether different nature. Numbers, one would assume, do not affect such questions, nor is it likely that—saving enormous changes in the ways in which young girls and boys are socialized, changes that we can scarcely project—time would alter the nature of this question. I can easily see such a problem remaining with respect to the work of women thinkers a hundred years from now.

The explosion in the biological sciences, not to mention the current work in neuroscience, may eventually yield some insight with respect to gender, but neural plasticity and most of the work extant today suggest, as has been claimed, that gender is very largely a social construct. The sticking point here is not whether it is a social construct; that much we can fairly take for granted. The hard area remaining is that it is a social construct that moves into place at a very early age. Studies of very young infants, particularly with respect to their patterns of interaction with their parents, suggest that the social demands for gender acculturation lead parents to treat male and female babies differently virtually from the day of their birth. In a society such as ours, where the media are also prominent socializers, much of the process has taken place by the beginning of elementary school. A recurring theme in the conversations of kindergarten and first- and second-grade teachers is the difference in play interaction style that is manifested between girls and boys, and the differences in topics chosen for writing, drawing, and creative activities.[20]

One result of the present project has been to take notice of the somewhat alarming fact that some among our women philosophers were actually recognized as having made philosophical contributions to a greater degree during their own lifetimes than they were at a later point. It is obvious from the work cited here that Anne Conway, Mary Astell, and Simone Weil were taken seriously by their male contemporaries, and that they were regarded as being significant and original contributors of their time. Despite the length and complexity of the *Principles,* Conway, for one, remains remarkably neglected, even though her work is a standard seventeenth-century philosophical treatise in every sense.

In other words, it is accurate to say that, if anything, gender became a more potent marker in the industrialized societies as greater leisure permitted men to construct a social view that required women to stay at home and, assuming a bourgeois scale of value, remain decorative objects. Thus Leibniz was able to recognize what Conway had achieved largely on the basis of More's descriptions, but this achievement seems virtually to have escaped the notice of later generations.

Projects of retrieval are simply as important as the social exclusion of the groups whose work they attempt to retrieve. We value work on the writings and thought of black American philosophers of the past because we know that, for a very long length of time, their thought remained almost unexamined.[21] Professional philosophical organizations and societies now routinely form colloquia and groups to work on the thought of American and non-American philosophers of Latino, Asian, or American Indian heritage.

It is probably an unfortunate truth that projects of retrieval on the work of women intellectuals will continue to be necessary for a very long time to come. It does not seem at all realistic to envision a future where no such projects of retrieval would come to the fore, or where they themselves would not make valuable contributions to the intellectual climate of the day. My project has been to examine the lives and work of eight women philosophers, women who were without exception recognized as thinkers by at least some of their contemporaries. What we can hope for the future is that such work will cease to become as urgent as it is today. It can be said with some poignancy, however, that there is little likelihood that that will happen anytime soon.

notes

Introduction

1. The work of John Blassingame, for example, shows us how the written and transcribed records of American slaves were archived. See Blassingame, *Slave Testimony* (Baton Rouge: Louisiana State University Press, 1977).

2. I address these issues to some extent in my *Worlds of Knowing: Global Feminist Epistemologies* (New York: Routledge, 2001).

3. See *Hypatia* 4 (Spring 1989). In her introductory essay to the issue, Linda Lopez McAlister, the editor, mentions that during her graduate work in philosophy, she did not recall "a single instance" where women philosophers were cited, especially with regard to the history of philosophy (1).

4. See Jane Duran, "Anne Viscountess Conway: A Seventeenth-Century Rationalist," *Hypatia* 4 (Spring 1989): 64–79.

5. See Marjorie Hope Nicolson, *The Conway Letters: The Correspondence of Anne Viscountess Conway, Henry More, and Their Friends, 1642–1684* (Cambridge: Cambridge University Press, 1930).

6. See Mary Ellen Waithe, *A History of Women Philosophers,* vol. 1 (Dordrecht, Neth.: Martinus Nijhoff Publishers, 1987).

7. Ibid., xx–xxi.

8. For evidence concerning the existence of Buddhist commentary written by at least one woman, see the work of the scholar Diana Paul.

9. Sylvia Plath, *The Unabridged Journals of Sylvia Plath,* ed. Karen V. Kukil (New York: Anchor, 2000), 98.

10. Sian Miles, "Introduction," in *Simone Weil: An Anthology,* ed. Sian Miles (New York: Grove Press, 1986), 4–5.

11. Ibid., 7 (second quote), 46 (first quote).

12. Ibid., 45.

13. *The Complete Works of Harriet Taylor Mill,* ed. Jo Ellen Jacobs (Bloomington: Indiana University Press, 1998), xix.

14. See the discussion, for example, in Evelyn Fox Keller, *Reflections on Gender and Science* (New Haven: Yale University Press, 1985).

15. See, for example, Stephen Greenblatt, *Learning to Curse* (Cambridge, Mass.: Harvard University Press, 1990).

16. Frank Kermode, "Art among the Ruins," *New York Review of Books,* July 5, 2001, 59.

17. Ibid.

18. Greenblatt, "Marlowe, Marx and Anti-Semitism," in *Learning to Curse,* 40–58.

19. See Cornel West, *The American Evasion of Philosophy* (Madison: University of Wisconsin Press, 1989).

20. Mary Astell, *The First English Feminist: The Writings of Mary Astell,* ed. Bridget Hill (Aldershot, Eng.: Gower, 1986), 31.

21. Kermode, "Art among the Ruins," 59.

22. See Nicolson, *Conway Letters.*

23. Henry More is said to have turned to Conway "as naturally as the needle turnes North." (Quoted in Aharon Lichtenstein, *Henry More: The Rational Theology of a Cambridge Platonist* [Cambridge, Mass.: Harvard University Press, 1962], 15.) One might then wonder, for example, about the characteristic atmosphere of the Cambridge colleges during this period.

24. See Greenblatt, "Learning to Curse," in *Learning to Curse,* 16–39.

25. Alice Jardine, *Gynesis* (Ithaca, N.Y.: Cornell University Press, 1985), 38–39.

26. See Duran, *Worlds of Knowing.*

27. See Hélène Cixous, "The Laugh of the Medusa," in *The Signs Reader,* ed. Emily Abel (Chicago: University of Chicago Press, 1984), 279–97.

28. Jardine, *Gynesis,* 115.

29. It is always somewhat surprising to see the various uses to which this term was put in European literature. Stuart Gilbert's translation of André Malraux's *The Royal Way* (New York: Vintage, 1951) consistently renders the characters' term for the Cambodian people as "natives," despite the fact that the reader might think this term to be well out of place in an Asian context.

30. See Edward Said, *Orientalism* (New York: Vintage, 1979).

31. Edward Said, "Jane Austen and Empire," in *The Edward Said Reader* (New York: Vintage, 2000), 347–67.

32. Ibid., 348.

33. See, for example, the work of C. L. R. James, in *The C. L. R. James Reader,* ed. Anna Grimshaw (New York: Routledge, 1994).

34. C. L. R. James, for one, was careful to address the question of whether or not blacks in the New World could be "revolutionary," although not classical proletarians. His answer to this question is that African diaspora cultures are inherently antibourgeois.

35. Max Horkheimer, "The End of Reason," in *The Essential Frankfurt School Reader,* ed. Andrew Arato and Eike Gebhardt (New York: Continuum, 2000), 28.

36. See, for example, Mead's *Sex and Temperament in Three New Guinea Societies* (New York: Simon and Schuster, 1929).

37. We do not, for instance, know enough about individuals assigned to the "berdache" roles in Native American societies.

38. See Oyeronke Oyewumi, *The Invention of Women* (Minneapolis: University of Minnesota Press, 1997).

39. Several issues of the journal *Hypatia* have been devoted to or have examined feminist work from around the globe, including Latin America and the former Eastern Bloc nations.

40. I have addressed these issues to some extent in my *Worlds of Knowing.*

Chapter 1: Hildegard of Bingen

1. One of the best sources for thoughtful commentary on the degree to which Hildegard's work is philosophical is Margaret Berger, ed. and trans., *Hildegard of Bingen on Natural Philosophy and Medicine: Translations from Cause et Cure* (Cambridge: D. S. Brewer, 1999). Berger has an admirable grasp of the interlinking of philosophical thought that drives a great deal of Hildegard's work in the natural sciences.

2. The latter, for example, is accorded a respected place in Frederick Copleston's *History of Philosophy* (Garden City, N.Y.: Image Books, 1962). Volume 2, part 1, 196–99, is devoted to Hugh, of whom Copleston writes: "To enter upon a discussion of Hugh's mystical teaching would scarcely be in place here; but it is worth pointing out that the mystical tradition of St. Victor was not simply a spiritual luxury; their [the Augustinians of St. Victor] mystical theology formed an integral part of their theologico-philosophical synthesis" (199).

3. Many of the extant commentaries on her work include lists of her writings in Latin and titles of the translations into English, if such are available. For lesser works, only German translations are available in some cases. See, for example, the list of her works and available translations in the notes to *Voice of the Living Light: Hildegard of Bingen and Her World,* ed. Barbara Newman (Berkeley: University of California Press, 1998), 193–94.

4. Catherine Villanueva Gardner, *Rediscovering Women Philosophers* (Boulder, Colo.: Westview, 2000), 149–74.

5. Ibid., 156.

6. Berger, "Introduction," in *Hildegard,* 12.

7. This is the rationale driving Gardner's work, as she states.

8. Constant Mews, "Religious Thinker: 'A Frail Human Being' on Fiery Life," in Newman, *Voice,* 58–59.

9. Hildegard, "Cause et Cure," in Berger, *Hildegard,* 35.

10. Ibid., 16.

11. Barbara Newman, *Sister of Wisdom: St. Hildegard's Theology of the Feminine* (Berkeley: University of California Press, 1987), 44.

12. Florence Eliza Glaze, "Medical Writer: 'Behold the Human Creature,'" in Newman, *Voice,* 131.

13. Copleston, *History of Philosophy,* vol. 2, part 1, 188–89.

14. Glaze, "Medical Writer," 136.

15. The late Arne Naess was the founder and originator of this movement, in which

the unity of all living things is emphasized. It distinguishes itself, typically, from "preservationist" movements.

16. Matthew Fox, "Foreword," in *Scivias,* trans. Bruce Hozeski (Santa Fe: Bear, 1986), xix. The Hozeski edition of *Scivias* is faulted by many, and there is a more scholarly version available in translation by Columba Hart and Jane Bishop (*Scivias,* trans. Hart and Bishop, with an introduction by Barbara Newman [New York: Paulist Press, 1990]). But it is the Hozeski version that is more widely available and that is at least partially responsible for current interest in Hildegard. I herein cite the Hozeski volume, while noting that Barbara Newman's superb introduction to the Paulist Press edition contains much valuable commentary on Hildegard's life and the relation of her thought to that of other thinkers of the time, including Hugh of St. Victor. Even Newman notes that the popularization of Hildegard through the work of Bear and Company has proven "useful and inspiring to many" (47).

17. Heinrich Schipperges, *Hildegard of Bingen: Healing and the Nature of the Cosmos,* trans. John A. Broadwin (Princeton, N.J.: Markus Wiener, 1998), 53. The work referred to as "LDO" is the Liber Divinorum Operum from the 1882 Paris edition of Hildegard's works in Latin.

18. Quoted in Berger, *Hildegard,* 57. Hildegard also notes in this passage that "due to the enclosure of the loins the fire of pleasure burns more strongly . . . in man" (ibid.).

19. See Gardner, "Knowing and Speaking of Divine Love: Mechthild of Magdeburg," in *Rediscovering Women Philosophers,* 149–74.

20. Ibid., 151.

21. Ibid.

22. Dronke, for example, repeatedly refers to the early age from which Hildegard began to manifest her gifts. On any construal, she regards herself as having had these gifts almost from birth, or at least from very early childhood. Peter Dronke, *Women Writers of the Middle Ages* (Cambridge: Cambridge University Press, 1984), 144–45.

23. Helen John, "Hildegard of Bingen: A New Twelfth-Century Woman Philosopher?" in *Hypatia's Daughters,* ed. Linda Lopez McAlister (Bloomington: Indiana University Press, 1996), 22.

24. See Andrea Nye, "A Woman's Thought or a Man's Discipline? The Letters of Abelard and Heloise," in McAlister, *Hypatia's Daughters,* 25–47.

25. Heloise, quoted, ibid., 29, as originally taken from MS. XV, in Etienne Gilson, *Heloise and Abelard* (Ann Arbor: University of Michigan Press, 1960).

26. Gardner has an interesting discussion of Mechthild and love in *Rediscovering Women Philosophers,* 163–65.

27. John Caputo, *More Radical Hermeneutics* (Bloomington: Indiana University Press, 2000), 1–2.

28. Greta Gaard, "Tools for a Cross-Cultural Feminist Ethics: Exploring Ethical Contexts and Contents in the Makah Whale Hunt," *Hypatia* 16 (Fall 2000): 9.

29. Hildegard of Bingen, *The Letters of Hildegard of Bingen,* vol. 1, trans. Joseph L. Baird and Radd K. Ehrman (New York: Oxford University Press, 1994), 48.

30. See the discussion in Evelyn Fox Keller, *Reflections on Gender and Science* (New Haven: Yale University Press, 1985).

31. Joseph L. Baird and Radd K. Ehrman, "Introduction," in *Letters of Hildegard,* 13.

32. Ibid., 19.

33. The extent to which this is the case globally is often difficult to estimate. To take but one example, Heinrich Zimmer's superb work on the philosophy of India indicates the rich and extensive Sanskrit (and other written) traditions of the subcontinent, traditions to which women seldom had access. Heinrich Zimmer, *Philosophies of India* (Princeton: Princeton University Press, 1951), 42.

34. Nancy Hartsock, "Standpoint Theories," paper delivered at the Pacific division meeting of the American Philosophical Association, March 1996, Seattle, Washington.

35. Berger, *Hildegard*, 60.

36. Sandra Harding, *The Science Question in Feminism* (Ithaca, N.Y.: Cornell University Press, 1986), 25.

37. Berger, *Hildegard*, 12.

38. Berger notes that the humoral conception is, in essence, pre-Socratic. Ibid., 15.

39. Many have claimed that the visions are related to what now would be claimed to be a medical condition, but there is no way to confirm this.

40. See Patricia Hill Collins, *Black Feminist Thought* (New York: Routledge, 1991), 261–62.

41. Sabina Lovibond, "The End of Morality," in *Knowing the Difference: Feminist Perspectives in Epistemology,* ed. Kathleen Lennon and Margaret Whitford (New York: Routledge, 1994), 74–75.

42. Alice Jardine, *Gynesis* (Ithaca, N.Y.: Cornell University Press, 1985), 100.

43. Copleston, *History of Philosophy,* vol. 2, part 1, 235.

44. This phrase originally occurs in the work of Evelyn Fox Keller. See her *Reflections on Gender and Science.*

45. Baird and Ehrman, "Introduction," *Letters of Hildegard,* 23.

Chapter 2: Anne Conway

1. See Carolyn Merchant, "The Vitalism of Anne Conway: Its Impact on Leibniz's Concept of the Monad," *Journal of the History of Philosophy* 17, no. 3 (1979): 255–69.

2. Marjorie Hope Nicolson, ed., *The Conway Letters: The Correspondence of Anne Viscountess Conway, Henry More, and Their Friends, 1642–1684* (Cambridge: Cambridge University Press, 1984), 46. There is a superb newer edition of this work, revised and with a detailed introduction by Sarah Hutton (Oxford: Clarendon of Oxford Press, 1992). The first edition, cited here and subsequently, however, is the standard Cambridge version. See also Hutton's *Anne Conway: A Woman Philosopher* (Cambridge: Cambridge University Press, 2004).

3. Ibid., 41–42.

4. Ibid., 46.

5. Ibid., 5.

6. Ibid.

7. Nicolson indicates that Ralph Cudworth, Jeremy Taylor, and Joseph Glanvill were frequent guests in the home, as well as Henry More. All were associated to some degree or other with Cambridge. Nicolson, *Conway Letters,* 6.

8. Anne Conway, *Principles of the Most Ancient and Modern Philosophy,* ed. Peter Loptson (The Hague, Neth.: Martinus Nijhoff, 1982), 164.

9. Merchant, "Vitalism of Anne Conway," 265–66.

10. A new edition of Conway's work appeared in the late 1990s, superbly translated and edited by Allison Coudert and Taylor Corse (*The Principles of the Most Ancient and Modern Philosophy* [Cambridge: Cambridge University Press, 1996]). This is the edition I will cite subsequently, unless noted otherwise. The work represents a new translation from the only extant Latin edition, itself apparently, according to most scholars, a translation of the once-English edition, which appears to have been lost to history. The new edition has the virtue of employing contemporary English, insofar as is possible, thereby alleviating some of the archaisms of the Loptson edition. The latter remains intriguing, however, both because of the high quality of Loptson's commentary and because the English employed in that edition is, of course, the English of Conway's time. For an extensive analysis of Conway's use of the Kabbala, see Coudert's introduction, vii–xxxiii. Another useful source is Allison Coudert, "A Cambridge Platonist's Kabbalist Nightmare," *Journal of the History of Ideas* 36 (Oct.–Dec. 1975): 633–52, wherein she argues for the somewhat controversial notion that the Lurianic Kabbala might be thought to be the single greatest catalyst of Conway's thought. See also Coudert, *Leibniz and the Kabbalah* (Dordrecht, Neth.: Kluwer, 1995).

11. Loptson's commentary is worth reading simply for its value as a guide to Conway's thought, whatever edition of her *Principles* is employed. See Loptson, "Introduction," in Conway, *Principles,* 1–60.

12. Conway, *Principles,* 10.

13. Ibid., 13.

14. Ibid., 35.

15. Ibid., 32.

16. A reproduction of this engraving appears in *Discover* magazine, November 2001.

17. J. A. Passmore, *Ralph Cudworth: An Interpretation* (Cambridge: Cambridge University Press, 1951), 18, 17.

18. René Descartes, excerpts from the *Passions of the Soul,* as quoted in *The Essential Descartes,* ed. Margaret D. Wilson (New York: New American Library, 1969), 363–64.

19. Conway, *Principles,* 20. Again, the influence of the Kabbala must be cited here. In addition to the other sources by Coudert, see also Allison Coudert, *The Impact of the Kabbalah in the Seventeenth Century* (Leiden: Brill, 1999). With respect to the intermingling, Coudert says: "In making this point, Conway accepts van Helmont's view that spirits continually pass into and out of individuals, joining them to their fellow creatures through a complex network of sympathetic emanations." Coudert, *Impact,* 205.

20. Nicolson, *Conway Letters,* 72.

21. Ibid., 81.

22. Conway, *Principles,* 45.

23. Ibid., 41.

24. Passmore, *Cudworth,* 11. Jacqueline Broad, in her *Women Philosophers of the Seventeenth Century* (Cambridge: Cambridge University Press, 2002), notes, "It is also possible that Masham had heard of Conway's writings" (117). For a comparison of Cavendish and Conway, see Lynette Hunter and Sarah Hutton, eds., *Women, Science, and Medicine: 1500–1700* (Gloucestershire, Eng.: Sutton, 1997).

25. Lois Frankel, "Damaris Cudworth Masham: A Seventeenth-Century Feminist Philosopher," in *Hypatia's Daughters,* ed. Linda Lopez McAlister (Bloomington: Indiana University Press, 1996), 129.

26. At least one contemporary work on women philosophers draws on the notion of imagined correspondences between philosophers to help illustrate the work of women who thought philosophically. See Cecile Tougas and Sara Ebenreck, eds., *Presenting Women Philosophers* (Philadelphia: Temple University Press, 2000).

27. Frankel, "Damaris Cudworth Masham," 130.

28. Ibid., 130–31.

29. Marjorie Nicolson, "The Real Scholar Gipsy," *Yale Review* (January 1929): 347–63. Again, see Allison Coudert's various works for excellent delineations of the Van Helmont circle of relationships.

30. Merchant, "Vitalism of Anne Conway," 255, 266.

31. According to Nicolson, the initial impetus for their meeting appears to have been medical. Nicolson, *Conway Letters,* 312.

32. In a letter to Conway of 1677, Henry More refers to the work as the "Apparatus of the Zoar." Ibid., 429.

33. The works most frequently cited are Carol Gilligan, *In a Different Voice* (Cambridge, Mass.: Harvard University Press, 1982), and Evelyn Fox Keller, *Reflections on Gender and Science* (New Haven: Yale University Press, 1985).

34. Richard H. Popkin, "The Spiritualistic Cosmologies of Henry More and Anne Conway," in *Henry More (1614–1687): Tercentenary Studies,* ed. Sarah Hutton (Dordrecht, Neth.: Kluwer, 1990), 104. Popkin is, of course, using the Loptson edition of Conway's work.

35. Ynestra King, "Healing the Wounds: Feminism, Ecology, and Nature/Culture Dualism," in *Gender/Body/Knowledge: Feminist Reconstructions of Being and Knowing,* ed. Alison M. Jaggar and Susan R. Bordo (New Brunswick, N.J.: Rutgers University Press, 1989), 116.

36. Popkin, "Spiritualistic Cosmologies," 106.

37. Writing of the ever-present cultural chasm between the secular and the religious, Giles Gunn has noted, "The stock of happiness being, as it were, in such comparatively short supply, is not most of the rhetorical and ritual machinery of the world's great religions designed precisely, as the majority of their modern interpreters have informed us, to cope with this unpleasant fact?" Giles Gunn, *Beyond Solidarity* (Chicago: University of Chicago Press), 118.

38. See, for example, Susan Bordo, *Flight to Objectivity* (Albany: State University of New York Press, 1987).

39. See Diana Paul, *Women in the Buddhist Tradition* (Stanford: Stanford University Press, 1985).

40. It is important to remember that Conway would have been cut off from immersion in daily activity not only by her own predilections, but by social class. Although Anne Conway was a mother for a brief period of time, we can hypothesize, for example, that tasks such as those having to do with caring for an infant would have been performed largely by many others. Conway's status as a viscountess cannot be overlooked in any examination of her life or work.

41. Nicolson, *Conway Letters,* 315.

42. These points are addressed by Conway most specifically in chapters 7 and 8 of the *Principles.*

43. I examine some traditions of Dravidian India that draw on comparable notions,

such as that of shakti, in my *Worlds of Knowing: Global Feminist Epistemologies* (New York: Routledge, 2001).

44. John Morrill, "The Stuarts," in *The Oxford History of Britain* (Oxford: Oxford University Press, 1999), 392.

45. See, for example, Edward Said, *The Edward Said Reader* (New York: Routledge, 1999).

46. That this was a staple of British commentary on Hindu India, for example, has been discussed in chapters 2 and 3 of my *Worlds of Knowing*.

47. I have given a more precise account of the substance and modal issues in Anne Conway's *Principles* in my article "Anne Viscountess Conway: A Seventeenth-Century Rationalist," *Hypatia* 4 (Spring 1989): 64–79.

48. Susan S. Stocker, "Problems of Embodiment and Problematic Embodiment," *Hypatia* 16 (Summer 2001): 31.

49. The genetic approach, presumably, is obvious; the "genealogical" approach is identified with Judith Butler and those thinkers who, like her, see the body as a social construction, or who write of the "semiotics" of the body.

50. See Stuart Brown, "Liebniz and More's Cabbalistic Circle," in Hutton, *Henry More,* 77–95.

51. Ibid., 86.

52. Of Spinoza, Conway writes: "For he confounds God and creatures, and makes one being of both." (Conway, *Principles,* 64.) Here, of course, she refers to Spinoza's well-known doctrine that God has an infinite number of essences, two of which are extension and thought. This has the corollary that all things that are, are in God.

53. For instance, two pieces, "Henry More and Witchcraft," by Allison Coudert, and "Mysticism and Enthusiasm in Henry More," by Robert Crocker, appear in Hutton, *Henry More,* 115–36 and 137–56, respectively.

54. Quoted in Stephen Greenblatt, *Learning to Curse* (Cambridge, Mass.: Harvard University Press, 1990), 18.

55. A wonderful work for general purposes on this topic is Antonia Fraser's *The Weaker Vessel.*

Chapter 3: Mary Astell

1. The back jacket of the Springborg edition of her works refers to her as a "High Church Tory pamphleteer." See Patricia Springborg, ed., *Astell: Political Writings* (Cambridge: Cambridge University Press, 1996).

2. Ibid., xi–xii.

3. Ibid., xv.

4. Ibid., xxix.

5. Florence M. Smith, *Mary Astell* (1916; New York: AMS Press, 1966). Although this work is somewhat out of date, it contains intriguing material in its opening chapter.

6. Ibid., 104.

7. Neither Springborg (*Astell,* xii–xiii) nor Smith (*Mary Astell,* 7–8) is able to shed any light on how this occurred, but it may be that the young, articulate woman, perhaps meeting other women in passing, was able to impress them with her wit and intelligence.

8. Smith, *Mary Astell,* 9.

9. This is how she is labeled insofar as her work is now included in the Cambridge Texts in the History of Political Thought.

10. Ruth Perry, *The Celebrated Mary Astell: An Early English Feminist* (Chicago: University of Chicago Press, 1989), 11. Once again, Jacqueline Broad's *Women Philosophers of the Seventeenth Century* (Cambridge: Cambridge University Press, 2002) is an excellent source, and the chapter on Astell reinforces the Cartesian nature of her views, while taking pains to point out the influence of John Norris.

11. Perry, *Celebrated Mary Astell*, 11.

12. Mary Astell, *Letters Concerning the Love of God,* as excerpted in Bridget Hill, ed., *The First English Feminist: Reflections upon Marriage and Other Writings by Mary Astell* (Aldershot, Eng.: Gower, 1986), 193–94.

13. Perry, *Celebrated Mary Astell*, 11–12.

14. Ibid., 13.

15. John Bowle, *The English Experience* (London: Phoenix Press, 2000), 347.

16. Mary Astell, *The Christian Religion*, in Hill, *First English Feminist*, 199.

17. Ibid., 202.

18. Ibid., 195.

19. Stephen Coote, *Samuel Pepys: A Life* (New York: Palgrave of St. Martin, 2001), 54.

20. Mary Astell, *Reflections upon Marriage,* in Hill, *First English Feminist*, 73. I have written a piece on Astell's various positions with regard to feminist issues. See "Mary Astell: A Pre-Humean Christian Empiricist and Feminist," in *Presenting Women Philosophers,* ed. Cecile Tougas and Sara Ebenreck (Philadelphia: Temple University Press, 2000), 147–54.

21. An excellent overview of the relationships the pamphleteers had to each other, and the nature of their authorships and responses, is given in Springborg, *Astell.* Springborg has a particularly astute introductory section to *A Fair Way,* in "A Note on the Text," 83–86. Her bibliography also contains full titles and publication dates for Astell's works; I am, of course, in general using shortened titles.

22. Perry (*Celebrated Mary Astell*) is an excellent source for how the Cromwellian period affected Newcastle and environs, ultimately having a pronounced effect on the family of Mary Astell.

23. Mary Astell, *A Fair Way with the Dissenters,* in Springborg, *Astell,* 90.

24. Perry, *Celebrated Mary Astell,* 42. Perry's careful delineation of the social structure of Newcastle at the time of Astell's birth is remarkable for its detail. She goes on to say, "The security of belief which resonates in her prose suggests the self-possession of one raised on the side of power, no matter how threatened it might be" (42).

25. I have made this argument in my "Mary Astell."

26. Perry, *Celebrated Mary Astell,* 50–51.

27. Bridget Hill, "Introduction," *First English Feminist,* 2.

28. Perry, *Celebrated Mary Astell,* 64.

29. Smith, *Mary Astell,* 8–9.

30. Perry, *Celebrated Mary Astell,* 66.

31. Springborg, "A Note on the Text," 84.

32. Perry has an excellent discussion of Norris's influence on Astell, and the extent to which each of them philosophized on the basis of extant disputes that are best seen in the light of Cartesianism, writ large, versus Locke's new work. As Perry says, "Like the earlier Cambridge Platonists, Norris resented the imputation, by those who sought to

'explain' Christianity, that religious belief implied the suspension of reason." Perry, *Celebrated Mary Astell,* 75.

33. I have made this point with respect to *Reflections* in my "Mary Astell."

34. Perry, *Celebrated Mary Astell,* 76–77.

35. Astell is replying to an essay from Norris's *Practical Discourses,* "A Discourse Concerning the Measure of Divine Love," and some ideas that were important to Astell are later recapitulated in Norris's *An Account of Reason and Faith.*

36. Perry makes this point repeatedly. See, *Celebrated Mary Astell,* especially, 106–9.

37. Ibid., 109.

38. Perry discusses these friendships at various points in *Celebrated Mary Astell.*

39. Hill, "Introduction," 23.

40. Ibid., 52.

41. Susan Moller Okin, "Philosopher Queens and Private Wives: Plato on Women and the Family," *Philosophy and Public Affairs* 6 (Summer 1977): 345.

42. Hill, "Introduction," 53.

43. Monique Canto, "The Politics of Women's Bodies: Reflections on Plato," in *The Female Body in Western Culture,* ed. Susan Rubin Suleiman (Cambridge, Mass.: Harvard University Press, 1986), 340.

44. Ibid., 339.

45. Okin, "Philosopher Queens," 349–50.

46. Kathleen Okruhlik, "Birth of a New Physics or Death of Nature?" in *Women and Reason,* ed. Elizabeth D. Harvey and Kathleen Okruhlik (Ann Arbor: University of Michigan Press, 1992), 63.

47. The term "feminist empiricist" is drawn from the work of Sandra Harding. See the discussion in Harding, *The Science Question in Feminism* (Ithaca, N.Y.: Cornell University Press, 1985).

48. Hilda L. Smith, "Intellectual Bases for Feminist Analyses," in Harvey and Okruhlik, *Women and Reason,* 19, 30.

49. Perry, *Celebrated Mary Astell,* 90–91.

50. The classic work of explanation in this regard is, of course, Nancy Chodorow's *Reproduction of Mothering* (Berkeley: University of California Press, 1985).

51. Astell, *A Serious Proposal to the Ladies, Part I,* in Hill, *First English Feminist,* 150.

52. Beverly Daniel Tatum, "Talking about Race, Learning about Racism: The Application of Racial Identity Development Theory in the Classroom," *Harvard Educational Review* 62 (Spring 1992): 1–2.

53. Astell, *Some Reflections,* in Hill, *First English Feminist,* 99–100.

54. See again my "Mary Astell."

55. Astell, *A Serious Proposal,* in Hill, *First English Feminist,* 153.

56. Geneva Smitherman, "'What Go Round Come Round': *King* in Perspective," *Harvard Educational Review* 51 (February 1981): 41.

57. Perry is able to flesh out her view of Astell with a meticulous examination of local historical records in the Newcastle area. This allows her to spend the better part of three chapters on Astell, her family, her environs, and the surroundings that produced her. See Perry, *Celebrated Mary Astell,* 3–97.

58. Ibid., 19.

59. Myra Reynolds, *The Learned Lady in England: 1650–1760* (Boston: Houghton

Mifflin, 1920), is a wonderful example of the range of work citing Mary Astell. In this compendium of information about women scholars and schooling schemes for women, her name appears no less than twenty times in the index.

60. Robert Halsband, *The Life of Lady Mary Wortley Montagu* (Oxford: Clarendon Press of Oxford University Press, 1956), 117–18. Halsband refers to Astell, intriguingly enough, as "the founder of the feminist movement" (117).

61. Perry, for example, says that she seemed to "welcome" death. Perry, *Celebrated Mary Astell,* 323.

62. Her letter to Archbishop Sancroft, for instance, is the source of extensive commentary by Perry. Ibid., 66–67.

63. Mary Astell, *The Christian Religion,* in Hill, *First English Feminist,* 198.

64. Mary Astell, *An Impartial Inquiry into the Causes of Rebellion,* in Springborg, *Astell,* 148.

Chapter 4: Mary Wollstonecraft

1. Mary Warnock, for example, lists her in her volume *Women Philosophers* (London: J. M. Dent, 1996).

2. Mary Wollstonecraft, *A Vindication of the Rights of Woman,* ed. Carol H. Poston (New York: Norton, 1975), 49.

3. Claire Tomalin, *The Life and Death of Mary Wollstonecraft* (New York: Harcourt Brace Jovanovich, 1966), 70–71.

4. Ibid., 96. Tomalin goes on to say, "Johnson was delighted: when Paine's Rights of Man appeared shortly afterwards, the names of Wollstonecraft and Paine were bracketed together as revolutionaries" (ibid.).

5. Ibid., 97.

6. Ibid., 93.

7. See Catriona Mackenzie, "Reason and Sensibility: The Idea of Women's Self-Governance in the Writings of Mary Wollstonecraft," in *Hypatia's Daughters,* ed. Linda Lopez McAlister (Bloomington: Indiana University Press, 1996), 181–203.

8. See Diana Coole, *Women in Political Theory: from Ancient Misogyny to Contemporary Feminism* (Boulder, Colo.: Lynne Rienner, 1993).

9. Ibid., 94. She goes on to say, with respect to dichotomies such as reason/passion, "In other words, she [Wollstonecraft] leaves these gender-related oppositions intact but would resolve all individuals into the superior (masculine) category" (ibid.).

10. Mackenzie, "Reason and Sensibility," 182.

11. Ibid., 198.

12. Wollstonecraft, *Vindication,* 14–15.

13. Ibid., 14.

14. Ibid., 12.

15. To be fair, in these paragraphs Wollstonecraft actually does mention European nations, but it is clear from context that she also thinks the European nations are capable of outgrowing these misguided forms of governance. Her venom is chiefly reserved for hereditary institutions, and, of course, the French Revolution—that quintessential product of the European Enlightenment—is one of the bulwarks of liberty against hereditary privilege. Somewhat later on, while criticizing Rousseau, she remarks that the Spartans were "scarcely human." Wollstonecraft, *Vindication,* 15.

16. Ibid., 14.

17. Ibid., 16.

18. Ibid., 24.

19. Tomalin claims that Wollstonecraft wrote *A Vindication of the Rights of Woman* in "six weeks." Tomalin, *Life and Death,* 105.

20. Ibid., 103–4.

21. Tomalin notes that Bentham suggested a "secret ballot and a literacy test." Ibid., 104.

22. Moira Gatens, " 'The Oppressed State of My Sex': Wollstonecraft on Reason, Feeling and Equality," in *Feminist Interpretations and Political Theory,* ed. Mary Lyndon Shanley and Carole Pateman (Cambridge: Polity Press, 1991), 113.

23. Ibid., 115.

24. Darlene Gay Levy and Harriet Branson Applewhite, "Women and Political Revolution in Paris," in *Becoming Visible: Women in European History,* ed. Renate Bridenthal, Claudia Koonz, and Susan Stuard (New York: Houghton Mifflin, 1987), 284.

25. Maria J. Falco, in her introductory essay to *Feminist Interpretations of Mary Wollstonecraft,* notes, "Twice she attempted suicide over his [Imlay's] rejection of her, but after the second attempt, her friends convinced her to get on with her life for the sake of her daughter, Fanny." Maria J. Falco, ed., *Feminist Interpretations of Mary Wollstonecraft* (University Park: Pennsylvania State University Press, 1996), 4.

26. Tomalin, *Life and Death,* 218.

27. Janet Todd, *Mary Wollstonecraft: A Revolutionary Life* (New York: Columbia University Press, 2000), 179.

28. Moira Ferguson, "Mary Wollstonecraft and the Problematic of Slavery," in Falco, *Feminist Interpretations,* 130.

29. Ibid.

30. Quoted in Miriam Brody, "The Vindication of the Writes of Women: Mary Wollstonecraft and Enlightenment Rhetoric," in *Feminist Interpretations,* Falco, *Feminist Interpretations,* 113.

31. In her own writings, Wollstonecraft refers to the French king, who was now known as "Louis Capet," as behaving "with more dignity than I had expected." Todd, *Mary Wollstonecraft,* 206.

32. Todd indicates, with her close scholarship of the time, that it sold thirty thousand copies. Ibid., 163.

33. Quoted, ibid., 165.

34. Ibid.

35. Levy and Applewhite, "Women and Political Revolution," 286.

36. Elizabeth Fox-Genovese claims that Wollstonecraft "ranks among the Enlightenment's first, great female heirs." Elizabeth Fox-Genovese, "Women and the Enlightenment," in Bridenthal, Koonz, and Stuard, *Becoming Visible,* 271–72.

37. Mackenzie, "Reason and Sensibility," 181–203.

38. Ibid., 191.

39. Alison Jaggar, *Feminist Politics and Human Nature* (Totowa, N.J.: Rowman and Allanheld, 1983), 37, 38.

40. Levy and Applewhite, "Political Revolution," 286.

41. Hélène Cixous, "The Laugh of the Medusa," in *New French Feminisms,* ed. Elaine Marks and Isabelle de Courtivron (New York: Schocken, 1981), 245.

42. Wollstonecraft, *Vindication,* 55.

43. Jaggar, *Feminist Politics,* 358.

44. Wollstonecraft, *Vindication,* 55.

45. Muller takes decided issue with still another critic, Mary Poovey, who, according to Muller, "accuses Wollstonecraft of adopting a gender-neutral voice that projects a tone of condescension." Virginia L. Muller, "What Can Liberals Learn from Mary Wollstonecraft?" in Falco, *Feminist Interpretations,* 54.

46. Ibid., 57.

47. Moira Ferguson, "Mary Wollstonecraft and the Problematic of Slavery," in Falco, *Feminist Interpretations,* 141 (second quote), 143 (first quote).

48. Ibid. 149.

49. Chapter titles are as they appear in the edition by Poston.

50. Wollstonecraft, *Vindication,* 76.

51. Carol Poston, "Mary Wollstonecraft and 'The Body Politic,'" in Falco, *Feminist Interpretations,* 85–104.

52. Ibid., 87.

53. Quoted from the second *Vindication,* ibid., 90.

54. Poston, "Wollstonecraft and 'The Body Politic,'" 93.

55. Miranda Seymour, *Mary Shelley* (New York: Grove Press, 2000).

56. Ibid., 23–24.

57. Ibid., 32.

58. Catherine Villanueva Gardner, *Rediscovering Women Philosophers* (Boulder, Colo.: Westview, 2000), 81–122. The title of the chapter is "Mary Wollstonecraft and the Separation of Poetry and Politics," and, pertinently, the chapter has a subsection entitled "The Second *Vindication* Is Not a Work of Enlightenment Philosophy," 92–95.

59. Ibid., 96–97.

60. Jaggar, *Feminist Politics,* 39.

61. Wollstonecraft, *Vindication,* 189.

62. Mary Wollstonecraft, *Maria, or the Wrongs of Woman,* ed. Janet Todd (London: Pickering and Chatto, 1991), 65. This edition consists of three works, two by Wollstonecraft and one by Mary Shelley, collected by Todd and published in one volume. It appears in the Pickering Women's Classics series and is fully titled and credited as *Mary, Maria and Matilda,* by Mary Wollstonecraft and Mary Shelley.

63. William Godwin, "Preface," in Wollstonecraft, *Maria,* 57.

64. Seymour, *Mary Shelley,* 33.

Chapter 5: Harriet Taylor Mill

1. There is some evidence that John Taylor was more than active in political circles. See "Introduction," *The Complete Works of Harriet Taylor Mill,* ed. Jo Ellen Jacobs (Bloomington: Indiana University Press, 1998); for a recognition of Taylor's knowledge of his wife's intellectual contributions, see xvi. All references to Jacobs in this chapter are to this volume, unless otherwise noted.

2. For an excellent overview of this leading concept in the work of the Mills, see Jonathan Riley, "Mill's Political Economy: Ricardian Science and Liberal Utilitarian Art," in *The Cambridge Companion to Mill,* ed. John Skorupski (Cambridge: Cambridge University Press, 1998), 293–337. As Riley notes, at the core of the theory is the notion that "an ideal liberal society would be composed of highly educated and productive workers . . . [who] respect each other's equal rights (including the right to liberty in purely self-regarding concerns)" (320).

3. Jacobs, introduction to "Ethics," *Complete Works,* 135.

4. Jacobs carefully notes watermark dates on all extant papers on which such dates are found so that we may ascertain the period of their composition with some degree of certainty; except for her published writings, HTM was not in the habit of dating her work. It should also be noted that since HTM published comparatively little, much of her remaining work is in holograph form and has been printed for the first time by Jacobs. As editor, Jacobs has supplied bracketed titles for fragments, drafts, or scraps that were found in the extant collection in the British Library of the London School of Political and Economic Sciences. In this text, I follow Jacobs and indicate only original publication dates for those few pieces, such as a piece on the life of William Caxton, that were published during HTM's lifetime. For complete citations, see Jacobs, *Complete Works,* and her "Textual Introduction," xxxvii–xxxix.

5. Harriet Taylor Mill, "The Nature of the Marriage Contract," in Jacobs, *Complete Works,* 17–18.

6. Jacobs, introduction to "Letters to John Stuart Mill," *Complete Works,* 319–20.

7. Alan Ryan, ed., *Mill: The Spirit of the Age, On Liberty, The Subjection of Women,* Norton Critical Edition (New York: Norton, 1997). The introduction is on pages ix–xlv; for the section on Harriet Taylor Mill, see pages xvi–xviii.

8. Alan Ryan, "Introduction," *Mill,* xvi.

9. Ibid.

10. Mill, quoted, ibid., ix. The text actually states that a "warm-hearted mother" is a "rarity" in England.

11. The reference to "faults of uncharitableness" is in the brief piece entitled by Jacobs "Sources of Conformity," in *Complete Works,* 137–42.

12. This particular piece is an unpublished letter to the editor of the *Reasoner* in response to printed work in that periodical. The letter is described by Jacobs as "sparked" by a previous letter that Harriet had sent to John herself, and Jacobs notes that, although the unpublished letter is cosigned, there is every reason to believe that Harriet had a significant hand in it. Jacobs, *Complete Works,* 157–58.

13. Jacobs notes in a footnote to the text at this point that the line of argument here sounds remarkably similar to some of the later arguments of Bertrand Russell.

14. Jacobs, *Complete Works,* 159.

15. Ibid., 159–60.

16. Ibid., 163.

17. Ibid., 161.

18. Alan Millar, "Mill on Religion," in Skorupski, *Cambridge Companion,* 177.

19. Jacobs, *Complete Works,* 160.

20. Ibid., 161.

21. Ibid., 162. (Jacobs has entitled this short paragraph "Christianity and Ethics.")

22. Millar, "Mill on Religion," 182.

23. That HTM is the author of the chapter entitled "On the Probable Futurity of the Labouring Classes" in the *Principles* is one of the few points that is pretty much beyond dispute. In her introductory pages to that chapter, Jacobs has an extensive quote from Mill's *Autobiography* that contains the following phrases: "[this chapter] . . . was wholly an exposition of her thoughts, often in words taken from her own lips." (Jacobs, *Complete Works*, 291.) On page 604 Jacobs lists the chapter as one of HTM's published pieces. Riley notes, in assessing Harriet Taylor Mill's contribution to the *Principles* as a whole, "By the time he published the third edition of his great treatise in 1852, he and Harriet Taylor . . . had firmly concluded." Riley, "Political Economy," 296.

24. Susan Moller Okin, "[Mill's Feminist Egalitarianism]", in Ryan, *Mill*, 331. Okin's chapter title is given in this somewhat unusual bracketed form because it is a direct excision from Okin's *Women in Western Political Thought* (1979; rpt., Princeton: Princeton University Press, 1992).

25. Jacobs, *Complete Works*, 315.

26. Harriet Taylor Mill, "Sources of Conformity," in Jacobs, *Complete Works*, 137–42. The editor dates this piece as 1832.

27. Ibid., 138.

28. Ibid., 297.

29. This portion of Mill's essay is taken directly from French documents and appears in French on pages 306–13 of Jacobs, *Complete Works*. The editor has provided a translation; HTM uses this information, presumably, not only because it is a direct financial testament with respect to the problems faced in forming a cooperative, but also because the original French text indicates the extraordinary change in the attitudes of the workers toward their work, and their lives in general, as a direct result of their success.

30. John Stuart Mill, *Autobiography*, ed. John Robson (London: Penguin Books, 1989), 145–46.

31. See Harriet Taylor Mill, "Source of Conformity," in Jacobs, *Complete Works*, 137–42.

32. Ibid., 138.

33. See the discussion of George Eliot in Catherine Villanueva Gardner, "George Eliot and How to Read Novels as Philosophy," in *Rediscovering Women Philosophers* (Boulder, Colo.: Westview, 2000), 123–48.

34. Gardner mentions some of Eliot's other work. Ibid., 131–34.

35. Ibid., 133.

36. Gardner mentions Eliot's "friendship with British Positivist . . . Frederic Harrison." Gardner, *Rediscovering Women Philosophers*, 124.

37. Gardner's chapter endnotes cite a number of works that deal, at least peripherally, with the general theme of Eliot-as-philosophical-thinker.

38. Josephine Kamm, *John Stuart Mill in Love* (London: Gordon and Cremonesi, 1977), 28.

39. This is the title of chapter 5, ibid., 44–47.

40. Ibid., 30.

41. Ibid., 34.

42. Jacobs, *Complete Works*, 5.

43. Kamm, *John Stuart Mill in Love*, 35–36.

44. James Morris, *Pax Britannica* (New York: Harcourt Brace, 1968), 118–19.

45. Intriguingly enough, there is an interesting strikeover in "Oppression of Women Due to Lack of Education" in Jacobs, *Complete Works,* at about twenty lines from the top of the piece. The sentence begins, "It is *not* wonderful that those white men who believe their own happiness to depend on other men's political degradation . . ." but the word "white" is struck out. It is not at all clear if the word was merely a slip of the pen, or if some other meaning was intended. One would suppose that the contemporary usage of such a term was not at all common in Britain during the 1830s, before the accession even of Victoria.

46. Sandra Harding, *Whose Science? Whose Knowledge?* (Ithaca, N.Y.: Cornell University Press, 1991), 13.

47. Jacobs, *Complete Works,* 5.

48. Kamm (*John Stuart Mill in Love*) has several excellent early chapters on the various permutations of the social circles in which both Mills, individually and as a couple, moved. She has a particularly striking analysis of the importance of the foursome of W. J. Fox, Eliza Flower, Harriet Taylor, and John Stuart Mill for all of its members.

49. Jacobs, *Complete Works,* 6.

50. Ibid., 293.

51. H. O. Pappe, *John Stuart Mill and the Harriet Taylor Myth* (Parkville, Victoria, Aust.: Melbourne University Press, 1960), 48.

52. Kamm, among others, insists upon JSM's comparative lack of experience with women before meeting Harriet. Kamm, *John Stuart Mill in Love,* 32.

53. Harding, *Whose Science?* 184–85.

54. Kamm, *John Stuart Mill in Love,* 14–15.

55. Hayek notes, "On the basis of the full account of this education which we possess, he has, in a recent study of child geniuses, been awarded the highest intelligence quotient of all recorded instances of specially precocious children." F. A. Hayek, *John Stuart Mill and Harriet Taylor* (Chicago: University of Chicago Press, 1951), 30.

56. Harding, *Whose Science?* 170.

57. There is some evidence that at least some of JSM's sisters were provided rigorous lessons in Latin and mathematics. See Hayek, *Mill and Taylor,* 286.

58. Ibid., 31.

59. Jacobs, *Complete Works,* 312.

60. Giorgio Agamben, *Homo Sacer* (Stanford: Stanford University Press, 1998), 5.

61. "The Nature of the Marriage Contract," in Jacobs, *Complete Works,* 18.

62. Ibid., 19.

63. Morris, *Pax Britannica,* 489.

64. Jacobs, *Complete Works,* 306.

65. Morris, *Pax Britannica,* 235.

66. For example, the title of the previously cited work by H. O. Pappe, *John Stuart Mill and the Harriet Taylor Myth,* is indicative of the sort of commentary previously published.

67. Kamm, *John Stuart Mill in Love,* 46.

68. Jacobs, *Complete Works,* 19.

69. Ibid., 6.

70. Hayek, *Mill and Taylor,* 25.

71. Jacobs, *Complete Works,* 168–70.

72. Ibid., 169.

73. Ibid.

74. Alan M. Dershowitz, *Shouting Fire* (New York: Little, Brown, 2002), 121.

Chapter 6: Edith Stein

1. See Sylvie Courtine-Denamy, *Three Women in Dark Times,* trans. G. M. Goshgarian (Ithaca, N.Y.: Cornell University Press, 2000). Interestingly enough, both of the other women alluded to in the title, who lived through the dark times of the Holocaust, are also philosophers.

2. The dissertation has been published and translated. One available edition is Edith Stein, *On the Problem of Empathy,* trans. Waltraut Stein (Norwell, Mass.: Kluwer, 1989).

3. Courtine-Denamy, *Three Women,* 11.

4. Ibid., 41.

5. Edmund Husserl, author's preface to the English edition, *Ideas,* trans. W. R. Boyce Gibson (New York: Collier, 1972), 15.

6. Rachel Feldhay Brenner, *Writing as Resistance: Four Women Confronting the Holocaust* (University Park: Pennsylvania State University Press, 1997), 62–63.

7. W. R. Boyce Gibson, "Translator's Preface," in Husserl, *Ideas,* 23.

8. Brenner, *Writing as Resistance,* 76.

9. Ibid.

10. Stein, *On the Problem of Empathy,* 112. The title of the section from which this quotation is taken is "The Existence of the Spirit."

11. Waltraut Stein, "Translator's Introduction," in E. Stein, *On the Problem of Empathy,* xvi–xvii.

12. Ibid., xxi–xxii.

13. Brenner, *Writing as Resistance,* 77. The quotation Brenner gives is from Hilda Graef.

14. Courtine-Denamy, *Three Women,* 25–26.

15. Augustine, *Confessions* (New York: Liveright, 1943), 154–55.

16. Edith Stein, "The Spirit of St. Elizabeth of Hungary," in *Writings of Edith Stein,* trans. Hilda Graef (London: Peter Owen, 1956), 50.

17. Stein, "The Knowledge of God," in *Writings of Edith Stein,* 75.

18. Paul Ricoeur, *Husserl: An Analysis of His Phenomenology* (Evanston, Ill.: Northwestern University Press, 1967), 9.

19. Ibid., 10.

20. Rachel Feldhay Brenner, "Ethical Convergence in Religious Conversion," in *The Unnecessary Problem of Edith Stein,* ed. Harry James Cargas (Lanham, Md.: University Press of America, 1994), 98.

21. Freda Mary Oben, "Holiness in the Twentieth Century," in Cargas, *Unnecessary Problem,* 10.

22. Ricoeur's account is very helpful here. As he says, "Phenomenology very clearly comes to bay with the paradox of solipsism, for only the ego is constituted primordially." Ricoeur, *Husserl,* 11.

23. Ibid.

24. Stein, "The Vocation of Man and Woman," in *Writings of Edith Stein,* 121.

25. Oben, "Holiness," 9.

26. Ibid.

27. Ibid., 10–11.

28. The Cargas volume (*Unnecessary Problem*) is a set of essays specifically designed to respond to this problem.

29. Courtine-Denamy, *Three Women,* 10.

30. Ibid., 20.

31. Peter Baehr, in his introduction to *The Portable Hannah Arendt,* notes, "It is man as *homo faber* who is most admired today, and productivity that is elevated to the highest level of social esteem." Baehr, *The Portable Hannah Arendt* (New York: Penguin Putnam, 2000), xxxi.

32. Ibid., xxvi.

33. See David Woodruff Smith, "Mind and Body," in *The Cambridge Companion to Husserl,* ed. Barry Smith and David Woodruff Smith (Cambridge: Cambridge University Press, 1995), 323–93.

34. For Scheler's placement in a list of Husserl's heirs, see the introduction, ibid., 1–44.

35. Smith, "Mind and Body," 354–55.

36. In the index to the *Cambridge Companion to Husserl,* Stein is cited no less than eight times.

37. Edith Stein, *Essays on Woman,* trans. Freda Mary Oben (Washington, D.C.: ICS Publications, 1987).

38. See Stein, "The Vocation of Man and Woman," in *Writings of Edith Stein,* 101–25.

39. Ibid., 121.

40. Martha Nussbaum, "Objectification," in *Philosophy and Public Affairs* 24 (Fall 1995): 249–91.

41. Ibid., 249.

42. Edith Stein is, for example, cited more than once in the index to a general clinical account of empathy as an introject, published in a series devoted to Freudian analysis. See Joseph Lichtenberg, Melvin Bornstein, and Donald Silver, eds., *Empathy,* vol. 1 (Hillsdale, N.J.: Analytic Press, 1984). Stein's work is cited in this volume in a piece by Louis Agosta, in a paragraph that begins, "Although the paths of Husserl and Freud never crossed . . ." (44). See Agosta, "Empathy and Intersubjectivity," in *Empathy,* 43–61.

43. Brenner, "Ethical Convergence," 98–99.

44. Hilda Graef's *The Scholar and the Cross,* a sort of intellectual biography, has the imprimatur. Hilda C. Graef, *The Scholar and the Cross: The Life and Work of Edith Stein* (Westminster, Md.: Newman Press, 1955).

45. Ibid., 50–51.

46. Ibid., 51.

47. Ibid., 32.

48. Dorothy Dinnerstein, *The Mermaid and the Minotaur: Sexual Arrangements and Human Malaise* (New York: Harper and Row, 1976), 53–54.

49. See chapter 2 of my *Worlds of Knowing: Global Feminist Epistemologies* (New York: Routledge, 2001), for an extended account of appropriation of parts of the northern Hindu traditions by women activists in India.

50. Woodward has a very helpful brief section on Stein in his book. Kenneth L. Woodward, *Making Saints* (New York: Simon and Schuster, 1990), 135–44.

51. This must certainly be a comparatively unremarked-upon facet of the controversy surrounding Stein's canonization. Ibid., 139.

52. The volume in question is Susan Rubin Suleiman, ed., *The Female Body in Western Culture* (Cambridge, Mass.: Harvard University Press, 1986).

53. Miles, "The Virgin's One Bare Breast: Female Nudity and Religious Meaning in Tuscan Early Renaissance Culture," in Suleiman, *Female Body,* 196–197.

54. Ibid., 196.

55. Miles, quoting from the Graef translation of Bernardino, "One Bare Breast," 202.

56. In striking commentary on the importance of the body for these beliefs, Miles notes, "In some images of the resurrected Christ, power appears to be a primary message; Christ is shown with an artfully draped but unmistakable erection." Ibid., 202–3.

57. Jane Roland Martin has made these points in several essays reprinted in more than one collection. One of the most recent, widely used in courses in education and in American graduate schools of education, is *Changing the Educational Landscape* (New York: Routledge, 1997).

58. My own local scholarly resource has more than one item on Stein in English that has not been checked out in approximately thirty years.

59. Henry Bordeaux, *Edith Stein: Thoughts on Her Life and Times* (Milwaukee, Wisc.: Bruce, 1959), vii.

60. Sister Teresia de Spiritu Sanctu, ODC, *Edith Stein* (London: Sheed and Ward, 1952), 99.

61. She is, for example, cited in the index to Donn Welton's *The Other Husserl: The Origins of Transcendental Phenomenology* (Bloomington: Indiana University Press, 2000), a number of times.

62. In his capacity as editor of *Tikkun,* Lerner has often pointed out that the Judaic tradition requires one to "honor the stranger."

63. Susanne Batzdorff, "Witnessing My Aunt's Beatification," in Cargas, *Unnecessary Problem,* 33.

64. Woodward, among many others, makes note of this fact. Woodward, *Making Saints,* 137.

65. Courtine-Denamy, *Three Women,* 4.

Chapter 7: Simone Weil

1. *Gravity and Grace,* for example, is such a collection; some have compared it to Wittgenstein's *Investigations* in terms of style and make-up. See Simone Weil, *Gravity and Grace,* ed. Gustave Thibon (Lincoln: University of Nebraska Press, 1995).

2. Francine du Plessix Gray, *Simone Weil* (New York: Penguin Putnam, 2001), 210–11. There are several biographies of Weil readily available; there seems to be general agreement that the richest, although perhaps less accessible, is that by Simone Petrement. The French edition is Simone Petrement, *La vie de Simone Weil* (Paris: Librairie Artheme Fayard, 1973); it was published in the United States as *Simone Weil: A Life* (New York: Pantheon, 1976). Petrement's work is particularly detailed insofar as her family is concerned. For example, on page 15 of the French edition, Petrement wrote, in describing

her family of origin: "Hommes d'affaires ou commercants, il n'y avait guere d'intel-lectuels parmi eux, sauf le docteur" (Businessmen or salesmen, there were hardly any intellectuals among them, except for the doctor [her father] [my translation]).

3. Gray, *Weil,* 212.

4. One such example is her devotion to the project of teaching herself Sanskrit. As Gray remarks, Weil had claimed that the Sanskrit characters had never served "as the vehicle of anything base." Ibid., 167.

5. Simone Weil, *Oppression and Liberty,* ed. Arthur Wills and John Petrie (Amherst: University of Massachusetts Press, 1973).

6. Ibid., 2.

7. Simone Weil, "Draft for a Statement of Human Obligations," in *Simone Weil: An Anthology,* ed. Sian Miles (New York: Grove Press, 1986), 201–2.

8. Gray, *Weil,* 81. Gray indicates that she is quoting the introduction to the French edition of *Oppression and Liberty,* first published by Gallimard in 1948.

9. There is lengthy documentation of Weil's questioning, indeed hectoring, of priests and others about the position of the church on a number of matters. Coles, for example, notes the extent to which Father Perrin was the recipient of these desperate requests for information. Robert Coles, *Simone Weil: A Modern Pilgrimage* (Woodstock, Vt.: SkyLight Paths, 2001), 121.

10. Ibid., 119.

11. Coles has an extended chapter on this topic. (Ibid., 23–41.) Some of the most in-teresting material is on 30–31.

12. Weil, "Draft," 207.

13. Gray, *Weil,* 46–47.

14. Weil, "Are We Heading for the Proletarian Revolution?" in *Oppression and Lib-erty,* 6.

15. Weil, "The Needs of the Soul," in Miles, *Anthology,* 87.

16. Weil, "Reflections Concerning the Causes of Liberty and Social Oppression," in *Oppression and Liberty,* 61–62.

17. Coles, *Simone Weil,* 108. Coles is citing sentences that appear in a section toward the end of *Need for Roots.*

18. Ibid. Marybeth Timmermann's English translation of *Pyrrhus and Cineas* appears in Simone de Beauvoir, *Philosophical Writings,* ed. Margaret A. Simons with Marybeth Timmermann and Mary Beth Mader (Urbana: University of Illinois Press, 2004), 89–149.

19. Weil, *Anthology,* 257–58.

20. See also Thibon's comment in his introduction to *Gravity and Grace* about God's consenting "to cease to be everything so that we might be something." Weil, *Gravity and Grace,* 21.

21. In her introduction to the anthology, Sian Miles notes that Weil was "conspicu-ous, and she felt it keenly." Weil, *Anthology,* 46.

22. See my "The Two Simones," *Ratio* 13 (September 2000): 201–12, for a piece that presents a direct contrast between the work of these two thinkers.

23. See Rachel Feldhay Brenner, *Writing as Resistance: Four Women Confronting the Holocaust* (University Park: Pennsylvania State University Press, 1997). The four women

compared, despite what would appear to be some disparities in their works and lives, are Anne Frank, Etty Hillesum, Edith Stein, and Simone Weil.

24. Ibid., 107.

25. Ibid., 114.

26. Eric Springsted has noted that "Weil herself never felt any particular kinship to her ancestry; indeed, she felt some hostility towards it and is almost never generous when discussing Judaism or the Old Testament, excepting some books such as Genesis, Isaiah, and Job." Eric O. Springsted, *Simone Weil* (Maryknoll, N.Y.: Orbis, 1998), 13.

27. Brenner, *Writing as Resistance,* 112.

28. Ibid., 101.

29. Ibid., 131.

30. Ibid.

31. Gitta Sereny, *The Healing Wound: Experiences and Reflections on Germany, 1938–2001* (New York: Norton, 2001).

32. Ibid., 1.

33. Nancy Chodorow, "Family Structure and Feminine Personality," in *Woman, Culture, and Society,* ed. Michelle Zimbalist Rosaldo and Louise Lamphere (Stanford: Stanford University Press, 1974), 58.

34. Eric Springsted notes that "Simone was, I think, no less brilliant than her brother. But her genius was very different." Springsted, *Weil,* 13.

35. Gray states, "But to my knowledge, no critic has fully elucidated the meaning of the following fable." Gray, *Weil,* 229.

36. Weil, "Prologue," in Springsted, *Weil,* 31.

37. See Staughton Lynd, "Marxism-Leninism and the Language of Politics Magazine: The First New Left," in *Simone Weil: Interpretations of a Life,* ed. George Abbott White (Amherst: University of Massachusetts Press, 1981), 111–35.

38. Ibid., 112.

39. See, again, Weil's *Oppression and Liberty.* Like all of Weil's work available in English, this collection contains pieces from a variety of periods.

40. White, "Introduction," *Simone Weil,* 1–12. The comments by André Weil are found on 10–11.

41. Ibid., 110.

42. J. M. Cameron, "The Life and Death of Simone Weil," in White, *Simone Weil,* 43.

43. Michele Murray, "Simone Weil: Last Things," in White, *Simone Weil,* 60.

44. Quoted, ibid., 61.

45. Thibon admits as much in his editorial comments. It is an accident of fate that Weil entrusted her notebooks to him; she had, in any case, intended to return to France.

46. See Simone Weil, *Formative Writings: 1929–1941,* ed. Dorothy Tuck McFarland and Wilhelmina Van Ness (Amherst: University of Massachusetts Press, 1987).

47. Weil, "Do We Have to Grease Our Combat Boots?" in McFarland and Van Ness, *Formative Writings,* 258.

48. Michele Murray, writing in White, *Simone Weil,* is one of the few commentators who seems willing to admit to the extent of Weil's obvious psychological ill health and its relationship to her work.

49. McFarland and Van Ness, "Introduction," *Formative Writings,* 20.

50. Ibid.

51. Coles, *Simone Weil,* 6.

52. Gray notes that, after her death, Weil's parents did little else "but recopy her manuscripts for posterity." Gray, *Weil,* 213.

53. Coles, *Simone Weil,* 49–50.

54. Ibid., 62.

Chapter 8: Simone de Beauvoir

1. The work of Margaret Simons, the Fullbrooks, and others has been paramount in this regard. They continue to forward the notion that at least some of the work that was originally attributed to Sartre began, in thought, with Beauvoir. Edward and Kate Fullbrook have two books that develop this thesis: the most important is perhaps *Simone de Beauvoir and Jean-Paul Sartre: The Remaking of a Twentieth-Century Legend* (Hemel Hempstead, Eng.: Harvester Wheatsheaf, 1993). This line of thought comes up again in their *Simone de Beauvoir: a Critical Introduction* (Malden, Mass.: Blackwell, 1998).

2. See Simone de Beauvoir, *The Ethics of Ambiguity* (New York: Citadel Press Books, 1996).

3. This episode is recounted, for example, in Francine du Plessix Gray, *Simone Weil* (New York: Penguin Putnam, 2001), 35.

4. Beauvoir, *Ethics,* 10.

5. Ibid., 19.

6. Simone de Beauvoir, *A Very Easy Death* (New York: Pantheon, 1965), 72–73.

7. Elaine Marks, "Encounters with Death in *A Very Easy Death* and the Body in Decline in *Adieux: A Farewell to Sartre,*" in *Simone de Beauvoir: A Critical Reader,* ed. Elizabeth Fallaize (New York: Routledge, 1998), 135.

8. Beauvoir, *Very Easy Death,* 60.

9. Mary Warnock, *Women Philosophers* (London: J. M. Dent, 1996), 145–54.

10. Beauvoir, quoted, ibid., 148.

11. Ibid., 150.

12. Annie Cohen-Solal, *Sartre: A Life* (New York: Pantheon, 1985), 215.

13. Beauvoir, *Ethics,* 46–54. This interesting material comes toward the beginning of the section entitled, in English, "Personal Freedom and Others."

14. Ibid., 46–47.

15. Ibid., 77–78.

16. Cohen-Solal, *Sartre,* 154–56, 182–83.

17. Beauvoir, *Ethics,* 82–83.

18. For a full development of the debate on how various influences played out in Beauvoir's philosophical development, see Margaret A. Simons, *Beauvoir and The Second Sex: Feminism, Race and the Origins of Existentialism* (Lanham, Md.: Rowman and Littlefield, 1999). The larger thesis of Simons's work is that much of Sartre's own thinking is directly influenced by Beauvoir.

19. Nancy Bauer, *Simone de Beauvoir, Philosophy, and Feminism* (New York: Columbia University Press, 2001), 164–65.

20. Simons's *Beauvoir and The Second Sex* contains an entire chapter on this topic (167–84).

21. See Iris Murdoch, *Existentialists and Mystics,* ed. Peter Conradi (New York: Penguin Putnam, 1998). The review piece entitled "Beauvoir's *The Ethics of Ambiguity*" appears on pages 122–24.

22. Murdoch is, of course, employing her terminology very loosely, as she herself admits.

23. Murdoch, *Existentialists and Mystics,* 122.

24. In *The Book and the Brotherhood* (London: Chatto and Windus, 1987) this sort of tension is especially powerful.

25. Bauer has an interesting section on the influence of Lacan on Beauvoir; see Bauer, "The Struggle for Self in *The Second Sex,*" *Simone de Beauvoir,* 200–237.

26. Murdoch, *Existentialists and Mystics,* 223.

27. I make such a comparison in "The Two Simones," *Ratio* 13 (September 2000): 201–12.

28. Simons, *Beauvoir and The Second Sex,* 169–70. For a full chapter of this work that is specifically on the relationship between Beauvoir and Wright, see "Richard Wright, Simone de Beauvoir, and *The Second Sex,*" 167–84.

29. Ibid., 169.

30. Some commentators have examined the intersection of "existentialism," or the "philosophy of existence," and work on black liberation. See, for example, Lewis Gordon, ed., *Existence in Black* (New York: Routledge, 1996). Among works almost entirely by black authors, Gordon includes a reprint of one piece originally authored by Sartre for *Le Figaro* in 1945.

31. Simons (*Beauvoir and The Second Sex*) addresses Sartre's failure in this regard at several points in her text; see esp., 51–53.

32. Bauer, *Simone de Beauvoir,* 22.

33. Simons (*Beauvoir and The Second Sex*) addresses this problem at length in her work; she provides detail on pages 62–71.

34. Simone de Beauvoir, *The Second Sex* (New York: Knopf, 1957), 238.

35. See Toril Moi, *Simone de Beauvoir: The Making of an Intellectual Woman* (Cambridge, Mass.: Blackwell, 1994). Moi pays Beauvoir a bit of a back-handed compliment: assuming that the text should be viewed as a philosophical work, she then finds numerous examples of serious, unresolved philosophical problems. One of the strongest chapters is "Ambiguous Women: Alienation and the Body in *The Second Sex,*" 148–78.

36. Quoted, ibid., 167.

37. Interestingly enough, Stendhal was apparently a favorite author of both Beauvoir and Sartre, and he is mentioned many times in their works.

38. Reyes Lazaro, "Feminism and Motherhood: O'Brien vs. Beauvoir," *Hypatia* 1 (Summer 1986): 94.

39. Moi provides what is perhaps the clearest analysis of the arcane intricacies of the French education system in the early chapters of *Simone de Beauvoir.*

40. Deirdre Bair, *Simone de Beauvoir: A Biography* (New York: Simon and Schuster, 1990), 438.

41. Deirdre Bair's excellent *Simone de Beauvoir* has a great deal of material on this relationship. One chapter centrally concerned with Algren's response to the amount of detail about their relationship in *The Mandarins* is "Not Exactly Our Story, But . . . ," 412–28.

292 Notes to Pages 240–51

42. Bair notes that, even as her mother aged and began to lead a more independent life, Beauvoir found it difficult to acknowledge any change in her. (Bair, *Simone de Beauvoir,* 440–41.) Beauvoir deals with similar issues in *Old Age,* trans. Patrick O'Brian (London: Andre Deutsch, Weidenfeld and Nicolson, 1972). This work was published in the United States as *The Coming of Age* (New York: Putnam, 1972).

43. Marks, "Encounters with Death," 135.

44. Beauvoir, *Very Easy Death,* 72–73.

45. Dawn Rae Davis, "(Love Is) the Ability of Not Knowing: Feminist Experience of the Impossible in Ethical Singularity," in *Hypatia* 17 (Spring 2002): 146.

46. This chapter, a crucial and somewhat underrated part of the text, can be found in Beauvoir, *Second Sex,* 139–98. It is immediately followed by the literary section, and the segment on Stendhal, already alluded to, is on pages 238–48.

47. Ibid., 140–41.

48. Ibid., 142.

49. Simone de Beauvoir, *The Mandarins* (New York: Norton, 1991), 36.

50. Ibid., 48.

51. Rosemary Radford Ruether, *Womanguides: Readings toward a Feminist Theology* (Boston: Beacon, 1985), 106.

52. Ibid.

53. Beauvoir, *Second Sex,* 141.

54. This sort of examination is made by Moi throughout her *Simone de Beauvoir,* especially in the later chapters.

55. Beauvoir, *Second Sex,* 331.

56. Bair, ibid., xxvii.

57. Barbara S. Andrew, review of *Identity without Selfhood: Bisexuality and Simone de Beauvoir,* by Mariam Fraser, *Hypatia* 16 (Summer 2001): 161.

58. Bair, for one, is straightforward in her account of these relationships, including the relationship with Natalie Sorokine during the 1940s that resulted in the loss of a teaching post for Beauvoir.

59. Beauvoir, *Second Sex,* 404. The chapter entitled "The Lesbian" is on pages 404–24. In general, much of the chapter takes a psychoanalytic stance.

60. Beauvoir, *Mandarins,* 52.

61. Beauvoir, *Very Easy Death,* 76–77.

62. Ibid., 67.

63. Ibid., 103.

64. As Beauvoir remarks, this report by Remy Roure was written "untruthfully." Ibid., 104.

65. Ibid.

66. A variation of this phrase is the title of the last chapter of Bair's book.

Conclusion

1. Richard H. Popkin is explicit about the influence of Descartes and the development of mathematics in general. See Popkin, "The Spiritualistic Cosmologies of Henry More and Anne Conway," in *Henry More (1614-1687): Tercentenary Studies,* ed. Sarah Hutton (Dordrecht, Neth.: Kluwer, 1990), 97–114.

2. A great deal of recent work in the past two decades goes some way to clearing the ground here, and I have referred to that work throughout this manuscript. Particularly helpful among recently published American volumes are Linda Lopez McAlister, ed., *Hypatia's Daughters* (Bloomington: Indiana University Press, 1996); Cecile Tougas and Sara Ebenreck, eds., *Presenting Women Philosophers* (Philadelphia: Temple University Press, 2000); and Catherine Villanueva Gardner, *Rediscovering Women Philosophers* (Boulder, Colo.: Westview, 2000).

3. I have made such contrasts in *Worlds of Knowing: Global Feminist Epistemologies* (New York: Routledge, 2001).

4. The *Chronicle of Higher Education,* June 7, 2002, examines a question making the rounds in academic circles: is biography helpful or necessary in deciphering the work of philosophers? Although almost all of the thinkers listed were male, Simone de Beauvoir was named, and Deirdre Bair's biography was mentioned.

5. An excellent example is Martha Nussbaum's *Therapy of Desire* (Cambridge, Mass.: Harvard University Press, 1994). Thinkers not even particularly well known, such as certain of the Skeptics, are brought to life by Nussbaum in this insightful work.

6. In thinking of the historical, we might want to note, for example, Astell's empirical bent, which shows up in her analysis of social relations. In this, she may be seen as a precursor of Hume.

7. I have investigated many of these issues in my *Knowledge in Context* (Savage, Md.: Rowman and Littlefield, 1994). A relevant work on the notion of intellectual collaboration and its products is Vera John-Steiner, *Creative Collaborations* (Oxford: Oxford University Press), 2000.

8. It is not only Marjorie Hope Nicolson's *The Conway Letters: The Correspondence of Anne Viscountess Conway, Henry More, and Their Friends, 1642–1684* (Cambridge: Cambridge University Press, 1984) that bears testimony to this; most scholarship on Conway's work gives central place to her relationship with More. See, for example, Hutton, *Henry More.*

9. Jo Ellen Jacobs, "Introduction," in *The Complete Works of Harriet Taylor Mill,* ed. Jacobs (Bloomington: Indiana University Press, 1998), xi–xxxv.

10. Diane Wood Middlebrook, *Anne Sexton: A Biography* (New York: Vintage, 1992), 340.

11. For more on these crucial matters, see Robin Lakoff, *Talking Power* (New York: Free Press, 1992).

12. This shows up particularly in her criticisms of religious institutions and conventional religious thought, as Jacobs indicates. See Jacobs, "Introduction."

13. It is worth remembering at this point that Brenner writes of a foursome of women, two of whom would ordinarily be thought of as diarists, and two of whom we have examined here as philosophers. What these women share in common is not only a response to the Holocaust, but a concern for how we live our lives with respect to other human beings. See Rachel Feldhay Brenner, *Writing as Resistance: Four Women Confronting the Holocaust* (University Park, Pa.: Pennsylvania State University Press, 1997).

14. In many of these cases, although it may sound simplistic, the distinction at which we are driving is probably best thought of as analogous to Gilligan's distinction between the "justice" voice and the "care" voice.

15. Conway is a particularly relevant figure here, for it has been only recently, with the

"historical" turn, that essays such as those employed here have appeared with respect to work from this period. It is worthwhile, for example, to compare Loptson's commentary on Conway, in the edition of her work pieced together by him (Anne Conway, *Principles of the Most Ancient and Modern Philosophy,* ed. Peter Loptson [The Hague, Neth.: Martinus Nijhoff, 1982]), with the commentary by Coudert and Corse in Anne Conway, *The Principles of the Most Ancient and Modern Philosophy,* trans. and ed. Allison Coudert and Taylor Corse (Cambridge: Cambridge University Press, 1996).

16. Coles, for one, feels strongly that Weil cannot be understood without reference to some Jewish history and doctrine. See the discussion in his *Simone Weil: A Modern Pilgrimage* (Woodstock, Vt.: SkyLight Paths, 2001).

17. Work by Lewis Gordon in the late 1990s, for example, asks these questions about Western African thought. See *Existence in Black* (New York: Routledge, 1997).

18. I have detailed these lines of argument in my *Philosophies of Science/Feminist Theories* (Boulder, Colo.: Westview, 1998).

19. I examine these questions at length in my *Worlds of Knowing.*

20. We can see how pertinent these differences are at a later point when we examine the current spate of books on the behavior of adolescent girls, reviewed by Carol Tavris in the *Chronicle of Higher Education,* July 5, 2002.

21. Alain Locke's work was, for years, almost unnoticed.

239, 241–42; and Edith Stein, 172–75, 178–79
Oyewumi, Oyeronke, 17

pain: and Mary Astell, 102–3; and Anne Conway, 68–69; and Simone Weil, 196–99, 201–4, 208–9, 211, 212, 216–19, 266
papacy, rise of, 27
Pappe, H. O., 154
Paris Commune, 197
passions: and Anne Conway, 62–63; and René Descartes, 31, 57–58; and Baruch Spinoza, 30–31; and Simone Weil, 216; and Mary Wollstonecraft, 108, 109, 110, 116, 120–22, 125, 127–29, 131, 133
Passions (Descartes), 57–58
Passmore, John A., 57, 60
patriarchal cleansing, 43
Paul, Diana, 67
Paul, St., 142
Pauline text, 25
Pax Britannica (Morris), 152
Pepys, Samuel, 84
perfectibilism: and Anne Conway, 54–58; and Mary Wollstonecraft, 109–10, 112–13, 115–16
Perry, Ruth, 81, 85–86, 88–89, 101, 102
personal freedom: and Simone de Beauvoir, 224, 229–32; and Harriet Taylor Mill, 138–49, 161, 163–64; and John Stuart Mill, 138, 140, 144–45, 147, 164; and Jean-Paul Sartre, 230–31; and Simone Weil, 196–98, 202, 212, 266; and Mary Wollstonecraft, 114
personality development, of Simone Weil, 209–11, 217
personal relationships: of Mary Astell, 9–10, 80, 89–90, 96–97, 102; of Simone de Beauvoir, 7, 222–24, 228, 232, 239, 245, 248, 252, 255–58, 261; of Anne Conway, 10, 51–52, 57–63, 68, 69, 76, 252, 255, 256; of Harriet Taylor Mill, 7, 137–39, 146, 150–61, 153, 154, 156, 160–62, 251–52, 255–58; of Edith Stein, 175; of Simone Weil, 6–7, 219, 224; of Mary Wollstonecraft, 106–7, 109, 116–17, 127–30, 133, 252, 255, 257
phenomenology: and Simone de Beauvoir, 224–25; and Edith Stein, 166–73, 176–78,

182, 184–85, 188, 192, 213, 259–60; and Simone Weil, 224–25, 260
Philosopher Queen (Plato), 91–92
philosophes, 112
Philosophical Fragments (Kierkegaard), 210
Physica (Hildegard of Bingen), 22
physis, 44
plague, and Anne Conway, 56, 75, 264
Plath, Sylvia, 5, 217
Plato, 25, 47, 51, 89, 91–93, 128, 195, 233–34
Platonists, 60, 62–63, 66, 72, 73–74, 97, 103
pleasures, and Harriet Taylor Mill, 144, 146, 161, 162
Plotinus, 51, 89
Popkin, Richard, 64, 65, 66
postcolonial theory, 13–15, 70–71
postmodernism, 14–15, 92, 160
Poston, Carol, 127–28, 130, 131
post post-theory: nature of, 12–15; and third-wave feminism, 42–45
poststructuralism, 92, 240, 246
power: and marriage, 158–59; uses of, 157–58
predestination, 141–42
Principles of Political Economy (H. T. Mill), 144–47, 153, 156–57, 163
Principles of the Most Ancient and Modern Philosophy (Conway), 52–57, 59–60, 68, 69, 71–73, 75, 76, 259, 268
Proclus, 89
progressive politics, 91, 101
property rights, 114
public shaming, of women philosophers, 7
puritanism, 84, 143
Pyrrhus et Cineas (Beauvoir), 231
Pythagorean women, 5

Quakerism, 65–66, 69

racism, 36
radical feminism, 127
Rationalists, 11, 45, 73
Rediscovering Women Philosophers (Gardner), 130–31
Reflections on Gender and Science (Keller), 37
Reflections on the Revolution of France (Burke), 107, 118–20
Reformation, 264
reincarnation, and Anne Conway, 55

JANE DURAN is a Fellow in Philosophy and Lecturer in the Humanities at the University of California, Santa Barbara. Her books include *Worlds of Knowing: Global Feminist Epistemologies; Philosophies of Science/Feminist Theories; Knowledge in Context: Naturalized Epistemology and Sociolinguistics;* and *Epistemics.*

The University of Illinois Press
is a founding member of the
Association of American University Presses.

———————————————————————

Composed in 9/13 ITC Stone Serif
with Helvetica Neue Extended display
by Type One, LLC
for the University of Illinois Press
Designed by Paula Newcomb
Manufactured by Thomson-Shore, Inc.

University of Illinois Press
1325 South Oak Street
Champaign, IL 61820-6903
www.press.uillinois.edu